WITHDRAWN

Peace without Victory for the Allies
1918–1932

940.312
M786p

Peace without Victory for the Allies
1918–1932

by
Sara Moore

Foreword
by
Forrest Capie

BERG
Oxford/Providence, USA

First published in 1994 by
Berg Publishers
Offices:
150 Cowley Road, Oxford, OX4 1JJ. UK
221 Waterman Street, Providence, RI 02906, USA

© Sara Moore 1994

All rights reserved.
No part of this publication may be reproduced in any form or by any means
without the written permission of Berg Publishers

Library of Congress Cataloging-in-Publication Data
A CIP catalogue record for this book is available from the Library of Congress

British Library Cataloguing in Publication Data
A CIP catalogue record for this book is available from the British Library

ISBN 1 85973 026 4

Cover illustration © The Illustrated London News Picture Library.

Printed in the United Kingdom by Short Run Press, Exeter.

Contents

ALLECHENY COLLEGE LIBRARY

CATMar1395

BNA 53.95

1-8-96

Contents

Contents

Contents

Foreword

Where does the blame lie for the First World War? If Germany is to be held responsible what payments should she have made after the war to recompense the Allied powers for the damage they suffered during the war? What damages were suffered, indeed how can the calculation of such damages be made? And was Germany in any position to pay such damages (called reparation payments) as were calculated? These and other associated questions, either explicitly or implicitly, have occupied historians for many years, and they were the questions which dominated the discussions and the negotiations in the 1920s. They are treated explicitly in Sara Moore's book.

Reparations payments have become common in modern times. They are the payments made by the loser to the winner as recompense for damage suffered in wartime. The most famous instance of these payments is that exacted from the Germans following World War I. A considerable literature was produced on the subject in the 1920s and 1930s, and very much more has been written by economists and historians in the last two decades. The present volume is a further contribution to the subject, but as will be seen from a perusal of the book this is a different approach.

Following the First World War the victorious Allies imposed a huge bill on Germany. Apart from having to pay all the costs of Allied occupation, she was also obliged to pay by means of specified annual instalments 132 billion gold marks. (i.e. $33b, or £6,600m. To give some indication of the size of that figure it represented about two years total British output at the time). Germany had to surrender the greater part of her merchant marine and all her navy, armaments, some industrial equipment and so on, although these were credited against the £6,600m. Not surprisingly such a sum was regarded by many as simply too much, and much of the following decade was taken up with negotiations over terms and amounts. One of the justifications for the large amount was that many of the Allies had debts outstanding to the US, and that this was more or less of the order of magnitude to offset these.

There were huge problems of adjustment in the world economy following what had been the greatest period of turmoil in more than a century at least. Germany had many problems. In 1922 the financial system there deteriorated sharply, the exchange rate oscillated with capital flows, and Germany pleaded for postponement of payment. In

Foreword

1923 the French and Belgians marched on the Ruhr with a view to securing their entitlement or forcing payment. The German currency collapsed in one of the worst hyper-inflations of modern times. A new plan – The Dawes – was designed and introduced in 1924. Controls were put on the German economy. Regular payments followed over the next few years, though it should be said Germany was also borrowing massively abroad at the time. When the flow of capital dried up at the end of the 1920s fresh problems arose and yet another plan was devised, the Young Plan, which took effect from April. However, the following year there was the Hoover moratorium.

A major problem with reparation payments was the impact brought about by the transfer of resources. The term 'transfer problem' was introduced into the literature by Keynes in 1929. The question was, which way would the international terms of trade move following a transfer? That is an important issue in international economics which is noted by Moore, but not one that is pursued at length.

What did Germany end up paying? This is difficult to be precise about. There are many estimates. One that has been quite widely accepted is that total payments made in the 1920s were 22.9b gold marks, quite substantial, but only a fraction of the original specification. While Keynes argued in The Economic Consequences of the Peace that the payments discussed at Versailles were excessive, others argue that Germany's ability to pay was greater than sometimes assumed. What is clear is that the original objective was negated by the American capital exports of 1924–29.

History acts as society's memory. We take actions today based, however subconsciously, on what we know of the past. What we know of the past is a combination of the work of investigation by the many hands and the perspective that derives from distance from sources not available in a consideration of the present. As a result we invariably have a better understanding of the more distant past than we have of the present or the recent past. Nevertheless, of necessity it remains an imperfect picture coloured, however subconsciously and in spite of the attempt at impartiality, by views and attitudes of the commentators. The picture is also continually being modified and even on occasions completely revised.

Sara Moore is not a professional historian, but an enthusiastic amateur and our perception of the past can be sharpened and our understanding furthered by incorporating a range of opinion, even that which falls outside the conventionally bounded world of professional history. More's argument is expressed forcibly. She rejects the view that the Allies' actions inevitably brought about the rise of Hitler, and argues that if the Allies had fought on for unconditional surrender in 1918, the former Prussian Empire would have been divided into its component parts and rendered relatively harmless. Instead Germany was treated magnanimously under the Treaty of Versailles.

The argument is that Germany then manipulated the international community in the decade after the war; the German economy was strong on the eve of the First World War and it remained strong in the 1920s and the 1930s. Further, it was the German deflation together with the assistance provided to the Soviet Union in undermining world agriculture in the 1920s that were the principal causes of the world depression at the beginning of the 1930s. Some of that argument is by now uncontentious but other parts will be doubted or challenged.

Moore has spent many years researching and writing this book. It is a passionate account and different in many ways from the normal work of the historian. But that is its strength. It draws on a large secondary literature and at the same time quotes extensively from the contemporary press and draws too on the private papers of many of the principal participants in the drama. It carries portraits of these leading figures and is enlivened by cartoons from the Press.

Introduction

One of the major misappprehensions of the 20th Century has been the supposed weakness of Germany before Hitler came to power. Before World War I, the building of German battleships was enough to raise alarm signals throughout the British Empire, while in 1993, all are agreed, 'The Bundesbank' is *The Bank that Rules Europe.*[1] Before Hitler came to power, however, Germany was said to be weak.

Not only was it weak, many thought, but it was the victim of injustice. Britons, it was said, had been happy to go to war in 1914. Yet when Germany accepted a compromise peace on the basis of the 14 points and principles, the Allies reneged on their altruistic promises and imposed a draconian peace.

In the words of George Kennan, New York columnist, writing on Remembrance Day in 1984:

'The vindictive madness of the British and French peace terms.. the economic miseries of the postwar years; the foolish attempts to draw the blood of reparations and war debts from the veins of the exhausted peoples of the Continent....assured that only twenty years later Europe would stand confronted with the nightmare of Adolph Hitler and a second vast military conflagration.'

It is a grave accusation to make that the Allies and America were somehow responsible for the rise of Hitler, and not one likely to endear the British people to the strong and populous German nation. But it is one which has been levelled at the Allies, not only by George Kennan in America, but also by a great many people in England.

One reason that the accusation has gained so much credence is because, until recently, it was alleged that we all 'fell into war' in 1914 but that Germany, alone, was held responsible.

This myth has been finally dispelled by the German Professor, Fritz Fischer's studies into the secret Austrian and Prussian archives which

1. Title of David Marsh's book (1992).

were opened to researchers in the 1950s. After the revelations of the secret files, Fischer's disclosures were investigated for many years until German historians were satisfied as to their veracity. British historian, Andrew Roberts, writing in 1991, has encapsulated modern opinion on the subject.

'In 1914, Germany was a thrusting, highly nationalistic parvenu power and quite clearly the aggressor, but this unpalatable fact was submerged into theories about the 'inherent instabilities of alliances' and the evils of secret diplomacy.'[2]

In Fischer's first book, entitled in English, *Germany's Aims in the 1st World War* and more explicitly, in German, *Grasp at World Power*, and his subsequent book, *War of Illusions*, Fischer shows how the German powers behind the throne seized upon what could be used as a racial insult to the German speaking nations, namely the murder of the Archduke Ferdinand in the Balkans in 1914, to unite the wavering Austrians behind the Prussian Empire's drive for world power. To persuade the vociferous anti-war Social Democratic Party to support the leadership, Germany's Chancellor, Bethmann Hollweg, managed to goad lumbering, autocratic Russia into ordering the mobilisation of her armed forces from the vast depths of her country before Germany mobilised its troops. Thus Bethmann Hollweg was able to present Germany as the victim of aggression.

After the war foreigners gradually began to be impressed by Germany's repeated pleas of innocence. Surely the country would not campaign so hard, they reasoned, if it had actually caused World War I. However, investigation reveals that those who were most active in making accusations against the 'war-guilt lie' had formerly been the most ardent advocates of war.

In the Autumn of 1929, Alfred Hugenberg, formerly Chairman of Krupps, caused consternation on the American stock market through his petition for a national referendum to have the whole German cabinet tried for treason, if it agreed to pay any more reparations, on the grounds that Germany was innocent of starting World War I. But his committee, included, not only Hitler, but also Justice Class, Chairman of the Alldeutsche Verband, Germany's pan German association before the war, and the Chairman of the Stahlhelm, Germany's anti-Republican, paramilitary, army veterans' organisation.

In 1913, the Alldeutsche Verband had aligned itself with the Farmers League to present a formidable pressure group to fight the growth of

2. Andrew Roberts. *The Holy Fox. A Biography of Lord Halifax*. p.49

democracy, by promoting aggressive, external aims as Germany's right as a superior nation.

Judge Class had been bitterly critical of the Kaiser's previous retreats from war in 1905 and 1909. In his anonymously published, fast selling book, *Wenn ich der Kaiser wär* (*If I were the Kaiser*, 1912) he advocated that we pursue 'an active foreign policy, indeed let us frankly say an 'aggressive' one.'

> 'A defensive war in this sense – as punishment for a vicious attack...is what an aggressive war by Germany would amount to if it was fought to forestall our enemies....France must be crushed...' and Russia 'be required to make territorial concessions which give us a better frontier at the same time as land for settlers.'[3]

Hugenberg, at that time Chairman of Krupps, the armament manufacturers, had the same ideas as his close friend, Class, but in his public position, he phrased them more carefully. Thus, on 25 April 1914, he looked forward to a possible war as a 'liberating trial of strength behind which beckons a clearer and wider horizon and the prospect of applying very much higher standards to our entire economic and political future than we have in our modesty done before.'[4]

The army had, for a long time, favoured war. Chief of the Prussian General Staff, Moltke, declared in December 1912:

> 'I believe a war to be unavoidable and: the sooner the better.' Moltke further declared that 'we ought to do more to popularise a war against Russia through the press, along the lines suggested by the Emperor.'[5]

After one month of war Class and Hugenberg produced a list of war aims. It had the approval of notable Ruhr industrialists such as Krupp von Bohlen und Halbach, and Herr Stinnes, who became, after the war, one of the richest men in the world. Stinnes advocated annexing the entire northern coast of France in order to make sure of owning its iron ore deposits. Yet Stinnes, Hugenberg, and friends, were the most strident of campaigners against the reparations after World War I, presupposing that they felt that they could bully the Allies over the issue. The German government had not dared tax heavy industry for the windfall

---

3. F. Fischer. *War of Illusions.* p.245–6. Extract taken from *Wenn ich der Kaiser wär* in Chapter entitled, 'Von den Grundzügen deutscher Machtpolitik'. (Concerning the main features of German power politics.)

4. Alfred Hugenberg. *Streiflichter aus Vergangenheit und Gegenwart*, Berlin, 1927, p.205

5. F. Fischer. *War of Illusions.* p.162. 'Admiral von Müller and the approach of War 1911–1914'. *The Historical Journal.* XII, 4 (1969) note 58.

profits it had made out of the war, and the articles in Hugenberg's 500 newspapers increasingly won the propaganda argument.

The British people were totally unprepared for World War I. It is true that, ever since before 1903, when Erskine Childers wrote his novel the *Riddle in the Sands* depicting a German plot to invade Britain, Great Britain had been alarmed by the threat of German aggression. Threats of war in 1905 and 1909 heightened British anxieties. But after an incident in the Balkans in 1912, which the German leadership judged was too irrelevant to unite the Prussian and Austrian Empires, Britain was impressed by Germany's peaceful intent. Germany waxed friendly in order to wrest Britain from her uneasy entente with France, and ensure her neutrality in the forthcoming war.

While the Europeans were hectically arming in 1912 and 1913, therefore, minorities in Britain, lulled by the German embrace, turned their backs on events in Europe and campaigned for their own sectional interests. Thus it was that the weak Liberal British government, on the eve of a World War, was almost beset by a general strike in England and civil war in Ireland.

British workers had been excited by the ideas of the left, just as in other countries. Mass production had opened up the possibility of a modicum of wealth for all. Thousands of workers, employed in giant factories, felt that, if they mobilised, they could apply political pressure to hasten the process. Marx and Engels, brought up in the Prussian mould, had thought in terms of revolution to secure the dictatorship of the proletariat. The militant left in England, did not canvass 'revolution' to gain its objectives, but it did think in terms of the 'collective ownership of the means of production, distribution and exchange.'[6] It had little respect for the government of the day, or Britain's traditional leadership.

Keynes was later to write of his and other young intellectuals' perception of Britain's traditional leadership before World War I:

> 'It did not occur to us to respect the extraordinary accomplishment of our predecessors in the ordering of life...We were not aware that civilisation was a thin and precarious crust erected by the personality and the will of a very few, and only maintained by rules and conventions skilfully put across and guilefully preserved...I can see us as water-spiders, gracefully skimming, as light and reasonable as air, the surface of the stream without any contact at all with the eddies and currents underneath.'

British socialists had an exaggerated respect for Germany's Social Democratic Party because it was the largest socialist party in the world, elected on the basis of universal suffrage and avowedly pacifist. But the

6. J. D. Caute. *The Left in Europe*. p.58. Resolution of the ILP at Bradford in 1891.

British did not understand its limitations. It was a powerful pressure group but it could not initiate legislation, only make suggestions and approve finance.[7] And it was bound to be prey to an appeal to patriotism. The lure of socialism was already waning anyway by 1913 in the face of the heady philosophy of pan Germanism.[8]

Unfortunately at the outbreak of war in 1914, filled with antiquated British prejudice against the French, Britain's labour party leader, Ramsay Macdonald, not appreciating the weakness of German socialism, undermined the future of his country by putting his faith in Germany's peaceful intent.

On 8 August 1914 he made his first accusation against Britain's participation in World War I, without ever having had any experience of foreign affairs:

> 'There is no doubt whatever but that, when all this is over and we turn back to it in cold blood and read it carefully so as to ascertain why England has practically declared war on Germany, we shall find that the only reason from beginning to end in it is that the Foreign Office is anti- German and that the Admiralty was anxious to seize any opportunity of using the Navy in battle practice.'

A week later he followed up this outburst with an article in the Labour Leader entitled 'Why we are at War' and subtitled 'A reply to Sir Edward Grey.' The article attempted to negate Britain's moral stance in going to war because of Germany's invasion of neutral Belgium. This time Ramsay Macdonald did not mention the Admiralty but blamed Britain's entangling entente with France and the 'secret' diplomacy of Sir Edward Grey for Britain's participation in the war.

The article was naturally translated post-haste by enthusiastic German propagandists. They published it in every paper in Germany and then translated it into the languages of all the neutral countries with which their country did business, to persuade them that Germany was not the aggressor and deserved continued wartime assistance. By December 1914 Germany would be accusing 'England' of starting World War I.

The moral maze of the responsibility for World War I has at last been

---

7. 'the Reichstag had no influence upon the composition and policy of the Imperial government, from which the deputies were expressly excluded...Its influence was confined to making suggestions which the government was at liberty to accept or refuse, to checking the proceeds and expenditure of the budget, and to passing such bills as did not affect the imperial prerogative of foreign and military affairs. The gulf which separated the government bench from the seats of the deputies was not bridged until October 1918.' S. H. Steinberg. *A Short History of Germany.* p.224.

8. C. Landauer (1959) *European Socialism.* I. p.374–82.

unravelled by Professor Fischer. But the Allies and America are still accused of being responsible for the rise of Hitler and the Second World War.

This is because none of those who fought for a conditional peace and against 'unconditional surrender' has liked to accept that their failure could have helped to precipitate another war. Only in 1939 was it revealed that President Woodrow Wilson's failure to demand 'unconditional surrender' from the Germans in 1918 was inspired as much by jealousy of Britain's high profile Empire as a belief in the 14 points in 1918.

Lloyd George was also eager to dodge the blame for not ordering his army, the most effective in the field, to appeal to opposition American public opinion and fight on for unconditional surrender in October 1918. He used his pen to great effect to put the blame on the British army, rather than the politicians, for the failure of World War I to prove 'the war to end all wars.' He told his secretary in 1934, after Hitler achieved power and Germany began re-arming, that 'he was very sick that Haig and Robertson were not alive. He intended to blow their ashes to smithereens in his fifth volume.' 'As a piece of sustained invective it could not be bettered' judged the military Historian, David French, 'As a piece of serious history it smacks of having been composed on the nineteenth hole.'[9]

British socialists were also unhappy to admit that they had made a terrible mistake in actively campaigning against 'unconditional surrender' in 1918. According to the historian, J. D. Caute when organised labour was in a powerful position with so many men in uniform in 1918, 'the Labour Party advocated the immediate nationalisation of land, railways, mines, electricity, industrial insurance, harbours and so forth, as well as the extension of social services and education on the basis of a steeply progressive income tax.'[10]

It seemed worth undermining the efforts of the British army to achieve overwhelming victory in the Autumn of 1918, when the German army was on the retreat, because President Wilson's envoy had promised British Trade Unionists' help towards their socialist ideals if they would support a peace on the basis of his President's principles. The unforseen consequence of not being able to control Germany's finances under the ill-defined terms of the Treaty of Versailles, however, was the destruction of British industry by German economic penetration after World War I and mass unemployment in Britain in the 1920s.

---

9. Taken from *War, Strategy, and International Politics. Essays in Honour of Sir Michael Howard* edited by Professor Robert O'Neill. p.152–3.
   10. J. D. Caute. *The Left in Europe.* p.58.

The left in Britain had had faith in the efficacy of German socialism to control the creed of Prussian militarism before World War I. They believed that it had been largely the 'revolution' in Germany which had forced the Kaiser to abandon his throne afterwards, not the ultimatum by President Woodrow Wilson that if the American government was not assured of the Kaiser's abdication 'it must demand, not peace negotiations, but surrender.'

After 1918 the German Social Democratic Party did have the power to initiate legislation. Disappointed British socialists were therefore quick to blame them for the failures of government in Weimar years when Prussian influences should rightfully have been castigated because so much power and influence was still beyond Governmental control.

British socialists have always identified their party with the protection of the oppressed. So they, like their leader, Ramsay Macdonald, were too ready to believe German tales of 'starvation' after World War I and blame Britain's historic enemy, but wartime ally, the French, for perceived German misfortunes.[11]

No-one liked to say how dominant Germany was before Hitler came to power. Little mention was therefore made of the devastation of Northern France and Belgium's mines and industry by the retreating German army in 1918, leaving Germany in a powerful economic position after the war. No mention was made either of the devastation of British industry by German industry in the early 1920s, caused by the low value of the German mark. The effect of the ultimatum of the Ruhr coal owners to the German government in 1923, to return to an eight and a half day underground and a ten hour day above, has somehow been forgotten in books on Germany's hyper-inflation and the subsequent coal strike in Britain. Hitler's attempted coup in 1923 naturally receives much attention, other coups naturally less. The German right's profligacy with finance in the 1920s has been too often blamed on German socialists. The impact of Hugenberg's letter to American industrialists in the Spring of 1929 has to be taken into account when considering the impact of his 'Bill against the Enslavement of the German people' on the American stock market in the Autumn. Germany is still considered

---

11. Diary 16.2.30 taken from *Ramsay Macdonald*. David Marquand. p.514, p.608. I am determined not to drift into the position in which Grey found himself. That gives France a free hand in determining European policy with Great Britain a bound follower. That will mean alliances & war, & I shall prevent it so long as I am in office.
Diary 22.7.31:
Over French conditions for offering Germany a loan during the banking crisis of 1931:
'Again & again be it said: France is the enemy, we shall pay with all our honour for that war...'

to have been weak during the banking crash of 1931, because of its large numbers of unemployed, despite the fact that it was the world's 'leading exporter.'

No-one wants to consider that those who were prepared to fight the world in 1914 for what they considered to be the greater long term good of Germany, could have, afterwards, been equally prepared to fight the world, in an economic sense, for the same purpose, using their citizens as soldiers in the campaign.

The dust is finally beginning to settle on interwar events. But as we enter into closer association in Europe, it is important that truth should prevail.

The Allies are still being falsely accused of imposing an iniquitous peace on Germany, leading to the rise of Hitler. Study does not support the allegation. It finds that America saved Germany from defeat in 1918, not denied it of victory as many Germans alleged between the wars. Far from dividing the former Prussian Empire after World War I into its component parts, as might have happened if the Allies had fought on for 'unconditional surrender,' (and was the justice meted out to the former Austrian/Hungarian Empire) it gave Germany a relatively magnanimous peace under the terms of the Treaty of Versailles.

As for those huge, 'crippling' reparations, readers will have to look at the small print and make up their mind whether the Allies were extortionate in their demands, and whether Germany was too weak to pay what was actually asked for, or whether it felt strong enough to defy the world, after the American troops had gone back to America.

Britain, by the 1930s, impressed by German protestations of innocence, decided that everyone was equally guilty of causing World War I.[12] After accusing Britain in December 1914, Germany had blamed Russia of causing the war in 1918, but by 1930 it would use the position of Ramsay Macdonald as head of the British government, to blame its old enemy 'England' again.

---

12. During monetary negotiation over the reparations at Lausanne in 1932, in the words of his biographer, David Marquand. p.722: 'without saying so in so many words, he (Ramsay Macdonald) implied that if they raised their bid the conference might agree to a political declaration, formally abrogating the hated war–guilt clause of the peace treaty.'

–1–

A Stab in the Back for Britain

1.1 America's Opposing Views

There probably never would have been any argument as to how the 1st World War had started if there had not been such a terrible muddle as to how the war had ended. In the Spring of 1918 the Germans had seemed to be carrying all before them. In the East their troops were in control from the Baltic Sea, through a great swathe of the Russian Empire down to the Black Sea, while in the West they were threatening Paris. Although the Allies fought off that challenge to their existence Winston Churchill, as Minister of Munitions, was still talking of troop requirements for 1919 and 1920 in the Autumn of 1918. Then suddenly it was all over and the Allies declared that they had won the war while the Germans soon maintained that they had never been beaten.

The man who was to dictate the peace, however, was neither one of the Allies nor their ex-enemy, Germany. It was President Woodrow Wilson, leader of the Democratic Party of America. In 1918 President Wilson's country was in an enviable position for a nation at war. The European contestants had been fighting for four long years and they were very tired while his numerous countrymen were still fresh and eager. Moreover his nation possessed in abundance that precious commodity so necessary in war, money. America was a young country, vast by European standards and full of confidence.

As Harold Nicolson said of the Allied European nations in relation to their 'associate' from America in 1919:

> 'We were all, at that date, dependant upon America, not only for the sinews of war but for the sinews of peace. Our food supplies, our finances, were entirely subservient to the dictates of Washington.'[1]

President Wilson had a high moral tone which appealed to many suffering Europeans:

1. Harold Nicolson. Peacemaking. p.41.

'The new things in the world are the things that are divorced from force,' he proclaimed on 5 June 1914. 'They are the moral compulsions of the human conscience.'[2]

The opposition Republican leader, Theodore Roosevelt, however, distrusted President Wilson's sentiments. He favoured fighting on for an old fashioned victory and insisting on 'unconditional surrender' by the German army. The election for the House of Representatives and a third of the Senate was due on 5 November 1918.[3]

1.2 The German Home Front

The German Home front was quiet in the Summer of 1918 in contrast to the dissatisfaction of 1917. Then the workers had taken up Lenin's slogan of 'self-determination without annexations or indemnities' and demanded a democratic regime in Germany based on universal suffrage. The German authorities used propaganda to counteract this demand which they depicted as being promoted by foreign saboteurs, Slavs, socialists and Jews.[4] Meanwhile they proposed, though did not enact, legislative reform of the Prussian State Parliament.[5]

The willingness of Lenin to come to terms with Germany enabled the German military dictatorship to disregard internal opposition to a rapacious peace. Opposition was stifled by using altruistic liberal phrases to justify taking over large sections of Russian territory.

Richard von Kuhlmann, Germany's foreign minister, wrote in his recollections in 1948 that he had used 'the right of national self-determination to undermine the point of peace without annexations' in his negotiations with the Bolsheviks:

'My plan was to entangle Trotsky in a purely academic discussion on the right of national self- determination and the possibility of applying it in practice, and to get for ourselves through the right of national self-determination whatever territorial concessions we absolutely needed.'[6]

In time Germany found that it 'absolutely needed' many of the territories that made up the former Russian Empire and it still had its eyes on more distant objectives when the battle on the Western front ran out of

2. Harold Nicolson. *Peacemaking*. p.37.
3. *Annual Register*. 1918. p.301.
4. V. R. Berghahn. *Modern Germany*. p.55-6.
5. Fischer. *Aims of Germany in the 1st World War*. p.398–9.
6. Kuhlmann. Erinerungen. pp.523f. Fischer. Aims of Germany in the 1st World War.

steam and the morale of the troops began to crumble. Germany imposed a strict censorship on adverse news and members of the Social Democratic Party (SPD), who were considered to be troublemakers were dealt with remorselessly. The historian, Sebastien Haffner, describes the feeling on the Home front in Germany in the Summer of 1918:

> 'The idea of a possible defeat had never seriously gained ground. Had there not been an unbroken succession of victories for four years? Was the Army not everywhere in enemy country? Had not Russia been forced to make peace? For the people in Germany the War consisted of hunger, worry for those 'out there' – and news of victories. They kept going, clenched their teeth and fought and starved and went on toiling – full of bitterness for those who despite all victories were not ready to make peace. That they would end by losing the War never entered their heads.'[7]

1.3 Soviet Peace Proposals

The Soviet peace proposals had been made on 19 November 1917. Then the German delegation had stunned the Allies by agreeing to Lenin's proposal for renunciation of annexations and reparations 'without exception and without any reservation' but with the cunning proviso that their proposal must be agreed by all belligerents, including such countries as Ireland, Morocco and India, within ten days, that is by 4 January 1918. The sheer impossibility of Allied agreement within the time stated demonstrated the nature of the German proposal. But those who chose not to look at the small print would hasten to condemn their own supposedly greedy and rapacious leaders for not immediately echoing such elevated statements. The ball was firmly back in the Allies' court.[8]

Naturally the socialists in Britain were angry at the lack of altruism emanating from their own leadership. A lot of water had passed under the bridge since Germany had invaded Belgium in 1914. Passchendaele had been a bloody and seemingly useless campaign while early success at Cambrai had made the reverse that followed all the more difficult to bear. The country had thought that it might win the war in the Autumn of 1917. Now the realisation was sinking in that, far from gaining military victory, Great Britain was about to go on the defensive. Maynard Keynes epitomised the thoughts of many pacifists on the left when he wrote to his mother in December 1917:

7. Sebastien Haffner. *Failure of a Revolution. Germany.* 1918–19.
8. Fischer. *Aims of Germany in the 1st World War.* p.488-9.

'My Christmas thoughts are that a further prolongation of the war, with the turn things have now taken, probably means the disappearance of the social order we have known hitherto...I reflect with a good deal of satisfaction that because our rulers are as incompetent as they are mad and wicked, one particular era of a particular kind of civilisation is nearly over.'[9]

William Ormsby-Gore, Secretary to the Cabinet, wrote to the Prime Minister to tell him of the tenor of the Labour Conference. The unions planned strike action over the threatened taking of trade unionists for the army, 'war aims,' food, and excess profits. Ormsby-Gore blamed much of the agitation on shop stewards rather than Trade Union leaders and pointed darkly to the fact that many of the more left-wing shop stewards, such as Gallacher, Murphy and Cassidy had 'Irish sounding names.' But he asserted that the left had declared that they would no longer support an offensive war:

'The idea is growing among the intelligentsia of the labour movement that any interest to the working classes must be obtained, not through military victory but by negotiation......The Labour leaders are asking the question whether a military victory is in itself desirable, even if it were possible after Cambrai.

'It would therefore seem absolutely essential that the long standing demand for clearer definitions of our war aims and those of France and Italy will have to be made if Labour is to be reassured.'[10]

On 20 December 1917 Lloyd George reiterated his rallying call of the previous June for the 'destruction of Prussian military power.'[11] But Arthur Henderson, leader of the Labour Party, called for the destruction 'of militarism not only in Germany but universally' at the Trades Union Conference at the end of the month. So when Lloyd George outlined his country's war aims, on 5 January 1918, he tailored his language so as not to upset Labour sensibilities, declaring that Britain had not entered the war 'to alter or destroy the Imperial constitution (Germany's) much as we consider that military constitution a dangerous anachronism in the twentieth century.' He stated Britain's aims to be[12]:

1. Belgium to be restored politically and economically.
2. Alsace-Lorraine to be returned to France.
3. Austria/Hungary to remain intact but Serbia, Montenegro and the occupied parts of France, Italy and Rumania to be restored.

9. R. Skidelsky. *John Maynard Keynes. Hopes Betrayed.* p.346.

10. *Lloyd George Papers.* F/23/2/1.

11. *Annual Register.* 1917. p.193.

12. Lloyd George Papers. Extracts from Certain Peace Statements made since January 1917. (2 Whitehall Gardens. 5.2.18) F/160/1/1.

Figure 1.1 Bertrand Russell, Maynard Keynes and Lytton Strachey at Garsington 1915
Reproduced with permission of Dr. M. Keynes.

4. The passage between the Mediterranean and the Black Sea to be neutralised and internationalised. Arabia, Armenia, Mesopotamia, Syria and Palestine to be recognised as separate national states, no longer under Turkey's wing, their form of government and, under whose supervision to be decided later.
5. The German colonies to be run for the benefit of the nations concerned and 'not for the benefit of European capitalists.'
6. An international body to be set up to settle disputes.
7. Although the Austrian/Hungarian Empire should remain intact the different nationalities should have self-government.
8. The Prussian Empire should remain essentially intact but, preferably under a democratic government. 'They, the British peoples, have never aimed at the break-up of the German peoples and the dis- integration of their state or country. Nor did we enter this war merely to alter or destroy the Imperial constitution, much as we consider that military constitution a dangerous anachronism in the twentieth century...Our point of view is that the adoption of a really democratic constitution ...would make it much easier for us to conclude peace with her. But that is for the German people to decide.'[13]

Lloyd George was not amused when President Wilson came out with a statement of his own war aims only three days later on 8 January. Lloyd George was an opportunist who was inclined to suit his message to his audience. President Wilson had been a professor of politics and, having adopted a viewpoint, stuck to it like glue. Nine of his points were remarkably similar to those of Lloyd George. This was unfortunate since Lloyd George's views on the colonial question were contrary to the current views of most Europeans and the majority of the British people. Also while allowing Britain's colonial states to work towards 'self- determination', Lloyd George had ruled it out for the Prussian Empire's recently acquired subjects from such ancient kingdoms as Saxony and Bavaria. If the proposals were adopted they would leave the Prussian Empire consolidated into one enormous country and the British Empire under threat. President Wilson had told Lloyd George that he would be displeased if Lloyd George's war aims differed materially from his own. Now he pounced on Lloyd George's speech and added some more points, one of which could only be described as hostile.

1. No secret international agreements.
2. Freedom of the seas.
3. Free trade.
4. A reduction in armaments consistent with national safety.

13. *Lloyd George Papers.* F/166/1/1.

5. An independent Polish state.
6. Russia was to be evacuated and left intact.

On the question of Germany President Wilson declared: 'Neither do we presume to suggest any alteration or modification in her institutions.'[14]

But the clause to which Britain objected most strongly was 'freedom of the seas.'

All seas are free in peacetime but Britain, so dependent herself on maritime shipments, had mounted a blockade to stop raw materials reaching Germany during the war. Lloyd George had had these words to say in Glasgow on 27 June 1917 on this matter:

> 'The freedom of the seas as the preliminary conditions of the free existence and peaceful intercourse of the peoples and the open door for trade by all nations have always belonged to the leading principles of German policy.'[15]

Lloyd George was filled with alarm and despondency about Wilson, whom he considered a victim of Irish and German propaganda. America had a large population of German origin before the 1st World War although many of these had been socialists expelled by Bismarck and were therefore not enamoured of the German Imperial regime. There were also many vociferous Irish in America who, now they were far from their former homeland, felt that they knew what was best for the old country and were determined to influence events. Lloyd George declared:

> 'The Irish are now paralysing the war activities of America. If America goes wrong we are lost.'[16]

However, in the end it was the Germans themselves who resolved all President Wilson's 'hesitations' when they rejected his fourteen points and concluded the Peace of Brest-Litovsk with the Russians. Count Hertling brusquely dismissed President Wilson's 14 points. The only ones that interested his strong industrial country were 'free trade', 'the freedom of the seas' and America's promise not to tamper with Germany's unrepresentative government. But he made it clear that no one was going to dictate peace to Germany. Germany was going to decide its own future. 'General peace is not possible so long as the integrity of the German Empire, the security of its vital interests, and the dignity of our Fatherland are not guaranteed. Until that time we must quietly stand by each other and wait.'[17]

14. *Annual Register*. 1918. p.290.
15. *Lloyd George Papers*. F/160/1/1.
16. *Lloyd George Papers*. F82/8/4.
17. *Lloyd George Papers*. F/160/1/1.

ALLECHENY 15 COLLEGE LIBRARY

1.4 Germany on the Offensive

Germany, however, did not 'quietly stand by' and wait. Following fast on the heels of its successful dissection of the Russian Empire, the German army fell on the tired forces of Europe with overwhelming numbers. Haig pleaded with his men in this desperate hour:

'Three weeks ago to-day the enemy began his terrific attacks against us on a 50 mile front. His objects are to separate us from the French, to take the Channel ports, and destroy the British Army.

'In spite of throwing already 106 divisions into the battle and enduring the most reckless sacrifice of human life he has yet made little progress towards his goal. We owe this to the determined fighting and self-sacrifice of our troops.

'Words fail me to express the admiration which I feel for the splendid resistance offered by all ranks of our Army under the most trying circumstances.

'Many of us now are tired. To those I would say that victory will belong to the side which holds out the longest.

'The French army is moving rapidly and in great force to our support.

'There is no other course open to us but to fight it out. Every position must be held to the last man; there must be no retirement. With our backs to the wall and believing in the justice of our cause, each one of us must fight on to the end.

'The safety of our homes and the freedom of mankind depend alike upon the conduct of each one of us at this critical moment.'[18]

We often think of World War I as mass massacre in the mud. Many men did die that way. The following extracts from Haig's account of the 1918 Spring offensive, however, illustrate the individual heroism of countless others:

'On March 27th, at Le Quesnoy, a detachment of 100 officers and men of the 61st Brigade, 20th Division,...was detailed to cover the withdrawal of their division, and under the command of their Brigade Major, Captain E.P. Combe, M.C. successfully held the enemy at bay from early morning until 6.p.m. at night when the eleven survivors withdrew under orders, having accomplished their task.'

'On April 9th the advanced posts of the 55th Division held out with the utmost resolution though surrounded, pinning to the ground those parties of the enemy who had penetrated our defences and preventing them from developing their attack...one machine gun...was kept in action although the German infantry had entered the rear compartment of the 'pill-box' from which it was firing, the gun team holding up the enemy by revolver fire from the inner compartment.'

18. *Annual Register.* 1918. p.27.

'During the morning, which was very foggy of April 12th several deter-mined attacks, in which a German armoured car came into action against the 4th Guards Brigade on the Southern portion of our line, were repulsed with great loss to the enemy. After the failure of the assaults, he brought up field-guns to point-blank range, and in the northern sector with their aid, gained Vieux Berquin. Everywhere except at Vieux Berquin the enemy's advance was held up all day by desperate fighting, in which our advanced positions maintained their ground when entirely surrounded, men standing back to back in the trenches and shooting to front and rear.

'In the afternoon the enemy made a further determined effort and by sheer weight of numbers forced his way through the gaps in our depleted line, the surviving garrisons of our posts fighting where they stood to the last with bullet and bayonet. The heroic resistance of these troops, however, had given the leading brigades of the 1st Australian Division time to reach and organise their appointed line east of the Forêt de Nieppe. These now took up the fight and the way to Hazebrouck was definitely closed.' [19]

1.5 American Casualties

President Wilson's patience with Germany was at an end. On 6 April he declared: 'There is, therefore, but one response possible for us: force, force to the utmost, force without stint or limit, the righteous and tri-umphant force which shall make right the law of the world and cast every selfish dominion down in the dust.' [20]

A new federal loan was raised by the American Government, 'the vic-tory loan,' and during the last seven months of the war many of the 10 mil-lion Americans liable for military service were rushed over to Europe's shores. The numbers who died in the Allied cause in 1918 were:

Killed:	32,842
Died of disease etc.:	17,015
Lost at sea:	13,554 [21]

There were also many casualties and some Americans were taken prisoner. The thought of the arrival of more and yet more, young, fresh American troops would deal a crushing blow to the morale of the German army. By October the American army had overtaken the British army in size. After France they would have the largest army on the battlefield. [22]

19. *Annual Register.* 1918. p.127 - from a dispatch by General Haig.
20. *Woodrow Wilson. Public Papers.* Vol. V. pp.198–202.
21. *Annual Register.* 1919. p.295.
22. *New York Times.*

1.6 Germany on the Retreat

At last, in the middle of July, the Germans suffered a reverse. The Prussian military high command's overweening ambition had at last outstretched itself. Soon the Allies were pushing the Germans back towards their homelands. On 8 August, the 'black day' as Ludendorff called it, the British army delivered a telling defeat on the Germans. By 3 September German ministers could no longer ignore the casualty figures. They were flatly told that 'The reserves of the central powers are running out.'[23] Peace initiatives could not long be delayed.

On 13 September the Daily Mirror recorded Von Payer, the German Vice-Chancellor's, first peace initiative. He reserved the right for Germany to keep its Eastern territorial acquisitions, especially Poland and Finland. Von Payer stated bluntly: 'We can never permit anyone to meddle with us in this matter.' 'Just as little will we submit to the Entente for its gracious approval or alteration of our peace treaties with the Ukraine, Russia and Rumania.' But Germany was prepared to withdraw from France and Belgium.

It obviously hoped that by doing a deal in the West it might be able to retain its Eastern Empire. And it was prepared to accommodate Allied sensibilities with regard to Germany's autocratic form of government if that was to be the price of peace. 'A great democratic peace campaign is being prepared for the delusion of the Allies' alleged the Daily Mirror.

Hot on the heels of this initiative, an Austrian note was sent, inviting all the belligerents to a peace conference. Then a hasty new German proposal was made to Belgium, providing that Belgium remained 'neutral until the end of the war.'

On 2 September the Allies had recovered the important Drocourt Queant-Switch line. Finally Haig secured his war cabinet's grudging permission to pierce the Hindenburg line and capture the Passchendaele Salient by making the position clear to them. 'The discipline of the German army is quickly going, and the German officer is not what he was.'[24] The loss of this wretched, much disputed territory proved the final straw to German morale.

The Germans had won their battle on the Eastern front with the help of the Russian Revolution, aided by German money, propaganda and

---

23. Schwertfeger. *op.cit.* pp.242.ff. Fischer. *Aims of Germany in the 1st World War.*
24. Schwertfeger. op.cit. pp.242.ff. Fischer. Aims of Germany in the 1st World War. p.630.

the clever manipulation of words.[25] But on the Western front they had lost 300,000 men at Verdun, 560,000 on the Somme, at least 260,000 at Passchendaele in 1917 and hundreds of thousands more on their 1918 Spring offensive[26] yet still had not achieved victory. On 28 September as the Allies, in 'bog-like conditions' surmounted the Passchendaele Salient, Generals Ludendorff and Hindenburg informed their Emperor that an armistice must be sought.

1.7 America's Peace Initiative

President Wilson had replied to Germany's peace initiative of 13 September by offering 'impartial justice' and a peace based on the 14 points on 27 September. But talk of the 14 points and principles did not figure as a reason for the desperate German generals to ask their Emperor to seek peace. Peace must be sought, the Generals told him because:

> 'The army could not wait forty-eight hours longer.'[27]...'Today the troops are holding their own; what may happen tomorrow cannot be foreseen...'

It was a terrible task to have to tell the Emperor of such a nation, many of whose commanders could conceive of no higher honour than dying for their country, that his territorial ambitions had come to naught. Germany was facing defeat.

Colonel von Thaer has supplied us with this vital evidence in his diary both of the collapse of the troops on the Western front and of the Generals' determination to throw the blame on the socialists for the 'mess.'

> 'When we had assembled, Ludendorff stepped among us, his face filled with the deepest grief, pale, but with his head held high. A truly beautiful Germanic hero figure! I had to think of Siegfried with the fatal wound in his back from Hagen's spear. He said roughly this. 'It was his duty to tell us that our military situation was terribly grave. Our Western front might be breached any day...There was no relying on the troops any longer...Thus it was to be antici-pated that in future with the help of the high battle morale of the Americans the enemy would gain a major victory, and break through on a very large scale; our army on the West would then get out of control and flood back across the Rhine in complete disorder, bringing revolution to Germany...For the above reasons no further defeat could be risked. The Kaiser had accepted his resignation.'

25. Fischer. *Aims of Germany in the 1st World War.* p.146–54. Also p.36–8. Kuhlmann: "It was only the resources which the Bolsheviks received regularly from our side, through various channels and on various pretexts, that enabled them to develop their chief organ Pravda, to carry on a lively agitation and greatly to expand the originally narrow base of their party."

26. *Haig. The Educated Soldier.* Verdun. p.191. Somme, Passchendaele. p.371–2.

27. *Preliminary History of the Armistice.* pp.40–2.

His Excellency Ludendorff added:

> 'For the moment we are therefore without a Chancellor. It is not yet clear who will take over. I have, however, begged H.M. now to draw into the Government those circles whom we have chiefly to thank for being in this position. We shall thus see these gentlemen moving into the Ministries. Let them conclude the peace that must now be concluded. Let them cope with the mess! It is their mess after all.'[28]

1.8 President Wilson's Vision of a Better World

Despite German military aggression in the Spring, President Wilson had still not lost his vision of a better world order where disputes could be settled without distress and bloodshed. The Treaty of Brest-Litovsk and the near evacuation of Paris had convinced him that 'force' was the only way to deal with the marauding Prussian Empire. However, when the tables were turned and Germany was on its knees, he felt more threatened by what he saw as the old imperialist nations, the British and French. The kowtowing of the Allied leaders had convinced him of the political weakness of those countries. He felt he could use his strength to create a better world. So, on the very day that the Allies were surmounting the Passchendaele salient, he offered new hope to the beleaguered Germany army. He placed his hope on the League of Nations, which he saw as a sort of godlike body, much as many Europeans envisaged President Wilson himself, to curb any renewed German ambitions and called for 'impartial justice.'

> 'The impartial justice.' President Wilson declared: 'must involve no discrimination between those to whom we wish to be just and those to whom we do not wish to be just. It must be a justice that knows no favourites and knows no standards but the equal rights of the several peoples concerned.'

The way President Wilson was going to mete out that 'impartial justice' was through the auspices of a League of Nations.

Indeed President Wilson declared that the 'League of Nations...is in a sense the most essential part, of the peace settlement itself.'

But he declared in a manner that must have brought worries to Empires like Great Britain that 'no special or separate interest of any single nation or any group of nations can be made the basis of any part of the settlement which is not consistent with the common interest of all.

28. Sebastien Haffner. *Failure of a Revolution. Germany 1918–19*. p.38.

'There can be no leagues or alliances or special covenants or understandings within the general and common family of the League of Nations.

'And more specifically there can be no special selfish economic combinations within the League and no employment of any form of economic boycott or exclusion except as the power of economic penalty by exclusion from the markets of the world which may be vested in the League of Nations itself as a means of discipline and control.

'All international agreements and treaties of every kind must be made known in their entirety to the rest of the world.'[29]

Despite the high moral tone of the President's words the leaders of Allied governments whose Empires had supported them through thick and thin during the war, could not but feel those Empires to be threatened by President Wilson's talk of 'no leagues or special ... understandings', 'and more specifically ... no special selfish economic combinations'. But what must have made them aghast was his talk of 'impartial justice, no matter whose interest is crossed' between them and the nations they had been fighting against for four years. These apprehensions were even more heightened because American Secretary of State, Robert Lansing, had just sent a letter to his President which read:

'We are receiving constant reports, the truth of which seems beyond question, that the retiring armies of Germany are destroying property and committing outrages in the territory which they are forced to evacuate, that the destruction is without any military benefit whatsoever, and that this deliberate lawlessness is inspired by malice and spite...'[30]

1.9 Domestic Strife in Britain

Although the British army was winning the war by the Autumn of 1918, the British Home front was not a happy place, weakening the resolve of Britain's elected leaders. In January Lloyd George had brought in universal male suffrage and the vote for women over thirty, enfranchising some 8 million extra voters.[31] Food rationing was also brought in to eke out the meagre food supplies. But still some workers were discontented.

---

29. *Annual Register.* 1918. p.296-7.
30. Ray Stannard Baker. *Woodrow Wilson. Life & Letters.* Vol.8. p.431. The letters of President Wilson have lately been republished by Princeton University Press, editor Arthur S. Link. *The Papers of Woodrow Wilson* leaves out some of the material in *Woodrow Wilson Life & Letters* but gives the whole text of letters rather than just extracts. Link gives the whole text of this important letter on page 135 of Vol. 51, published in 1985.
31. *Annual Register.* 1918. p.51–2.

There had been a cession of shop floor unrest in those desperate months of March and April. However, in the fateful month of July, when the future of Europe still hung in the balance, the Ministry of Munitions had put an embargo on employers taking on more men because they were needed for the war. Strikes then broke out in the key munitions industries on the grounds that the embargo violated 'the liberty of the worker in the free disposal of his labour.'[32] 12,000 skilled workers downed tools at Coventry on 23 July, while on 26 July 300,000 munitions workers threatened to strike if the embargo was not lifted. Over 100,000 workers were said to be already idle in Birmingham. Despite Lloyd George's statement of war aims in January army recruitment figures had fallen dramatically in 1918 as can be seen from the following table.

Total joining the armed forces:

1914	1,186,357
1915	1.280,000
1916	1,190,000
1917	820,646
1918	493,562[33]

But Lloyd George rallied his nation firmly. First he issued a stern declaration that if the strikers didn't return to work 'they will become liable to the provisions of the Military Service Acts'. Then, on the fourth anniversary of Britain's entry into the war, he issued a timely reminder of national aims:

> 'We are in this war for no selfish ends. We are in it to recover freedom for the nations which have been brutally attacked and despoiled, and to prove that no people, however powerful, can surrender itself to the lawless ambitions of militarism without meeting retribution....To stop short of Victory for this cause would be to compromise the future of mankind.
> 'The great autocracy of Prussia will still endeavour by violence or guile to avoid defeat and so give militarism a new lease of life. Having set our hands to the task we must see it through till a just and lasting settlement is achieved. HOLD FAST!'[34]

On 19 August the *Daily Mirror* reproduced letters from the soldiers at the front echoing Lloyd George's message, begging their friends on the shop floor to support their war efforts:

> 'People at home have no idea of the feeling overseas amongst the men, and they will be considerably surprised when they come home....'

32. *Annual Register.* 1918. p.122.
33. Stevenson. *British Society. 1914–45.* p.65.
34. *Annual Register.* 1918. p.129

'The lads out here will stick it all right if you only keep on backing them up as you are doing.'

'Let us have a clean sweep of our Huns in the trade unions, who misrepresent us in Parliament and out of it.'

However despite Lloyd George's rallying words, and the pleas of soldiers at the front, there were a depressing number of strikes in August and September. On 19 August, women on the London buses demanded the right to an equal war bonus pay as the male employees. The strike soon spread to Bath, Brighton, Hove, Bristol, Folkestone, Hastings and Weston-super-Mare. After ten days they were awarded the bonus. Meanwhile strikes had broken out among the miners and women workers in transport and tailoring. On Saturday 30 August the Police went on strike demanding an increased war bonus, union recognition and the reinstatement of ex-Police Constable Thiel, provincial organiser of the nascent union and delegate to the London Trades Council. Lloyd George agreed to all their requests on condition that the men went back to work immediately. Sir Edward Henry, Commissioner of the London Police, resigned.

It soon became clear that, as in Germany in January 1918 when a million workers went on strike in support of their colleagues in Russia, the primary reason for the strikes in the Autumn of 1918 was political. They did, however, for a time seem to threaten the very life of the nation. The success of the Police Officers' strike encouraged the Firemen to threaten to follow suit. While on 16 September the Lancashire cotton spinners went on strike, followed by the railwaymen. Both these disputes endangered the success of the British army in France and Belgium. The army and the navy had to be called in to ensure supplies and ammunition for the troops, operate the ambulance trains and even to distribute food for the civilian population.[35]

The Trades Union and Labour Conferences showed the shop floor's political confidence. With victory in sight they wished to put pressure on their government to accept peace on the basis of the fourteen points. A clear-cut victory would have meant recriminations against them for not supporting the war in 1918; besides so many of the fourteen points were similar to the points that Lloyd George had outlined for them as war aims in January. So they were prepared to fight for a compromise peace, even though they were taking the risk, which must have seemed slim at the time, that they might 'give (Prussian) militarism a new lease of life.'

The Trades Union Congress on 3 September called for solidarity between the young Labour Party and the trade union movement. It laid down 5 principles for peace.

---

35. *Annual Register*. 1918. p.136.

THE TRAITOR.

Figure 1.2 The Traitor
© Punch

1. It held that an International Labour and Socialist conference was an essential preliminary to peace.
2. It called on the Socialists of the Central Powers to state their war aims in response to the memorandum of Inter-Allied labour.
3. It demanded Labour representation at the Peace Conference.
4. It urged the government to initiate peace negotiations immediately the enemy, either voluntarily or by compulsion, evacuated France and Belgium.
5. It expressed belief in the principle of the Socialist International as the safest guarantee of the world's future peace.

Sam Gompers, President of the American Federation of Labour, attended this conference and he also attended Labour's second conference on 17 September which was attended by delegates from socialist organisations in France, Italy, Belgium, Serbia and Greece. The object was to determine common war and peace aims and the main result was a decision to adopt 'the fourteen points of Mr. Wilson as the war aims of Allied Labour.'[36]

1.10 The Fight Goes On

September was a wearing month for the Home front. There was a dreadful shortage of coal at the power stations, hardly enough even to supply Britain's ships, but Milner begged the Prime Minister not to withdraw more men from the depleted British fighting lines, saying that the miners could work harder.[37]

Lloyd George complained that the arriving American troops were not being used to reinforce the British army but being used for the relief of the French 'whilst our men are left...to hold the mud through the winter.'[38] He ordered that pressure should be put on the Americans to support the British army as well as the French since it was British ships which were bringing American soldiers to Europe.

A virulent flu swept the British Isles killing 761 people a week in October in London alone. It did not begin to abate till the first week of November.[39]

Despite being weakened by the dreadful influenza virus sweeping the

36. *Annual Register.* 1918. p.138.
37. *Lloyd George Papers.* F/38/4/20.
38. *Lloyd George Papers.* F/38/4/20.
39. *Annual Register.* p.138–9.

country and alarmed by the severity of the strike action, the overwhelming majority of the British people wanted to fight on for a clear-cut victory in 1918. Lloyd George spoke for the British people when he declared on 15 September:

> 'Prussian military power must not only be beaten but Germany herself must know that. The German people must know that if their rulers outrage the laws of humanity, Prussian military strength cannot protect them from punishment ... Unless this is accomplished, the loss, the suffering, and the burdens of this war will have been in vain.'[40]

So how did the Allies come to accept a compromise peace which enabled the Germans 'by guile...to avoid defeat' and be able to tell their populace that they had never been defeated in battle?

1.11 A Compromise Peace Plan

On 6 October 1918 the news swept Britain that Germany had grasped at the lifeline offered by President Wilson at the end of September. Although this meant Germany foregoing the whole of its newly acquired Eastern Empire, the Allies must have been bitterly aware that the 14 points had originally been offered to Germany in January 1918, when the fortunes of the Allies had been at their lowest ebb. It had been summarily turned down by Germany at that time and the British army alone had suffered over 600,000 casualties since,[41] in what could only be called an imperialist offensive by Germany. The *Daily Telegraph* commented wryly of the new Chancellor, Prince Max's initiative:

> 'The German Chancellor is favourably impressed with Mr. Wilson's speech of January 8 as a basis of peace negotiations – a speech which had been familiar to everyone in Germany for two months and more when the last German bid for a crushing victory was made this spring. We would refer him to a speech made by Mr. Wilson shortly before the utterance of 8 January in which he said:
> 'This menace of combined intrigue and force, which we now see so clearly as the German power, a thing without conscience or honour or capacity for covenanted peace, must be crushed.'

President Wilson, however, chose not to remember the Allied and American dead of 1918. Now that the German army was on its knees he was more worried by what he termed 'British navalism' and French

---

40. *Lloyd George Memoirs*. Vol.VI. p.3251.
41. J. Terraine. *To Win a War*. p.149.

thoughts of revenge. He therefore made an encouraging reply to Germany's overture and the leaders of the Allies looked on helplessly and with increasing suspicion while President Wilson talked to their enemy without consulting them.

The prospect of peace talks had a marked effect on the Allies in Europe. British, French, and Italian politicians, excluded from President Wilson's discussions with Germany became alarmed lest he make a separate peace. The French and the British armies, who had fought so well as a team, now began to show suspicion of each other too.

This was the moment when the *Foundations of Germany*, Ellis Barker's documentary account of Prussian history and attitudes should have been circulated to generals and politicians alike, for in commenting on the Prussian campaign of 1761-62 he wrote:

> 'At the end of the last campaign in the opinion of all statesmen Prussia was lost. After the battle of Kunersdorf, scarcely 10,000 men of Frederick's army remained and they were a flying mob. However, when the Austrian general urged the Russian general to finish off the Prussian rabble he replied:
> 'I have done enough during this year. I have won two battles which have cost Russia 27,000 men...It is not right that the Russian troops should bear the brunt and do all the fighting.'[42]

There is no doubt that Field Marshall Haig felt this way in October 1918. The prospect of peace had had a dramatic effect on the French army who must have despaired at times of ever ridding the Germans from their soil. Haig remarked of the French army that it was 'worn out and has not been really fighting latterly. It has been freely said that the 'war is over' and 'we don't want to lose our lives now that peace is in sight.'[43] The French supremo Foch, for whose reinstatement Haig had campaigned in order to save Paris in the Spring (Foch had lost his command in 1916 accused of wasting too many French lives) had put forward a plan for armistice terms without any reference to Haig, or indeed, it appears to the wishes of his President, Poincaré. The terms which he submitted to Lloyd George and the French Prime Minister, Clemenceau, represented 'unconditional surrender' in every respect except that the Germans would be able to march back to Germany brandishing their weapons. Why he proposed to offer this valuable propaganda weapon to Germany when it was obviously contrary to the wishes of Poincaré is not known. By October 1918 the rifle strength of the Allies with the newly arrived Americans outnumbered the Germans by 2:1.[44] The

---

42. J. Ellis Barker. *The Foundations of Germany*. (1916) p.102.
43. Robert Blake. *Private Papers of Douglas Haig*. p.326.
44. *Annual Register*. 1919. p.276.

British had held the line in the Spring of 1918 and in the Autumn they had captured 200,000 prisoners and 2,510 guns compared to the French armies 133,720 prisoners and 1,880 guns. Foch had even had to borrow Haig's second army to reinstate the Belgian king.[45] So, although Foch had been made supremo, tact, at least, would have dictated a common initiative.

But Foch did not seek a common political initiative from the leader of the army which had given so much support to his country. Old jealousies of France returned, to which were added suspicions of the newly arrived American troops. Haig pleaded for a compassionate peace.

> 'The British army has done much of the fighting latterly, and everyone wants to have done with the war, provided we get what we want. I therefore advise that we only ask in the armistice for what we intend to hold and that we set our faces against the French entering Germany to pay off old scores. In my opinion, under the supposed conditions, the British army would not fight for what really is not its affair.'[46]

There is no doubt that the sentiments that Haig was expressing would probably have been echoed by many in the British army. Haig had considered the German army beaten. He recorded in his diary.

> 'Saturday September 28th. The object of the day's operations is to get the Clercken-Passchendaele Ridge as a base for further operations. Reports from the Cambrai sector of my front are also most satisfactory. The enemy seems to be falling back without offering much resistance to the east of the Scheldt. I visited Head Quarters, the Third army before lunch and had a talk with Byng. He now thinks that the enemy on his front shows signs of 'cracking.'
> 'October 1st. I motored with C.G.S. to Head Quarters, third army (near Baupaume) and had a talk with Generals Byng and Rawlinson. Both consider that the enemy has suffered very much, and that it is merely a question of our continuing our pressure to ensure his completely breaking.'

On 5 October Germany announced in the Reichstag that it had made a peace initiative on the basis of the fourteen points. Ray Stannard Baker, President Wilson's Press Secretary, reported the effect that this bombshell produced on Germany's previously uninformed populace. 'Panic on the Berlin Stock Exchange was reported, shipping and armament shares being especially affected.'

On 10 October General Haig wrote in his diary: 'We have got the enemy down, in fact, he is a beaten Army, and my plan is to go on hitting him as hard as we possibly can, till he begs for mercy....I think the

---

45. *Private Papers of Douglas Haig.* p.326.
46. Robert Blake. *Private Papers of Douglas Haig.* p.334.

situation is highly satisfactory for us, and the results of our victories will be far-reaching.'[47]

However, the war was not yet over and Lloyd George had warned in July 'Prussia will still endeavour by violence or guile to avoid defeat and give militarism a new lease of life.'

1.12 Germany Requests Peace

On 5 October President Wilson had received Germany's first note asking for peace on the basis of his points and principles, while Prince Max stated in the German Reichstag that the socialists' famous 'peace resolution' of July 1917 had been adopted by the government and that the Reichstag itself would now be assuming 'a more important position in the governance of the Empire.' He declared, however, that should Germany not receive a satisfactory answer to her note he had every confidence in his army's ability to continue the struggle.[48]

Wilson's reply arrived promptly on 8 October. It stated that he wanted to make sure that the Germans accepted all his points and principles and that he could not grant Germany peace as long as Germany and its Allies remained on foreign soil. Finally he wanted to know whether Prince Max was speaking for all Germans.[49]

In haste, on 12 October, Germany sent another note to America. It agreed to all his points and principles. It affirmed that Germany spoke for all its Allies in agreeing to evacuate foreign soil. And it declared that it spoke for the German Chancellor and all the German people.

The prospect of peace without annihilation had a dramatic effect on the morale of the German army in the field.

On Saturday 19 October Haig reported:

'Our attack on the 17th met with considerable opposition ...the enemy was not ready for unconditional surrender.'

On 1 November he recorded:

'The determined fight put up by the enemy today shows that all the divisions in the German army are not yet demoralised.'[50]

It was essential now that the Allies and their associate, America, stood

47. Robert Blake. *Private Papers of Douglas Haig.* p.328–31.
48. 'German notes to America'. See under Germany. *Annual Register.* 1918. p.202.
49. 'American notes to Germany'. See under America. *Annual Register.* 1918
50. Robert Blake. *Private Papers of Douglas Haig.* p.332–9.

firm to defeat what had become close to a German religion – the myth of the Master Race and the all conquering Prussian army. It was not even as though President Wilson had the authority to give succour to the Germans. The 1916 Presidential elections had been close with all the Eastern States (except for Ohio and possibly New Hampshire) voting for America's participation in the war. Only late results from the middle and far west finally returned President Wilson to the White House with a workable majority.[51] His majority in the Senate had been reduced to eight, however, while control over the House of Representatives rested with a handful of Progressives and Independents. Now the Congressional elections, due on 5 November, were coming closer by the day and the American Press objected most strongly to anything less than 'unconditional surrender.'[52]

Theodore Roosevelt, the Republican leader, had made his position plain on 7 October 1918:

'I am living in constant anxiety now of a sudden plunge of the Administration for a negotiated peace. At this point, if we make an armistice we have lost the war and we shall leave Germany about where she started. I am sure that the American people want a complete victory and an unconditional surrender.'[53]

On 24 October he even hinted that for America to grant Germany peace on the basis of the fourteen points without the support of the Senate, might be unconstitutional.

'As an American citizen, I most earnestly hope that the Senate of the United States, which is part of the treaty-making power of the United States, will take affirmative action against a negotiated peace with Germany. I earnestly hope that on behalf of the American people it will declare against the adoption in their entirety of the fourteen points of the President's address of last January as offering a basis for a peace satisfactory to the United States.

'Let us dictate peace by the hammering guns and not chat about peace to the accompaniment of the clicking of typewriters...Moreover we should find out what the President means by continually referring to this country merely as the associate instead of the ally of the nations with whose troops our own are actually brigaded in battle...'[54]

---

51. Arthur S. Link. *Woodrow Wilson and the Progressive Era*. p.247.
52. Baker. Woodrow Wilson. Life and Letters. Vol.8. p.455. Quoted from the Baltimore Sun: "Absolute surrender is the sine qua non for peace, the condition precedent to the consideration of terms. The fact to be constantly in mind is that this is not a war against a nation or a combination of nations, but against a great criminal which has deliberately organised to conquer and plunder the world."
53. R. S. Baker. *Woodrow Wilson. Life and Letters*. Vol.8. p.458.
54. R. S. Baker. *Woodrow Wilson. Life & Letters*. Vol.8 p.510–11.

1.13 German Industrial Sabotage

It was a timely warning to the American President because it was becoming evident that the Germans on their retreat were not behaving in the conciliatory manner embodied in the philosophy of President Wilson's points and principles.

In *Die Industrie im besetzten Frankreich bearbeitet im Auftrage des Generalquartiermeisters* (Munchen 1916) the Germans had described in 482 pages what they were going to do to beat French competition if they were forced to retreat: 'Coal mines: the districts will be unproductive for years to come owing to the removal of machinery and the flooding of shafts...France will have to buy her machinery from Germany...Textiles: the French textile industry will during the war have lost its markets. To reconquer them, and to derive some use of the terrible blow suffered by the textile industry in occupied regions, it is particularly important for Germany to start its intact industries working as quickly as possible after the war...'[55] This policy was put into action on their 1918 retreat. On 9 October, one week after the Germans started negotiating with President Wilson on the terms of a charter that was to end all wars, they were reported to be 'hard in flight, blowing up bridges and burning villages.'[56]

On 17 October German newspapers printed an official declaration stating that their armies had received orders to cease all devastation 'unless absolutely forced to follow this course by the military situation for defensive reasons.' Before this directive was implemented, however, Cambrai, Laon, and Lens had been looted and burned.[57] The *New York Times* reporter in December 1918 described how the Germans had operated in Belgium.

'This morning I visited the great Cockerill plant at Seraing near Liege. It is the largest engineering concern in Belgium and was founded 100 years ago. In normal times it employs 10,000 hands. The area covered by the works is immense and the multitude of buildings present the appearance of a town...Now not an ingot of steel can be made at Cockerill's for the Germans with devilish ingenuity have dismantled the essential machinery and either smashed it up or taken it off to Germany... A favourite method was to drop heavy weights on the machinery from a rolling crane. As one of the directors explained to me, the Germans deliberately aimed at crippling Belgian industry for several years so as to enable their own mills and factories to capture markets.'[58]

55. E. Mantoux. *The Carthaginian Peace.* p.91.
56. R. S. Baker. *Woodrow Wilson. Life & Letters.* p.467. (American) Relations. 1918. Supp.2. p.7901.
57. R. S. Baker. *Woodrow Wilson. Life & Letters.* p.483–4.
58. *New York Times.* 12.12.18.

Figure 1.3 Textile Mill in Lille, where machinery was wrecked by the Germans in October 1918 Produced with permission from the Imperial War Museum.

Under the terms of the armistice the German command would be ordered to reveal all the destructive measures that it had taken such as the poisoning or pollution of wells or springs, the return of gold appropriated from the National Bank of Belgium, return of barges etc.[59] Clemenceau, speaking at the peace conference was also to plead with President Wilson for the return of France's cattle:

> 'The strongest wish of the French peasants on the border is to recover their cattle stolen by hundreds and thousands and which they can now see feeding on the German side of the frontier. These peasants keep on crying out: 'After all we have won, can't the Germans be made to give us back our cattle?'[60]

Finally, one week before the armistice was signed: 'Germany gave notice to the Belgian coal mines that all men were to be brought out of the pits, materials delivered to Germans and the mines destroyed.'[61] It was only after a strong American protest that the Swiss minister in Washington transmitted a denial of this order.

1.14 Dedication and Discipline of British Army

On 22 October under a heading entitled 'British push on in ocean of mud' the New York Times commented on the discipline and dedication of the British army at the battle front (in contrast to the strikes and discord emanating from Britain itself).

> 'The year is waning and the weather, breaking today, was truly foul in the aspect around Courtrai, with a heavy drizzle for hours putting a wet blanket of mist over the fields and blotting out the view of villages and towns in this country of lowlands.
>
> 'The British troops slogged through water pools and trudged down rutty tracks with the mud splashing them to their neck, while lorries surged along broken tracks swung around shell craters and skirted deep ditches. Gun teams with all their horses plastered to their ears with mud travelled through the fog to take up new positions beyond the newly captured towns.
>
> 'All this makes war difficult and slow and what is amazing is the speed with which the armies are following up the German retreat like a world on the move, with aerodromes and hospitals, telegraph and transport, headquarters staffs and labour companies, all the vast population and mechanism which make up modern armies, across battlefields like the craters of the moon to country forty miles from their old bases.

59. *Annual Register.* 1918. p.153. Armistice Terms. p.155–6.
60. F. W. Foerster. *Europe and the German Question.* (1937) p.259.
61. R. S. Baker. *Woodrow Wilson. Life and Letters.* p.550. American Foreign Relations. 1918. Supp 2. p.790.

'It is a wonderful achievement, due to the industry and effort of every single man from the corps commanders to the road menders, working in the mud. One never hears any order given to hurry up or make haste. 'Carry on there' is the usual phrase of an officer with the rain dripping down his neck as he stands by a German pill-box with a watchful eye on his labour party, but the men do whatever job is theirs with a quiet industry which helps the army on and the man with the shovel, as well as the man with the rifle, is doing his level best to get a move on, and that is the way the army is moving.

'More cities are slipping into British hands and the enemy is being hustled faster than he wants to go and he cannot stop the weight of things bearing down on him with relentless and dreadful pressure.'[62]

1.15 American Media Dissatisfied with Compromise Peace

President Wilson and the Germans had penned notes to each other while Allied politicians remained impotent in the wings. But there was now a surge of feeling from President Wilson's own unconsulted constituents at home which could not be ignored. Americans had an election for their House of Representatives coming in two weeks time but President Wilson was not going to let them have a say on the vital issue of war and peace. The latest vague, unsatisfactory note from the Germans, on the 20 October, had especially incensed them. A flood of newspaper articles reflected their fears. They felt America was being hoodwinked. American newspapers up and down the country reflected their anxiety.

The *New York Tribune* commented bitterly: 'They (the Germans) have manoeuvred for an armistice which would save their precious Fatherland from an invasion, and lead to a peace conference based upon Mr. Wilson's conditions, which provide for Germany's restoration to free seas and free trade, and omit to mention moral punishment or reparation.'

'If that is what the American people have been fighting for let them hold their peace. If not then now is the time to speak.'

The *Boston Globe* felt that the President was being manipulated by left wing opinion in Allied countries: 'The ink and paper of the German reply to President Wilson are new; but it is the same old handwriting. Item by item the note reveals its insincerity. The problem propounded to the President by it is twofold: how to keep the internal front in Germany disunited – German liberals against German militarists – by insistence on genuine democratic reforms, and how to avoid alienating the sympa-

62. *New York Times.* 22.10.18.

thies of the more extreme popular parties in the Entente who may be (as we were once) disposed to accept the official professions of the present Government at their face value.'

Most newspapers urged their President to drop all discussion until the Germans had agreed to 'unconditional surrender.'

The *Boston Herald* declared: 'We hope the President will break off these negotiations by proclaiming at once the keynote of the situation. This keynote is unconditional surrender. Unconditional surrender is not alone the sole course for us, but it is the best for our enemies. The German people and their rulers must trust to the magnanimity of the Allies. The hour of reckoning has come, and the reckoning cannot be a matter of bargain and sale.'

The *Philadelphia Inquirer* maintained: 'The German note is mere bosh. It is a clumsy mixture of special pleading, of hypocrisy, of an effort to prolong discussion, and of downright lying. If any reply is sent to it, that reply should go in precisely two words – unconditional surrender.'[63]

The *Chicago Tribune* echoed its demand: 'From the German response it is apparent that the ruling powers at Berlin now look complete defeat in the face. It is inevitable that Germany's representatives will concede as little as they can without running the danger of bringing the present diplomatic interchanges to a brusque close...There is but one mind in America on this war – that it shall go on to victory, to the utter destruction of Prussian militarism.'

While the *New York* Journal of Commerce declared: 'a snivelling appeal to the President of the United States to approve of no demand 'irreconcilable with the honour of the German people' cannot change the fixed resolution of the Allied Governments and peoples to demand atonement.'

The *New York Times* also quoted from the British newspapers showing how many of them echoed the American point of view:

The *Daily Chronicle*: 'If Solf's present proposal, as it is not improbably may be only a piece of diplomatic huckstering, a stage along the downward pathway of surrender, which he desires to make gradual, but knows to be inevitable, well and good. We can wait until he reaches the bottom, but nothing should be done to encourage him or his people to think that in any event they can induce us to meet them half way down.'

The *Daily Mail*: 'The new Hun note is no reply at all. Quite characteristically, it reaches the world at the very moment of the news of the sinking in the Irish Sea of the steamer Dundalk by a Hun submarine.'

The *Morning Post* maintained that 'Germany enjoys all the advantages possessed by an unscrupulous liar over an honest man.' 'The

---

63. *New York Times*. 22.10.18. p.3.

Allies', it asserted luridly 'demand the unconditional surrender of 'this dehumanised people' because until 'these enemies of the human race' are compelled openly to take knowledge of their utter defeat there can be no peace in the world.'

On 14 October 1918, the *Daily Mail* reproduced a prophecy from the *American Everybody's Magazine* of September 1918 entitled:

THE GREAT WAR OF 1938

And the subtitle,

IF ONLY WE HAD SEEN IT THROUGH IN 1918

The article started:

> 'These are words that with inexorable certainty will be wrung from our agonized lips twenty years from now – if, in these tremendous moments of world-struggle, we falter, relax, and in weariness fall short of finishing our task now and for all time.'

In the lengthy subsequent article it went on to try to describe the bloodshed and misery of a second world war.

President Wilson had fallen 'short of finishing' his 'task' of defeating Germany but had hoisted instead what might have been interpreted as a white flag. The declaration by Germany that it would approve of no demand 'irreconcilable with the honour of the German people' showed how dangerous this could be.

The *Daily Telegraph* showed its concern:

> 'What Germany desires to do is go on talking. Equally clearly the interest of the Entente Powers lies in exactly the opposite direction. It is time an end was put to negotiations, which so long as Germany is in her present mood can obviously lead to no result.'

President Wilson could ignore popular opinion in England, but an election was coming up in America in barely two weeks time.

On 23 October 1918 he made his final condition to the German people. He would grant them peace if they got rid of their Emperor.

> 'If it (the American Government) must deal with the military masters and the monarchical autocrats of Germany now, or if it is likely to have to deal with them later in regard to the international obligations of the German Empire, it must demand, not peace negotiations, but surrender.'

When the German negotiators agreed to force their Emperor to abdicate, President Wilson agreed to offer them peace, unaware that, although

Kaiser Bill had made many bellicose remarks before World War I, it had been the powers behind the throne that had steeled his nerve to go to war in the final days of July 1914.

Happy in the belief that he had secured democracy permanently in Germany, President Wilson turned his attention to the Allies to force them to accept peace on his terms.

1.16 President Wilson's Pressure

President Wilson's speeches during the war had been full of lofty principles. Privately, however, he was not without some of the old fashioned sentiments he had so lamented in the Allies.

In 1916 he had been outraged at the British Empire's high-handedness in searching American ships in the enforcement of their blockade against Germany.[64] Before he had made his speech about 'impartial justice' on 28 September 1918 he had confided to Joseph P. Tumulty:

'There are many things in it which will displease the imperialists of Great Britain, France, and Italy.[65]'

Later, writing to Colonel House in his private code (no. 6 31 October) he declared that:

'Congress will have no sympathy whatever with spending American lives for British naval control.'

While just before the armistice he confided:

'Nelson Page will tell you how busy the English propagandists are destroying our prestige and building up their own in Italy.'[66]

His anti-French and anti-British sentiments boded ill for the future of an enforceable peace in Europe.

Up to that point the elected leaders of the Allied nations had not been asked whether they would like to grant Germany a compromise peace. On 29 October House had his first meeting with the Allies at the Quai d'Orsay to give them an ultimatum. Naturally the Allies made

64. Woodrow Wilson. *Revolution, War and Peace*. p.428.
65. Ray Stannard Baker. *Woodrow Wilson. Life and Letters*. Vol.8. p.538.
66. R. S. Baker. *Woodrow Wilson. Life and Letters*. p.527.

objections to the fourteen points, Britain being particularly anxious about the 'freedom of the seas.'

Whereupon House declared that the logical consequences would be for the President to say to Germany: 'The Allies do not agree to the conditions of peace proposed by me and accordingly the present negotiations are at an end.' 'I pointed out', recorded House 'that this would leave the President free to consider the question afresh and to determine whether the United States should continue to fight for the principles laid down by the Allies.'[67]

After he had made this statement he reported that the Allies became very excited and that Balfour declared it was clear that the Germans were trying to drive a wedge between the President and the Allies.

House ignored this and merely told the Allies to make drafts by the next day of where they could and could not agree with the President's proposals.

He telegraphed to his President to show him how he was going to put the pressure on:

'It is my intention to tell Prime Ministers today that if their conditions of peace are essentially different from the points you have laid down and for which the American people have been fighting, that you will probably feel obliged to go before Congress and state the new conditions and ask their advice as to whether the United States shall continue to fight for the aims of Great Britain, France and Italy.

'I told the British privately you anticipate that their policy would lead to the establishment of the greatest naval program by the United States that the world had ever seen. I did not believe that the United States would consent for any power to interpret for them the rules under which American commerce would traverse the sea. I would suggest that you quietly diminish the transport of troops giving as an excuse the prevalence of influenza or any other reason but the real one...I feel confident that we should play a strong hand and if it meets with your approval I will do it in the gently and friendly way almost certain to prevail.'

As soon as Colonel House had sprung 'his bombshell' the next fateful afternoon Lloyd George and Clemenceau looked at each other significantly...Clemenceau decided to abandon 'the preparation of a French draft and to accept the British.'

67. R.S. Baker. *Woodrow Wilson. Life & Letters*. p.530-1. "the last thing they want is publicity." p.554. Col. House. to Wilson, private code no. 6. "I consider that we have won a great victory...This has been done in the face of a hostile and influential junta in the United States." Ray Stannard Baker from his notebook: "Wilson's great fight is before him...Our only hope lies in the masses underneath, the worker."

1.17 British Compromise

It is difficult today to understand why Lloyd George chose to accept a compromise peace when a substantial majority of the American people were crying out for 'unconditional surrender.' Pershing, the American General, had just written a thirteen point document to the Supreme War Council stating his view that the Allies military position was excellent and that they should press home their attacks until they forced the enemy to surrender unconditionally. 'Anything short of capitulation', he maintained, 'postpones if it does not make impossible the imposition of satisfactory peace terms, since Germany could in such case resume hostilities if the terms were not satisfactory to her.'

He also warned sombrely: 'An armistice would lead the allied armies to believe this the end of fighting and it would be difficult if not impossible to resume hostilities with our present advantage in morale in the event of failure to secure at a peace conference what we have fought for.'[68]

There were reasons, however, for Lloyd George's decision to accept a compromise peace.

Firstly, so pre-occupied had he been with strikes and disturbances at home, he had obviously been unaware of the magnitude of the British army's great Autumn successes on the battlefield. Foch had even to ask him to send a telegram to Haig in October to congratulate him on the British army's achievements.[69] The tired French army could not give Clemenceau the bargaining counter which realisation of the moral fibre of the British army could have given Lloyd George.

Secondly, there was the attitude of the shop floor worker in Britain to contend with. Some authorities feared that 'Bolshevism' could spread from Russia to England's green and pleasant land. So far Lloyd George had appeased the shop floor militants but they had demanded peace on the basis of the fourteen points.

Thirdly, Lloyd George himself was in sympathy with so much that was expressed in the fourteen points. So many of them, indeed, were his own points. There was an election coming up in Britain too in a month's time. If he decided to fight on for 'unconditional surrender' the right would gain the ascendancy in Britain while Lloyd George would be further alienated from his supporters on the left of the Liberal Party.

Fourthly, opportunist that he was himself, Lloyd George obviously

---

68. *The Private Papers of Douglas Haig.* Vol.51. – gives the full text page 524.
69. R. Blake. *Private Papers of Douglas Haig.* p.331.

Figure 1.4 Colonel House and President Wilson
Colonel House, 29th October 1918: 'It is my intention to tell Prime Ministers today that if their conditions of peace are essentially different from the points you have laid down ... that you will probably feel oblig-ed to go before Congress and ... ask their advice as to whether the United States shall continue to fight for the aims of Great Britain, France and italy.'
© Hulton Deutsch

did not appreciate President Wilson's sincerity. Wilson was a genuinely principled man although his prejudices sometimes obstructed his comprehension. Lloyd George imagined that President Wilson was like so many others who could be bought off with promises of material gain. When he suggested to House on 29 October that America should become trustee for the German East African colonies after the war while Britain assumed a protectorate over Mesopotamia and perhaps Palestine, House reported cynically back to his President that the British 'would like us to accept something so they might freely take what they desire' while the outraged President in his secret code replied that there would be no difficulty about peace terms 'if the Entente statesmen...have no selfish aims of their own which would in any case alienate us from them altogether.'[70]

Fifthly, the Allies obviously did not take the President's points and principles or indeed the man himself sufficiently seriously. They were impressed by the fact that he left all the details of the armistice to Foch, giving rise to the belief that they would be given similar rein at the Peace Conference. There was a very good reason for the President's action, however. He was not in charge of the military situation. It was not until January 1st that Bonar Law would write of Wilson: 'He is a bigger man than I thought.'[71]

Lastly Lloyd George's commander in the field, General Haig, had also advised against continuing the fight. Lloyd George had not rated Haig's advice highly during the war, and Haig was not the senior commander on the battlefield in 1918. Nevertheless, a strong demand for a continued push for 'unconditional surrender' by him, in cooperation with General Pershing, would have been difficult to resist in view of the overwhelming Allied superiority of 2:1 'in the fighting lines' by October 1918.[72]

As the aftermath of World War I began to look more and more like defeat for Britain, and Germany began to show renewed signs of militarism, the principle players began to write their memoirs to justify their actions. The venomous attacks against the British army, and General Haig in particular, by Lloyd George in his memoirs, published in 1936, could be construed as an attempt by him to pass the buck for his failure to insist that President Wilson listen to the voices of the American people and press on for 'unconditional surrender' in October 1918.

70. R. S. Baker. *Woodrow Wilson. Life and Letters*. Vol.8. p.528.
71. *Lloyd George Papers*. letter re. President Wilson, given to Mr J. Davies. 1/1/1.
72. *Annual Register*. 1918. p.276. Figures from the American War Department.

1.18 The Downfall of the Kaiser

President Woodrow Wilson had demanded the downfall of the Kaiser. The question was, how to make him depart?

The revolution that was to cause his downfall and convince the Allies and their associate from overseas, America, that Prussian militarism had at last been defeated, erupted on the 3 November. The 'weirdest of all revolutions' according to the historian, Sebastien Haffner, was sparked off by the German Naval High Command's decision to order its ships to put to sea to fight the enemy ten days before the armistice. The German government was in the final stages of its peace negotiations with President Wilson at this point and had expressly ordered the cessation of the U-boat war before this extraordinary order was given.[73]

It is understandable for a country's military High Command to urge its armed forces to throw themselves into battle in the final stages of war in order to gain the best possible advantage from peace. But in this case the action was inappropriate. Peace terms had already been accepted by Allies and enemy alike and America was far more likely to be sympathetic to Germany if it showed itself to be weak rather than strong. The only stumbling block preventing a greater acceptance in America of President Wilson's fourteen points appeared to the Germans to be the continued presence of the Kaiser as head of state in Germany.

Solf, German Secretary of State for Foreign Affairs wrote: 'The abdication of the Emperor as an undeniable result of Wilson's policy, would strengthen the latter's position and would probably make it possible for him to carry out his program despite all opposition.'[74]

In this connection a naval victory would definitely have been counterproductive. It would have convinced the die-hards in America that Germany must, at all costs, be defeated. Yet the entire German fleet was secretly ordered to put to sea in direct contravention of the new democratic Government's Authority. This order was too much for the German sailors to accept. There had already been a history of trouble in the navy. When these men received the incredible order to put out to sea in direct opposition to the new, democratic government, two ships refused to sail. But when the ships that 'had mutinied and those which had not yet mutinied aimed their giant guns at each other from the closest proximity, the mutineers surrendered.' The officers abandoned their grandiose plans to engage the British navy. The sailors were arrested en masse and taken to prison where they faced court martial and the execution squad.

73. Erich Eyck. *The Weimar Republic.* Vol.1. p.41.
74. *Preliminary History of the Armistice.* pp.133–4.

Meetings took place in protest and a great march was formed. However, the march was stopped by a patrol and when the sailors did not obey orders to disperse, nine were killed and twenty nine wounded. The march scattered but one sailor managed to kill the head of the patrol, Lieutenant Steinhauser. The 'revolution' had begun.

The sailors solicited support from other regions and were overwhelmed by the response. By 8 November all the major West German cities were in the grip of revolution 'the garrisons elected soldiers' councils, the workers elected workers' councils, the military authorities capitulated or fled, the civil authorities, scared and cowed, recognised the new sovereignty of the workers' and soldiers' councils.'[75]

Gradually the revolution gathered momentum until it seemed unstoppable. Even the soldiers drafted into Berlin made no resistance to public opinion and opened the gates of their barracks to the rebels. The factory workers poured out towards the city centre from the industrial estates. The Government divined that the only way to stop the revolution was for the Emperor to abdicate.

The Emperor tried to prevaricate. Finally the Chancellor lost his patience. The official pronouncement was read out:

'The Emperor and King has decided to renounce the throne.'[76]

Where he was to go to nobody knew but Hindenburg found a way out of the difficulty with his careful language.

'In an extreme emergency crossing the frontier to Holland might be considered' he declared repeatedly.[77]

Ludendorff wrote dramatically of that day: 'On November 9th, Germany lacking any firm hand, bereft of all will, robbed of her princes, collapsed like a house of cards.'[78]

But the workers were not satisfied. Rosa Luxembourg and Karl Liebknecht might have been the theoreticians of the extreme left but the men with the organisation were the shop stewards from the great factories. These men now planned to take the running of the country out of the hands of the new democracy.

Prince Max had resigned the Chancellorship because his name smacked too much of the old order. So now the new President, Ebert 'compared to the Prince merely a lowly tailor's son' had to face this new threat to democratic rule. Prince Max of Baden had handed over the keys of government to six socialists, three of whom supported the revolutionary soldiers' and workers' councils and wanted them integrated into government by the back door. In fact they were already almost

75. Sebastien Haffner. *Failure of a Revolution.* p.57.
76. Sebastien Haffner. *Failure of a Revolution.* p.74–5.
77. Sebastien Haffner. *Failure of a Revolution.* p.57.
78. *Ludendorff's Own Story.* Vol II. pp.348–53.

knocking on the front door also. From his lonely room in the Chancellor's palace on that November day, the tailor's son could hear the revolutionaries marching towards him from their stronghold in the Imperial Palace. How could he defend his country from these desperate men? To whom could he turn? It was the voice of General Gröner of the Military High Command that came to his rescue. The army would support him.[79]

One month later Herr Ebert was made to pay the price for this support. Under Foch's armistice terms the Allies had allowed the German soldiers to march back into Germany with heads held high and their weapons at their sides. On 12 December President Ebert was impelled to give them a heroes' welcome in Berlin. His words were to become engraved on the consciousness of the nation. 'I salute you, who return unvanquished from the field of battle.' The legend of the 'stab in the back' had begun.[80]

The 'weirdest revolution of them all' had been convenient for the old guard. For it was the revolution that finally convinced a doubting world that Germany was truly beaten. The revolution enabled the old guard to get rid of the Emperor and thus provide the enemy with a scapegoat and yet they could blame the socialists for expelling him. The revolution also would presuppose the Allies to be lenient to Germany in case 'Bolshevism' should rear its head again while reinforcing the belief in the average German citizen that Germany needed a firm hand to govern it. As an independent observer, more than seventy years later, one might almost say that the revolution had been engineered. Where were the soldiers like Lieutenant Steinhauser, who with one small patrol dared defy thousands of striking sailors on 3 November? And what about the men like Hitler who from his hospital bed wrote these despairing words at the end of the war:

'Everything went black before my eyes as I staggered back to my ward and buried my aching head between the blankets and pillow...The following days were terrible to bear and the nights still worse...During the nights my hatred increased, hatred for the originators of this dastardly crime.'[81]

The revolution in Berlin had been almost bloodless. On 8 November Richard Muller, leader of an illegal group of conspirators, had watched by the Halle Gate in Berlin as 'Heavily armed columns of infantry, machine-gun companies and light field artillery moved past me in an endless stream towards the heart of the city.'[82] Yet not one of these men fired a shot in anger against the mild-mannered revolutionaries as the

79. Sir John Wheeler Bennet. *Nemesis of Power*. p.21.
80. Sir John Wheeler Bennet. *Nemesis of Power*. p.31.
81. Allan Bullock. *Hitler. A Study in tyranny*. p.60. *Mein Kampf*. pp.176.
82. Sebastien Haffner. *Failure of a Revolution*. p.69.

pressure built up for the abdication of the Emperor. Were they there, one might ask oneself, to stop an insurrection or to encourage it until it had accomplished its task?

Whether manipulated or not the revolution turned out to be both opportune and fruitful. No one in Allied countries wanted Germany to disintegrate into chaos. President Wilson seemed to have achieved the right balance.

Suddenly Germany seemed worth saving. The American electorate still voted against President Wilson but not by such an overwhelming majority as might have been expected. It was enough, however, to give control both of the Senate and the House of Representatives to the Republicans. In England when a Prime Minister loses an election he has to resign. The President of America has a much stronger position. But it is not absolute. President Wilson could make war and he could make peace but any treaty made after that war would have to be passed by the American legislature in which the Republicans now had a majority.

It was a point which he would have done well to remember.

1.19 Signing of the Armistice

In 1893 General Graf von Haeseller addressed his troops in occupied Lorraine as follows: 'Our civilisation must build its temple on mountains of corpses, an ocean of tears and the groans of innumerable dying men.'[83] The elite of the Prussian army sacrificed itself on the Western front that desperate October to ensure that the Prussian Empire's enemies didn't waver in their determination to grant Germany a compromise peace. As had been the case for the last eighteen months the British army bore the brunt of the fighting to drive the German soldiers from French and Belgian soil. The casualties in the British army for the month of October 1918 amounted to 5,438 officers and 115,608 other ranks.[84]

On 11 November the armistice was signed. After most wars it is customary that the Generals put their signature to their nation's defeat but in this case the Allies accepted a civilian signature. Herr Erzberger, the Social Democrat head of the German delegation, spat out his nation's triumph at the ceremony that was supposed to humble him.

'The German nation which for fifty months has defied a world of enemies will preserve...its liberty and unity.

'A nation of 70 million people suffers but does not die.'[85]

---

83. F. W. Foerster. *Europe and the German Question.* p.56.
84. J. Terraine. *Haig. The Educated Soldier.* p.471.
85. *The Memoirs of Marshall Foch.* pp.477. *et seq.* Baker. *Woodrow Wilson. Life and Letters.* p.583.

Between them the French and the British nations comprised just over 80 million people. Both countries had large Empires, but by opting for peace on the basis of the fourteen points with its right of 'self- determination' for all people who spoke the same language, they had cemented the formerly independent German-speaking states that comprised the Prussian Empire into one country, while digging a grave for their own Empires.

For now there was much rejoicing. Victory bells rang out all over the world. Everyone could see the magnitude of Germany's distress. Germany was now in the grip of revolution and her Kaiser had been forced to abdicate.

Even Theodore Roosevelt, bitter opponent of President Wilson, felt elated by this turn of events as he wrote to his English friend, Arthur Lee (Lord Lee of Fareham) on the 19 November:

'When the war first broke out I did not think the Kaiser was really to blame. I thought he was simply a tool; gradually I was forced to realise that he was one of the leading conspirators, plotters and wrongdoers.'

He still had no good words for what he conceived President Wilson's intentions to have been: 'Namely, double-cross the Allies...and get a negotiated peace which would put him personally on a pinnacle of glory in the sight of every sinister pro-German and every vapid and fatuous doctrinaire sentimentalist throughout the world.'

The President, he maintained, knew he could bully the Allies:
'The probably necessary kowtowing performed in front of him by almost all the British leaders and by the great majority of the French leaders, made him certain that they would accept what ever he did.'

But he was immensely reassured by Foch's armistice terms which he thought would become the basis for the actual settlement:

'The comparison between Foch's Twenty-Three points which were actually adopted in the armistice and Wilson's Fourteen show the difference between the shifty rhetorician who wants an indecisive peace and the resolute soldier who will accept only the peace of overwhelming victory.'[86]

He was also relieved by the fact that the Republicans had 'carried the House by a substantial, and the Senate by a bare majority' for true parliamentarian that he was himself he expected the President now to take account of Republican views.

The German newspaper, the *Berliner Tageblatt*, stated that 'the election of a Republican Congress rendered it impossible for Germany to

86. *Lloyd George Papers*. F31/2/24. Box 111.T. Roosevelt.

hope that Mr. Wilson would be able to give them the kind of peace that was reasonable – in other words, pro-German.'[87]

Thankfully at last the weary British left the crater-torn fields of France and returned to their green and pleasant fields at home. Their elected leaders chose to disregard the fact that when they talked of asking the total cost of the war to the Allies, £24,000 million from Germany, President Wilson declared that he would be asking for 'no indemnities.'[88] Both statements seemed preposterous. The Coalition government under the leadership of Lloyd George won a landslide victory on 14 December on the war's successful result and the expected line it would take over the peace and President Wilson received a rapturous welcome from the British people. As always he dazzled with his rhetoric.

> 'I believe' President Wilson told the crowds at Manchester 'that ...men are beginning to see, not perhaps the golden age, but an age which at any rate is brightening from decade to decade, and will lead us some time to an elevation from which we can see the things for which the heart of mankind is longing.'[89]

To the Allies so much had already been accomplished. The Prussian army, once the terror of Europe, had been reduced to an undisciplined rabble. Proud Germany had been reduced to chaos. So they were touched with sympathy when a new cry emanated from the Fatherland. Its populace was starving.

87. E. Eyck. *The Weimar Republic*. Vol I. p.41.
88. *New York Times*. 12.12.88.
89. *Annual Register*. 1918. p.169.

–2–

President Wilson Changes his Mind

2.1 Food Shortages

It was in the George V Hotel in Paris that the victors met to decide the fate of the world. But actually who the victors were had not yet been decided because victory in a compromise peace depends on who makes the biggest compromises.

On 12 December the reporter from the *New York Times* had been surprised to find that there was so much more food in the shops in Germany than in France. In order, it was said, to appease the revolutionary population, the granaries had been thrown open and six months supplies had been consumed within six weeks.[1] Then the government of the Fatherland threw itself on the mercy of the Allies and their great associate from America. Germany was starving, it was said, and all the country wanted was to buy food for her population – and what was more it had the money to pay for it. Germany had a nest egg of 2,550,240,000 gold marks sitting in her coffers on armistice day compared to 1,253,199,000 in August 1914, waiting to be spent on food.[2]

The French, whose cindered cities of Cambrai, Laon and Lens had scarcely stopped smouldering from Germany's destruction, claimed that the money belonged to them. They could still see the cattle that had been driven from French pastures, grazing on Germany's side of the border. But the Americans from the mid-west farming belt, far away from the scene of the tragedy, were more sympathetic towards Germany's plight than the French.

Germany had been supplied with 270,000 tons of fats and condensed milk for the payment of 4,000,000 in gold marks on 12 January 1919 but that was all. Germany pleaded for more.

Understandably America had been concerned at reports of revolution in Germany, the ex-Fatherland for so many Americans. They had

1. *New York Times*. 12.12.18.
2. *New York Times*. 26.2.24.

wanted the destruction of autocracy but not the elimination of the whole fabric of society. Now the tales of actual 'starvation' emanating from the Fatherland tore their hearts. But it was not only their hearts that were affected but also their purse strings.

American farmers had done well out of the war. European farmers had gone to fight in increasing numbers, leaving their lands at home under-tilled. American farmers had taken advantage of this situation to increase their production. Great Britain had been a very profitable market and, until President Wilson had thrown his weight behind the Allies in 1918, the neutral countries, Holland, Denmark, etc., had taken vast amounts of American produce and then passed them on to Germany.[3] In the Spring of 1918 that avenue was closed, however, and then, on 8 January 1919, the British withdrew their monthly buying orders for American food. Herbert Hoover who had been appointed food administrator in 1917, wrote an agonized letter to President Wilson on the seriousness of the situation – 400 million pounds of pork alone in America – held at war prices:

> 'If there should be no remedy to this situation we shall have a debacle in the American markets, and, with the advances of several hundred million dollars now outstanding from the Banks to the pork products industry we shall not only be precipitated into a financial crisis but shall betray the American farmer who has engaged himself to these ends. The surplus is so large that there can be no absorption of it in the United States and it, being a perishable product, will go to waste.'[4]

There was an official embargo on the sale of raw materials to Germany until it had signed the Treaty of Versailles. However, American humanitarian and commercial interests softened towards expenditure on the vital needs of Germany, especially when the money otherwise was merely to be used for reparations' payments. Germany, beleaguered by revolution, no longer appeared a threat to America. The rapacious Allies did.

Germany's leaders insisted that they didn't want charity. They were prepared to pay for the food they needed. Yet, although President Wilson did make an arrangement for the Allies to go on buying the food at expensive wartime prices and then sell it on to neutral and enemy countries to circumvent his nation's embargo, none apparently was getting through. For in February Germany made a bitter protest:

> 'Throughout this period, and up to to-day, the German people have not had the benefit of one gram of food, of fats, or of milk, more than they formerly

3. *Annual Register.* 1918. p.189.
4. R. S. Baker. *Woodrow Wilson & World Settlement.* (1923) Vol. II. p.338.

had...We make sacrifice after sacrifice, and in giving up our goods we are reaching the very limit of poverty. We do not want the food that we need as gifts; we want to buy it. Nevertheless, its delivery is postponed more and more, and we are suffering from hunger. If the Entente wishes to annihilate us, it at least ought not to expect us to dig our own grave.'[5]

Hoover complained in his letter on 4 February that 'events were reaching an unbearable crisis. Bolshevism was spreading into starving Germany owing to the fact...that the French, by obstruction of every financial measure that we can propose...have defeated every step so far for getting them the food which we have been promising for three months.'[6]

President Wilson, never much enamoured of France, was becoming thoroughly irate over what he considered France's rapaciousness over gold, land and every other issue and 'despite being smitten with a temperature of 103, looking utterly beaten, worn out, his face haggard and one side of it and the eye twitching painfully' was determined not to allow French greed to prevail over the gold marks lying in the German Treasury or over any other issue. His battleship, the George Washington, then under repair in America, was ordered to be made ready at once to return to France.

Ray Stannard Baker describes that day, 7 April:

'I went up to see President Wilson at 6.30 – the first time since he fell ill and had a long talk. I found him fully dressed, in his study, looking thin and pale. A slight hollowness around the eyes emphasised a characteristic I had often noted before – the size and luminosity of his eyes. They are extraordinarily clear and he looks at one with a piercing intentness...Nevertheless he was still determined not to give way over gold or anything else.
"Then Italy will not get Fiume?" I asked.
"Absolutely not – as long as I am here", he said sharply.
"Nor France the Saar?"
"No."
"The time has come to bring this thing to a head", he said.
"House was just here and told me that Clemenceau and Klotz had talked away another day...I will not discuss anything with them any more...We agreed among ourselves and we agreed with Germany upon certain general principles. The whole course of the Conference has been made up of a series of attempts, especially by France, to break down this agreement, to get territory and to impose crushing indemnities. The only real interest of France in Poland is in weakening Germany by giving Poland territory to which she has no right." '[7]

5. R. S. Baker. *Woodrow Wilson & World Settlement*. (1923) Vol. II. p.346.
6. R. S. Baker. *Woodrow Wilson & World Settlement*. (1923) Vol. II. p.40 & p.346.
7. R. S. Baker. *Woodrow Wilson and World Settlement*. (1923) Vol. II. p.60.

2.2 The Arrival of John Maynard Keynes

In the matter of food for gold, however, President Wilson found himself a new ally in the shape of Great Britain's premier, Lloyd George.

Britain had finished the war with a terrible shortage of ships while Germany's merchant ships had escaped largely unscathed. If Germany had been an abjectly defeated nation it would have had to hand over its ships as a matter of course in reparation for all the British ones its submarines had sunk. Austria had already surrendered her ships to her detested neighbour, Italy.[8] But as this was a compromise peace for Germany, negotiations had to be entered into, then subterfuge undertaken to explain the matter satisfactorily to the anti-German British public.

Lloyd George sent a young idealistic economist from the Treasury, Maynard Keynes, to argue Britain's case with the man both he and President Wilson considered the key man of the German delegation, Dr. Melchior, 'representing the great industrial interests.'[9]

The altruistic Keynes found Melchior to be an enchanting person. He described his first meeting with him and the rest of the German delegation.

> 'A sad lot they were in those early days, with drawn, dejected faces and tired staring eyes, like men who had been hammered on the Stock Exchange. But from amongst them stepped forward into the middle place a very small man, exquisitely clean, very well and neatly dressed, with a high stiff collar, his round head covered with grizzled hair shaved so close as to be like in substance to the pile of a close-made carpet, the line where his hair ended bounding his face and forehead in a very sharply defined and rather noble curve, his eyes gleaming straight at us, with extraordinary sorrow in them, yet like an honest animal at bay. This was he with whom, in the ensuing months I was to have one of the most curious intimacies in the world, and some very strange passages of experience – Dr. Melchior.'[10]

The Germans could have imposed a levy on the profitable war industries to pay for the food for their population. However, they insisted on their right to use their gold reserves for this purpose. For America who had made and was continuing to make so many loans to Europe, it must have been music in her ears to find one country who was actually able and prepared to pay for her commodities.

One can understand Lloyd George's anxieties over the shipping shortage. Many of the German ships were passenger ships and there was an acute lack of such vessels in England to carry the American and

8. *Lloyd George Papers*. F35/3/4.
9. R. S. Baker. *Woodrow Wilson & World Settlement*. Vol. II. p.498.
10. J. M. Keynes. *Dr. Melchior. A defeated enemy*. p.20.

Canadian troops home. Five men were killed and 23 wounded in Canadian riots in March, frustrated at the delay in being repatriated. The Americans were restive too.[11] Meanwhile there were fears that ships of the International Mercantile Marine Co. a combine of British and American shipping built up by an American, J.P. Morgan in 1902 but still controlled and run by the British, would revert to foreign control and be whisked back to America now that they had been bought by the American government.[12] The shipping position was critical. On top of this there was a damaging ship repairers' strike. Coal and other commodities were stacked on the quayside while the men refused to undertake vital repairs. It was essential that Germany handed over her ships.

Lloyd George blamed the French for Britain's difficulties. If only they would be reasonable over their insistence on retaining the gold for reparations, instead of allowing it to be used to feed the German population, he was sure that he could make Germany hand over its ships. But the French insisted that Germany could tax its iron and steel industries, which had made so much money out of the war, to pay for the needs of its people.

The frustrated British decided to put economic pressure on the French to force them to change their minds. On 19 February, Keynes told the French that Britain could no longer support the French franc. But the pressure did not have the desired effect. The French franc plummeted, followed by the British pound.[13]

On 4 March Keynes was due to meet the Germans again to discuss the problem. This time, however, the meeting was to be on German soil. Keynes looked forward to seeing the desperate food situation for himself.

He 'wondered what the streets would look like, whether the children's ribs would be sticking through their clothes and what would be in the shops.' He never received a proper impression since the delegation slept and worked in the train they had arrived in.[14]

A pacifist by nature and a sincere believer that all ordinary people everywhere had been cruelly misused by their leaders during the war for their own selfish ends, Keynes felt acutely the distress that the Germans must have felt at not being permitted even to feed their population by the rapacious Allies. He described his second meeting with Melchior:

'I looked across the table at Melchior. He seemed to feel as I did. Staring, heavy-lidded, helpless, looking as I had seen him before, like an honourable

11. *Annual Register.* 1919. p.41.
12. *Lloyd George Papers.* F/35/3/1.
13. Skidelsky. *Keynes.* Vol. I. p.359.
14. J. M. Keynes. *Dr. Melchior. A defeated enemy.* p.17.

animal in pain. Couldn't we break down the empty formalities of this Conference, the five-barred gate of triple interpretations, and talk about the truth and the reality like sane and sensible persons?'

They moved to a room where they were alone.

'I was quivering with excitement, terrified out of my wits at what I was doing, for the barriers of permitted intercourse had not then begun to crumble, and the somewhat emotional Melchior wondered what I wanted ... I tried to convey to him what I was feeling, how we believed his prognostications of pessimism, how we were impressed, not less than he, with the urgency of starting food supplies...that they (the Germans) must make up their minds as to the handing over of the ships; and that, if only he could secure a little latitude from Weimar, we could between us concoct a formula which would allow the food supplies to move in practice and evade the obstructions of the French...We both stood all through the interview. In a sort of way I was in love with him.'[15]

Melchior promised that, if the British could persuade the French to relinquish their rights over the gold, he could guarantee that the German government would hand over the country's merchant fleet. This greatly relieved the British government.

Although Lloyd George had favoured the British soldiers fighting under the direction of the French generals, Nivelle and Foch, during the war, when it came to peace his prejudice against the French nation rapidly returned. He perceived a new rapprochement between the Americans and the British. He declared that the Americans were becoming 'more and more anti-French', while he, himself, found the French 'extraordinarily greedy.'

At a meeting on 8 March, Lloyd George pulled out his trump card on the matter of gold for ships. It was a telegram from General Plummer on the food situation:

'Please inform the Prime Minister' the General telegraphed, 'that in my opinion food must be sent into this area by the Allies without delay...The mortality amongst women, children and sick is most grave, and sickness due to hunger is spreading. The attitude of the population is becoming one of despair, and the people feel that an end by bullets is preferable to death by starvation...I request therefore that a definite date be fixed for the arrival of the first supplies.'[16]

The French weakened but still M. Klotz declared that the Germans could pay for the food in any way they pleased but not with the gold

15. J. M. Keynes. *Dr. Melchior. A defeated enemy.* p.48–50.
16. J. M. Keynes. *Dr. Melchior. A defeated enemy.* p.59.

which must stand as surety for France's reparations. In a fit of rage Lloyd George gave the men around the Conference table a display of his lashing tongue, especially aiming his words at the French Jew, Klotz. Keynes recorded:

> 'Never have I seen the equal of the onslaught with which that poor man was overwhelmed. Do you know Klotz by sight? – a short, plump, heavy-moustached Jew, well-groomed, well-kept, but with an unsteady roving eye, and his shoulders a little bent in an instinctive deprecation. Lloyd George had always hated him and despised him; and now saw in a twinkling that he could kill him. Women and children were starving, he cried, and here was M. Klotz prating and prating of his ''goold.'' He leant forward and with a gesture of his hands indicated to everyone the image of a hideous Jew clutching a money bag. His eyes flashed and the words came out with a contempt so violent that he seemed almost to be spitting at him. The anti-Semitism, not far below the surface in such an assemblage as that one, was up in the heart of everyone. Everyone looked at Klotz with a momentary contempt and hatred; the poor man was bent over his seat, visibly cowering. We hardly knew what Lloyd George was saying but the words 'goold' and Klotz were repeated, and each time with exaggerated contempt. Then, turning, he called on Clemenceau to put a stop to these obtrusive tactics otherwise, he cried, M. Klotz would rank with Lenin and Trotsky among those who had spread Bolshevism in Europe. The Prime Minister ceased. All round the room you could see each one grinning and whispering to his neighbour ''Klotzky''.'[17]

Under the impact of this tirade the French delegation gave way over the gold. Admiral Wemyss was authorised to accept the surrender of the German fleet. The food trains started to roll into Germany.

Tales of starvation reinforced the impression in England that Germany was truly beaten. Stories of bloody confrontations between the new, democratically elected German government and its workers touched the hearts of solid, sensible British citizens who formerly had little sympathy with Germany's plight but were now being subjected to increasingly violent shop floor action themselves. The country rallied to its leadership in their humanitarian gesture over the food while suspicions of the intentions of Britain's traditional enemy, France, returned.

Whether Germany actually was starving, however, was another matter. Keynes, himself, couldn't help wondering why Germany seemed so much less concerned by their country's food situation than the Allies during those three months.

> 'It was a curious feature of the negotiations of the next three months that British anxiety over the German food supplies was, so far as concerned its

17. J. M. Keynes. *Dr. Melchior. A defeated enemy.* p.61–2.

urgency in point of time, decidedly greater, to all appearance, than the anxiety of the Germans themselves.'[18]

Indeed Keynes tells us that General Plummer's emotive telegram had not been prompted by the conditions he had seen in Germany but in response to a telegram received from Paris that morning. The confrontation with Klotz over the telegram had been stage managed. It had all been a ploy to gain the ships for Britain.[19]

Statistics do not bear out the assertion of the German delegate, Count Brockdorf-Rantzau in his speech on receiving the Treaty of Versailles proposals on 7 May 1919:

'Hundreds of thousands of non-combatants were killed with cold deliberation, after our adversaries had conquered and victory had been assured to them.'[20]

On the contrary, the statistics show that the German populace fared no worse than other Europeans after the war and far better than the French. It was, after all, the French cattle who were feeding on the German side of the border, not the reverse – and it was statistically the French who died from cold, malnutrition and disease in 1919. They even suffered a drop in their population whilst the German population increased. Statistics show the depths of their misery.

In Germany in 1919, there were 1,299,404 births and 1,017,284 deaths, an increase of 282,120 in the population of 59,858,284. While in France there were 503,606 births and 736,541 deaths in the population of 39,209,000, a decrease in the population of 232,935.[21]

The Germans must have been pleased about the outcome in Paris. Their ships were old and needed repair. Rebuilding them would provide work for the redundant workers from their massive armament factories. The payment of cash for commodities would strengthen the friendship between their country and America. Besides a precedent had been created. The needs of Germany could take precedent over the payment of the reparations. In future, whenever there was a conflict between the needs of Germany and the payment of reparations, Germany would cry 'starvation.'

18. J. M. Keynes. *Dr. Melchior. A defeated enemy.* p.30-1. 'I was never quite clear in my own mind how far this was due to concealed reserves known to the Germans but not to us.'

19. J. M. Keynes. *Dr. Melchior. A defeated enemy.* p.59.

20. R. S. Baker. *Woodrow Wilson & World Settlement.* (1923) Vol. II. p.504.

21. *Statesman's Yearbook.* (1923) Germany. p.972. France. p.896.

2.3   Churchill and the Maintenance of Conscription

Lloyd George had hastened to disband the British army which had been Britain's one strong bargaining weapon at the end of the war. He hoped that General Pershing and his American soldiers would assume the role of defenders of the Peace. However, Pershing had to decline that honour as he had received orders that the American troops in Europe were to be disbanded four months after the Peace Treaty had been signed.[22] Churchill was soon pressing for the maintenance of conscription, despite election promises. There were fifty four French divisions left in Northern France but they were said to be 'weak.' While Haig wrote in his diary:

> 'If the existing '(British)' orders are continued, by the middle of February there will be no organised Army of occupation left. How then can our Government hope to dictate peace terms to the Germans?'[23]

So Britain had to promise to send 10 Troop divisions to Germany and renege on the political promise made by Lloyd George over returning to a voluntary army, by conscripting two divisions of cavalry. The German army comprised 400,000 fully armed men[24] so it was a sensible decision for the Peace Conference delegates to decide that Germany should reduce its army to 100,000 troops under the terms of the Peace Treaty.

Germany had been proud and excited by its enormous Eastern Empire in 1918. But the exhausted and depleted nation (1,950,000 dead) was in no mood to try and recover it now. Besides, its leaders' whole strategy over the peace had been to try and ingratiate itself with the Americans to counter the demands of the Allies. So the beloved Eastern Empire, including parts of the great Teutonic Kingdom, Prussia, gained by the sword and symbolic of Germany's might, had to be relinquished in order to satisfy President Wilson's wish to give re-established Poland access to the sea.

But when it came to demanding reparations President Wilson had made his position clear. He had declared in December that he would be asking for 'no indemnities.'[25]

22. Robert Blake. *The Private Papers of Douglas Haig*. p.352.
23. Robert Blake. *The Private Papers of Douglas Haig*. p.351.
24. The Allies initially proposed to allow Germany to retain an army of 200,000 men (R. Blake. *Private Papers of Douglas Haig*. p.356.) but Germany's regular army of 400,000 men in December 1919 and its auxiliaries outnumbered the British army. *The Times*. 2.1.20.
25. *New York Times*. 12.12.18.

2.4   War Debts to Britain

Britain's Lord Cunliffe and Lord Sumner, 'the heavenly twins', as Keynes called them, had been chosen to argue the Allied case. They were both experienced negotiators. Viscount Sumner, born John Hamilton, impecunious younger son of a Manchester iron merchant, rose to become one of Britain's leading judges after having specialised in commercial work at the bar. He was made a Lord in 1912.[26] Lord Cunliffe was a former Governor of the Bank of England. Ever present in their Lordships' minds must have been the consideration that they would have to fight President Wilson's negotiators for every penny owed to the Allies because President Wilson had declared that he would be asking for 'no indemnities.' But there were other considerations to be borne in mind too.

They were aware that the bill for the material damage done to France came close to 1 billion pounds. So the amount secured for France had to be substantial.

But Britain, though only superficially scarred by the bombing of her East coast towns,[27] had mortgaged her future to help her wartime Allies. She too needed to be repaid for her sacrifice. During the wartime years the German finance minister, Herr Helfferich, had consoled his long suffering savers and taxpayers by telling them how much more the war was costing Britain than themselves.[28] And this was no less than the case. The mere logistics of transporting men and munitions across the Channel was expensive. In addition the British had had to pay hard currency to transport iron ore perilously across the ocean, while Europe's excellent rail network could carry Germany's free ore from occupied France to the Ruhr.

Britain was owed £1,683,500,000[29] by her Allies and the dominions. But how could she ask France to repay £508,000,000 in her present state or even Italy £467,000,000 without reparations? As for the £568,000,000 she had lent to Russia, it was unlikely that the Bolsheviks would ever honour the debts incurred by the Imperial regime. On the other hand the rich and not overwhelmingly friendly Americans would be certain to ask for the £850,000,000 owed to them.[30] Meanwhile the Germans, having devastated their neighbour's industries, would be certain to take over their trade unless some financial restraints were put

26. *Dictionary of National Biography.* p.392–3.
27. A Temple Patterson. *Jellicoe.* p.73.
28. A Temple Patterson. *Jellicoe.* p.73.
29. War debts to Britain. A. J. P. Taylor. *English History. 1914–45.* p.74.
30. A. J. P. Taylor. *English History 1914–45.* p.169.

upon them. As for the dominions who had fought so bravely in the war and at such great cost to themselves, not to mention smaller countries like Portugal, they too needed to feel that they had been repaid for their sacrifice.

However, their Lordships' primary reason for asking for heavy reparations was their belief that Germany had started the war. The destruction Germany had created on its last retreat merely increased their conviction that Germany must be adequately weighed down with debt for the foreseeable future to stop it creating a pot of gold to enable it to fight again.

Before talking figures Lord Sumner and Lord Cunliffe had to make sure that the terms of reference were right. A whole lot of unfortunate words had been spoken on the subject of reparations which the two negotiators had to have clarified in the Allies favour before they could negotiate a satisfactory agreement. They were aghast that the Americans were talking of excluding 'war costs' from the bill. Article 19 of Foch's armistice terms had expressly stated 'With the reservation that any future claims and demands of the Allies and the United States of America remain unaffected, the following financial conditions are required: Reparation for damage done.'[31] The Allies therefore submitted bills for the costs of the war.

However, John Foster Dulles maintained that Secretary of State Lansing's note of 5 November in which he declared that 'compensation will be made by Germany for all damage done to the civilian population of the Allies and their property by the aggression of Germany by land, sea, and air' precluded the Allies from charging Germany the costs of the war, assessed by all at £24 billion.[32]

The Allies knew that not even Germany could make full amends for the war. Who can atone for a million empty homes with no breadwinner to support them? But they realised that the formula espoused in Secretary of State Lansing's note would lead to a destitute France, a bankrupt Britain and a renascent Germany. So the debate continued.

Lord Sumner and Lord Cunliffe's arguments were so persuasive that Mr. Dulles had to cable President Wilson in America to arbitrate over the question of whether justice should prevail or whether the President still felt bound by Secretary Lansing's note. It was then that Wilson cabled the extraordinary words which were to have so much influence among Western liberals.

President Wilson was having a hard time over his concept of the League of Nations on his short trip back to the United States. He was accused of excluding (Republican) partners in the Senate from the Peace

---

31. *Annual Register.* 1918. Public Documents. p.156. General Clauses. XIX.
32. E. Mantoux. *The Carthaginian Peace.* p.100. Burnett. Vol. I. p.27.

Conference, 'his partners in treaty-making', and 'of making the impossible demand that whatever he saw fit to agree to must be accepted without debate or amendment.' But his troubles at home merely stiffened his resolve to be strong to those he felt he could dictate to, the Europeans. He sent word to the Conference that the Americans 'were bound in honour to decline to agree to the inclusion of war costs in the reparation demanded.' Using the royal 'We' he declared: 'We should dissent and dissent publicly if necessary, not on the ground of the intrinsic justice of it, but on the ground that it is clearly inconsistent with what we deliberately led the enemy to expect and we cannot now honourably alter simply because we have the power.'[33]

The suggestion in the President's words that Germany had not been defeated on the battlefield but had laid down their arms solely at his request would disturb liberals increasingly after the war and give much ammunition to the Germans. But the 'heavenly twins' and the British public knew that Germany had been defeated and wanted 'justice' done. The debate continued.

At length the Americans agreed to include 'war costs' in the reparations but in order not to make their decision look like a defeat a complicated verbal formula was devised. The Allies did not assert their right to war costs. Instead the Treaty affirmed the responsibility of Germany for causing all the damage done in the war and therefore, by definition, their duty to pay to put it right.

And so it was that the famous 'war-guilt' clause came into existence, to 'affirm' Germany's responsibility for causing all the damage. The text is as follows:

'The Allied and Associated Governments affirm and Germany accepts the responsibility of Germany and her Allies for causing all the loss and damage to which the Allies and Associated Governments and their nationals have been subjected as a consequence of the war imposed upon them by the aggression of Germany and her allies.'

Keynes's judgement of this formula was that it is 'only a matter of words, of virtuosity in draughtsmanship which does no one any harm and which probably seemed much more important at the time than it ever will again between now and judgement day.'[34]

But in this particular instance his judgement was incorrect. Germany's agitation over the 'war- guilt' clause was to 'poison the moral life of Europe for the next twenty years.'[35]

33. E. Mantoux. *The Carthaginian Peace.* p.100. Burnett. Vol. I. p.27.
34. J. M. Keynes. *The Economic Consequences of the Peace.* p.141.
35. E. Mantoux. *The Carthaginian Peace.* p.141.

2.5 Charging War Costs and Pensions

The Allies had not felt strong enough to defy America and demand their right to war costs for 'damage...as a consequence of the war' but they had won them by negotiation. However, the negotiators were still not happy with the terms of reference dictated by Lansing's unfortunate note of 5 November. For its wording seemed to infer that a man whose house had been demolished by the fighting would receive recompense while a man whose injuries had rendered him unable to work could claim nothing. Not only was this intrinsically unjust but it discriminated against the British and their dominions' claims for compensation from the effects of the war.[36]

The matter of pensions was becoming a political issue in Britain. General Haig had refused any title or peerage until his men had secured adequate pensions and gratuities. He reasoned that people would soon forget the service done by their armed forces after peace came and enumerated the many tales of hardship which his mutilated ex-soldiers were having to endure, unfit for work but without recompense from the Government.[37] So Lloyd George 'snatched' at a guileful suggestion from Smuts[38] 'that war pensions were a legitimate civil damage' and asked him 'to intercede with President Wilson to get the principle accepted.'

General Smuts of South Africa, untainted with British nationality, was known to be an ardent advocate of the League of Nations, the project most dear to President Wilson's heart. He overcame the reservations of the President with the argument that Lansing's note of 5 November had meant that, while direct military expenditure such as a soldier's upkeep could not be charged for, 'what was or is spent on the citizen before he became a soldier, or after he has ceased to be a soldier, or at any time on his family, represents compensation for damage done to civilians and must be made good by the German government under any fair interpretation of the above reservation. This includes all war pensions and separations allowances.'[39]

This was enough to satisfy both President Wilson and his aide, Dulles who declared: 'Whatever one's personal views may be, anyone who considers this subject in a spirit of fairness can hardly deal in a contemptuous and offhand way with the sincere and reasoned judgement of men such as General Smuts.'[40]

36. R. Skidelsky. *J. M. Keynes. Hopes Betrayed.* Vol. I. p.356.
37. Robert Blake. *The Private Papers of Douglas Haig.* p.345, p.348.
38. A. J. P. Taylor. *English History 1914–45.* p.183.
39. P. M. Burnett. *Preparations at the Paris Peace Conference.* Vol. I. pp.773f.
40. Letter to *The Times.* 16.2.20.

The case for charging 'war costs' and 'pensions and separations allowances' had been won by the negotiators after much delay and worry for Parliament. However, unless the sums demanded and received from Germany were substantial none of these arguments mattered at all.

Lord Sumner and Lord Cunliffe knew that Germany had boasted that its economy was the second strongest in the world (after the United States) pre-war.[41] Now the country was rapidly running down the value of its paper currency[42] reducing the value of the amount it had to return to its citizens on the one hand while undercutting the price of British goods in the market place on the other.[43] Lord Sumner and Lord Cunliffe, however, scaled down their original assessment of the reparations' sum to be demanded to £8 billion[44] to be paid by instalments in gold, timber and coal. Ceded property (schools, post offices, official buildings erected by Germany in returned provinces such as Alsace) and material were also to be credited against the reparations demands.

John Foster Dulles, the American delegate, however took the line that there had been a contract with Germany and that the Allies could ask for no more than £5 or £6 billion in total and he was backed up by the American banker, Thomas W. Lamont, in his assessment of what Germany could pay.[45]

An indecisive Lloyd George, trying to juggle between the demands of the Conservatives in Parliament who demanded 'justice', the cries of Labour who called for mercy and 'the German financial agents at Senlis' who told everybody that 'the Germans cannot pay much and if pressed to pay will decline to sign the Treaty'[46] declared that 'No trade was at present moving anywhere in Europe'[47] and called in his economist, Keynes, who had performed so well over the food issue to try and canvas support for lenient financial terms.

Keynes asked the advice of the City. The City, still hopeful of recovering some of the money they had lent to Germany before the war[48] advised asking for the lower figure.

However, Sumner and Cunliffe refused to budge on the sum they had

41. G. Borsky. *The Greatest Swindle in the World.* p.34. Helfferich. Deutschlands. Volksvohsland. Berlin. (1913) pp.98–9.

42. *Annual Register.* Finance and Commerce. p.69. By the end of the year the paper currency was worth approximately a third of its former value 200 to the £ as compared to 67.50. Parity with Britain in gold marks was 20.41.

43. *Lloyd George Papers.* F13/1/14.

44. R. Skidelsky. *J. M. Keynes.* Vol. I. p.364.

45. R. Skidelsky. *J. M. Keynes.* Vol. I. p.363–4.

46. R. Pound and G. Harmsworth. *Northcliffe.* Letter from Northcliffe to Kennedy Jones.

47. R. S. Baker. *Woodrow Wilson & World Settlement.* Vol. II. p.289.

48. Shroeder Wragg Historical Leaflet. Nearly all the major banking houses except Schroeder Wragg had lent copious sums to Germany before the war.

worked out. The issue provoked intense anxiety in Britain. Britain had been the Allies' major banker during the war. Unless her government were firm she would end up, weakened, paying for it, while Germany lived to fight another day.

It had been Lord Northcliffe's newspapers which had originally put the pressure on Lloyd George to give a pledge that 'those who started the war must pay to the last farthing.' It was not that Lord Northcliffe believed that the Germans would be able to pay 24 billion pounds – he actually caused the Crewe House assessment of what the Germans could pay to be syndicated worldwide on the very day that this figure was being bandied about – but he feared that unless the Allies adopted a strong negotiating position they would receive no liquid assets at all from Germany and that Britain therefore needed the force of public opinion to strengthen the resolve of the Prime Minister.

Northcliffe had spent six months in America during the war promoting Britain's cause and he knew how many friends Germany had in high places there. He was also aware of the economic threat posed by post- war Germany. Pound and Harmsworth, his biographers, explain his outlook:

'Political considerations, apart, his American experience of the previous year had opened his eyes to certain facts of economic geography which he felt could not be ignored by the British side at the peace talks...in spite of her certain and probable losses, Germany's economic assets were greater than those of the United Kingdom...Moreover, the Germans in retreat, with their own mines and industrial plants intact, had gone to work with high explosives and oxy-acetylene flame on the French and Belgian mines and factories with the object of eliminating future competition...Northcliffe believed that Germany might also eliminate British competition, notably in coal exports, by dodging reparations in cash and forcing British taxpayers to make yet more sacrifice in order to reconstruct their industries as well as to repay money borrowed from America to finance their Allies.

'He was unwilling to accept the Milner view, for example, that the Germans should be 'let off' in order that they might be free to deal with the Bolshevik threat...For the moment, Northcliffe was more impressed by information, which had come to him by secret sources via Crewe House, that the Bolshevik threat to Germany was being deliberately exaggerated by German agents who hoped to influence the peace talks. 'Do not let paper exaggerate Bolshevism in news and headlines' he had telegraphed to Marlowe of the *Daily Mail*...Northcliffe feared that the British people might be 'cheated.' That possibility supplied the motive for his newspaper campaigns which harassed the Coalition Government throughout the Versailles Peace Conference and the several conferences that followed. Underlying it was his deep mistrust of the politicians...He had divined a missing element of fervour in Lloyd George's patriotism – love of England.'[49]

49. R. Pound. & G. Harmsworth. *Northcliffe*. p.678–9.

Bonar Law, acting Prime Minister at home in Lloyd George's absence, had received an extraordinary letter in answer to his calls for information as to what was going on at the Conference:

'My dear Bonar
I did not realise until I received your letter that this last week you were not getting any progress verbal of our deliberations, in as much as there are no secretaries present at the Council of Four. If I had only thought of it I would have dropped you a note now and again to inform you what progress was being made.'[50]

Bonar Law asked Lord Staffordham to show the letter to the King but declined to show it to the rest of the Government.

Northcliffe felt that British interests were being sold down the river. He expressed as much to his brother, complaining about 'Bonar Law's halting statements as to financial reparation' in the House of Commons which he found 'exasperating to a degree.' He maintained:

'I personally have no intention of spending the rest of my life swotting to pay excess profits tax and supertax for the benefit of Germany, if I can help it. I do not believe the tales of German hard-up-ness. I know if we let her, she will dodge and cheat.'[51]

370 members of Parliament, the equivalent of the entire Conservative Party and 40 of Lloyd George's Liberals, sent a telegram to Lloyd George as follows:

'The greatest anxiety exists throughout the country at the persistent reports from Paris that the British delegates, instead of formulating the complete financial claim of the Empire, are merely considering what amount can be exacted from the enemy. This anxiety has been deepened by the statement of the Leader of the House on Wednesday last.
'Our constituents have always expected – and still expect –that the first action of the peace delegates would be, as you repeatedly stated in your election pledge, to present the bill in full, and make Germany acknowledge the debt, and then to discuss ways and means of obtaining payment.'[52]

Lloyd George responded to the Conservative M.P.s protests by lumping them with Northcliffe who was felt to be ambitious and self-seeking. Frances Stevenson, LLoyd George's secretary (and mistress) reported in her diary that it suited his purpose to 'play the brothers (Northcliffe and Rothermere) off against each other' at this juncture. 'He has made up his

50. *Bonar Law*. F101/3/38.
51. R. Pound & G. Harmsworth. *Northcliffe*. p.712.
52. Frank Owen. *Tempestuous Journey*. p.538.

GIVING HIM ROPE?

GERMAN CRIMINAL (*to Allied Police*). "HERE, I SAY, STOP! YOU'RE HURTING ME! [*Aside*]
IF I ONLY WHINE ENOUGH I MAY BE ABLE TO WRIGGLE OUT OF THIS YET."

Figure 2.1 Giving him Rope?
© Punch

mind to attack Northcliffe and declare war to the knife. He says that Northcliffe is intent on trying to oust him, so he (L.G.) is going to attack him now in order that people may know that Northcliffe's motives are purely personal, and that he may be discredited from the outset. He told me part of his speech before he left, and I must say it is very clever and amusing and will make Northcliffe very sorry for himself.'[53]

No doubt it did. For Lloyd George chose to attack Lord Northcliffe in the House of Commons in a speech which was sure to be widely reported and to which Lord Northcliffe, not being a member of Parliament, could not reply.

Ray Stannard Baker had been surprised and dismayed at Lloyd George's unreliable temperament at the Peace Conference.

'He seemed to have no guiding principles whatever. He was powerfully on one side one day and powerfully on the other the next. He was personally one of the most charming, amiable, engaging figures at Paris, full of Celtic quick-silver, a torrential talker in the conferences, but no one was ever quite sure, having heard him express an unalterable determination on one day, that he would not be unalterably determined some other way on the day following.'[54]

Lloyd George had promised his electorate 'Fullest indemnities from Germany.' But he had seemed not to be giving his negotiators his 'fullest' support at the Conference. Keynes's biographer, Skidelsky, declares that the reason for his change of heart was that he 'feared a war of revenge.' But he forgot that appeasement had merely whetted Germany's appetite pre-war. He was also nervous of asking his country-men to fight again. He had promised them 'no conscription' at the general election and hurried to dismantle Britain's fighting men.[55] Yet now the Americans were preparing to take their men back home and Britain would have to bear the brunt of enforcing whatever had been agreed at the Conference. Temperamentally a man who enjoyed talking rather than coercing, he had often bought peace before from the disaffected workers by making concessions over money. Now he hoped that con-cessions over money would make the Germans agree to the peace with-out the Allies having to resort to threatening a resumption of war.

'What I want is peace' he declared, 'I am prepared for any concession that will enable us to conclude...They must sign; with concessions they will sign...Warburg said that with concessions they would sign...We must con-clude.'[56]

53. Francis Stevenson. *Lloyd George. A Diary.* p.179–80.
54. R. S. Baker. *Woodrow Wilson & World Settlement.* Vol. II. p.509.
55. Robert Blake. *The Private Papers of Douglas Haig.* p.350.
56. A. Tardieu. *Le Sleswig et La Paix.* pp.246–7. *The Carthaginian Peace.* p.62.

But Lord Sumner and Lord Cunliffe would not give way. In the end, M. Klotz, the French finance minister, finally helped Lloyd George extricate himself from the negotiators whom he had appointed. M. Klotz felt that it would be better to leave the full amount to be decided to May 1921 and meanwhile ask for £1,000,000,000 to be paid on account.

But even this interim payment Lloyd George felt was a large amount for the Germans to accept. Now, however, the economist Keynes came up with an idea which seemed to present salvation. It was in the middle of April that Keynes devised his 'Grand scheme of rehabilitation of Europe.' General Smuts had just been to Austria to see conditions at first hand. He came to see Keynes and told him of the pitiful state of Central Europe. Keynes could divine no way that money could be extracted from 'destitute' countries such as Austria and Germany to pay reparations.

With this spectre in mind Keynes first stated his position that the wartime debts should be cancelled. Failing this he devised a grand scheme whereby the Americans loaned Germany the £1 billion payable on 1 May 1921 and Germany in turn repaid it to the Allies. It was to be a copper-bottomed scheme, carefully worked out, so that, should Germany renege on the deal, each Ally would guarantee a portion of Germany's repayments. Lloyd George sent a long covering letter. But the Americans were not impressed.[57]

2.6 The Future Of Poland

Lloyd George could not make any more concessions to the Germans over the question of money but there were other matters which Germany vexed over, especially Poland, much of which had been part of the Prussian Empire for the last 140 years and was now to be made an independent entity again under the terms of 'self- determination.' Under the terms of the Peace Treaty Germany was to be allowed to keep the ancient kingdom of Prussia, land of the Teutonic knights and medieval battles, but it was to surrender the rest of Poland which had only been part of the Prussian Empire for 140 years. As Poland would be land-locked, however, it was to be allowed a corridor to the sea and the ancient city of Danzig was to be internationalised. The Conference also proposed, in view of the fact that Germany was the dominant supplier of coal in continental Europe, to remove part of coal bearing Upper Silesia

57. R. S. Baker. *Woodrow Wilson & World Settlement.* Vol. II. p.509. *Papers of Woodrow Wilson.* Vol.60. (1989) Diary of Dr. Grayson. p.18.

from the Germans and give it to Poland to make it a viable economy.

A lot of noise emanated from Germany over the loss of any part of Polish soil. Danzig was said to be a 'German' city. The proposed Polish Corridor defied the laws of reason while the loss of Silesian coal would cripple the German economy. President Wilson sent his envoy, Dr. Lord. to Poland to advise him what the result would be if a referendum was held in Silesia.

Dr. Lord said that the people would vote to be part of Poland if they had free elections but that it was impossible to hold them at the moment because they couldn't be conducted impartially.

> 'Just at present, in spite of the Republican government of Germany, they are having a veritable reign of terror in Upper Silesia which is as bad as anything that went on under the Imperial Government, and such a state exists there that they have been arresting every prominent Polish leader; they have been placing people on trial charged with being guilty of high treason for the crime of having made speeches in favour of union with Poland, or collecting money in favour of Polish national causes.'

He said that all the wealth and power was in the hands of a very few rich and the Polish population was completely dependent upon these German landowners and capitalists for their livelihoods. He concluded soberly

> 'I can think of few countries where the countryman finds it so dangerous to express his opinion at the polls.'[58]

However Lloyd George insisted that 'self-determination' should prevail as enshrined in President Wilson's 14 point charter. No doubt British socialists applauded Lloyd George's determination to stick to his principles. But his insistence on holding a plebiscite in Silesia could also have been labelled a concession to Germany who, as the small Kingdom of Prussia, had won Silesia at the cost of 213,000 of its approximately 6 million population in the 18th century[59] and was in no mood to lose it now.

2.7 Lloyd George's Economic and Social Policy

Lloyd George, although a member of the Liberal Party, found himself in

58. R. S. Baker. *Woodrow Wilson & World Settlement*. Vol. II. Doc. 48. *Papers of Woodrow Wilson*. Vol.60. (1989) p.54–5.
59. J. Ellis Barker. *Foundations of Germany*. p.104.

sympathy with many socialist doctrines, particularly in their view of the desirability of the control of industry by the state. He had had no faith in the British industrialists' management of their companies during the war. He had received much acclaim for his time as Minister of Munitions when he had secured the rapid expansion of the armament industry from its small pre-war base. This had led him to 'control' other wartime industries. By 1918 nearly all Britain's major industries were under some sort of Government control. The mines, iron and steel and munition factories were directly under Government control and even the food and drink and hosiery businesses were largely controlled by the state.[60]

Lloyd George had received some criticism for the management of all these enterprises[61] and in the chill post-war climate he would soon abandon his identification with the unhappy, unprofitable industrial sector. Temperamentally, however, he believed that he could manage Britain's industry better than those who had engaged in it before and more to the benefit of those who worked there too.

A committee had been established at the Conference to co-ordinate social legislation. It contained nine recommendations:

1. The labour of a human being is not to be treated as an article of commerce.
2. Employers and workers shall be allowed the right of association for all lawful purposes.
3. No children shall be employed in industry before the age of fourteen. No one between the ages of fourteen and eighteen shall be employed on work which is harmful to physical development or which interferes with education.
4. The worker is entitled to a wage adequate to maintain a reasonable standard of life.
5. Equal pay shall be given to women and men whose work is of equal value.
6. A weekly day of rest, including Sunday or its equivalent.
7. Limitation of hours of work in industry on the basis of an eight-hour-day subject to special climatic or industrial conditions.
8. Foreign workmen lawfully admitted into any country shall be ensured the same treatment as nationals in matters concerning their status as workers.
9. A system of inspection shall be instituted to ensure the enforcement of regulations for the protection of workers.[62]

60. *Lloyd George Papers*. F/2/5/14.
61. *Lloyd George Papers*. F/8/76.
62. *Annual Register*. 1919.

In view of India's reservations the recommendations were not legally binding but were intended to provide a goal for nations to aim at. President Wilson had rewarded those in Allied countries who had fought for peace on the basis of his 14 points rather than 'unconditional surrender' by giving his seal of approval to their ideals.

Although the piece of paper remained a major step forward as a statement of intent, as it was not internationally legally binding, it depended on the desire of individual nations for its implementation.

However, the unfortunate outcome of socialists fighting for peace on President Wilson's terms, in order in part to achieve those nine precious recommendations, was that they would cling to their belief in the righteousness of their decision to seek a peace on the basis of the 14 points in the face of increasing evidence that they had made the wrong decision.

So now Germany had the rising tide of socialism in favour of a lenient peace, President Wilson whose aim was said to be 'Peace without Victory'[63] in order to moderate the ambitions of the European 'victors', and Lloyd George who sympathised with socialist causes and 'feared a war of revenge.'

2.8 Socialists in Favour of Lenient Peace Treaty

President Wilson had been sure of the righteousness of his path until the unforgettable day he met the Germans. They had been excluded from the Peace Conference until the terms had been worked out. Now the apparently humbled nation, racked by 'revolution', had come to hear its fate. President Wilson knew perfectly well that the German army could have been annihilated in October 1918, that the Allied armies and those of their American associate outnumbered those of the Central Powers by 2:1 by November, that the 1,950,000 bright, young, American boys newly stepped-ashore from the boats from America could have marched to Berlin to demonstrate to all the destruction of 'Prussian militarism.' But he had preached forgiveness and the absence of revenge. He had saved Germany. Every word, every gesture of that unforgettable day when the 'victors' met the vanquished in the Galerie de Glaces at Versailles, therefore, was indelibly engraved on his memory. To begin with, in contrast to the Allies' spokesman, Clemenceau, the German delegate, Count Brockdorf-Rantzau, sat down as he spoke and he spoke with a decision and confidence that rang round the Chamber:

63. Cooper. *The Warrior and the Priest*. p.312. Lodge on 'Peace Without Victory. p.315.

'We are under no illusion as to the extent of our defeat and the degree of our want of power....We know the power of the hatred which we encounter here, and we have heard the passionate demand that the victors shall make us pay as vanquished and shall punish those who are worthy of being punished. It is demanded from us that we shall confess ourselves to be the only ones guilty of the war. Such a confession in my mouth would be a lie. We are far from declining any responsibility for this great World War having come to pass and for its having been made in the way in which it was made...but we energetically deny that Germany and its people, who were convinced that they were waging a war of defence, were alone guilty...The hundreds of thousands of non-combatants who have perished since November 11 by reason of the blockade were killed with cold deliberation, after our adversaries had conquered and victory had been assured to them. Think of that when you speak of guilt and punishment.'[64]

As with all subsequent pronouncements by the Germans on the subject, this statement on Germany's war-guilt, was primarily meant for consumption by the audience at home. The Germans who eventually signed the Peace Treaty were branded as traitors when they returned and Herr Erzberger was later murdered.

The assembled company, however, were outraged, not least for Count Brockdorff-Rantzau's calculated discourtesy in failing to rise to give his speech.

Lloyd George wanted to hit Count Brockdorf-Rantzau,[65] presumably for using the propaganda weapon he had handed to him over the 'starvation' issue, so adroitly. On the matter of 'war- guilt' no one knew exactly what had happened in the last few days before the war broke out. But every American knew how Germany had been trying to incite Mexico to invade America's southern states, in the Spring of 1917, at the very moment when President Wilson was clutching at their spurious peace offer to the Allies.[66] The evidence of the vengeance they had reaped on their retreat through France had been observed by all.[67]

The Germans were presented with the Treaty on May 7 but they took six weeks before they would agree to sign. They staged large, showy demonstrations against the Treaty on the grounds that it contravened the terms on which they had agreed to lay down their arms, namely President Wilson's precious 14 points and principles. They proclaimed that Germany had been cruelly deceived, stirring up feelings of injury and outrage amongst their unfortunate, uninformed local population, and agonies of self doubt in liberal and socialist circles abroad.

64. *Annual Register.* 1919. p.178–9.
65. Francis Stevenson. *Lloyd George. A Diary.* p.183.
66. Barbara Tuchmann. *The Zimmermann Telegram.* p.146.
67. R. S. Baker. *Woodrow Wilson & World Settlement.* Vol. II. p.503.

Figure 2.2 " 'Nothing but the 14 Points'. A Berlin demonstration against the Peace Terms of the Allies."
© The Illustrated London News Picture Library

Lloyd George was concerned that the Treaty should be 'expedient as well as just.' Mr. Hoover (later President Hoover) also thought that the question of expediency ought to be raised. Mr. Hoover asked President Wilson: 'Apart from all questions of justice, how far does the question of expediency come in?'

President Wilson responded:

> 'In order to get them to sign, do you mean?' Mr. Hoover agreed: 'In order to get them to sign. It strikes me that that is a more important thing than the question of justice or injustice because the weighing of justice and injustice, in these times is pretty difficult.' President Wilson, however, presented a firmer line. He declared: 'Nobody can be sure they have made a just deci-sion. But don't you think that if we regard the Treaty as just, the argument of expediency ought not to govern, because after all we must not give up what we fought for? We might have to fight for it again.'[68]

President Wilson was a man of principle, determined not to be governed by expediency. But Lloyd George, with an unhappy industrial atmos-phere at home, was horrified at the thought of persuading the shop floor workers to return to the battlefield again and felt that expediency in the shape of concessions was the only way to get the Germans to sign and keep his shop floor militants happy.[69] Tardieu, later French Prime Minister, describes the time:

> 'Those were atrocious days. Mr. Lloyd George thoroughly alarmed by the consequences either of a refusal to sign or of a crisis in Germany, suggested unthinkable concessions on almost every point...The work of two months was threatened with ruin.'[70]

President Wilson complained of the British delegation: 'From the rea-sonable to the unreasonable, all the way round, they are all unanimous in their funk.'[71]

But the French would not make any more concessions and the British eventually heard their fears were groundless anyway. The Germans had made up their minds to sign.

Finally the Germans met their 'conquerors' again in the famous

---

68. E. Mantoux. *The Carthaginian Peace*. p.156–7.

69. *Annual Register*. 1919. p.78-9. For shop floor agitation. For Lloyd George's atti-tude towards the Peace Treaty, *Papers of Woodrow Wilson*. Vol. 60. (1989) 'Lloyd George told Baruch how anxious he was to meet the German viewpoint in certain circles but failed to be frank with him and did not mention the fact that the reason he has changed his attitude is due to the pressure that has been brought to bear upon him by the Liberal and Labour elements in Britain.'

70. A. Tardieu. *Le Slesvig et la Paix*. p.120.

71. R. S. Baker. *Woodrow Wilson & World Settlement*. Vol. II. p.503.

Galerie des Glaces at Versailles to sign the peace that was to end all wars.

According to Ray Stannard Baker, President Wilson's Press Secretary, 'the atmosphere was crowded and over-staged' and lacked the atmosphere of the previous occasion when the Peace Treaty had first been handed to the Germans.[72] The publication of a statement by General Smuts, criticising the Treaty, in his view, disturbed the harmony of the occasion.[73]

Smuts did say of the Treaty: 'It re-established peace; it marked the passing of Prussian militarism; and it set up the League of Nations.'[74]

But General Smuts had ambitions to become President in the forth-coming South African General Election and a large section of the pro-German South African electorate were antagonistic towards the 'victorious' British Empire.[75] So, having secured 'pensions and separations allowances' for South Africans who had fought in the war and the enduring gratitude of the British people who thought of him as a friend, he now prepared to give comfort to Germany by criticising 'the territorial boundaries' given by the Treaty, the 'guarantees', the 'punishments', and the 'indemnities' and he encouraged the Germans to renege on the Treaty's provisions by declaring:

> 'The real peace of the peoples ought to follow...and amend the peace of the statesmen.'[76]

Only one clause had been added to the Treaty since it was shown to the Germans. It related to France. After four long years of war she still did not feel secure. She wanted protection against armed attack from Germany but had only secured the support of the United Kingdom provided that America supported her too.

> 'Whereas His Britannic Majesty is willing, subject to the consent of his Parliament and provided that a similar obligation is entered into by the United States of America, to undertake to support the French Government in the case of an unprovoked movement of aggression being made against France by Germany.'[77]

72. R. S. Baker. *Woodrow Wilson & World Settlement.* Vol. II. p.503.

73. R. S. Baker. *Woodrow Wilson & World Settlement.* Vol. II. p.520.

74. R. S. Baker. *Woodrow Wilson & World Settlement.* Vol. II. p.520.

75. Sarah Gertrude Millin. *General Smuts.* Vol. 2. Chapter entitled 'Boers in Paris'. p.248, p.272–3, p.460. '1920 election fought on the issue of secession from England.'

76. Sarah Gertrude Million. *General Smuts.* Vol. 2. p.275–6. There is an interesting side-line to this. Botha, South Africa's ailing Premier, (died August 1919) wished to sign in order give South Africa dominion status. Smuts did not wish to sign. So 'Lloyd George suggested to Smuts that his proper course was to sign under protest. He was not precluded from issuing his critical statement as soon after as he chose immediately indeed, upon signing.'

77. *Annual Register.* 1919. p.182.

Figure 2.3 The Big four of the Peace Conference. 28th June 1919.
Lloyd George, Orlando, Clemenceau, and President Wilson
President Wilson had originally delcared of the French: 'Theirs was the
ancient policy. To the victor belongs the spoils'. Now he shared their
apprehensions.
© The Illustrated London News Picture Library

Support for France now came from an unlikely quarter. President Wilson had come to the momentous and brave decision that he had made a terrible mistake about the French. To begin with he had been convinced that the French were old-fashioned imperialists. 'Theirs was the ancient policy. To the victor belongs the spoils.'[78] Now he shared their apprehensions. It was the French who were prostrate and suffering, not their enemies the Germans. He wanted his countrymen to guarantee their safe future, if not in the name of the United States, at least in the name of the League of Nations.

But, having brought so many men all the way over from America once and then not used them to enforce surrender, he realised that it would be an awesome task to persuade his infuriated countrymen ever to undertake the exercise again. The Republicans, uninvited to the Peace Conference, turned down out of hand the proposal to risk America involving itself in Europe's affairs again.

So President Wilson put his faith in public opinion, which had helped him so well in the past, and planned an enormous tour of America to canvass support for his plan for a League of Nations to help the French nation if it was attacked again.

'One of the most interesting things that I realised after I got to the other side of the water' he told a gathering at St. Louis on 5 September 1919, 'was that the mental attitude of the French people with regard to the settlement of this war was largely determined by the fact that for nearly fifty years they had expected it, that for nearly fifty years they had dreaded, by the exercise of German force, the very thing that had happened, and their constant theme was: 'We must devise means by which this intolerable fear will be lifted from our hearts. We cannot, we will not, live another fifty years under the cloud of that terror.' The terror had been there all the time and the war was its flame and its consummation.'[79]

A few days later at Minneapolis he repeated this message:

'I believe my fellow countrymen that the only people in Europe who instinctively realised what was going to happen and what did happen in 1914 was the French people...'

He had been no less concerned for the future of the new-born nations of South East Europe as he explained in his speech at Indianapolis on 4 September 1919: 'Those very weak nations are situated through the very tract of country – between Germany and Persia – which Germany had meant to conquer and dominate, and if the nations of the world do not

78. R. S. Baker. *Woodrow Wilson & World Settlement*. Vol. 2. p.2.
79. E. Mantoux. *The Carthaginian Peace*. p.59. Address at St. Louis.

maintain their concern to sustain the independence and freedom of those peoples, Germany will yet have her will upon them, and we shall witness the very interesting spectacle of having spent millions upon millions of American treasure and, what is much more precious hundreds of thousands of American lives...to do a thing which we will then leave to be undone at the leisure of those who are masters of intrigue, at the leisure of those who are combining wrong influences to overcome right influences, of those who are the masters of the very things we hate and mean always to fight. For my fellow citizens, if Germany should ever attempt that again, whether we are in the League of Nations or not we will join to prevent it. We do not stand off and see murder done.'[80]

---

80. E. Mantoux. *The Carthaginian Peace*. p. 50. Speech at Indianapolis. 4.9.19.

–3–

Resolute Germany and Weakened Britain

3.1 Britain Goes to the Polls

On the 14 December 1918, a cold, grey, rainy day the British had gone to the polls to elect a post-war government. There was not a great deal of competition because Lloyd George's coalition Liberals and the Conservatives decided to continue their alliance. Ranged against them were merely the nascent Labour party and the discredited Liberals led by Asquith. The Labour Party had initially 'carried a resolution in favour of the Labour party co-operating with the government until the terms of Peace had actually been agreed upon and signed.'[1] But their members, especially the mining fraternity, were concerned that they would not have sufficiently powerful positions in the post- war coalition Parliament. On the eve of the election (10 December) Lloyd George summed up the Coalition programme in the following points:

1. Trial of the Kaiser
2. Punishment of those responsible for atrocities.
3. Fullest indemnities from Germany.
4. Britain for the British, socially and industrially.
5. Rehabilitation of those broken in war.
6. A happier country for all.[2]

The government won a sweeping victory that day, the thirteen million new voters registering their voice for a peace based on justice rather than mercy. The Unionists with their 338 votes comprised by far the largest votes in Parliament but they had decided to continue their coalition with Lloyd George's Liberals, giving them 484 votes in all.'

Asquith's Liberals managed to gain only 28 votes so that the Labour Party with its 50 votes secured itself the respectability of being the

1. *Lloyd George Papers*. F.5/6/4.
2. *Annual Register*. 1918. p.163.

official opposition with all the publicity that that ensures. Normally the voice of someone representing 62 members might be somewhat drowned by the thunder emanating from those representing 484 but although Labour had won little support from the voters, and the Labour party leadership itself was moderate and responsible, shop floor militants went instantly into action to put pressure on Government ministers to bend their ear to the socialist cause.

New Police grievances were placated with the promise of an inquiry but strike fever soon spread. On 24 January the Shipwrights and Blacksmiths' societies met the Minister of Labour. About 20,000 shipyard and engineering workers stopped work in Glasgow and about 10,000 shipyard workers in London. Dock workers also went on strike. The shop stewards on the Clyde attempted to organise a general strike, warning that they had hitherto adopted 'constitutional methods' but henceforth they would use 'any other methods which they might consider would be likely to help their cause.' As Lloyd George was at Versailles, Bonar Law took charge. The shortage of shipping was acute. One fifth of the nation's shipping had been destroyed in the war and more was lying idle for want of repair.

Bonar Law decided to be firm in response to militancy and disorder. He declined to talk to the militants as their leaders were already in discussion with the employers. 12,000 troops and six tanks were called in to deal with the unrest.[3] There was some rioting and 'a general strike' was proposed on 6 February but support for it soon evaporated. Bonar Law told the electricity workers who had promised that London 'would be plunged into darkness' over demands for a forty hour week that anyone leaving work without notice would be fined severely or sent to prison.

However, the industrial trouble was not yet over. A triple alliance was formed between the transport men, the railwaymen and the miners 'who had been starved, kicked, and kept in miserable houses for generations' to achieve political ends.[4] They called it 'direct action.' Lloyd George, briefly back from the negotiations at Versailles, tried conciliation. An industrial disputes committee would be set up with representation from all sides to try to head off trouble. But that did not satisfy the miners.

President Wilson's ideals had captivated the imagination of all groups in the Allied world but 'self-determination' was the principle which men found most appealing post-war. It certainly excited the miners. They not only wanted control of their industry, they preferred an easier life. They demanded nationalisation and a six hour day. Ormsby-Gore

3. Stevenson. *British Society 1914–45*. p.101.
4. *Annual Register*. 1919.

Figure 3.1 Oliver 'Asks' for More
© Punch

the previous January had identified the shop steward's movement as 'embittered against society' not socialism but 'Marxian syndicalism, revolutionary in its aims and methods, aiming at the overthrow of the existing social and economical order by direct action.' Their kind of revolutionary socialism had been shown in the elections to have no support among the British public but as Germany seemed to be in the grip of revolutionary activity, Britain's politicians could have speculated that concessions on hours worked would not be too damaging.

They decided to agree to the Sankey report, which proposed a seven hour day being shortened to six in 1921 if circumstances allowed. Bonar Law wrote to his Prime Minister:

> 'As regards arresting the leaders and so on, I agree with you in thinking that that would not be a wise procedure to take now but I think it is quite possible that after the strike has broken out and we have public opinion, as I believe, entirely on our side, it would then be the right thing to introduce such a Bill.'[5]

These were strong words but the shortening of the working week would have unhappy effects in the future. For the ensuing loss of production meant a shortfall for the year of some 70,000,000 tons[6] just when Europe was in crying need of coal. But instead of the concession satisfying the miners, it appeared to reinforce their faith that the day was near when the working man would be able to have control over his place of work if only more pressure was applied.

400,000 American miners also went on strike in 1919 demanding a six hour day and a 60% increase in wages.[7] Majority republicans refused to allow President Wilson to make concessions to the strikers. The lights went out in middle America. Huge factories employing thousands of people stood idle. The strike went on for weeks. But eventually the miners went back to work with only marginal concessions. A sinister plot was uncovered to spread the strike to other industries. Out of 4116 suspected 'Bolsheviks' held, 2,800 were detained for deportation.[8]

3.2 Bolshevik Disturbances

If Britain had been deceived into imagining that the Germans, like themselves, would behave in a weak and supplicatory manner towards their miners, because of the 'Bolshevik' disturbances in their country, they

5. *Lloyd George Papers*. Bonar Law File.
6. *Annual Register*. 1919. p.73.
7. *Annual Register*. 1919. p.282.
8. *The Times*. 5.1.20.

were to be mistaken. Although there was much bloodshed in Germany in the Spring of 1919, it did not mean that the 'revolutionaries' were in the ascendancy, quite the reverse. In Germany the old guard, through accusing the socialists of 'stabbing the nation in the back' had already achieved moral ascendancy over their socialist ideals. They responded to the miners postwar desires for a better life in a martial manner.

When the miners threatened a general strike and demanded that a Factory Council system of managing the mines be set up, the Government brought in the army. In April another strike occurred over the issue of disarming the free-corps and the delay in implementing the eight hour day which had been promised by the SDP. The government issued martial law. There was bloody confrontation. Eventually the precious eight hour day, promised in the 'November revolution' was won. Surface workers were granted an eight hour day and underground miners worked seven and a half.[9] But strikers were not feared any more in Germany. They were on the defensive. The free-corps remained at large, aching to confront those enemies of the Fatherland who had dared to go on strike and conspire with the enemy while their comrades had fought and died on the western front. The mining industry prospered however. In 1922 some 50,000 more workers were employed in the mining industry than in 1913, including 20,062 women, 43,474 juveniles and 130 children under the age of 14.[10]

Where was the German revolution that had swept the Kaiser from office in November 1918? It had been buried under a carpet of blood. The revolution had, in fact, at first been little more than a peace movement and so, by its very nature non-violent. Only in its last days had any sort of coherent policy emerged. It had not even taken over the printing presses in November.

Men like Hitler had been curiously silent that November but after the Kaiser had gone they re-emerged. Ebert had requested help from the army in dealing with the perceived threat to constitutional rule. In the first five months of 1919 'freikorps' were raised to help liberate the land from 'revolutionaries.' But these men, though they put a curb on 'Bolshevism,' were no lovers of democracy. Over 480,000 fighting men[11] had been on the victorious Eastern front at the end of the war. They could not believe that the morale of their army in the West had collapsed. They were outraged at what they perceived to be a 'stab in the back' against the army in the west. Captain Gengler, encapsulated the thoughts of many when he wrote in his diary on 21 January, 1919:

9. *New York Times.*
10. *Statesman's Yearbook.*
11. Information from John Terraine, taken from British Official History, Military Operations in France and Belgium 1918, vol. III p.253.

'The day will come when I shall get my own back on this government and unmask the whole pitiful, miserable pack.'[12]

The Conservative paper, *Deutsche Tageszeitung*, uncensored even in those critical November days, spoke for more sober citizens when it declared on 10 November:

'Words cannot suffice to express the indignation and the grief ... Germany, yesterday still unconquered, now left at the mercy of her enemies by men bearing the name of Germans...'

It asserted that the German socialists knew that peace was in the offing, it was merely a matter of facing the enemy for a few more weeks, perhaps only a few days, with a firm unbreached front to extract tolerable conditions from him. In this situation they hoisted the white flag.

'This is a perfidy that can never and shall never be forgiven.'[13]

The Home front simply could not believe that their nation had been so close to defeat when they had won such immense victories in the Spring. Although a Prussian captain had confided to a reporter from the *New York Times* that even the French Army alone could have beaten them without difficulty. 'They were completely at the mercy of the Allies – literally beaten to a frazzle.'[14] This fact had not been allowed to permeate the Home Front. The returning soldiers, marching back into Germany, in good formation, into an uninvaded, scarcely unscarred country, had been greeted with the words: 'Welcome, brave soldiers, your work has been done, God and Wilson carry it on.'[15] They had been treated to a heroes' welcome in Berlin.

L. James of the *New York Times* had recorded the defiant majority public opinion on 12 December: 'Defeat has not sorrowed the German people...They regret the sinking of the Lusitania, not because it was inhuman but because it was a mistaken policy which brought America into the war. The Germans are not sorry for the war. I have been told dozens of times by German citizens here that they are sorry the war stopped, for they thought they might have won.'[16]

So there was general support for the government's decision to recruit the 'freikorps' to deal with the threat to established authority posed by the strikers and revolutionaries. They responded to their orders with

12. Sebastien Haffner. *Failure of a Revolution*. p.159.
13. Sebastien Haffner. *Failure of a Revolution*. p.103.
14. *New York Times*. 12.12.18.
15. Paul Johnson. *A History of the Modern World*. p.105.
16. *New York Times*. 12.12.18.

Figure 3.2 Germany deceiving herself! Soldiers of the enemy armies return to Berlin as 'undefeated'.
© The Illustrated London News Picture Library

PUNCH, OR THE LONDON CHARIVARI.—January 29, 1919.

THE FIRST GERMAN VICTORY.

[The German Elections have resulted in a signal defeat for the Extremists.]

Figure 3.3 The First German Victory
© Punch

enthusiasm. Between 1,200 to 1,500 'enemies of the state' were shot in Berlin alone in March, at a cost to the freikorps of merely 75 dead and 38 missing.[17]

3.3   Germany's Industrial Strength

Germany's military and industrial hierarchy were confident that they had regained control of their country from far left socialist ideology. Industrially they were also confident. In 1919 Germany could be said to have been the OPEC of continental Europe in the supply of that vital source of power, coal. France's mines were out of action, Germany's currency was competitively priced and the British mines were suffering from industrial action. Germany possessed a partial monopoly over coal in central Europe[18] making Italy, France and Belgium dependant on her largesse.

The decision to give a coal mining area to Poland in 1921 in order to make it a viable economy, would arouse an enormous uproar in the Fatherland. But the area finally given to Poland had produced only 32.3 tons of coal in 1913 out of a total production of coal and lignite of 210 tons. In addition, it was to be allowed duty free into Germany so that German industry would not suffer. By 1926 Germany had so little need of Polish coal that the economists advised creating a barrier to keep imports out, despite the fact that Germany was busy filling British export orders whilst British miners were out on strike.[19]

One can see, on the map, the great ironworks of Longwy- Brie, just across the border from Germany. The annexation of these ironworks had been one of Germany's prime aims of the war.[20]

Longwy-Brie ore, however, was difficult to work. It needed top quality coal to operate it and that coal came from the Ruhr. The *New York Times* describes the history of the problem:

17. Gordon A. Craig. *Germany 1866–1945*. p.410.

18. Etienne Mantoux. *The Carthaginian Peace or The Economic Consequences of Mr. Keynes*. Etienne Mantoux was an economist, killed in the last days of World War II. Professor Laski wrote to the *Manchester Guardian* after hearing of his death: 'I thought him one of the ablest students who had ever come my way.'

19. Etienne Mantoux. *The Carthaginian Peace*. p.82–3. E. Storm. *Geschichte der Deutschen Kohlenwirtschaft von 1913–26*.

20. Fritz Fischer. *The Aims of Germany in the 1st World War*. Bethmann Hollweg. 9.9.14. p.104. 'The ore-field of Brie, which is necessary for the supply of our industry to be ceded in any case.'

August Thyssen: 'incorporation of the Brie basin would raise the iron ore prodcution of Greater Germany to 61.4 million tons which with the production of the Belgian and French works would lead to German domination of the market. It would therefore be only a question of a little time before Germany caught up and passed America'.

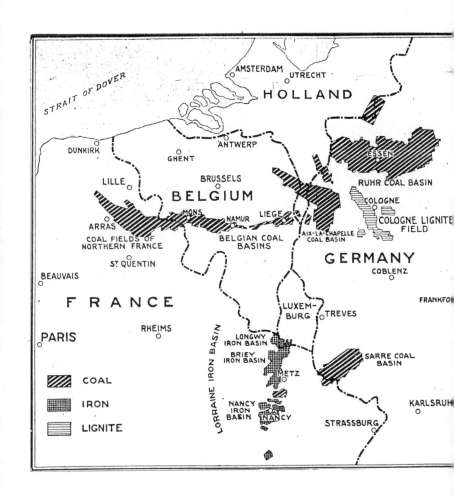

Map 3.1 France's Longwy Briey Ore-Field and Germany' Coal.

'The situation of France becomes imminently perilous the moment Germany is able to work the Ruhr unhampered because of the industrial axiom that normally iron always goes to coal rather than coal to iron. Since it requires three tons of coal to smelt a ton of ore the saving in transportation in sending iron to the mines is overwhelming and thus it is in the coal fields, not the iron fields that great industries spring up.

'It is only in the past generation and a half that the problem now confronting France has arisen. The development and adequate exploitation of Lorraine iron and Ruhr coal have been so recent that in 1871, when Bismarck sought to cripple France forever by the annexation of much of Alsace-Lorraine, he was so badly advised by his experts that he permitted France to have the territory which before long became the enormously rich Briey iron basin and thus his vanquished rival became richer in iron than Germany.[21]

It was the Thomas blast furnace, invented in Britain, which enabled iron to be extracted from ore with a high phosphorous content. It enabled a greater use to be made of machinery all over the world. The close proximity of the French ore field to the German border, however. made the danger of war that much greater from a nation that believed in 'blood and iron.'

Germany had coveted France's Longwe-Brie ore field but after the devastation Germany wrought on her retreat the French iron and steel works would be inoperable for one or two years anyway, giving Germany the industrial advantage in those vital years after the war.[22] Thereafter France would still have to sell her iron to Germany if she wanted the best price for it.

Yet it was not only the powerful iron and steel industry that was looking to gain from other countries post-war weakness, the whole of German industry was ready to take the war from the battlefield into the shops. The ubiquitous reporter from the *New York Times* reported on 12 December 1918:

'It is true that in some respects Germany is ready for a trade war. They have undoubtedly a considerable stock of glassware, cutlery, electrical appliances, photographic materials and iron and steel goods stored up for exportation if the Allies will allow it...I visited a big iron works, admirably equipped and using electrical power throughout, whose manager said proudly that he had enough mine pumps built during intervals of big gun order, by which he admitted he had made enormous profits, to supply all the flooded mines of France and Belgium.'[23]

21. *New York Times*. 2.12.23.

22. 'Die Industrie im besetzen Frankreich: bearbeitet im Aufrage des Generalquartier-meisters'. Munchen 1916. Quoted in Etienne Mantoux The Carthaginian Peace. p.91. Lloyd George. The Truth about the Peace Treaties. Vol. I. pp.441–3.

23. *New York Times*. 12.12.18.

Russia had been eliminated at least for a decade as an industrial competitor and whereas Bethmann Hollweg's aim of September 9 1914 that France 'must be so weakened as to make her revival as a great power impossible for all time'[24] had not been accomplished the £830 million pounds worth of material damage done to France would take a long time to put right and would receive precious little help from the Fatherland.

There was not only 'the 1,800,000 hectares of good French agricultural land, filled with bomb craters, trenches, barbed-wire and spent shells to be restored before it could be used for agriculture, there were the 2,245 kilometres of destroyed railway lines to be repaired, 1,160 bridges had been destroyed, 1,073 kilometres of canals rendered inoperable, 550,000 houses destroyed and 460,000 tons of industrial material, stolen and carted off to Germany.'[25]

Before World War I the then director of the German Reichsbank, K. Th. Helfferich, had assessed Germany's wealth at £16,000,000,000 and its national income at £2,150,000,000, compared to Britain's national wealth which he assessed at £12,500,000,000 and her income at £1,710,000,000. He declared that Germany was the richest country in the world with the possible exception of the United States.[26] The pan-German Rheinisch-Westfaelische Zeitung, reviewing A. Steinmann-Bucher's book, Das Reiche Deutschland, boasted: 'The German people should keep in mind what Steinmann-Bucher is proclaiming. 'We have five million soldiers more than the Britishers and 50,000 million gold marks more in national wealth.'[27]

The war had cost the central powers £12 billion while it had cost the Allies, £24 billion.[28] Of that £24 billion 5 or 6 billion had been lent by Britain to Russia and might never be repaid. Germany was weary at the present, but the prospects looked bright for the future.

3.4 Germany's Propaganda War

As the German military and industrial hierarchy were confident that they were winning the propaganda war at home they went on the offensive over the Peace Conference to which they had not been invited.

By far the major victory that the former Prussian Empire had won

24. Fritz Fischer. *Aims of Germany in the 1st World War*. p.103.

25. *New York Times*. 1.2.20.

26. Helfferich. Deutschland. Volkswohlstand. Berlin 1913. *The Greatest Swindle in the World*. G. Borsky. p.34.

27. G. Borsky. *The Greatest Swindle in the World*.

28. G. Borsky. *The Greatest Swindle in the World*. p.35.

Map 3.2 Prussia in 1815.

Map 3.3 The 'German' or Prussian Empire between 1871 and 1914.

from a peace based on President Wilson's points and principles, was that nationality was to be defined on the basis of language so that while the 400 year old Austrian Empire was decimated by the Peace, Bismarck's 50 year old Prussian Empire remained essentially intact.

Bismarck had unified the German speaking nations by creating fears of aggression from their external neighbours, the Austrians, Danes and French. German philosophers such as von Treische had sweetened the pill of defeat for such states as Hanover, Hesse and Saxony, who had had the temerity to fight the Prussians,[29] by spreading the Gospel that they were still part of an all-conquering superior race by 'uniting'[30] with Prussia.

'Their dynasties are ripe and over-ripe for the annihilation which they deserve...As Prussian citizens they will soon discover if they have not already learned in this war from the elevating spectacle of Prussian patriotism that the human heart is richer and better when it has a fatherland.' Only 'unconditional surrender' could have disproved this axiom.

Nevertheless, the fact remained that a state like Bavaria had an 800 year old history and was larger in size than Holland. She had much more in common with Catholic Austria than Protestant Prussia and had only been part of the pre- Bismarck loose association of states known as the German Confederation, in case of an invasion by France. Now she, in common with all the other 39 individual states that had made up the German Confederation before Bismarck's time, was to be branded with guilt for a war that members of the Prussian Empire had been told was a war of self-defence. Hegel, the German philosopher, had promoted the virtues of a war which would unite the German states under the banner of the omnipotent state[31] but in fact it was the perceived injustices of the peace that would cement the German speaking people in 1919.

To conceal its relief that the heart of the Empire remained intact and to give credence to the myth promulgated among its people that the war on the battlefield had never been lost, Germany threw its propaganda machine into making an immense issue about each small province or chunk of land that the Treaty of Versailles had removed.

29. Steinberg. *A Short History of Germany*. p.218.

30. Bismarck on the human costs of 'unification' - 'But for me three great wars would not have taken place, eighty thousand men would not have been killed and would not now be mourned by parents, brothers, sisters and widows.'
Crankshaw. *Bismarck*. p.344. Constantin Franck on the virtues of the Confederation as opposed to the 'Bismarckian Empire' – 'Impotent and imperfect as the Confederation may have been, one thing cannot be denied, namely, that it was of paramount importance for the whole European system...It operated moderatingly, it was in fact an instrument of peace. Its dissolution in 1866 made the whole European system lose its former stability so that from that moment onward the relations of all European states became based upon bayonets, and the whole continent groans under the burden of militarism.' (1879).

31. Bertrand Russell. *A History of Western Philosophy*. p.711.

TERRITORIAL CHANGES IN EUROPE 1919–24

KEY

- - - - NATIONAL BOUNDARIES 1924

TERRITORY LOST BY GERMANY

TERRITORY LOST BY AUSTRIA HUNGARY

TERRITORY LOST BY RUSSIA

Danish-speaking Schleswig was given back to the Danes. Alsace, originally a loosely federated German state before Louis XIV's time, was given back to France in ruins and Prussia was broken up to give Poland back a homeland. This was undoubtedly the greatest blow of all, especially to the Prussian nobles and landowners.[32] Ominously East Prussia remained, a cuckoo in the nest, threatening Poland, just like the two halves of the kingdom of Prussia had threatened the state of Hanover in pre-Bismarck days.

Indeed it was to the East that the former Prussian Empire, now called Germany, had hoped to expand, and this was demonstrated by its terms at Brest-Litovsk in 1918: Lithuania and Courland, were to be annexed, the Russian part of Poland, although not formally annexed, was also to become an area of 'direct' German influence. Estonia, Livonia and the Southern Russian territory of Georgia were to become 'territories of territorial and administrative dependency.' The Ukraine was to become an area of 'closest involvement with Germany' while the fate for Rumania was to become a territory 'of political and economic connection.'

'Spheres of influence and raw material bases' were demanded by Germany from the Kuban and the Land of the Don Cossacks, while Armenia and Azerbaijan were to become the Transcaucasian Republic, 'closely connected with the Central Powers.' Finally the name of the Crimea was to be changed. It was to become the Tartar Republic, an area of German settlement.[33]

It was no wonder that the old guard ranted at the Treaty of Versailles. They had to blame someone for their foolishness. For had they not risked all by throwing their troops against the Allies in the Spring of 1918 President Wilson would have been unable to restrain them from retaining their Eastern Empire.

As a penalty for their greed the Empire now had even to forfeit parts of Prussia to the Poles. It was Germany's conquest of Prussia, originally part of Poland, which had given Germans their philosophy of their right to rule. The recovery of their lost Prussian territory became a major preoccupation with many of the old guard during the interwar years.

---

32. In December 1924 Count Brockdorff-Rantzau proposed Russo-German collaboration 'to push Poland back to its ethnic borders.' *Stresemann Papers*. 7129H.
Gottfried R. Treviranus (11.2.30) 'We have not forgotten the wound on our Eastern flank and the lopping off of the Vistula district. We have not forgotten how shabbily Woodrow Wilson urged the unnatural severing of East Prussia and to what a hybrid plight Danzig was condemned. The future of our Polish neighbours...can be insured only when Germany and Poland are no longer kept in eternal unrest over frontier injustices.'
33. Fritz Fischer. *Aims of Germany in the 1st World War*. p.547.

3.5 German Colonial Empire

The Prussians had managed to 'unite' the 39 states of the German Confederation but they had been less successful with their other conquests.

Finding the lack of subservience of the local Alsatian population intolerable, one of the young Prussian Army officers, Lieutenant Forstner, had promised a present of 10 marks to any of his soldiers if they stabbed a 'Wackes' (local expression for a native of Alsace) who insulted them. The indignation caused by this order and subsequent commands had repercussions all over Germany and eventually was brought up in the Reichstag. But the Prussian Minister for war, General Falkenhayn, defended the Lieutenant by declaring that 'what they had to deal with was not the degree of a lieutenant's offence, but a determined attempt by Press agitation and abuse to exercise an unlawful influence upon the decision of the authorities.'[34]

Under the new, more democratic rules of procedure enacted in 1912 the Radicals and Socialists managed to secure a vote of censure against the unrepresentative[35] government. It was passed by 293 votes to 54. However the Military Court of appeal reversed a forty-three days imprisonment sentence against Lieutenant Forstner who had struck a lame cobbler over the head with his sword for insulting him with 'contemptuous cries', by upholding his plea that 'it was only an ordinary military sword and had not been specially ground for the occasion.' In the Prussian Upper House Count von Wartenburg declared that 'the Army must not be exposed to democratic impulses lest Germany should become like England, which had 'a life President at the head of a Republic.'[36] The Danes and the Poles suffered similar indignities.[37]

Although Germany made a tremendous protest at the loss of its European territory at Versailles, it removed a strand of opposition within their country.

The Germans also made a fuss over their Colonial Empire which was stated to cover an area more than nine times the size of the United Kingdom.[38] In Germany's colonial Empire in Africa men like Lieutenant Forstner had more rein to act as they pleased to subdue the native population without the Press and the democrats in Parliament

34. *Annual Register.* 1913. p.318–20.
35. 'Unrepresentative. The elected members of Parliament had the power to deny finance but not to propose legislation. *Annual Register.* 1914. p.306.
36. *Annual Register.*
37. *Annual Register*, Poland. p.316–7. Schleswig. p.321.
38. J. Ellis Barker. *Foundations of Germany.* p.213.

breathing down their necks. The Reichstag had passed a resolution in favour of the abolition of 'serfdom' by 1st January 1920 but the government responded by stating that those born after 1905 were already free and that it would be 'highly dangerous' to set a date for complete abolition.[39]

Germany had fought many wars in South West Africa to 'pacify the natives.' In 1893 and 1894 Germany was at war with the Hottentots. In 1896 the Khauas Hottentots and Hereros revolted. During 1897 and 1898 Germany fought the Zwartbooi Hottentots. In 1904 the great rising of the Hereros occurred. It took up to 20,000 troops, £20,000,000 and three years to subdue them.

During the war the Prussian Commander in Chief, general von Trotha made this proclamation to the Hereros:

'I the great General of the German soldiers send this letter to the Herero nation. The Hereros are no longer German subjects. They have murdered and robbed, they have cut off the ears and other members of wounded soldiers, and now they are too cowardly to fight. Therefore, I say to the people: Whosoever brings one of the chiefs to one of my stations shall receive 1000 marks, and for Samuel Mahero I will pay 5000 marks. The Herero nation must now leave the country. If the people do not I will compel them with the big gun. Within the German frontier, every Herero with or without a rifle, with or without cattle, will be shot. I will not take over any more women and children, but I will either drive them back to their people, or have them fired on. These are my words to the nation of the Hereros.
The Great General of the mighty Emperor,
von Trotha.'[40]

After three years of war they obeyed. 180,000 natives had been killed in the campaigns. There was no one left to work because those men, women and children who had not been exterminated, had taken the hint and vanished over the borders into neighbouring lands. Although most of South West Africa is semi-desert it has also been said that 'large parts of German South West Africa and German East Africa lie at so high an altitude above the sea that the climate is moderate, bracing, and extremely healthful.'[41] The Prussians had built strategic railway lines. They also constructed some substantial, empty towns, with huge schools, magnificent public buildings, statues and parks. But the ordinary emigrant German had a more progressive view of life. He escaped to America.

Nevertheless prominent Germans had been inordinately proud of

39. *Annual Register*. 1914. p.311.
40. J. Ellis Barker. *Foundations of Germany*. p.223.
41. J. Ellis Barker. *Foundations of Germany*. p.215.

their colonies. It mattered not that the colonies had contained 'hardly 25,000 whites altogether and contributed only 3% of the total of their (Germany's) trade.'[42] It had annoyed the military and industrial hierarchy that the map of the world had been covered by a sea of British red and French blue. They believed that Germany's economic strength should have been reflected materially on the map of the world. They wanted a 'place in the sun.' That ambition had not been quenched by the events of 1918.

So Germany would complain bitterly at the Treaty of Versailles. The country would cry that its heart had been ripped out by the Allies at a peace which it wasn't permitted to attend. It had been starved, it had been humiliated and recovery might take half a century to achieve. Germany's Hanovarian, Saxon and Bavarian citizens would forget the fact that they had lost their own identity in the common outrage at the territory that was being stripped from the 'Fatherland' and the guilt that was being thrust upon it in what they had always been told was a war of defence. Yet essentially the spirit of Prussia was still healthy, as shall be examined in later chapters, even if its ambitions were yet to be fulfilled. Meanwhile Great Britain, victorious on paper with even larger extensions to the British Empire, would find its whole existence undermined by President Wilson's peace with its principle of 'self-determination.'

42. *Annual Register.* 1914. p.312.

–4–

The Economic Consequences of the Peace

4.1   The Role of General Smuts and John Maynard Keynes

The story of the Peace Conference recorded the names of two people who were to have an indelible effect on international opinion's conception of post-war Germany and its ability to pay reparations, General Smuts and John Maynard Keynes.

General Smuts was a curious choice for Lloyd George to have included in his war cabinet. An ambitious introvert with a towering brain and a limp-handshake manner, he had fought a bitter propaganda war against Britain during and after the Boer War[1] as well as fighting British troops in the field.[2] The British had been enduringly grateful to him for advocating South Africa's support for the allies in the Great War[3] but it was a fine point whether he had done this out of affection for Britain or fear of the Germans, so close in South West Africa, too close in view of South Africa's reserves of gold. South Africans fought bravely and to great effect in World War I and in South West Africa they forced 'unconditional surrender' on their foes.

The post-war Peace Treaty negotiators had reason to be grateful to

1. Sarah Gertrude Millin. *General Smuts*. Propaganda during the Boer War. The Kruger Millions. p.131. A century of wrong. p.113, p.192–4. For propaganda after the war Miss Hobhouse. *Chinese Slavery*.

2. See Chapter XIX. Commandant. *General Smuts*. p.147.

3. At the start of the 1st World War Prime Minister Botha sent a cable that the Union 'recognised its obligations to the Empire and was prepared, in the event of war, to defend its own territory.' p.304–305.
However the Germans 'accidentally' crossed the border into South Africa, counting on Boer support. (We expected a triumphal rebellion in South Africa. p.310.)
Smuts spoke in the South African Parliament supporting the Prime Minister's view that there should be an offensive against German South Africa.(now Namibia) p.308.
July 3rd.1915. Seitz, German Governor General suggested an armistice – each side to keep the territory it now occupied, a neutral zone to be created, prisoners exchanged. 'His own troops and Germany's were now in a position of unusual strength.' Seitz surrendered the next day. It was the Allies first wartime success.

General Smuts for being instrumental in persuading President Wilson to change his mind over allowing pensions and separations allowances to be chargeable as reparations. President Wilson felt close to the General, who was an enthusiastic supporter of the League of Nations. The General privately envisaged the League as a strong protective force to guard South African interests instead of his country having to rely on and kowtow to the British Empire. So now that the German menace had apparently receded, he was an ardent advocate of peace on the fourteen points, the League of Nations and leniency to a suffering Germany, many of whose nationals were now resident in South Africa and would hopefully vote for him shortly to be Prime Minister. A practised propagandist, he bent the ear of the young economist, John Maynard Keynes, who had dealt with the Germans over the food issue and had wondered 'whether the children's ribs would be sticking through their clothes' but had never been able to take a proper look.

Keynes came from a cloistered academic family and had been brought up by German nannies in his youth. At Cambridge he had joined a set of non-conformist iconoclasts, brilliantly talented but without experience of the outside world. Lytton Strachey, the leader of this group, younger son of a distinguished general but physically infirm, campaigned against his friend's involvement in the war. Keynes's moral dilemma grew worse as the war dragged on and the casualty figures mounted. After Germany's peace offer of December 16th 1916 had been turned down by the Allies Lytton Strachey sent Keynes a letter:

'Dear Maynard, Why are you still at the Treasury?
Yours, Lytton.'[4]

Keynes was not to know that the German peace offer was merely an excuse for Germany to justify the use of unrestricted submarine warfare to her people. By 1917 he was writing to his friend Duncan Grant:

'I work for a government I despise whose ends I feel criminal.'[5]

There had to be a better way of conducting one's affairs than through this dreadful carnage. Although the Allies started winning battles in late July and August 1918 it still seemed as though the war would never end. That is why President Wilson's ringing cry for a new world order held such an emotional appeal for so many people, not just pacifists like him.

Harold Nicolson in 'Peacemaking', written in 1933, describes his feelings at the Peace Conference:

4. Paul Johnston. *A History of the Modern World*. p.29.
5. Paul Johnston. *A History of the Modern World*. p.30.

'In the main tenets of his political philosophy I believed with fervent credulity ... I believed, with him, that the standard of political and international conduct should be as high, as sensitive, as the standard of personal conduct. I believed, and I still believe, that the only true patriotism is an active desire that one's tribe or country should in every particular minister to that ideal. I shared with him a hatred of violence in any form, and a loathing of despotism in any form. I conceived, as he conceived, that this hatred was common to the great mass of humanity, and that in the new world this dumb force of popular sentiment could be rendered the controlling power in human destiny.'

It was in this light that idealists approached the peace conference with the highest expectations. They were excited by President Wilson's high moral principles, his 'intrinsic justice' his 'open covenants of peace openly arrived at.' There had to be a better way of doing things by consensus rather than by compulsion and using the force of public opinion seemed to be the best way to go about it.

Harold Nicolson, writing in 1933, when the Allies decided to abandon charging Germany reparations, maintained that not all President Wilson's high ideals had been adhered to by the Conference in forming the Treaty.

Keynes, in 1919, felt that, he himself, was responsible for the Treaty's lack of slavish adherence to the fourteen points. He found a sympathetic, understanding friend in 'guileful'[6] Smuts who confided that he himself was hoping to create 'a favourable atmosphere ... in which to help the public virtually scrap this monstrous instrument'.[7]

Smuts had used people like Keynes before, during and after the Boer War. They had written letters to *The Times* about matters such as the 'Chinese slavery' issue which helped cause the downfall of the unfriendly British Conservative government in 1905. He hoped to promote a similar head of steam against the Treaty of Versailles.

Sensing an ambivalent attitude in Lloyd George, Smuts had bombarded him with emotive letters on the proposed clauses of the Treaty of Versailles, denouncing the territorial clauses and describing the power given to French and Belgian industrialists to re-appropriate their machinery as 'industrial looting.' 'The coal demands' he deemed would 'cripple' Germany's industry, while he opined 'that the reduction of her armed forces would simply hand over Germany to anarchy.'9 but 'the most dangerous provision of the Treaty,' he opined 'was the occupation of the Rhine for fifteen years.'

Keynes was also a ready listener to his counselling. The solemn

6. A. J. P. Taylor. *English History. 1914–45.* p.183.
7. Sarah Gertrude Millin. *General Smuts.* Vol. II. p.256.

evenings spent together discussing the iniquities of the Peace fuelled Keynes's indignation. He had wanted to right the wrongs of his continued presence at the Treasury during the war by alleviating the conditions of Germany's apparently abject defeat afterwards. But his grand plan for America to loan Germany the first £1,000,000,000 due in reparations had been brusquely turned down by the Americans. Thomas Lamont of J.P. Morgan's Bank had even called the scheme: unsound in conception and impracticable in execution.'[8]

Keynes had been horrified by the publication of the draft Treaty. On May 7th Smuts wrote to Mrs. Gillett:

'Poor Keynes often sits with me at night after a good dinner and we rail against the world and the coming flood.'[9]

On the 14th May 1919, tired and miserable, Keynes wrote to his mother:

'It must be weeks since I've written a letter to anyone, but I've been utterly worn out, partly by work partly by depression at the evil round me. I've never been so miserable as for the last two or three weeks; the Peace is outrageous and impossible and can bring nothing but misfortune behind it. Personally I do not believe the Germans will sign though the general view is to the contrary.... Certainly if I was in the Germans' place I'd rather die than sign it.'[10]

On 29 May there was a conference to deal with the reparations clauses in the Treaty with Austria. At the Conference Britain had assembled both the hard-liners, Sumner and Cunliffe, and Keynes. Keynes had been told by Smuts of the critical food situation in Austria and he stated that it was 'wholly impossible for Austria to make reparations along the lines proposed. People were starving on a large scale ... A large part of the population were without clothing.' He recommended that an independent body go and visit Austria 'with power to require reparation payments, if this should seem desirable, but also with power to recommend loans to Austria in case this should seem indispensable.'[11]

Lord Sumner in careful language disassociated himself from Keynes's view. In fact it seems astonishing that Lloyd George had him on his delegation at all. Keynes had dragged himself out of bed in order

8. R. Skidelsky. *Keynes. Hopes Betrayed.* p.336, p.369. Keynes Financial Scheme. Text. R. S. Baker. *Woodrow Wilson & World Settlement.* p.341.

9. R. Skidelsky. *Keynes. Hopes Betrayed.* p.372.

10. Keynes to Mrs. Keynes. 14.5.19. R. Harrod. *Life of Keynes.* p.249.

11. *B.L.H. Lamont Papers.* 169–11.12. Memorandum of Conference held at the Ministry of Finance to deal with reparations' clauses in the Treaty with Austria. R. Skidelsky. p.373–4.

to appear and was obviously in a poor physical and emotional state. It is true the City had warned that 'collection' of reparations from Germany was liable to be difficult and costly but that gave all the more reason for the Allies to put on a united front and not create a precedent by letting one of the Central Powers off. Lloyd George had a mandate from his electorate for a peace based on justice which it was his duty to honour or Great Britain's own future could be at stake. One can only believe that the unduly sensitive Lloyd George was using the unhappy Keynes to demonstrate to his would-be supporters on the left that he had tried his hardest to ameliorate the terms to the central powers in case his worst fears came true and the Allies were forced to take up arms against Germany again. The anti- conscription 'triple alliance' were threatening 'direct action' while a specially convened meeting of the Labour Party also called for some of the 'harsh' provisions of the peace to be removed with regard to Germany and for Germany to be admitted to the League of Nations.[12]

In contrast to Germany, Austria had suffered incredibly harshly territorially under the terms of the Treaty because the extent of her defeat had been more complete. Yet there was no reason to suppose that the shortage of food in Austria was anything but temporary and the principle of reparation had to be applied even if the sums demanded were small and payment was deferred.

Lord Cunliffe and Mr. Dulles pointed out to Keynes that the figures given to Keynes had been arrived at after consultation with experts, including Dr. Alonzo Taylor who had but recently been to Austria and was deeply appreciative of the frightful food conditions, but these were concentrated on Vienna ... where alone the situation was acute.'[13]

Keynes took to his bed again. He confided to his mother on June 1st 1919:

'Partly out of misery for all that's happening, and partly from prolonged overwork, I gave way last Friday and took to my bed suffering from sheer nervous exhaustion ...

'My first idea was to return to England immediately, but General Smuts, with whom I've been working very intimately for changes in this dammed Treaty, persuaded me that it was my duty to stay on and be available if necessary for the important decisions of these present days, declaring that one can only leave the field of battle, dead. However, the business will soon be determined and then, I hope in two or three days at latest, I return to England forever ... I dragged myself out of bed on Friday to make a final protest before the Reparation Commission against murdering Vienna, and did achieve some improvement.'[14]

12. *Annual Register*. 1919. p.78–9.
13. *B.L.H. Lamont Papers*. 169–11.12. See no. 11. p.374. R. Skidelsky. 30.5.19.
14. J. M. Keynes to Mrs. Keynes. 1.6.19. R. Harrod. *Keynes*. p.252.

On the 5th of June he wrote to the Prime Minister after he had left Paris and the Treasury:

'Dear Prime Minister,
I ought to let you know that on Saturday I am slipping away from this scene of nightmare. I can do no more good here. I've gone on hoping even through these last dreadful weeks that you'd find some way to make of the Treaty a just and expedient document. But now its apparently too late. The battle is lost. I leave the twins (Sumner and Cunliffe) to gloat over the devastation of Europe and to assess to taste what remains for the British taxpayer.'[15]

It was in this mood of despair and desperation that he turned to General Smuts:

'Dear General Smuts,
I left Paris on Saturday, having first pretty completely burnt my boats by letters to the Prime Minister and others. So I must now be considered a private citizen again – thank heaven.
    I hope immensely that you may come to the conclusion that some public explanation of what is really happening and a protest against it is now the right course. If so, I am at your service – by pen or any other way.'[16]

Smuts replied:

'My Dear Keynes,
Thank you for your note. I was sorry that you had cut the painter. Not that you did not have every reason. But it is never advisable to act under the impulse and influence of such a strain as you had been passing through ...
    And as to the future. I think it would be very advisable for you as soon as possible to set about writing a clear, connected account of what the financial and economic clauses of the Treaty actually are and mean, and what their probable results will be. It should not be too long or technical as we may want to appeal to the plain man more than to the well-informed or the specialist.'[17]

Smuts decided in the end that it would be better not to let the impulsive Keynes's pen loose against the Treaty. Smuts had made a public protest on signing the Treaty, stating that he was only signing it so that the world could get down to the task of rebuilding its future. The statement had been well received by the Prussian element at home. So he wrote to Keynes to quell any emotional outburst he might be thinking of making:

15. R. Harrod. *Keynes*. p.253.
16. *Smuts Papers*. 1012. p.221. Vol. 22. no.57.
17. Hancock and van der Poel. *Smuts Papers*. 1013. Vol. 22. no. 159.

'After giving the matter my closest consideration I have seen no great profit in a regular attack on the Treaty. It is past and nothing can undo it except time and the great Mercy which works away all our poor human follies. Better to be constructive. My protest on signing the Peace has had a great effect both here and on the Continent. And tomorrow I publish a statement of farewell, which will put my views even clearer than they have been expressed before. We will find many opportunities to help the world, especially when the real trouble over the Reparation and financial clauses begins with Germany.'[18]

Smuts indeed was about to put the boot in with his farewell speech.

'The brutal fact is that Great Britain is a very small island on the fringe of the Continent, and that on that Continent the seventy odd million Germans represent the most important and formidable national factor. You cannot have a stable Europe without a stable, settled Germany.'[19]

He had underlined the fact, now that it was too late to alter it, that the Allies had so welded the different nations that had comprised the Prussian Empire indissolubly together under the terms of the Treaty of Versailles that they would have little alternative but to appease the powerful German nation if she chose to be awkward about complying with its reparations clauses –an assertion which, in time, only Poincaré refused to believe.

However, Keynes was not to be put off writing his book. Had not Smuts himself denounced the Treaty to Lloyd George in emotive language? A great injustice had been done to Germany.

Keynes was under the illusion, as so many British and Germans were, that the German army had only stopped fighting because of its government's faith in President Wilson's fourteen points. President Wilson's statement in which he had initially declined to include 'war costs' in the amount to be charged to Germany 'not on the ground of the intrinsic justice of it, but on the ground that it is clearly inconsistent with what we deliberately led the enemy to expect and cannot honourably alter simply because we have the power' could only have strengthened his conviction that the war had ended solely because of the President's intervention.

Thereafter the Allies had proposed, in his eyes, an iniquitous peace, contravening many of the terms of the fourteen points upon which Germany had laid down her arms. As he wrote in his final chapter:

'Never in the·lifetime of men now living has the universal element in the soul

---

18. *Smuts Papers.* 1054.
19. *Smuts Papers.* 1057.

of man burnt so dimly.'[20] His quest was to embody in each person in Britain an enduring awareness of guilt for their iniquity.

In the Autumn he was invited by some Dutch financiers to discuss the financial situation in Europe. He couldn't help sending for Herr Melchior. He wanted to see him again. Afterwards he disclosed:

> 'I began to wonder at the impulse which had caused me to send for Melchior, for no such idea had entered my head before I left England, and what possible purpose this interview could serve. All the same I wanted to see him immensely. At last the door opened and he came in.
>
> 'It was extraordinary to meet without barriers, we two who had faced one another so often in opposition and etiquette and constraint. Those Paris negotiations seemed to be absurd and to belong to a dream; and after a moment's emotional embarrassment we settled down to a long rambling gossip as two ordinary people. He told me of the last days at Weimar, and the struggle over the signature of the Treaty, his own resignation, how these days had been the most dreadful of all, how Erzberger had deliberately betrayed to an agent of the English government the decision of a secret cabinet meeting between Noske, David and himself, in which it had been decided that in any event they must sign, and how he Melchior, believed that it was out of a knowledge of this decision that Lloyd George finally decided to abandon his efforts towards moderation. Melchior's emotions were towards Germany and the falsehood and humiliation which his own people had brought on themselves, rather than towards us. I also understood most clearly, then for the first time, how dwellers in Eastern Germany look to the East and not Westwards. The war for him had been a war against Russia; and it was the thought of the dark forces which might now issue from the Eastwards which most obsessed him. I also understood better than before, what a precisian he was, a strict and upright moralist, a worshipper of the Tablets of the Law, a Rabbi. The breach of promise, the breach of discipline, the decay of honourable behaviour, the betrayal of undertakings by the one party and the insincere acceptance by the other of impossible conditions which it was not intended to carry out, Germany almost as guilty to accept what she could not fulfil as the Allies to accept what they were not entitled to exact – it was these offenses against the Word which so much wounded him.'[21]

This was a very revealing passage because any intimation from Herr Melchior that there had been some collusion between the German finance minister, Herr Erzberger, and the British had to be taken as gospel. Warburg had said that 'with concessions they will sign' and Herr Melchior was a partner of Warburg's. Keynes continued his narrative:

20. *The Economic Consequences of the Peace.* p.279.
21. *Keynes. Dr. Melchior.* (Two Memoirs) p.69–71.

'As we talked on, the morning passed and it began to seem ridiculous to me that we should not lunch together openly, like any other couple. So I asked him to my hotel, where a German American Jew, Paul Warburg, brother of Melchior's Hamburg partner, but one of the leading financiers of the United States and formerly the chief spirit of the Federal Reserve Board, was also to be my guest. We strolled through Amsterdam, and Melchior, who knew it well, took me on our way to see a courtyard of ancient almshouses, which conveyed to him, he said, most perfectly the intimate atmosphere of the town. It was a charming spot, indicative of order and of retirement.

'My book was not then out, and I had with me the manuscript of my chapter on the President. After lunch I read it to them. We went upstairs for privacy, this time to my bedroom not Melchior's. I noted its effect on the two Jews. Warburg, for personal reasons, hated the President and felt a chuckling delight at his discomforture; he laughed and giggled and thought it an awfully good hit. But Melchior as I read, grew ever more solemn, until at the end he appeared almost to be in tears. This, then, was the other side of the curtain; neither profound causes, nor inevitable fate, nor magnificent wickedness. The Tablets of the Law, it was Melchior's thought at that moment, had perished meanly.'

These were not the people Keynes should have showed his book to in the hope of getting a disinterested judgement on its arguments. Paul M. Warburg, it is true, was most highly regarded in United States banking circles. No one could doubt his love of his adopted country. He had become a naturalised American 'a score of years ago' and his only son had enlisted in the airforce as soon as the United States entered the war against Germany.[22] But the fact remained that he was an American, looking at matters from an American point of view, which did not always coincide with that of the Allies, and that he had felt it necessary to resign from being Vice- Governor of the Federal Reserve Board, the 'mainstay of the nation's banking system' after the war because his brother had been one of William II's two closest advisers.[23]

But Melchior was a worse choice as confidant because he had been the representative of Germany's 'great industrial interests' at the Peace Conference.[24] Germany's 'great industrial interests', had identified their future with the military during the war. Alfred Thyssen had had a document conveyed to the Government on September 9th 1914, at a time when Germany's military ambitions looked like being fulfilled, in which he demanded the incorporation, amongst others, of Belgium and

22. Viereck's *American Monthly*. September 1918.
23. Fritz Fischer. *Aims of Germany in the 1st World War*. p.16.
24. R. S. Baker. *Woodrow Wilson & World Settlement*. Vol. II. p.498. Later industry changed its mind about Melchior and protested against Stresemann's wish to have 'a cooler personality like Melchior' rather than Schacht who in his opinion 'possesses a certain excess of temperament' as Germany's delegate at the Young Plan Conference.

the ports of Calais and Dunkirk in the West, and in the East, the Baltic provinces.[25] While Vögler, as spokesman for the iron and steel industry, told the Chancellor, Michaelis, on August 29th 1917 that 'they were prepared to carry on the war for another ten years for the sake of Longwy-Brie.'[26] These men were furious that their ambitious plans had come to naught. Their representative at the Peace Conference could not give Keynes the impartial advice he so desperately needed.

Macmillans had agreed to print Keynes's book as they had already printed his treatise on *Indian Currency and Finance* but this time, instead of sharing the profits and costs on a 50/50 basis it was agreed that Keynes would take the risks himself and pay for the book's publication. For some inexplicable reason the printers R. & R. Clark of Edinburgh elected to send the copies by sea to London.

R. F. Harrod, Keynes's biographer, takes up the story:

'A ship carrying 2000 copies was driven eastwards by storm and finally wrecked; the copies were thrown overboard in order to lighten the load.'

The book was reprinted and reached London – this time by one of Britain's reliable steam trains.

The Times was very censorious and wrote its review under the heading COMFORT FOR GERMANY.

'Mr. Keynes has written an extremely "clever" book on the Peace Conference and its "economic consequences." It is the work of an erudite university don who was attached as adviser in the British Treasury during the war. He represented the Treasury officially at the Peace Conference up to June 7th, 1919. He also sat as deputy for the Chancellor of the Exchequer on the Supreme Economic Council. In his preface he states that "he resigned from these positions when it became evident that hope could no longer be entertained of substantial modifications in the draft terms of the Peace." The purpose of the book is, he avers, to set forth "the grounds of his objection to the Treaty or rather, to the whole policy of the Conference towards the economic problems of Europe." He adds that they "are entirely of a public character and are based on facts known to the whole world."

'Readers are thus prepared for a critical economic treatise. In some respects they will not be disappointed. In others they will be surprised, amused, shocked and not a little mystified. How came it, they may ask, that the man who could write the pages of incisive portraiture, not to say caricature, that fill the chapter on "The Conference", came to hold the position of Technical Adviser to one of the most Technical Departments of the State? How, unless his bias had been throughout akin to that of the conscientious

25. H. H. Herwig and Neil Heyman. *Biographical Dictionary of World War I.* (See Erzberger.)
26. Fritz Fischer. *Aims of Germany in the 1st World War.* p.259.

objector, could he place the Allies persistently on the same moral level as
Germany in regard to the war?'

'Assuredly the Peace Treaty is defective. Undoubtedly many of its features may need revision. The League of Nations should provide the machinery for such revision. But, if this necessary work be approached in
forgetfulness of German guilt, of palliation of German crimes, of undifferen-
tiated anxiety to help Germany to escape the consequences of her felony, it is
not only bound to fail, but its failure will wreck whatever remains of inter-
Allied solidarity that brought German schemes to naught. If the war taught
one lesson above all others it was that the calculations of economists,
bankers and financial experts who preached the impossibility of war because
'it would not pay' were perilous nonsense. Germany went to war because she
made it pay in 1870–71 and believed she could make it pay again. She nearly
succeeded. Were she now to be placed in control of the resources of Russia
and to be let off with a practically optional payment for reparation, what
would prevent her, a few years hence, from renewing the struggle as mistress
of Russia with a secretly-trained army, officered by veterans, and holding all
Europe and Asia to ransom? Mr. Keynes may be a 'clever' economist. He
may have been a useful Treasury official. But, in writing this book, he has
rendered the Allies a disservice for which their enemies will, doubtless, be
grateful.'[27]

The full amount of reparations to be demanded from Germany had been
postponed till 1921. But the overt purpose of Keynes's book, *The
Economic Consequences of the Peace*, was to show that large sums
could not be extracted from the Fatherland.

Before being killed in action in the closing days of the Second World
War, the incensed son of Paul Mantoux, the interpreter at the original
Conference at the Treaty of Versailles, wrote a book refuting Keynes's
claims. He entitled it: *The Carthaginian Peace or the Economic
Consequences of Mr. Keynes*. He went through Keynes's economic
analysis, line by line, showing that heavy reparations could have been
paid by an economy as powerful as Germany's and concluding that the
money that should have been thus spent in the 1930s had gone on re-
arming The Fatherland instead.

But it was not the wearisome economic pages that the general public
leafed through but the racy sketches of the leading personalities acting
out their drama at Versailles. This was the secret of the book's success
when it arrived in America, one month after its British publication.

Wilson had made a great omission when he failed to take any prominent Republicans with him to the Peace Conference. He was the head of
the world's most powerful nation but unless he could produce a plan for
peace which his Parliament would support, other lesser nations, seeing
America's lack of resolve, would start picking quarrels again. The foun-

27. *The Times*. January 5th, 1920.

dation of his plan for peace was the establishment of the League of Nations, a forum where national disputes could be resolved without recourse to war.

Although the Republican leader, Theodore Roosevelt, had opposed President Wilson's moves for 'peace without victory' in the Autumn of 1918, as soon as he felt sure that victory had indeed been won he hastened to declare his support for Wilson's plan:

'The United States cannot again completely withdraw into its shell ... We need not mix in all European quarrels nor assume all spheres of interest everywhere to be ours' maintained the pragmatic Roosevelt 'but we ought to join the other civilised nations of the world in some scheme that in a time of great stress would offer a likelihood of obtaining settlements that will avert war.'[28]

He still doubted the League's efficacy in preventing war, stating privately: 'We have an anti-vice crusade ... Everybody is aroused. The movement culminates in a big meeting and we adopt resolutions abolishing vice. But vice isn't abolished that way.'

And he was determined that the League should not become a 'Meddlesome Matty.'[29] But having four sons who had fought in the war, his youngest, Quentin, dying, Roosevelt was prepared to throw his influence behind the League of Nations movement in the interests of a unified approach to the Peace.

'I believe that such an effort made moderately and sanely ... will be productive of real and lasting international good.' But Roosevelt himself was to die, only two days after speaking these words, on 5 January 1919.[30]

It is difficult to over-estimate the extent of this disaster for those who had fought for 'unconditional surrender' on the allied side.

'At the Peace Conference England and France can get what they wish so far as America is concerned,' wrote Roosevelt to Bryce in November, 'if, while treating Wilson with politeness, they openly and frankly throw themselves on the American people for support in any vital matter.'[31]

This may have been an exaggeration of his powers to sway the American people. But they had been behind Roosevelt's desire for fighting for a clear-cut victory in November 1918.

Lloyd George, torn between left and right, didn't know quite what he

28. J. M. Cooper. *The Warrior and the Priest.* p.333.
29. J. M. Cooper. *The Warrior and the Priest.* p.333–4.
30. J. M. Cooper. *The Warrior and the Priest.* p.333–4.
31. J. M. Cooper. *The Warrior and the Priest.* p.334.

wanted out of the Peace Conference, but both the French and Britain's Conservatives knew that they needed justice and an enforceable peace. It would have been difficult for President Wilson to have completely disregarded Republican opinion during the Peace Conference if Roosevelt had still been alive, thus gaining a Peace with teeth, with the all-important American endorsement of its clauses.

But when Roosevelt died, American Republicans shrank into isolationism. They had come over to Europe to deal the Germans a crushing defeat but when they arrived they had been sent back home again before they could deliver the telling blow. Roosevelt had labelled the fourteen points when they had first been proclaimed in January 1918, 'a Judas kiss', a 'high-sounding speech to cloak ignoble action.'[32] Ordinary Republicans, uninvited to the Peace Conference and no more aware of what was going on than the uninformed British electorate, felt that 'high-sounding speech to cloak ignoble action' summed up what was going on behind their backs at Versailles.

Republicans had reacted with increasing hostility towards President Wilson's concept of the League of Nations during the months when he was far away in Europe so on his return he was greeted, not with acclaim, but with suspicion.

How could the President, in this situation, tell the Republicans his fears and forebodings that he had made a terrible mistake?

This proud, reserved man could not bring himself to confide in the Republican Senators who were willing to discuss the setting up of a League of Nations with only 'mild reservations.'[33] Having failed to demand 'unconditional surrender' he felt that the League, in undiluted form, was the only way to keep German ambitions in check. So he lectured the disenchanted Senators:

'Dare we reject it and break the heart of the World?' and set forth on a nationwide tour, hoping that the 'dumb force of public opinion' would force the Republicans to endorse the League wholeheartedly.

On 25 September 1919, the emotional strain of his personal crusade overcame the President. At Pueblo, in Colorado, he was overcome with exhaustion and his doctor cancelled his remaining engagements. He returned to Washington. On 2 October he suffered a severe stroke and

32. J. M. Cooper. *The Warrior and the Priest*. p.331.
33. Link. Woodrow Wilson. Revolution, War and Peace. See - The Fight for the League of Nations. p.109. The great sticking point, Article 10 'guaranteed the political independence and territorial integrity of every member nation throughout the World.' Senator Lodge for the Republicans refused to agree to American troops being used in the field of battle without the agreement of the American Parliament. p.123.
p.122 – shows how close President Wilson came to accepting the Republicans recommendations before he had his stroke.

the whole of the left side of his body and his face became paralysed. He nearly died. Had he done so the grief stricken nation would probably have rallied to his memory and ratified his Treaty with only marginal changes.

But he did not die. And, when he recovered, his physical enfeeblement made him more irrational emotionally. He remained President. He clung to power. But he became even more stubborn. Any signature on the Treaty of Versailles by America was better than none for there were other clauses in the Treaty besides the League designed to keep German ambitions in check, the trial of war offenders – and the reparations – which Germany could not lightly ignore if America endorsed them. But the President would accept no alterations in his charter for the League of Nations so the future of the whole Treaty lay in the balance.

In Europe the Allies were incensed and alarmed at the delay in getting the Treaty ratified by the American Parliament. The Europeans had considered it very much America's document. Naturally therefore they could not understand the delay in America, especially when Great Britain in particular had bent over backwards to try and conform to President Wilson's ideas on peace.

But it had been this very identification of British ideals with those of the sickly, long-serving, unpopular President which had most kindled hostility amongst the American people. Frank H. Simonds of the Maclure Newspaper Syndicate explains why:

> 'To understand the situation one must go back a year and recall the fact that at the November election in 1918 Mr. Wilson appealed to the people to elect a Democratic House of Representatives as an evidence of his future purposes. These future purposes were accurately understood to include a trip to Europe on behalf of the League of Nations.'

The result of that election was a decisive defeat for the President. Under similar circumstances in Great Britain or France the responsible ministry would have resigned since the control of the House of Representatives, as well as the Senate, passed to the opposition.

Spared the need to resign, Mr. Wilson persevered in his determination to go to Europe. But he went against the will of a majority of the American people who clearly indicated by their votes and by their feelings grave doubts about his intentions. At the outset of his European visit Mr. Wilson was welcomed on all sides with unprecedented enthusiasm as the duly authorised representative of his country.

When Mr. Wilson began to speak in the name of the American people, declaring that they desired a certain form of peace there was a renewal of American resentment, since Mr. Wilson had never submitted to the American people any draft of his programme and the American people had rejected a 'blank cheque' at the November elections.

It had been easy for Germany's friends to build on this resentment and to imply that there must be some dark plot if Great Britain was so eager to accept a peace on the basis of the fourteen points, many of which, on the face of it, were so contrary to her interests. Frank H. Simonds continued:

'As the Conference in Paris progressed, and it became clear that Great Britain was supporting Mr. Wilson almost without reservation, popular suspicion began to concentrate upon British purposes. The majority of the American people did not believe in Mr. Wilson's policies and they did not believe that any considerable number of Englishmen believed in them. They saw in the British championship of Mr. Wilson a deliberate effort to make use of Mr. Wilson's alleged idealism to involve the United States in world affairs to the ultimate profit of Great Britain and the immediate peril of the United States.'

All Autumn long the battle raged over the small print of the concept of the League of Nations. The Republican Senators were determined that no President would be as unconstitutional ever again as to take the law into his own hands over the issue of war and peace. Meanwhile, the enfeebled President remained closeted in his abode, unyielding on any changes in the wording of the League provisions. Presumably his resolution sprang from a very justified belief that Americans would be most unwilling to fight Germany again after this fiasco. But discord and delay could have done nothing but encourage the Germans to resolve to ignore the provisions of the Treaty.

At last the bitter Europeans resolved that they could wait no longer for what they considered to be America's Treaty to be ratified. Germany's army was real and threatening in contravention of the Treaty. While Berlin's lights blazed and she exported coal to Switzerland and Holland, cold Paris lay in darkness, deprived of reparations' coal. The Treaty of Versailles needed to be given American ratification to give it bite.

The *New York Times* described the situation:

'Tonight the streets of Paris will be dark, but the streets of Berlin will not.'

Premier Millerand pointed out that whereas under her treaty engagements Germany was bound to send monthly shipments to France of 1,000,000 tons of coal, she sent less than 500,000 tons last month to France and at the same time sold coal to Holland and Switzerland. 'The Premier did not think it just that the streets of Paris remained dark while those of Berlin remained lighted.'[34]

34. *New York Times.* 3.2.20.

Meanwhile in Britain the miners were outraged that housewives should find coal expensive and scarce while coal was exported to France. It was a freezing Winter. It was essential from every point of view that the Treaty be officially signed and its provisions enforced before the militarists got the upper hand in Germany to reinstate the Emperor.

The European Allies and the Parliamentarians in Germany signed the ratification document in the middle of January but still the battle raged on in America. Representatives of 20,000,000 people[35] brought a petition pleading for the politicians to ratify but the politicians were still hopelessly divided on the issue of apparently lessening the power of the Constitutional government in the United States in favour of the League of Nations. Since President Wilson was determined not to weaken the wording of the League of Nations provisions, however, it had to be those on the Republican side who would waver in their opposition in the interests of getting the Treaty through.

It was at this point, however, that the words of the English economics expert, Keynes, electrified the nation. For they told the country what they had secretly suspected all along, that America in general, and President Wilson in particular, had been 'bamboozled' by the Europeans. Keynes's portrait of the President is unforgettable. The *American Monthly*, the propaganda newspaper founded to promote Germany's cause during the war, quoted it at length in their magazine, stating that they found the portrait of the President the most significant part of the *Economic Consequences* of the Peace.

> 'Perhaps the most brilliant is the chapter in which Mr. Keynes cruelly psycho-analyses the character of T. Woodrow Wilson.
> 'When President Wilson left Washington he enjoyed a prestige and a moral influence throughout the world unequalled in history.'

But afterwards:

> 'The disillusion was so complete that some of those who had trusted most, hardly dared to speak of it ... The President was not a hero or a prophet; he was not even a philosopher, but a generously intentioned man, with many of the weaknesses of other human beings and lacking that dominating intellectual equipment which would have been necessary ... His temperament was not primarily that of the student or the scholar; he had not much even of that culture of the world which marks M. Clemenceau and Mr. Balfour as exquisitely cultivated gentlemen of their class and generation ... He was not only insensitive to his surroundings in the external sense; he was not sensitive to his environment at all. What chance could such a man have against Mr.

35. *New York Herald.* 2.2.20.

Lloyd George's unerring, almost medium- like sensibility to everyone immediately around him ... ?

'The poor President would be playing blind man's buff in that party ...

'The President was like a Nonconformist Minister, perhaps Minister, perhaps
a Presbyterian.

'In fact, the President had thought out nothing. When it came to practice
his ideas were nebulous and incomplete. He had no plan, no scheme, no
constructive ideas whatever for clothing with the flesh of life the
Commandments which he had thundered from the White House. He could
have preached a sermon on any of them or have addressed a stately prayer to
the Almighty for their fulfilment, but he could not frame their concrete appli-
cation to the actual state of Europe ... Not only was he ill-informed – that was
true of Lloyd George also – but his mind was slow and unadaptable. There
can seldom have been a statesman of the first rank more incompetent than
the President in the abilities of the Council Chamber ... He did not remedy
these defects by seeking aid from the collective wisdom of his lieutenants ...
He could write notes from Sinai or Olympus; he could remain unapproach-
able in the White House, or even in the Council of Ten, and be safe. But if he
once stepped down to the intimate equality of the Four, the game was evidently up.'[36]

By 1924 this 'economic' work had been read, in the opinion of Sir
William Beveridge 'By – at a moderate computation – half a million
people who never read an economic work before and probably will not
read one again.'[37]

Naturally the League's opponents seized on the book as ammunition.
Its words must have been music in their ears.

No Republican Senator could have dared go as far as to declare himself:

'There can seldom have been a statesman of the first rank more incompetent
than the President in the agilities of the Council Chamber ...'[38]

But now that someone else had said it for them they did not hesitate to
pass the good word around America.

They had found the President's mind 'slow and unadaptable.' They
had also been sure that he had been 'bamboozled' by the Europeans. Of
course their objections to the Treaty were almost exactly the opposite to
those put forward by Keynes. Senator Lodge and the Republicans'
objection to the Treaty was centred on the League of Nations, the one
provision on which Liberals like Keynes were united in approval. They
had thought the Treaty too soft, Keynes considered its provisions

36. Viereck's *American Monthly*. March 1920.
37. Quoted in E. Mantoux. *The Carthaginian Peace*. p.6.
38. J. M. Keynes. The Economic Consequences of the Peace. p.40.

crippling. Never mind his drift, the Republicans must have argued, Keynes's inflammatory language would serve as excellent ammunition to confirm suspicions that the naive President had been 'bamboozled' by the Europeans and that America must reserve the right to plough her own course.

Before Keynes had proclaimed on the Treaty of Versailles influential Americans had not taken much interest in the Fourteen Points. The only matter on which they were determined was for America not to become involved in the machinations of the League of Nations. Now, however, they began to study the small print of the President's precious points and principles and they decided that, far from the Europeans agreeing to the principle of self-determination as laid down by Mr. Wilson, every greedy European power, and even Europe's dominions had been laying their hands on extra territory under the guise of the 'mandate system.' For instance:

South Africa had been given a mandate to look after German South West Africa.

Australia had been given a mandate to look after New Guinea.

Great Britain had been given a mandate to look after German East Africa, Palestine and Trans Jordan while France was to look after Syria and the Lebanon.

Indeed almost all the major countries at the Conference seemed to have grabbed territory, with the notable exception of America. Every red-blooded Republican oozed with anger when he thought of how America had been shortchanged by the Europeans. German children might be 'starved and crippled' by the Treaty, Americans had also been taken for a ride. Pacifist Democrats had always thought of all Europeans as Imperialists to justify their position. Now erstwhile pro- European Republicans did too. It was no good the President suddenly having a change of heart about who was the guilty party. The 'expert' Keynes had given a graphic account of how their President, a gauche, inept mortal from the New World, had been taken in by the Old.

Now the Republicans were free from popular reaction against their isolationism. Their crusade against the League of Nations had been shown to be a stand taken in the national interest, not done out of petty selfishness and indifference towards the fate of Europe. It was the Europeans who had made this Treaty which the economic expert had said was so disgraceful, not America. President Wilson had been hoodwinked, more worldly-wise Republicans left out in the cold. Sentiment cooled towards signing the Treaty, identified as it was with an unpopular, maladroit President. The partially recovered President's insistence on making the Treaty of Versailles, with the wording of the League of Nations unaltered, his main plank in the forthcoming

Presidential elections, spelt disaster for the Treaty's ratification, dragging as it did, a matter of national importance, into the to and fro of party politics.

There remained however a great reserve of sentiment dedicated to the ratification of the Treaty. The only hope for its ratification was for enough Democrats to cross the floor of the House to vote with the opposition for the acceptance of the Treaty with the Lodge reservations to the League of Nations. 21 senators did cross the floor of the House to vote with the opposition but it was not quite enough. The all important two-thirds majority which would have meant America's vital endorsement of the Treaty of Versailles was missed by just seven votes.[39] The purpose of Keynes's book, apart from being a cry from the heart, had been to campaign for American funds to be used to rehabilitate Europe and help Germany fund her reparation debt. Keynes's earlier scheme of April 1919 had invoked strong language among Americans. Assistant Secretary Leffingwell had described it as 'Preposterous.' The *Sun and New York Herald* was kinder about the new scheme. It had applauded every other aspect of Keynes's book. Over his grand scheme to help Europe it merely contented itself with commentating:

'Here for the first time one feels the limitations of the academic mind.'[40]

American economists cannot be blamed for thinking of Keynes as 'a man with more imagination than good sense' as Stephen A. Shucker declared in his book, *The End of French Predominance in Europe*, for Keynes himself did not seriously seem to be campaigning on behalf of the Allies as much as for Germany. Indeed he had written in his book:

'If I had influence at the United States Treasury I would not lend a penny to a single one of the present governments of Europe.'[41]

The American government concurred in that belief. They had funded and fed most of the governments of Europe since the war. They had lent them an unprecedented amount of money. It was time to turn their attention again to their own country.

The *Sun and New York Herald* commented soberly:

'Not even the universal financial and economic disaster which the spring may have in store in Europe is likely to convince the people of the United States of the wisdom of the entire cancellation of inter-Allied indebtedness

39. Link. *Woodrow Wilson. Revolution, War and Peace.* p.122.
40. *Sun and New York Herald.* 2.2.20.
41. J. M. Keynes. *The Economic Consequences of the Peace.* (1919) p.267.

incurred for the purpose of the war and the creating of a great international loan, which are the principal remedies Keynes proposes.'[42]

4.2 Eyck's Criticism of Keynes

As a sequel to its success in America *The Economic Consequences of the Peace* was translated into German. Erich Eyck, a former lawyer, journalist and Social Democrat politician who was forced to leave Germany when Hitler came to power, wrote about its effect on German public opinion in his book, *A History of the Weimar Republic*, which was translated and printed by Harvard University Press.

Like *The Times* in Britain, Eyck attested to Keynes's qualifications to speak on economic matters and paid tribute to his 'able style of writing.' But he criticised the main reason Keynes gave for writing his book against the Treaty, which Keynes had stated as being the, in his eyes, illegal 'inclusion of the reparations demands for widows and the wounded' in the total sum to be demanded, as this clause had only been included at the behest of Keynes's friend, General Smuts. It was obvious, therefore, that Smuts was playing a double game and that the rest of the words that he had poured into Keynes's ears emanated not from truth but from self- interest.

Keynes had been convinced that the Germans had laid down their arms in the Autumn of 1918 solely out of reverence for the fourteen points so to him each syllable of the 14 points had been sacred and the inclusion of the help to Britain's wounded in the reparations clauses, inexcusable. In fact, he had equated the crime of the 'inclusion of the reparations demands for widows and the wounded' with Germany's violation of Belgian neutrality in 1914.

Erich Eyck however did not like this sort of talk. He had harsh words for what he called Keynes's 'doctrinaire prejudices'. 'This danger becomes all the greater when he fails to restrict his writing to the fields of his competence.'

Eyck's most important point was that Keynes did not understand the German people or their country.

'Most important of all was Keynes's failure to realise that in Germany, where his book naturally was read with great interest and approval, he was dealing with a reading public radically different from the Englishmen he knew. In England political self-criticism, that is, the critical examination of the policies of one's own country, not only is

42. *Sun and New York Herald.* 2.2.20.

traditional, it also fails to reflect upon the critic's patriotism in any way. In Germany this sort of national self-criticism is considered objectional and unseemly. Keynes's ecstatic German readers never asked themselves what would have befallen a countryman of theirs who had dared to criticise Bismarck's Peace of Frankfurt even half as sharply. General Voel von Falkenstein had had Johann Jakoby arrested and brought to prison for opposing the annexation of Alsace-Lorraine as a violation of 'a people's right to self-determination' ... When Jacoby came out of prison he was ostracised by his party and had to resign.

Eyck registered his surprise that in contrast, although 'Keynes's book made him, to be sure, quite unloved by the English government of that time,' he went on to have a brilliant career, 'ending up in the House of Lords.'

Eyck went on to explain the disastrous effect Keynes's book had had on the German people.

> 'Thus it was that his manifesto had a quite different effect in Germany from what Keynes himself had wished. For it served as a complete confirmation to all those who had been shrieking about the 'shameful peace' and the 'Diktat of Versailles'; those who insisted that the primary, indeed the single, purpose of German policy should be to circumvent the Treaty; those who branded as treason any policy of "fulfilment" or rapprochement; and those who sensed a pleasant relief from any feeling of guilt over their violation of Belgian neutrality once Keynes had accused the Allies of an equivalent violation of international morality.'

Eyck paid tribute to Keynes's economic arguments for a 'reduction of the reparations to an economically feasible sum' but added that 'they were comprehended by only a small minority of his German readers, while his sharp condemnation of the way the reparations were dealt with in the Treaty burned itself indelibly into every German mind, where it generally was simplified into the conclusion that one was justified in opposing any and every reparations' bill.'

He went on to state:

> 'No German with any serious hope of a political career dared even imply the thought that Germany was legally obligated to pay for even part of the damage she had inflicted on the neighbours she attacked. And if the Germans finally went so far as to attribute all their economic ills not to their having lost a war but simply to the reparations that they paid, Keynes cannot be relieved of his share of the blame.'

Eyck finished by demonstrating how disastrous Keynes's 'portraits' of Wilson and Clemenceau were.

'For what could be more welcome to a German nationalist than a description of President Wilson as a 'blind and deaf Don Quixote' who let an avenging Clemenceau lead him around by the nose? ... Why should the German reader ponder France's need for security if Keynes could so glibly ignore it?'

He concluded 'It is therefore little wonder that ninety-nine of every hundred Germans were convinced they had been duped by the armistice, and little wonder too that they left themselves excused from any careful examination of Wilson's fourteen points to see whether and to what extent the Points had been violated by the peace. This mental attitude began to nourish the 'stab in the back' legend. Thus to the two villains who had betrayed Germany, the armistice and the revolution, was added yet a third: 'that old Presbyterian Wilson'.

For, 'What could be more soothing to the German conscience than to see an Englishman blame the President of the United States for everything that had gone wrong?'

–5–

Down with Erzberger; Down with the Mark

5.1 Introduction

The most important requisite of any democratic system is that it enjoys the support and respect of the population of the country. It is their forum, their chance to make their wishes heard. Many of the German public never gave Germany's new system of Government, the Weimar Republic, that precious enthusiasm and support which was so vital for its continuing survival in the difficult times which lay ahead. They felt that democracy had been inflicted on them by the socialists and President Wilson. If ever the socialists fell into disfavour, therefore, and President Wilson's peace was discredited, the whole system of government which their combined efforts had brought into being, would be under threat. That being said there was much enthusiasm, among a large section of the public, for the Weimar Republic, when elections were first held in January 1919. Naturally the ex-Empire was to be a federal republic but it aimed to become truly one country. The individual states were to be called 'lands' in the future and it was proposed that the new, more centralised government could impose direct taxation on the 'lands' as well as the indirect taxation which was all that Bismarck had felt strong enough to levy.[1] Parliament was to be modelled on the American example but with proportional representation. Everyone over twenty one years of age was to be given the vote.[2]

Proportional representation meant that the President of Germany had more power within his own domain than the President of the United States had in his country. American democracy was a two party system, so the President could rely on powerful opposition to any sweeping measures that he chose to make. In Germany proportional representation

1. 'Unrepresentative.' The elected members of Parliament had the power to deny finance but not to propose legislation. *Annual Register.* 1914. p.306.
2. E. Eyck. *A History of the Weimar Republic.* p.73. Gerhard und Richard Thoma. *Handbuch des Deutschen Staatsrechts.* p.324.

led to many different parties and this gave the President a wide hand in deciding how the country should be run. The most important weapon in the German President's armoury was the power to dissolve Parliament and call for new elections under certain clearly defined circumstances. He also was in overall command of the armed forces, could dismiss and appoint the Chancellor, call for national referenda on matters of national interest and represent Germany in foreign affairs. It has been said that many a king would have been happy to have the powers that the Reichspresident possessed but his term of office was only for seven years.[3]

The first Reichspresident, Friedrich Ebert, had impeccable democratic credentials, being the son of a tailor. However he had incurred the enmity of many on the right by formulating the Reichstag's famous 'peace resolution' in July 1917, and leading a strike in the munitions industry in 1918, ensuring him little support from the old military and industrial hierarchy.

Ebert's party during the war had been the Social Democratic party or SPD In January 1919. There was much support for this party. It won 163 seats, nearly twice as many as any other party. The Social Democrats had pursued a pacifist socialist line before the war but had been persuaded by the mobilisation of Russia's troops that the Reich was under threat and had to fight to protect herself.

Before the war the Social Democrats had been nominally impotent but public opinion had been on their side over the treatment of minorities and many other issues. After the war, although they had at last been given the longed-for legislative power they had lacked in the old Parliament, they rapidly lost cross party public support over the allegation that they had 'stabbed the nation in the back,' limiting their power to enact any sweeping legislation.

The Social Democrats' enemies, the German Nationalists or DNVP who followed an unambiguously pro-monarchist and anti- republican line, won only 42 seats out of 421 in the first elections after the war.[4] From the beginning, however, Germany was to be ruled by coalitions.

Besides what could be called the two main protagonists, the German Nationalists, small in number but supported by powerful heavy industrial interests, and the SPD, numerous but weak in political muscle, there were other moderate well- supported parties whose influence declined as extremism grew in Germany in 1923 and again in the 1930s.

The People's Party, led by Gustav Stresemann, although prepared to leave the question of the return of the monarchy open, was in sympathy

3. E. Eyck. *The Weimar Republic*. Vol. I.
4. E. Eyck. *A History of the Weimar Republic*. Vol. I. p.68.

with the DNVP in those early post-war years, Stresemann's pan-German wartime policy and his support for unrestricted submarine warfare in 1917 brought him only 21 seats in January 1919.[5]

The newly-formed Democratic Party, the DDP, had been brought into existence to produce a strong centre party. It included a wide shade of political opinion.[6] The idea was to merge the old National Liberal Party with Stresemann's People's Party to create a strong centre party, but as, in the end, merger plans were dropped, it actually succeeded in dividing rather than uniting the centre. High hopes were entertained for it at its conception, however, and it secured 75 seats at the first elections.

There was already one party of the centre, the 'Centre' party. But that was identified with the Catholic Church. Catholics had been harassed in Bismarck's time. Even in the Great War it had been difficult for a Catholic to achieve much advancement in the army. Only Lutheran Prussians were considered to have the moral fibre for command. So is it unlikely that those from Protestant parts would have wished to vote for the Centre Party. But it still gained 88 seats in the January 1919 elections, making it the second largest party. Soon, however, the Bavarian members of this party were to split and form their own group, the Bavarian People's Party or BVP.

There was also the Independent Social Democratic Party which identified its future with the communist cause. It gained 11 votes. Much of the power however, in Weimar years, remained outside Parliament.

There were two other groups of people who were part of government but not part of elected government. These were the civil service and the judiciary. They were not changed or re- elected when the monarch was deposed but were guaranteed their jobs in view of the service they had rendered to the community in the past. Their outlook remained hostile to the new order. Of the creation of the fledgling republic in Germany, the historian Gordon A. Craig would write: 'It is no exaggeration to say that it (The Weimar Republic) failed in the end partly because German officers were allowed to put their epaulettes back on again so quickly and because the public buildings were not burned down, along with the bureaucrats who inhabited them.'[7]

The Ruhr industrialists were not part of government, or elected, but by virtue of their immense industrial muscle, they were able to shape the policies of government that affected their industrial livelihood.

5. E. Eyck. *A History of the Weimar Republic.* Vol. I. p.61. He had wished to see German ownership of Calais which he had envisaged as a 'German Gibraltar on the Atlantic.'

6. E. Eyck. *A History of the Weimar Republic.* Vol. I. p.60.

7. Gordon A. Craig. *Germany 1866–1945.* p.396.

5.2   The Legend of Prussian Militarism

The legend of 'Prussian militarism' which the Allies had tried so hard
to extinguish in the Great War had been created by the Great Elector,
Frederick III of Brandenburg, (1657-1713) when he played off the
ambitions of invading Poles and the Swedes to carve himself out an
Empire, calling on all German speaking people to fight together to
eject the enemy from their soil.[8] The Elector was the first of a series of
warlike Hohenzollern kings. They took their creed from the Teutonic
knights who had subdued the Pruzzi in Poland in medieval times and
created an enormous Empire in an alien land. The Empire had vanished but the inspiration remained. Although its possessions were
scattered, Brandenburg/Prussia became a sizeable kingdom, imbued
with the medieval military spirit. Under the Great Elector's grandson,
Frederick William II, it became a soldier state, with each individual
citizen subservient to the needs of the army.[9] Frederick William's son,
Frederick the Great, and Bismarck in the nineteenth century made the
words 'Prussian militarism' feared throughout Europe. Although the
advent of democratic ideas brought an urge for individualism, the
habit of obedience remained strong in Germany, reinforced by the
Lutheran religion and the philosopher Hegel's doctrine of the omnipotent state, the German God and the positive values of war.[10] The wife
of a German officer who reviewed letters written by German students
from the front in the 1st World War had this to say of the influence of
Martin Luther in shaping the German's conception of his responsibility
towards the state.

> 'For centuries,' she wrote, 'German history has been marked by the gigantic
> persistent cleavage first opened by Luther's gigantic personality when he
> attempted to dam the revolutionary forces which his doctrine of salvation
> had released, by demanding unconditional submission to the ruler, no matter
> what his character and the spirit that inspires him. For centuries, right down
> to the present day, Germany had been suffering from the consequences of his
> teaching that man's intellect and will must play no part in determining his

8. S. H. Steinberg. *A Short History of Germany.* (1944) p.118, p.292.
9. S. H. Steinberg. *A Short History of Germany.* p.142–3.
10. Bertrand Russell. *A History of Western Philosophy.* p.636. 'Fichte and Hegel
(1770–1831) were philosophic mouthpieces of Prussia and did much to prepare the way
for the later identification of German patriotism with admiration for Prussia.' p.710.
Hegel on the State: 'the state is the actually existing realised moral life'; 'all the spiritual
reality possessed by a human being he possesses only through the state.' p.711. 'States are
not subject to ordinary moral laws.' p.711. Hegel on war: 'War has a positive moral
value.' 'War has a higher significance ... through it the moral health of peoples is preserved in their indifference towards the stabilising of finite determination.'

outer life, in which he has only to submit in silence to his superior's command. Henceforward the German was no longer responsible for the exterior
conduct of his life. Blind obedience replaced responsibility.'[11]

The civil service, the judiciary, and the returning army officers, were
therefore lost in the new postwar democratic world with its shifting
sands of public opinion and no firm hand to guide.

5.3 Intrinsic Justice

The Peace Treaty was handed to the Germans on 7 May 1919. But they
took a long time to agree to its terms. The Socialist government were
already under fire from the general public for believing in President
Wilson's talk of 'intrinsic justice.' They asked Hindenburg whether the
army could not fight again. He answered that they could in the East but
not in the West. However, he continued that he preferred 'honourable
annihilation to a disgraceful peace'[12] thus passing the responsibility for
any decision onto the unhappy politicians.

Just as the politicians were about to negotiate to try and ameliorate the
peace terms, the German fleet at Scapa Flow, due to be handed over to
the Allies under the Peace terms, was scuttled, and the French flags in
the Berlin armoury, burned.

Any hopes that the Germans might have had for concessions were
dashed by the public fury emanating from these acts. President Wilson
declared that he finally realised that when he was dealing with the
Germans he was not dealing with honourable men. Clemenceau, proclaimed that the time for words was past and that the Germans must
accept or reject the Peace document in its entirety within the next 24
hours.[13]

Although the form of government ushered in by the peace made with
President Wilson represented the summit of all the SPD's hopes, the
government felt it necessary to resign rather than be identified with its
terms. No-one wanted the stigma of signing. But even the anti-
Republican German Nationalists knew it had to be signed, otherwise the
Americans would never return home. So a new government was formed
and the Treaty agreed to, four hours before the deadline.

11. F. W. Foerster. *Europe and the German Question.* p.332.
12. E. Eyck. *A History of the Weimar Republic.* p.102.
13. 1919 Peace Documents. VI. 605.613. E. Eyck. *A History of the Weimar Republic.*
Vol. I. p.103.

5.4 Erzberger and German Devaluation

If the burly Herr Erzberger had been called upon to make any concessions on behalf of his country in return for Allied concessions they
would have centred on stabilising the mark which was to finish the year
worth one third its previous value.[14] The President had made Erzberger
his finance minister on 28 June, just before the treaty was signed. On 8
July Erzberger laid before Parliament 10 drafts of new tax bills which
had been prepared by his predecessor. These proposed stabilising the
currency and raising the sum of 80 billion marks (approximately £4 billion) by means of taxation and a levy on property, to shift the burden of
paying for the war from those with fixed incomes to those with assets
like land and houses which would maintain their value in an inflation.
No wonder Herr Erzberger confessed to Parliament that he felt frightened when placing these bills before it.

There was immediately a ferment in the country. To begin with central government had never before had the effrontery to tax the individual
states. And now this new untried government was presenting them with
these enormous levies, seemingly solely for the payment of the reparations when President Wilson, himself, had declared in December 1918
that he would be charging 'no indemnities.' Despite this, Erzberger had
specifically declared that his government would 'do all in their power to
pay the reparations due.'[15]

The government also proposed a Commission of Inquiry which
would prove, once and for all, that the socialists had not been the guilty
ones who had started the war and led the country to this catastrophic
defeat. Angry questions about the conduct and ending of the war were
being asked on every street corner. How could it happen people wanted
to know? How could the German race be disgraced? They felt that their
questions should be answered and the proper blame firmly placed on the
culprits. This being so it had been perhaps unwise of Herr Erzberger to
propose to place a swingeing tax on the old guard before he had established to all and sundry that it was they who had sued for peace and not
the socialists. Large sections of the middle-classes would be paying this
tax too and they were already condemning the socialists for believing in
President Wilson's woolly verbiage. But it was Hindenburg's evidence
which crucified the socialists.

Field-Marshall Paul von Hindenburg's name had not been sullied by
the events of the Autumn of 1918. He had remained in Germany, not

14. *Annual Register.* 1920. Official Rate. 20.43. Actual Rate between 120 and 365.
15. *New York Times.* 6.1.20.

guiltily escaped to Sweden like General Ludendorff. The man who had repulsed the invading Russians at Tannenberg had always retained his hero's image. When he came to give his evidence to the Committee of Inquiry, therefore, on 8 November 1919, all stood out of respect when he entered.

For his part, however, he treated the members of the Inquiry with the greatest disdain. Ignoring all procedure and all interjections, he read out a prepared statement. In this document he told the Court, and avid newspaper reporters from all over the world, that Germany had been stabbed in the back in the Autumn of 1918, that the German armies and her leaders had always done their utmost for the country and that they had been deserted by the political parties and the nation. For proof of his story he gave as his testimony that 'some English general had said that the German army was knifed from behind.'[16]

It was this British corroboration of the German general's testimony which convinced the ordinary German conservative that its army had indeed been undefeated and had been betrayed by the socialists' naive faith in President Wilson's empty phrases. Egon Larsen in his 'Weimar Witness' tells how the story originated. Major-General Malcolm, head of the British military mission in Berlin, was unwise enough to ask the former military dictator, Ludendorff, to dinner, after the latter had recovered his nerve and returned to Berlin from Sweden. Ludendorff launched into a tirade against the 'traitors' who had started a revolution at home just as the army was about to win the war. It was then that the British general betrayed the fact that he didn't know how the war had ended. Instead of indignantly saying that the German army had been on its knees when Ludendorff and Hindenburg asked President Wilson for peace, he astonished the General by repeating the German nation's propaganda message:

'Do you mean to say that you were stabbed in the back?'
He innocently asked the, no doubt, astonished General.

'Yes, yes, we were stabbed in the back.'[17]

General Haig, whose successes in the Autumn of 1918 had been little acclaimed while his mistakes in 1917 were to become ingrained on the nation's consciences, was in no position to refute any statement of General Hindenburg's which was relayed by bright young newspaper columnists to every corner of the globe. And which Allied politician would like to proclaim that their army had had the German armies crumbling before them, but that the politicians had let them off the hook, under the pressure of an American President who did not even have the support of his own electorate?

16. E. Eyck. *A History of the Weimar Republic*. Vol. I. p.138.
17. J. Wheeler Bennet. *Hindenburg*. p.238.

The Germans realised that if a senior figure in the British army had not known what was going on on the Western front, the wider world would not know either. So the legend of 'the stab in the back' became gospel to Germans and Allies alike.

5.5 Poacher Turned Gamekeeper

In Germany there was a relief that at last the great dilemma was over. At last the middle-classes knew for certain that socialists were the culprits who had led them to this catastrophic defeat. It need never have happened. Before the Field Marshall had given his evidence Herr Helfferich, the war-time Minister of Finance, had accused the independent's representative on the subcommittee, a Jew named Oscar Cohn, of having used Russian money to buy the revolution that stabbed Germany's army in the back.[18] Now they believed him. How bitter the exhausted nation must have felt. How impotent. Those who had been on the Eastern front at the end of the war had always been convinced that they would have won but for President Wilson's intervention – and those who had fought in the West were not going to tell their compatriots at home that their morale had crumbled. No wonder the Germans refused to fly their flag at half-mast when President Wilson died in 1925. He was the major villain of the peace. He had offered the German nation 'intrinsic justice', 'impartial adjustment of colonial claims', 'open covenants of peace openly arrived at' and he had reneged on his promises.

But there were other villains too, at the head of government, weak, unpatriotic, susceptible to political hot- air and even to bribery. Both Germany's Chancellor, Herr Scheidermann and his Minister for Defence, Herr Noske, were accused of corruption. They were forced to set up a Committee of Investigation before the public prosecutor finally acquitted them.[19]

The old guard fared better with their attacks on Herr Erzberger. The assertive Herr Erzberger was not prepared to accept the findings of the Committee of Inquiry which his government had set up and which, because of Hindenburg's evidence, had laid the blame for the loss of the war on the socialists. He maintained in public that Ludendorff and Hindenburg had asked for the peace and that the Conservatives were responsible for the start of the war. Furthermore he declared that 'the

18. E. Eyck. *A History of the Weimar Republic*. Vol. I. p.136.
19. *New York Times*. 24.1.20.

Figure 5.1 Imperial Chancellor Bethman-Hollweg during the war with the then Vice-Chancellor, Dr Karl Helfferich. In the background Gottlieb von Jagow, Secretary for Foreign Affairs.
© Hulton Deutsch

court at Leipzig would prosecute those guilty of inexcusable acts if Germany's enemies would furnish lists of such persons to the Government.'[20]

Herr Helfferich, former wartime finance minister and architect of the method of financing the war effort by borrowing (gold coins were changed for paper marks) was determined to defeat this democratic upstart with his costly financial notions and unpatriotic outlook. He wrote a book entitled: *Down with Erzberger* which was so full of the most disgraceful accusations that Herr Erzberger felt it necessary to take out a libel suit against him.

Herr Erzberger was in the position of poacher turned gamekeeper as he had been spokesman for Germany's heavy industry at the beginning of the war, and in September 1914 had come out in favour of widespread German annexations, including Belgium and France's iron ore field at Longwe-Brie.[21] When he made accusations against the German political and industrial establishment he spoke with authority. It was not surprising, in the circumstances, that the full weight of the Nationalist newspapers should be ranged against the one man who was brave enough to stand up and tell the truth. In fact, although Helfferich was the man standing in the dock it was soon apparent that he had turned the tables on the plaintiff. The finger of accusation from the start was on Erzberger.

In his article Helfferich had made many accusations concerning Erzberger's wartime conduct. Prestigious Bethmann Hollweg, wartime Chancellor till 1917, was called to the witness stand. He declared, under oath, that he could not possibly have made a statement that Erzberger had attributed to him because at the time he was already bound by a resolution of the Federal Council.[22] At this the State Attorney, in an almost unprecedented move, changed sides and opposed Erzberger. Helfferich further accused the Jewish Erzberger of being cynical, two-faced and corrupt. He insisted that Erzberger's method of finance with its emphasis on taxation would lead to the ruin of the country. There had already been one unsuccessful attempt on Erzberger's life. After hearing Helfferich's words, a patriot, overwhelmed by the force of Helfferich's argument, managed to wound Erzberger in the shoulder. Erzberger had to flee to Switzerland while he cleared his name on a tax evasion charge. The judge had always silenced him when he spoke anyway while

20. *New York Times*. 6.1.20. Re the fairness of the subsequent trial for libel which Erzberger brought against Herr Helfferich. *New York Times*. 25.1.20. 'It is significant that the court allows Helfferich to speak at great length, while insisting that Erzberger shall be brief.'

21. H. Herwig and Neil M. Heyman. *Biographical Dictionary of World War I.*

22. E. Eyck. A History of the Weimar Republic. Vol. I. p.145.

Helfferich's lengthy statements were even recorded in the Press before he proclaimed them in court. Then the judge pronounced sentence. He spent little time in censuring Helfferich. However, Erzberger was declared guilty of mixing politics with business, of being untruthful, and engaging in politics to the detriment of his country.

'Down goes Erzberger, up goes the mark' chanted Herr Hugenberg's newspapers. On meeting Erzberger Keynes had called him 'fat and disgusting.'[23] Small, middle-class savers must have agreed with him. Here was a two-faced socialist trying to impose swingeing taxes on them, when all the time he was fiddling taxes himself. But if they imagined that Herr Erzberger's downfall would lead to the stabilisation of the mark they were to be disappointed. Herr Erzberger had been the only one to come up with a stabilisation scheme which would defeat those who wished to debase the currency and he had been discredited.

An inspection of the minutes of the Federal Council later revealed that the resolution that Bethmann Hollweg had spoken of, and which had led to Erzberger being publicly condemned as 'untruthful' had not been passed till several weeks after his alleged statement had been made.[24] It appeared as though it was Bethmann Hollweg who had been mistaken on this occasion, not Erzberger, but Erzberger received the public condemnation. The taint of venality and corruption fell on the fragile Democratic government. The truth about the origins of the war, its ending and the merits of taxation vanished out of sight. The omens were bad for the payment of the reparations.

These were desperate times for the Allies. While Berlin's lights blazed and Germany exported coal to Denmark, Holland and Switzerland, cold Paris lay in darkness, deprived of coal as reparations.[25] Meanwhile Germany's fragile democracy was under attack from the anti-Republican forces of the right and its military were assembling an enormous army.

Although Bonar Law refuted a statement in *The Times*, as regards numbers of the German armed forces, stating that they were grossly exaggerated, The Times replied with details on 1 January 1920 under the heading 'OVER A MILLION MEN.' These forces consisted of:

The Reichswehr (Regular army) 400,000
Land forces of the Reichsmarine (Regular navy) 12,000
Zeltfrelwilligen (Emergency volunteers) 150,000–200,000 Einwohnerwehr (Civic Guards) 300,000–400,000 Sicherheitspolizei 40,000–50,000

23. *New York Times*. 13.3.20.
24. E. Eyck. *A History of the Weimar Republic*. Vol. I. p.145.
25. *New York Times*. 3.2.20. Anger in Britain at scarce coal being exported to France instead of being used at home. *The Times*. 12.1.20.

The Times also enumerated the number of machine guns, howitzers and aircraft in organisations such as the Sicherheitspolitzei (public safety police) and compared the total figures of men under arms in Germany with those of Britain's armed forces which in December 1919 amounted to 185,000 men.[26]

The Allies hastened to try to put the provisions of the Treaty of Versailles into operation. They had waited at length for America to ratify the Treaty their President had conceived. But Americans, cheated of victory in 1918, and tired of their long-standing, sanctimonious President, were in no mood to tie themselves to League of Nations' legislation, embroiling them in another, inconclusive war in Europe. The Allies could wait no longer for America's endorsement. They realised that, unless they acted fast to assert their authority, they would be facing a coup d'etat in Germany. On the 10 January 1920, the Treaty was finally inaugurated, without America's endorsement.[27]

5.6 The Kaiser on Trial

On the 16th January, under Article 227 of the newly ratified Treaty, the Allies asked Holland to hand over the ex-Emperor, 'Kaiser Bill', for trial.

But Holland, aware of the proximity of Germany's enormous army and reaping rich rewards from Germany's switch of trade from Antwerp to Rotterdam, refused to surrender the ex- Emperor. If and hopefully when the associate power (U.S.A.) eventually signed the Treaty and was willing to take a full part in the League of Nations, it hinted, it might be different.[28]

The same fate befell Article 228 of the newly ratified Treaty, concerning war criminals.

The Allies had consequently produced a paper-bound book of more than two hundred pages containing the names of 890 persons or groups with their rank and accusations against them. It was a painstakingly assembled and impressive document and heading the list of war criminals were Field Marshals Hindenburg and Ludendorff. Admiral von Tirpitz and Ex-Chancellor Bethmann Hollweg also figured prominently.[29]

Viereck's *American Monthly*, a small circulation newspaper, dedicated to relaying German propaganda in the United States, portrayed

26. *The Times*. 1.1.20.
27. *Annual Register*. 1920. p.158–9.
28. *Sun & New York Herald*. 24.1.20.
29. *Sun & New York Herald*. 8.2.20.

exactly the uproar created in rightist circles in Germany by this demand:

'A united Germany rebuked the indecent demand of the Allies for nine hundred Germans, including Hindenburg, Ludendorff and Bethmann-Hollweg. If the German government surrendered even one of its heroic leaders no German in the world could ever lift his head again. There is nothing in the peace treaty that justifies the "extradition" of any one except persons accused of specific crimes ... The idea for the Allies' blacklist must have originated in the mind of a madman.'

The weakened German democratic government truthfully asserted to the Allies that it was simply in no position to carry out this provision at present. Indeed, there was absolutely nothing the Allies could do to enforce the Treaty, however many German democratic signatures were on it. Germany had a million men with weapons and its old guard was just about to try and restore the Emperor.

In October 1918 Robert Bosch, the industrialist had declared: 'We may have to put out the fire with water from the dung heap even if it stinks a bit afterwards.'[30] 'The fire' was the approaching Allied armies which threatened to destroy the German established order, and 'the water from the dung heap,' the democrats. Now the peace had been signed, and the Americans had gone home, they were not needed any more. After Erzberger's crushing defeat by Herr Helfferich, Dr. Kapp, a royalist, declared that the government was inefficient, corrupt and had outlived its usefulness. Elements of the army captured Berlin and hoisted the Imperial flag. Simultaneously reports of unusual activity emanated from the Kaiser's house in Holland. Once more President Ebert was faced with a desperate situation. He had only one card left, to appeal to the workers:

'Cease work! Stifle the opportunity of this military dictatorship! Fight with all the means at your command to retain the republic. Put all differences of opinion aside. 'Only one means exists against the return of Wilhelm II. That is the cessation of all means of communication. No hand may be moved. No proletarian may assist the dictator. Strike along the whole line.'[31]

The effect of his words was miraculous. The workers downed tools. There was a total strike. They had always imagined that it had been largely their efforts that had ousted the Emperor in the first place. Naturally they now overplayed their hand and tried to promote a genuine revolution for which there was little public support. The army was called in to put it down and it also marched without permission into the

30. S. Taylor. *Germany 1918–33*. p.5–6.
31. *Annual Register*. 1920. p.177–8.

demilitarised Rhine zone to quell the disturbances there. The horrified French retaliated by occupying German territory with coloured troops which provoked the anger of the German race, which in those racialist days considered coloured troops inferior. The right wing Press were able to make much of the insult. In the elections afterwards the moderates lost power in the Reichstag at the expense both of the extreme right and the extreme left.[32] The elected government thankfully reduced the size of the army to conform with the statutes of the Treaty of Versailles. But it knew it was under seige. Both the extreme right and the extreme left were indulging in propaganda campaigns to woo the moderate voter. But the cards were stacked in favour of the establishment. Although numerically few, they controlled the media, the money men, the army and the judiciary. From now onwards the socialists would always be having to look over their shoulder. The old guard could not seize power against the wishes of the people but they would increasingly be attempting to run the country behind the democratic facade.

Meanwhile continental Europe's strongest industrial nation would redouble its propaganda efforts over the reparations and the Allies, put on the defensive, would be repeatedly forced to scrutinise the small print of the Treaty of Versailles to see if the 'master race'[33] had been short-changed.

5.7 German Vested Interests

German industry was dominated by a few, very powerful industrial families who were not above meddling in politics if they felt it suited their interests. In 1916 Germany's foreign minister, Jagow, was found to be complaining with reference to the industrial magnate, Herr Stinnes's aims in the East:

> 'Germany cannot frame her ends exclusively to meet the interests of heavy industry.'[34]

32. *Annual Register.* 1920. p.181.

33. Bertrand Russell. Re Hegel on the 'master race.' 'The principle of historical development, he (Hegel) says, is national genius. In every age there is some one nation which is charged with the mission of carrying the world through the stage of the dialectic that it has reached.' Bertrand Russell's opinion on how modern Germans regarded Hegel's message. 'In our age, of course, this nation is Germany.'

34. F. Fischer. *The Aims of Germany in the 1st World War.* p.229-230. Letter to the Japanese Minister, Ushida. 'This lad Stinnes is a pusher, who is trying to force our policy into his own spheres of interest.'

Post-war Herr Stinnes was reputed to own some 4,500 businesses in Russia, Rumania, Italy, Scandinavia, Spain, Luxembourg, France, Britain, Holland, Belgium, North America, China, Japan, Portugal, Switzerland, Persia and many other places. Stinnes was an anti-social man with an Assyrian beard and ill-fitting clothes but he had personally built his family coal and transport concern, Siemens, Rheinalbe, Schuckert Union into one of the most powerful conglomerates in the world.[35]

When he was chosen by the Reichminister, Dr. Simons, to meet the Allies at Spa in June 1920 to explain the 'technical difficulties,' which had caused a short fall in the reparations, he did not waste time with idle pleasantries.

Dr. Simons and Secretary Bergmann, the German representative on the Reparations Committee, called Herr Stinnes, as the industry's coal expert, to explain the nature of the difficulties which were holding up the vital reparations' deliveries of coal to the Allies. Herr Stinnes made no mention of manpower troubles, problems with extraction etc. in his reply. Instead he decided to use the occasion, as a political platform, to defy the Treaty of Versailles.

'I rise in order to be able to look the hostile delegates straight in the eyes' he opened.[36] Men like him had been thwarted of defying the Treaty of Versailles by restoring their Emperor only by force of public opinion in the Spring. Had they been able to reinstate William II there is no doubt that they would have defied the Allies on every single provision of the Treaty. As it was Stinnes contented himself with trying to whip up 'the dumb force of human sentiment' by referring to the Allies as our 'insane conquerors.'[37]

Pale with anger, M. Hyman the Belgian foreign minister, declared: 'What would have happened with such a man if he had been in the position of conqueror?'[38] Marshall Foch and the British General, Wilson, began preparations for marching into the Ruhr, even though Herr Stinnes threatened that all coal reparations would be cut off if they did. In the end, the German minister, Simon, appealed to Lloyd George and the matter was resolved with a concession by the Allies. Interestingly the concession concerned the matter of food. A cash credit of five gold marks was to be credited on each delivered ton of coal, the sum to be used for food to feed the German miners.[39]

35. Guttmann & Meehan. *The Great Inflation.* p.112–3.
36. E. Eyck. *A History of the Weimar Republic.* Vol. I. p.167.
37. E. Eyck. *A History of the Weimar Republic.* p.167.
38. Viscount d'Abernon. *An Ambassador of Peace.* Vol. I.
39. E. Eyck. *A History of the Weimar Republic.* Vol. I. p.168.

5.8   America Withdraws from Europe

After the Treaty was ratified by the Europeans, America felt she could wash her hands of her European Allies, on whom she had lavished so much of her food, her money and even the blood of her young men. Herbert Hoover stated America's case for retiring from the unhappy European scene.

> 'I disagree emphatically with the statement being circulated by European propagandists, both as to the volume of European financial needs from the United States and as to their suggestions that the great bulk of these needs cannot be met by ordinary commercial credits ...   The American people are finding $7.000.000 a month in charity for feeding 3,000,000 children and fighting disease. If we contribute the bread supply on government credit to these starving cities plus business credits, we will be doing our share of world responsibility.'[40]

Of Keynes's idea for the cancellation of inter-Allied debts in order to get the world economy functioning again, the *Sun and New York Herald* commented: 'Not even the universal financial and economic disaster which the Spring may have in store in Europe is likely to convince the people of the United States ... of the wisdom of the cancellation of inter-Allied indebtedness.'

In fact America was not feeling rich any more. She certainly could not afford any more largesse. She had lent huge sums of money to Europe and it would be some time before it was repaid. She needed to replenish her nation's coffers. But she was having trouble with the Germans 'dumping cheap German wares' on the American market, undermining the price of her own goods and putting up the import bill.

On 2 February 1920 Dr. H. Harty, technical adviser for the Reparations Commission, spoke of the inroads that the German dye industry was making in America by January 1920:

> 'The threat to the American dye interests lies in the fact that until American manufacturers can take care of all the American needs Germany can charge extortionate prices for those dyes which we do not manufacture. She is manufacturing dyes on a large scale and because of the present low value of the mark she will be able to underbid the American dye producer in an open competitive market.'

Dr. Harty had been immensely impressed by his tour of the German dye

---

40. *New York Times*. 7.1.20.

manufacturers ('his plants are even greater than before the war') and by the bustling economic climate.

'Everywhere there were signs of activity' he wrote. 'The same confidence characterised the industrial German as had been recorded by the military German in his first advances on Belgium.'[41]

On 11 February 1921 America asked the Germans to furnish their tariff department with details of employees working conditions and 'all available data on German production' to see if Germany was indulging in unfair trade. The Germans protested that their employees were highly paid and 'would work only six hours a day' but the Committee demanded data from every important German export industry dealing with the U.S.[42]

On 21 September 1922 the Fordney-McCumber Tariff Act was passed by the American President, Warren Harding, the highest in American history. No public reason was given for this blanket tariff which was bitterly resented by Britain, France and Italy. 'Wall Street issued repeated warnings that Europe could not pay what it owed America if the latter raised its tariff walls so high as to bar out European goods but the warnings fell on deaf ears.'[43] How could the American President tell his countrymen that defeated Germany was driving America's powerful industry into the ground? So all the Europeans had to suffer.

In his study of the *Weimar Republic* (1988) Eberhalb Kolb of the University of Cologne contrasted the prosperity of the German worker with the British at that time:

'Whereas in Britain in 1921 over 20% of workers were unemployed, in Germany at that time there was practically full employment with rising wages, adjusted ever more frequently to rising price levels.'

5.9 Protectionism in Europe

In April 1919 Lloyd George had had to report that 'No trade was moving anywhere in Europe.'[44]

In August 1919 the Prime Minister promised the House of Commons that in implementing 'Free Trade' as promised under the terms of the

41. *New York Times*. 1.2.20.
42. *New York Times*. 13.2.21.
43. *Annual Register*. 1922. p.285.
44. R. S. Baker. *Woodrow Wilson & World Settlement*. p.289.

Treaty of Versailles 'the Government would seek emergency powers to check any flood of imports that might arise.'[45]

On 20 November 1920 in a speech to the Federation of British Industries he declared:

> 'We are pledged to do everything we can to shield the industries which were discovered during the war to be essential industries for the defence of the country. We are pledged to do something, in so far as the government can, to deal with the exchange situation, so that the exchange situation in Europe may not be utilised as a means for destroying our industries. These things we are pledged to do.'[46]

But he did not carry out his promises. British industry was already struggling under the weight of taxation and excess taxation to make up for the profits it had made in the war. In addition it had to contend with German industry, protected by an extremely cheap rate for the mark. Shipbuilding followed the rest of British industry into decline. Meanwhile, subsidised German shipbuilding, prospered. By 1922 German shipbuilders lay second only to Britain in the number of ships built in the world.[47]

1920-21 was a dreadful year of poverty for Europe. The price of coal, wheat, wool etc., dropped by half but still nobody had any money to pay for them. On the export market German coal was bought because it was so much cheaper. British trade drooped. Farmers went bankrupt and the government considered the drastic course of cutting wages despite the promise of strike action by the miners. Plans for nationalisation were discarded. Lloyd George abandoned his precious government controls while making it clear in public that all the present industrial difficulties were due to the inadequacies of Britain's industrialists.

Britain's financial experts however explained the matter differently. It appeared that Germany's currency was being manipulated to Britain's disadvantage. In his explanation of what he called 'collapsed exchange dumping', C. Patrick Duff explained the situation for the Prime Minister:

> 'Thus, suppose the value of the sterling in England is in the relation of 200 marks to the pound, but that Germany is not able to purchase all that she requires abroad. The exceptional demand in Germany for certain foreign currencies drives up the mark price of sterling until it reaches say 250 marks to the pound. Then, while the internal value of the mark equals 200 to the pound, the external value of the mark equals 250 to the pound. The difference between the two, that is 50 marks, constitutes a virtual bounty on exports.'[48]

45. *Lloyd George Papers*. Baldwin File. c/8. F/3/1/13.
46. *Lloyd George Papers*. Baldwin File. c/8. F/3/1/13.
47. *Annual Register*. Finance & Commerce. 1922. p.91.
48. *Lloyd George Papers*. Baldwin File. C/F/3/1/13.

5.10 German Unwillingness to Meet First Reparations' Payment

Germany was due to pay the first £1,000,000,000 of its reparations' obligations by 1 May 1921. Then the final bill would be decided and presented. The Reparations Commission, labelled by the German delegation at the Treaty of Versailles as having 'greater rights than the Emperor possessed' was in reality a sober, painstaking body of men dedicated to the sympathetic interpretation of President Wilson's principles.[49]

However, in January 1921 it had to disclose Germany's total unwillingness to meet its initial obligation. 84 million marks (£4.2 million) had been received so far by the Commission but this payment had been made not by Germany but France and Denmark as credits to Germany for property received under the Treaty. 3.8 milliard marks had been deducted kindly by the Commission to pay for Germany's food and raw materials. In return she had sent back the sheep and cattle stolen by the retreating army, some coal but no money at all.[50]

Meanwhile the *New York Times* reported on 9 March that between them Hugo Stinnes and the Mannesmann concern had gained control of all the Austrian iron and steel interests. Herr Hugenberg, the right-wing German Newspaper magnate, lately of Krupps, had bought most of the Austrian newspapers too.

49. E. Mantoux. The Carthaginian Peace. p.1233–5.
The full text of the German protest against the Reparations Commission: 'German democracy is thus annihilated at the very moment when the German people were about to build it up after a severe struggle ... The Commission, which is to have its permanent headquarters outside Germany, will possess incomparably greater rights than the German Emperor possessed; the German people under its regime would remain for decades shorn of all rights, and deprived ... of any independence of action ... in its economic or even its ethical progress.'
The Reparations Commission reply:
'The observations of the German delegation present a view of this Commission so distorted and so inexact that it is difficult to believe that the clauses of the Treaty have been calmly or carefully examined. It is not an engine of oppression or a device for interfering with German sovereignty. It has no forces at its command. It has no executive powers within the territory of Germany; it cannot, as is suggested, direct or control the educational or other systems of the country. Its business is to ask what is to be paid; to satisfy itself that Germany can pay; and to report to the Powers, whose delegation it is, in case Germany makes a default.'
27.4.19. Lloyd George found the original wording enabling the Commission to demand payment 'in the form of properties, chattels, commodities, business rights' etc. 'too stiff.' President Wilson agreed. 'What he wanted was to avoid even the appearance of a forced Brest-Litovsk Treaty.'
50. *Reparations Commission*, IV. Statement of Germany's obligations. pp.5ff. E. Mantoux. *The Carthaginian Peace*. p.137.n.

Dr. Melchior and Secretary Bergmann had made their approaches to the Reparations Commission from the standpoint that Germany was a 'Besserungschein', a bankrupt debtor, who could only promise to pay the Allies, as and when economic conditions improved.[51] The British, aware that Germany had exported a third more goods to Britain in 1919–20 than she had imported from her (£31,073,000 compared to £21,535,000) were naturally incensed.[52] It was not only the French and the Danes who were feeling the chill blast from the 'stocks of glassware, cutlery, electrical appliances, photographic materials and iron and steel goods' that had been 'stored up for exportation'[53] at rock bottom prices, British industry was also reeling under the blow. Lord Northcliffe's fears of 'spending the rest of my life swotting to pay excess profits tax and supertax for the benefit of Germany' were being amply fulfilled. The hardline conservatives in the coalition demanded payment or retribution.

5.11   France Receives No Money

The French were also furious that they had received no money for the devastation of their homeland. Had not the Reparations Commission just proclaimed that the internal debt of Germany was 4.178 marks paper per head, while that of France was 5,353 francs paper per head? The external debt of Germany was stated to be 40 marks paper per head while that of France was 2,101 francs paper per head. The Reparations Commission judged that the German pre-war wealth of 350,000,000,000 marks prewar had not materially decreased. Dividends of 20 to 100 per cent by German companies were common. Germany was in the lucky position of being able to use all its funds to develop its export industries whereas the unhappy French had had to find money to reconstruct their devastated lands and still they received no recompense. M. de Lasteyrie, official reporter of the finance committee of the French Parliament declared:

> 'France must be paid. If Germany refuses, France must go in herself and exact payment.'

He was applauded by the entire house.[54]

51. E. Eyck. *A History of the Weimar Republic.* Vol. I. p.170.
52. *Annual Register.* 1921. p.26. Finance and Commerce.
53. *New York Times.* 12.12.18.
54. *New York Times.* 13.4.21.

5.12   Allies Occupy German Cities

Stinnes's widely reported words at Spa, however, had stiffened the
mood of the German population, putting pressure on their government.
Reichminister, Dr. Simons, made a tour of the country, ranting at the
debt collection efforts of the Reparations Commission and declaring
that the value of the Saar and the goods delivered to the Allies amounted
to not the £400,000,000 accepted by the Commission but much more
than the whole £1,000,000,000 demanded by the Allies.[55] He further
inflamed public susceptibilities by playing on the war guilt issue. The
London Conference of 1 March could not have opened under more
inauspicious circumstances.

By 3 March Lloyd George could no longer resist pressure from
British 'die-hards' and the French. The British Prime Minister declared
that the Allies would occupy the cities of Düsseldorf, Duisburg and
Ruhroht and meanwhile impose an 'advalorem levy' not exceeding 50%
on incoming goods, the proceeds of which were to be credited against
the reparations account, unless the Germans agreed to hand over their
reparations due by 1 May or, at least, make satisfactory counter proposals. Far from making any satisfactory proposals the Germans threatened
not to make any reparations payments at all unless they were allowed to
keep Upper Silesia with its coal deposits, so necessary to the viability of
the Polish economy.

On 8 March the Allies had to fulfil their threat. They occupied the
towns of Düsseldorf, Duisburg and Ruhroht.

5.13   Debasement of Currency Eliminates Wartime Debt

On 27 April 1921 the Allies demanded £6,600m in reparations from
Germany over fifty years the sum to include ceded property, coal etc.
Britain and Germany had both had a national debt of £7,500m[56] in 1918
but Germany's depreciating currency had eliminated three quarters of
its internal debt. France's £6,400 debt had been swelled by the unrepaid
costs of repairing wartime devastation. The small print of the reparations' agreement, however, revealed the demands to be less than draconian. The demands were to be divided into A, B, and C Bonds. As the C
Bonds were only to be issued when the German payments were suffi-

55. E. Eyck. *A History of the Weimar Republic*. Vol. I. p.174–5.
56. German figures. Reichschuldenkommission. U.K. Figures. Statistical Abstract for
the U.K. French figures. The War finance of France. G. Jéze and H. Truchy.

cient to cover the sinking funds and charges connected with the A and B Bonds, and not one penny of the already overdue A Bonds had actually been received, the C Bonds, from the first, looked more like a public relations' exercise to satisfy alarmed public opinion at home, than a serious desire to batter the economic life out of Germany. In the opinion of the Historian, Gordon A. Craig in his Germany 1866–1945, they 'represented ... a fairly empty threat to turn the screw harder if the Germans were not co-operative. To all intents and purposes, the German debt had been set at 50 billion gold marks.'[57] (£2,500,000,000 approx.)

One can understand English desires for reparations. By 1921, by dint of currency manipulation, Germany's bill for reparations and internal debt, was, in effect, less than Great Britain's. Germany could afford a reparations' levy of £100,00, plus a tax on exports, and still repay its citizens, in some measure, for their patriotism during the war. Britain's yearly interest on its National Debt was £345,000,000. The excess profits' tax which has netted £300,000,000 for the British Exchequer in 1919/20,[58] should be levied in Germany. The Allied occupation of Dusseldorf, Duisburg and Ruhroht had not produced any money on the table so, on 5 May, the Allies issued Germany with a further ultimatum. Germany was given seven days to agree to fulfil its disarmament obligations, agree to pay the £600,000,000 already overdue, try its war criminals and agree to the new terms for reparations' payments. The penalty for non- cooperation, the occupation of the Ruhr.[59]

Germany was in a ferment over the reparations' proposals. If its own small savers, its patriots, had had to suffer degradation and penury, why should it succour the small savers in 'decadent' Britain and France? Had not the widely quoted British expert declared that to demand sums like these would be 'one of the most outrageous acts of a cruel victor in civilised history.' The enormity of asking this immense and impertinent figure from a country which had laid down its arms 'solely' out of faith in President Wilson's high minded principles, engulfed the nation. Germany was filled with outrage, indignation and disgust.

The question has to be asked, however, whether the Allies were really trying to force a draconian peace upon a crushed foe as Keynes asserted or whether Germany's recalcitrance was due to 'the powers behind the throne' feeling strong enough to resist the combined demands of the Allies?

'Either the German government does not intend to carry out its treaty

57. Gordon A. Craig. *Germany 1866–1945.* p.440. Charles S. Maier. *Recasting Bourgeois Europe. Stabilisation in France, Germany and Italy in the Decade after World War I.* (Princeton 1975) pp.241–2.

58. *Annual Register.* 1920. p.60. Finance and Commerce.

59. *Annual Register.* 1921. p.47.

obligations or it has not the strength to insist, in the face of selfish and shortsighted opposition, upon the necessary sacrifices being made.'[60] In fact, there is evidence that Germany, itself, had expected more severe terms than those produced in the ultimatum. Germany had appealed to the recently elected American President, Harding, to persuade the Allies to accept alternative reparations' proposals.

On viewing Germany's proposals, however, the President found them 'unacceptable' and declined to transmit them to the Allies.

Although there was an enormous outcry in Germany when the total figure which the Allies proposed to charge, was known, Secretary Bergmann, the Germans reparations expert, found that the actual Allied reparations' proposals were no more severe than those that Germany, itself, had devised and America had declined to submit on its behalf.[61] No one was going to divulge this information however. There was an enormous outcry against the reparations in Germany. Under the threat of invasion of the Ruhr, Germany agreed to the Allies reparations' demands. The British reduced the import duty on German goods to 26%. The proceeds were credited against the reparations.[62]

A new government was formed in Germany to undertake the odious duty of fulfilment. It was headed by Dr. Wirth, finance minister in the previous government. He included in his cabinet, the brilliant Jewish heir to the world famous A.E.G. company, Walter Rathenau. It was an unusual and controversial choice which caused a sensation in Germany. Although a member of the Democratic party, Rathenau had never even been offered a place in the Democratic party's ballot owing to his independence of thought. 'It must have seemed an act of Providence' when Wirth asked the rich, talented but 'lonely', and to some extent unloved man to join his cabinet.[63]

Dr. Wirth promised a policy of fulfilment over the reparations and Rathenau attempted to put it into action. He did manage to circumvent the machinations of the central bank (formerly bank of Prussia) to some extent by arranging deals in kind as reparations to French individuals. He was much criticised for this.[64] But actual money, gold, was demanded by the schedule agreed with the Allies under threat of invasion in May, and this was to be delivered by the end of August.

Before this happened, however, an event occurred which was to have world-wide repercussions. Herr Erzberger had managed to clear his

60. E. Eyck. *A History of the Weimar Republic.* Vol. I. p.177.
61. E. Eyck. *A History of the Weimar Republic.* p.179.
62. *Royal Institute of International Affairs Survey.* 1929. p.121.
63. E. Eyck. *A History of the Weimar Republic.* p.185.
64. Weisbaden Agreement, concluded 6–7.10.1921. Accepted by the Reichstag with one dissenting voice – Herr Helferrich. *Annual Register.* 1921. p.176–7.

name of perjury and tax evasion. So, having been re-elected to Parliament by his faithful Wurtemburg electorate, he decided to resume an active political career. But on August 26th, before he had time to resume the offensive against his former detractors and set the record straight over how the war had ended, he was murdered by two former army officers, Schultz and Tillessen.[65]

Foreign confidence in Germany collapsed. The value of the mark tumbled.

Astonishingly, however, with the aid of short-term credits[66] the government did manage to scrape together the 1,000,000,000 gold marks (approximately £50 million) to pay the initial instalment of the reparations, due four days after Erzberger's death, but the value of the mark plummeted.

Dr. Wirth divined a threat to the constitution from so much glee at Erzberger's murder. His government pushed through new measures designed to combat sedition in newspapers but there was such an outcry against the 'dictatorial manner' with which the law was applied that he felt forced to repeal it.[67]

The government managed to make the November 500 million mark instalment of the reparations, agreed with the Allies after the Spring ultimatum. Then it requested a moratorium. After deliberation, the knotty question of Germany's ability or willingness to pay was shelved until yet another conference was convened in January 1922.

The opponents of democracy and 'fulfilment' had 'won' over the Erzberger episode. Every time the Jewish Herr Erzberger had shown his face, the mark had plunged in value. People now equated its present lowly state as being the direct result of the reparations payments, not realising that the first cash reparation payment had not been made till 31 August 1921 and this with the help of loans from abroad.

People were being reduced to penury by the fall in the value of the mark and they blamed their slavish Democratic government with its policy of 'fulfilment'. They declared that the government were 'the bailiffs of King Mammon' and that the new national flag contained 'the yellow stripe of Jewry.'[68]

65. E. Eyck. *A History of the Weimar Republic.* p.188–9. 'What Erzberger's enemies could never forgive was his going to Compiegne to sue for peace.'

66. E. Mantoux. *The Carthaginian Peace.* p.139.

67. *Annual Register.* 1921. p.183.

68. Schulthess' Europatscher. E. Eyck. *A History of the Weimar Republic.* p.190.

–6–

Who was Driving Whom to Bankruptcy in 1922?

6.1 German Compensation from Turkey

On 6 January 1922 the new conference was convened at Cannes to discuss Germany's failure to live up to its agreement of 8 May 1921, when it had promised, under threat of invasion, to pay its reparations under an agreed schedule. Under this schedule payments were next due on 15 January and 15 February 1922.[1] But the German government had, in effect, declared itself bankrupt.

It is interesting to conjecture what Germany would have done under similar circumstances if France had declared herself unable to pay. During the war Germany's ally, Turkey, had exhausted her financial resources in the fight against the Entente. Naturally the Turks expected, in view of their human and material sacrifices, suffered in a common cause, that their debts would be reduced or indeed entirely remitted by their grateful ally. But for this the Germans demanded 'real compensation.' A detailed report of the economic concessions to be made was drawn up:

(a) The hard coal deposits of Heraklea, which should be secured by liquidating the French company and transferring the concession to Germany;

(b) The Turkish copper mines of Arghana Maden, which were owned by the Turkish state, should be transferred to Germany;

(c) The iron and zinc deposits of Berlia and Bulgar to be brought under German control partly by liquidating the French company, partly by transferring Turkish rights to Germany;

(d) The Baghdad railway's claims on the oil of Upper Mesopotamia and Mosul must be realised under all circumstances, as must the safeguarding of transport to the Persian Gulf by the acquisition of

---

1. *Annual Register*. 1922. p.161.

the majority of shares in the shipping companies of the Euphrates, the Tigris and the Shatt-el-Arab;

(e) The phosphate deposits on the Hejjas line and at Es-salt must also be transferred to Germany, as must the asphalt deposits in the Yamuk Valley and at Ladikiye;

(f) Complete possession of Turkey's ore supplies to be achieved by the liquidation of the Borax Company, which would give Germany the borazite deposits at Panderma and the transfers of the Turkish concessions for the manganese ore deposits in the Vilayet of Bursa would give Germany the means of refining the steel.

Germany was not going to allow an ally off with its debts even if that ally was fighting alongside Germany in the field of battle.[2]

But Germany had not even been France's friend but her foe who had inflicted gross physical injury on her. Grass roots French opinion was therefore infuriated by their country's failure to achieve just recompense.

They were especially incensed when their Premier, Briand, seemed to retreat from his former firm position over the reparations. The forthcoming instalment of the reparations' schedule was due on the 15 January. However, although Rathenau promised to pay the reduced sums of 720,000,000 gold marks and 1,450,000,000 value of goods in kind, agreed by the Commission on condition that Germany's tax collection methods improved, no gold was put on the table.[3] On the contrary the German government's allegation that the Reparations Commission was interfering in the nation's internal affairs was greeted with an outburst of popular indignation at home. Dr. Wirth himself declared the interference to be incompatible with President Wilson's principle of self-determination.[4]

The Reparations Commission, put on the defensive, humbly declared that it had no intention of 'trespassing on Germany's sovereignty.' So, 'monetary inflation, tax evasion, public expenditure and capital flight continued as fast as ever.'[5] The only concrete result of the conference appeared to be an agreement to meet at yet another conference, in Genoa, in three months time.

Lloyd George was influenced by his political position at home with a divided Liberal Party, an increasingly divided Conservative Party and a pro-German Labour Party[6] rapidly gaining ground, in the abject

---

2. Fritz Fischer. *The Aims of Germany in the 1st World War*. p.585.
3. *Annual Register*. 1922. p.162.
4. Karl Bergmann. *The History of the Reparations*. (1927) p.121.
5. Etienne Mantoux. *The Carthaginian Peace*. p.140.
6. See letter in *The Times*. 10.2.23.

economic conditions prevailing. The French Press viewed his apparently equivocal position and his influence on Briand with the deepest suspicion. Lloyd George seemed to have forgotten the 'series of overlapping shell craters, half-full of yellow, slimy water,'[7] whose restoration needed to be paid for, nor the '438,000 (Frenchmen) martyred in German prisons' and 'the systematic destruction of her (France's) industrial districts in the North and in the East.'[8]44 He appeared not to understand their worries that the Prussian army could strike again. When he attempted to instruct Briand on how to play the game of golf in the balmy Cannes breezes, instead of discussing how to make the Germans pay their debts, it was too much for the stricken French Parliament in Paris. They ejected Briand and re-instated their hard-line ex- President, Poincaré, as Premier, a man who was determined to exact the letter of the law from Germany. What was the nature of France's new mentor?

6.2 The Return of President Poincaré

Poincaré was a small, neat, punctilious man with a formidable intellect and a prodigious capacity for work. He had had an impressive career, being asked to become Finance Minister for France before the age of 30.[9] In 1911 he became Prime Minister. In 1913 he was invited to the supreme honour of becoming President of France. Before his career in Parliament he had been lawyer to the French iron ore magnates of Longwe Brie and his association with them in dealing with the coal magnates had convinced him that the only language the Germans understood was grim resolve.

He and his Prime Minister had felt particularly impotent on learning of Austria's harsh ultimatum to Serbia at 5 pm. on the 23 July 1914, after their boat had left St. Petersburg on its voyage home from their Russian State visit.

> 'In our floating home there reached us only the deadened echoes of the outside world. We received nothing precise, either from St. Petersburg or from Paris. We were more and more anxious in our solitude and in our remoteness and the Sunday passed away without bringing us, lost between the sky and the waves, positive news from land.'[10]

7. *Lloyd George War Memoirs*. IV. p.2208.
8. E. Mantoux. *The Carthaginian Peace*. p.20–221. Memorandum of the French Government on the Fixation at the Rhine of the Western Frontier of Germany. 26.2.19.
9. Sisley Huddleston. *Poincaré*. p.29.
10. Sisley Huddleston. *Poincaré*. p.63–4.

Figure 6.1 President Poincaré
'... each time we have desired to be conciliatory towards Germany she has abused our conciliatory overtures. Each time, on the other contrary, that we have shown ourselves firm, she has receded. Germany does not understand the language of right; she understands on the use of force.'
© The Hulton-Deutsch Collection

– 148 –

On their return to France the Prime Minister withdrew the French troops 10 kilometres (6 miles) behind their frontier to avoid giving the Germans any excuse to invade.[11]

In those days in France the Prime Minister had the executive power, while the President's post was largely ceremonial, so Poincaré could do little during the war. He objected to Foch allowing the German troops to withdraw into the German heartland, flags flying, drums beating, after the war had finished, but had to watch impotently. He sent letter after letter to Versailles after the war, opposing appeasement. To him France's frontier should be on the Rhine, the only natural defence against Germany's superior numbers.

He defended his attitude to negotiations with Germany through research.

'I have studied all the documents relating to the Morocco affair. There results from this study a conviction: it is that each time that we have desired to be conciliatory towards Germany she has abused our conciliatory overtures. Each time, on the other contrary, that we have shown ourselves firm, she has receded. Germany does not understand the language of right; she understands only the use of force.'[12]

The Great War had failed to kill that military spirit because it was not prosecuted to the finish, allowing Germany to still retain an enormous army in December 1919 before the Treaty of Versailles was inaugurated. He believed that every new concession renewed Germany's confidence and scorn for the Allies.

After his departure from the Presidency Poincaré had launched a campaign in the Press against the catalogue of concessions at Versailles. However, he who had most strenuously opposed the Treaty of Versailles now clutched at this piece of paper as the only available weapon to ensure his nation's security.

6.3 Lloyd George and Poincaré

There could hardly have been a greater contrast between the new French Premier and the British Prime Minister. True they were both small men. However, whereas Lloyd George liked to make a deal, Poincaré was a 'bigoted legalist.' Lloyd George enjoyed the company at Great Houses.

11. *Annual Register*. 1914. p.282.
12. M. Stephane Lausanne. *Les Hommes que j'ai vue*. Sisley Huddleston. *Poincaré*. A Biographical Portrait. p.71.

Poincaré, at first, refused to preside over official banquets at all, and later, only occasionally, 'on the ground that even the appearance of participating in any kind of pleasure is undignified and even offensive after the tremendous tragedy of the war.'[13]

Lloyd George's first interview with Poincaré on 14 January 1922 was not a success. Lloyd George wanted another conference to sort out the reparations' dilemma. Poincaré declared that a Reparations Commission had been set up under the Treaty of Versailles to deal with the matter. Conferences could only make its job more difficult by undermining its authority.

Lloyd George offered Poincaré a Security Pact, guaranteeing to go to the aid of France if France were attacked. Poincaré ungratefully asked precisely what this meant in numbers of soldiers, ships and guns.

'Everything we have, all our force, just as we did in the late war' declared Lloyd George.

But Poincaré was not satisfied. He appeared not to believe Lloyd George's word. He wanted a precisely worded military convention. Lloyd George flew into a rage.

'If you cannot take the pledged word of the British people you had better consider the Draft Treaty withdrawn. Britain's word has always been her bond. There was no military convention in existence before the Great War. Merely our word. We kept it as France and the world knows. There are some things which cannot be set down in black and white. Britain gives you her word. If you don't accept that, then consider the Draft Treaty at an end. Choose between the two.'[14]

Flying into a rage had worked in the past. But not with Poincaré. Poincaré did not want the British to waste lives trying to defend French soil, just to show a bit of resolution so that, if there was a danger of invasion, it could be nullified.

6.4 The Treaty of Rapallo

Lloyd George loved conferences with their publicity and air of bustle. Poincaré did not. There had already been thirty peace conferences since the war.[15] But a new conference had already been arranged in April, at Genoa, before Poincaré returned to office, and Lloyd George had high

13. Sisley Huddleston. *Poincaré*. p.30.

14. Owen. *Tempestuous Journey*. Biography of Lloyd George. p.578, p.599. Also, A. J. Sylvestor. *The Real Lloyd George*.

15. Owen. *Tempestuous Journey*. p.595.

hopes for it. The British sent 92 delegates. Poincaré sent his vice-Premier. The Americans declined to take part.[16]

Lloyd George had hoped to score advantage for Britain, at the Conference, by encouraging Soviet Russia to ask for reparations from Germany. For their part the Germans were to promise not to trade with the Russians until they agreed to pay their war debts. The plan misfired. Under the Treaty of Rapallo 'impoverished' Germany not only waived all national claims against the Soviets, but also all private claims by German nationalists for compensation, provided that the Russians treated other claimants in the same way. Unsubstantiated rumours swept the Conference that the firm of Krupp had obtained the right to manufacture war materials in Russia.[17] The Allies came home empty-handed.

It was the rich, brilliant, Jewish, loner, Herr Rathenau, that had been pressurised by Baron von Maltzen to make his historic agreement with the Russians, in the greater interest of the Fatherland.[18] German industrialists had been determined to pre-empt any moves towards Allied rapprochement with the Communists. They were willing to throw everything into the battle for Russia's valuable friendship, including their citizens' Russian investments. The precedent that they established over non-repayment of Russian war debts would deal a crushing blow to the French and British Exchequers. But the blow to the German people was almost worse. The loss of their Russian investments, when their German investments were daily being reduced to waste paper, would embitter the German people.

6.5 Loss of Russian Investments

Despite Germany feeling rich enough to renounce all Governmental and private debt in Russia, when the time came for it to pay its next instalment of the reparations due on 31 May, it declared that it would need to borrow the money, once again, from its unhappy creditors, to meet its obligations. Americans on the Committee, such as Pierpont Morgan and Benjamin Strong, wished to see whether the reparations total, fixed just a year ago in May 1921, could not be reduced. Then at least one would not have the agony of trying to extract money from Germany. Britain

16. Owen. *Tempestuous Journey.* p.615.

17. *Annual Register.* 1922. p.164.
Eyck in *A History of the Weimar Republic* states that what they wanted to establish in Russia was an air force. p.205. See also Rabenau: Seeckt. p.308–9. 'Whenever our policy in the West has run aground it has always been wise to try something in the East.'

18. He boasted that he had figuratively 'raped Rathenau that night.' Blucher. Weg nach Rapallo. p.149. E. Eyck. *A History of the Weimar Republic.* p.207.

agreed.[19] Then, at last, Germany might agree to stabilise its currency and Britain could get her men back to work. But France refused. The debts incurred restoring Northern France were reaching alarming proportions and her population was baying for reimbursement. Meanwhile, German savers were not at all happy with seeing an elected member of their government renounce all their Russian investments, just when their own government bonds had fallen to such pitiful levels. Walther Rathenau had been blamed for the debasement of the German currency because, after telling American compeititors in 1920 that he intended to take advantage of the mark's depreciation and the resulting low German labour costs to reconquer export markets, he had put pressure on the government to continue with the debasement of the mark to 'keep unemployment under control.'[20] Helfferich, the former Secretary of State, publicly accused Rathenau of the 'pulverization of our middle class' by adopting a 'fulfilment' policy over the reparations, which had led to 'the frightful devaluation of German money'[21] while negating Germany's just claims in Russia.

The right-wing Press voiced their anger and frustration. Now that Herr Rathenau had done his job they seemed to feel that he could be made the scapegoat for any losses that the public incurred. 'Bolshevik', 'Traitor', 'Jew.' These epithets were hurled at Rathenau and on 24 July, two blue-eyed, blond-haired, Nordic-looking Germans, Kern and Fischer, took the law into their own hands and murdered him.[22]

The Police managed to corner the pair in Saarlack Castle, near Kosen, but were unable to question them. Kern was shot after a lively exchange of gunfire. Whereupon Fischer shot himself. Although the police had failed to extract any information from the culprits as to who else was involved in the shooting, the German Chancellor, Joseph Wirth, felt well enough informed to stand up in the Reichstag and put the blame firmly on the old guard and the reactionary Herr Helfferich. For he pointed at him and declared: 'The enemy stands on the right.'[23]

Later a monument would be erected by the Nazis at Saarlack Castle in memory of Herr Rathenau's heroic murderers.

Herr Rathenau's murder undermined political stability in Germany. Left-wingers redoubled their demands for the prosecution of the war offenders, Ludendorff and Hindenburg – and Karl Helfferich, the architect of Germany's inflationary policy, who was known to be openly pro-royalist.

19. *Annual Register*. 1922. p.165.
20. Stephen A. Schuker. *American 'Reparations' to Germany 1919–1933*. (1988) p.21.
21. Kessler. *Rathenau*. p.362. E. Eyck. *The Weimar Republic*. Vol. I. p.212.
22. E. Eyck. *The Weimar Republic*. Vol. I. p.213.
23. E. Eyck. *The Weimar Republic*. p.217.

Radicals were outraged by the sight of the old Imperial flag flying over a castle in Madgeburg. In reply to their demonstration against it, the castle's owner, Count Gneisenau, told his guards to open fire from the tower with rifles and a machine gun. They killed two men and a thirteen year old boy. The demonstrators fled but returned when they had armed themselves. They disarmed the outnumbered security police, who had been hurriedly called to the scene, removed their machine guns, grenades and rifles and used them to storm the barracks of the now discredited security police.[24] There was trouble in Singen and Baden too while in Berlin protestors broke the busts of Bismarck and von Moltke.[25]

This caused alarm in the currency markets. The mark shed fifty percent of its previous value in three weeks. On 12 July Germany asked the alarmed Allies for a moratorium on its reparations, not only for the current year but also for the years 1923 and 1924.[26] Also, ominously Germany now asked for a 75% reduction on its pre-war private loans. It was becoming more and more costly to avoid biting the bullet over the reparations.

6.6 Prosperity in Germany

On the same day that Germany had requested a moratorium on its reparations, T. Walter Williams, special correspondent of the *New York Times*, went to Germany to investigate the situation. Under a heading entitled: PROSPERITY SEEN IN GERMAN JOURNEY he declared that a German banker had told him that his country 'would continue to haggle with the Allies until they agreed to what Germany considers a reasonable amount.'

'If France still refused to listen to reason (so far France had not received any money at all in reparations) the mark would go lower and lower until it became worthless. Finally the currency would be 'washed out' and the government would be bankrupt as a nation, but not industrially or commercially.'

In his article T. Walter Williams did not stipulate what amount Germany would consider reasonable to pay but he did comment on the full shops in cities like 'Frankfurt-on-Oder, Berlin, Hanover, Dortmund,

---

24. *New York Times*. 6.7.22.
25. *New York Times*. 6.7.22.
26. *Annual Register*. 1922. p.165. E. Mantoux. *The Carthaginian Peace*. p.140.

Düsseldorf, Duren and Cologne, full of all kinds of pretty, luxurious things, including watches and jewellery' – and the absence of 'maimed men' in the streets. 'There is possibly some section where these cripples are but I have not seen them, nor the blind soldiers led about as they are in London and Paris by their relatives or friends.'

He was impressed by the clean and comfortable railway trains and he noticed 'that every sideline was occupied with freight trains loaded with all kinds of machinery, from ploughs to locomotives on the way to Russia, Denmark, and other countries. Goods to Turkey and Asia Minor, where they are forbidden to be imported, are shipped to Rotterdam, with French trade marks on them, and the same thing applies to Greece.'

> 'All through the Near East German goods can be seen for sale. British firms in Egypt are ordering machinery from Germany because it costs less than 50% of the price of the British made article ... Two thirds of the goods now imported into Palestine are being carried in German ships.'[27]

6.7 Devastation of British Industry

The exasperation and anger felt by the English business community over the persistent desire to let Germany off her debts when she was driving Britain out of business was summed up in a report in *The Times* on 18 April 1922:

> 'The greatest fraudulent conspiracy in the history of the world is now being enacted in Germany with the full concurrence and active support of its 60 or 70 millions of people. And this conspiracy is brazenly enacted under the very noses of the Allies. Germany is teeming with wealth. She is humming like a beehive. The comfort and prosperity of her people absolutely astound me. Poverty is practically non-existent. It is all the other way ... And yet this is the country that is determined she will not pay her debts ... They are a nation of actors ... If it wasn't for the fact that the German is guiltless of humour, one might imagine the whole nation was bent on perpetrating an elaborately laborious practical joke.'[28]

On 7 July 1922 Winston Churchill wrote a desperate plea to Lloyd George:

> 'Suppose we were confronted by tremendous importations from Germany at prices out of all relation to anything we could produce, and this was due to

27. *New York Times.* 10.7.22.
28. *The Times.* 18.4.22. Reprinted in *When Money Dies.* A Fergussen. 1975. p.81.

the extraordinary fall in the Mark, surely the remedy would be to proceed by embargo and licence until conditions become more normal. Embargo and licence are undoubtedly effective, whereas a trumpery 33% duty bears no relation to the present fluctuations of the exchange.'[29]

The devastation of British industry by German dumping in those post-war years has been compared to the physical devastation wrought by the retreating Germans in France in October 1918.

6.8 A Revision of the Treaty

John Maynard Keynes was not concerned with the devastation being caused to British industry, however, but with the hardship which the depreciation in the value of the mark was having on the lives of Germany's citizens, a depreciation which, in his new book on the reparations, entitled *A Revision of the Treaty*, he attributed not to internal German political and economic considerations but to the Allies' onerous reparations' demands. In *A Revision of the Treaty* Keynes estimated Germany's citizens' real income in 1920 at less than 6d. a day – 'the equivalent in purchasing power in England of something between 9d and 1s.' And he estimated that the reparations demands of the Allies would remove 50% of this pitiful amount.[30]

'Would the whips and scorpions of any Government recorded in history have been efficient to extract nearly half their income from a people so situated?' He protested emotively.[31]

However, 'Alpha' writing in the New York Times in September 1923 refuted Keynes's accusation.

'The statements of Mr. Keynes in A Revision of the Treaty up to now never refuted, are that the French claim as presented to the Reparations Commission was vast indeed, a fantastic exaggeration beyond anything which it would be possible to justify under cross-examination' and conceived in a spirit 'so grasping, faithless, and extravagantly unveracious as to defeat in the end its own objects ... were based on a mistake by Keynes in his method of exchange calculation and have no foundation in fact.'[32]

29. *Lloyd George Papers.* F/10/3/17.
30. E. Mantoux. *The Carthaginian Peace.* p.114.
31. J. M. Keynes. *A Revision of the Treaty.* (1922) p.84. Also, E. Mantoux. *The Carthaginian Peace.* p.114–15.
32. *New York Times.* 7.10.23.

The ordinary French people, slipping over the border to eat miraculously cheap cream cakes, agreed with him. They could not fail to marvel at the magnificent railway stations and public buildings of all kinds that were being erected in the Fatherland. Germany's infrastructure was being modernised with money that should have gone to France.

In his book *The Carthaginian Peace* or T*he Economic Consequence of Mr. Keynes*, written in 1945, the French economist, Etienne Mantoux, would complain bitterly of Keynes's mistake: 'It was with arithmetic of this calibre that the legend of a destitute Germany was engineered after 1918.'[33]

6.9 Strikes in Germany

It appears that the article in the New York Times entitled PROSPERITY SEEN IN GERMAN JOURNEY had not been telling the whole truth when it said that only the question of settling the reparations to its own personal satisfaction was holding up Germany's payments of her debts to the Allies. When he threatened that unless Germany received satisfaction 'the mark would go lower and lower until it became worthless. Finally the currency would be 'washed out' and the government would be bankrupt as a nation but not industrially or commercially', the 'Well-known' banker, to which the article referred, seemed to be sketching a scenario which had already been seriously contemplated.

There were two considerations which appeared to be affecting industrialists' reasoning. The first was the ever present background of Germany's unpaid internal debts. Those citizens with assets, like houses or land, had done well out of the Great Inflation but if Germany was shown not to be bankrupt its many citizens, who had lived on their savings before the war, would begin asking for the return of their money when Germany stabilised its currency.

The second consideration was summed up by Herr Stinnes, reputedly the richest of all Germany's industrialists:

> 'I do not hesitate to say that I am convinced that the German people will have to work two extra hours per day for the next ten or fifteen years ... The preliminary condition for any successful stabilisation is, in my opinion, that wage struggles and strikes be excluded for a long period..We must have the courage to say to the people: 'For the present and for some time to come you will have to work overtime without any payment.'[34]

33. E. Mantoux. *The Carthaginian Peace*. p.115.
34. Stinnes to National Economic Council. Oct. 1922. Part quoted in S. Taylor. *Germany 1918–33.*

1922 was a record year for strikes. Most of these disputes, however, were merely concerned with the workers wishing to maintain their standard of living in the face of the ever diminishing value of the mark. Up to now, although many pensioners and rentiers were destitute, those in work had more or less maintained the value of their take home pay. If the mark was stabilised, without national bankruptcy, the supporters of the right would be penniless while the supporters of the left still had money in their pockets, and the power that goes with money, to defy those who wished to rule them. For these reasons it appears that a 'washed out' currency and national bankruptcy was an attractive option for those who ruled Germany.

6.10   How Much Money Could Germany Pay?

The question of how much money Germany could pay was still a matter of intense argument amongst the Allies as Germany had largely succeeded in discrediting the Reparations Commission by abusing it from the start with inflammatory language.

The Germans had declared of the powers and intentions of that sober, painstaking body.

> 'German democracy is thus annihilated at the very moment when the German people were about to build it up after a severe struggle ... The Commission, which is to have its permanent headquarters outside Germany, will possess incomparably greater rights than the German Emperor ever possessed, German people under its regime would remain for decades shorn of all rights and deprived, to a far greater extent than any people in the days of absolutism, of any independence of action, of any individual aspiration in its economic or even in its ethical progress.'[35]

In view of the success of his books, Keynes's assertion that 'these comments were hardly an exaggeration' must have carried weight. Although Winston Churchill had commented on 7 July that the low rate of exchange for the mark was enabling German industry to drive British industry into the ground he must have been impressed by Keynes's hypothesis, later refuted by Mantoux and 'Alpha' of the *New York Times*, that German workers were excessively poorly paid. For he declared:

> 'I may add that I am very sceptical over the Germans being willing to embark on unprofitable exportations ..for any lengthy time. It is a pretty poor

35. E. Mantoux. *The Carthaginian Peace*. p.133.

business for a country to go on exchanging the work of a hundred men for a hundred hours in return for the work of seven men for seven hours, or something like that. Remember that it is the heart-beats of human energy that are exported, and drops of human sweat.'[36]

And, to add insult to injury Keynes alleged that the demands of the reparations took 50% of the Germans miserable pay. No wonder the sympathies of the British people started to stretch towards Germany.

6.11 Moratorium on Reparations

On 12 July Germany had asked for a moratorium on its reparation debts. No doubt mindful of this, the Americans hastened to remind their European 'associates' that they had been patiently waiting for them to start repaying capital and interest on the war debts due to them. It was time to put them on a proper basis.

On 1 August the famous Balfour note was issued. In it Britain offered to cancel many of the war debts owed to her. But Britain declared that, unless America let her off her American war debts, she had to ask her Allies to pay a sufficient amount to cover the repayment of those debts. Balfour was in fact asking America for a similar inter-Allied cancellation of debt as Keynes had in December 1919 in *The Economic Consequences of the Peace*.[37]

The idea had been firmly turned down by the Americans then and it was greeted with even more indignation now. Americans were furious at being dragged into European squabbles. They had withdrawn from the European scene which had caused them nothing but trouble and discord. But they had been magnanimous enough to wait until now before asking for some return on the money they had lent to Europe during the war. Now, at last, when the small shopkeepers, teachers, civil servants etc. who had loyally bought bonds to support the Allies' war effort, were looking forward to a return on their investment, the British were asking for cancellation. Even if their wish was not granted it was bound to lead to a further collapse in the bonds quoted value. The Americans were outraged.

Americans had also 'invested' 960,000,000 quality dollars, since the war, in what had turned out to be worthless German paper currency. If only, the many caring Americans of German extraction argued, the Allies had not insisted on those extortionate reparations, they could have

36. *Lloyd George Papers*. F/10/3/17.
37. *Annual Register*. 1922. p.93–4. For reaction in America – see. p.287.

Figure 6.2 The Debtors
© Punch

justified their investment and multiplied their money, not seen it degenerate into waste paper.[38] Americans were definitely not feeling rich any more. In September they would be bringing in their blanket tariff against foreign goods. The French were equally outraged by the Balfour note. Their anger is exemplified by Poincaré's reply:

'When Germany formulated her fresh demands for a moratorium, the British Government, without consulting France, publicly declared that the German wish should be granted, and at the same time England in a note reminded France that she was a debtor country. We were greatly surprised that a kind of eventual demand should be thus addressed to us at the very moment when Germany was announcing that she would not pay and when England was supporting Germany's demand. The coincidence was, to say the least, regrettable. If England required to be immediately paid for what France had purchased from her during war, and if, at the same time, she deferred the payment of reparations, she would reduce France to the necessity of turning to those of her Allies who were her debtors, and thus France would be invited to recover from Italy, Rumania and Serbia the sums demanded which she was not allowed to recover from Germany. I need not say that we could not allow ourselves to be placed in such a strange position. We are not dreaming of calling upon our Allies to pay at this moment. We want to recover our bill against Germany first. Until we do, it is morally and physically impossible for us to discharge our debt to our British friends, and they will understand that we on our side do not wish to dun our common friends.'[39]

In reply to Germany's demand for a moratorium, Poincaré demanded sanctions – Allied control of Germany's finances, its foreign currency, its export licences, revenues from forests and mines, a 60% share of some of its factories, a customs barrier etc.[40] As the Germans were allowed to pay monetary reparations in the form of Treasury Bills for the rest of the year they technically met the terms of the Treaty of Versailles.[41] However, as the mark continued to plummet the Belgians would not be happy for long with being paid in depreciating paper. If Germany shortchanged them in deliveries of coal or timber they would be happy to support drastic action.

6.12 Violation of Neutral Zone by Turkish Troops

The reparations' issue was coming to a head. Lloyd George could avoid

38. *Annual Register*. 1922. p.288.
39. Sisley Huddleston. *Poincaré*. p.133.
40. *Royal Institute of International Affairs Survey*. 1920–23. p.180.
41. E. Mantoux. *The Carthaginian Peace*. p.140.

it no longer. Germany was in default of its reparations' obligations and it was menacing Britain's trade. There is evidence that Lloyd George was even worried about Germany renewing military hostilities against Great Britain. Although he had been reassured by his private secretary M.P.A. Hankey on the 27 July, that Sir Auckland Geddes's 'tale of a projected (German) aeroplane and poison gas attack on London'[42] was not possible, Lloyd George had been sufficiently perturbed to make extensive enquiries from the astonished armed forces as to its feasibility.

So he tried to forget the Germans by concentrating his mind upon the Turks. During the war he had sought to defeat 'Prussian militarism' by undermining the fighting spirit of its ally Turkey. On 4 August 1922 Lloyd George prepared the world for another Eastern adventure by giving such fulsome praise to the fighting qualities of the Greeks in Asia Minor that the Greek High Command sought fit to reproduce it in their *Order of the Day.*

'I do not know of any army that would have gone as far as the Greeks have gone. It was a very daring and a very dangerous military experiment. They established a military superiority in every pitched battle.' enthused Lloyd George.[43]

Lord Ronaldshay commented on this speech in his book on Curzon:

'It was at this psychological moment, when the suspicions of the Turks as to the next move by Greece were thoroughly aroused, that Mr. Lloyd George's evil genius prompted him to make a speech which, in the circumstances of the time, could only be regarded by Greeks and Turks alike as an encouragement to the former to seek a decision by force.

'Whatever may have been Mr. Lloyd George's object in making his speech there is not the smallest doubt as to its effect. Both in Athens and in Angora it was interpreted as a thinly veiled invita tion to Greece to renew the struggle.'[44]

Lloyd George must have been happy that the speed with which events developed in the Middle East saved him from having to take sides in the ominous developments in Europe.

Lord Curzon had not been consulted about the Greeks and the Turks when the Allies had discussed carving up Asia Minor in 1919. He did not share Lloyd George's admiration for Greece's fighting prowess.

'Was it to be believed' he asked 'that the Greeks who cannot keep order five miles outside the gates of Salonika would be allowed contentedly to occupy and administer a great city like Smyrna or a province like Aidin?'[45]

42. *Lloyd George Papers.* F/26/28.
43. Owen. *Tempestuous Journey.* p.632.
44. Ronaldshay. *Life of Lord Curzon.* p.298–9.
45. Ronaldshay. *Life of Lord Curzon.* p.265–6.

His worst fears were realised when, twenty two days after Lloyd George's much publicised remarks, the Turkish army fell on the Greeks. The retreat of the Greek army quickly became a rout. Despite British ships lying in the bay, the Turks burnt Smyrna to the ground and every Greek man, woman or child who had not managed to climb aboard a ship to escape, was massacred. Then the Turks turned north towards the areas round the Dardanelle Straits, an area declared neutral under the Peace agreement and protected by a force of Allied troops.[46]

Lloyd George decided to send a communiqué announcing his cabinet's intentions to reinforce the troops at the disposal of Sir Charles Harrington, the Allied Commander in Chief in the Mediterranean, with orders to oppose any infringement of the neutral zones by the Turks. The dominions were horrified to read in the Press, before hearing a word from the British Government, that their countries had been asked to take part in a military action against the Turks.[47] The French were adamant that they were not going to take part. A hasty consultation in Paris looked like finding a formula to settle the matter with the Turks by negotiation. Then a revolution occurred in Greece and King Constantine fled the country.[48] The Turkish troops under their leader, Mustafa Kemal, violated the neutral zone. General Harrington was ordered to send an ultimatum. Had it been delivered war might have resulted. But General Harrington chose to ignore it.[49] The British people by this time were thoroughly incensed by the so-called Chanak affair that it led to the collapse of the government. The Labour Party had always believed that all leaders of governments were imperialists anyway. Now more Conservative folk were beginning to share their convictions.

Bonar Law was a tired sick man when he rescued the Conservative Party from the utter extinction of being identified with Lloyd George's imperialistic adventures in the Autumn of 1922.[50] The chain-smoking ex-metal merchant had only been a compromise leader of the Conservative Party in 1911.[51] His party had not held office independently for twenty two years. It was, additionally, bereft of nearly all its nationally known figures. They had stayed with Lloyd George. The *Daily Express* drew a penline sketch of Lloyd George's new home in Vincent Square.

46. *Annual Register*. 1920. Gives Allied peace terms for Turkey. p.239.
47. Ronaldshay. *Life of Lord Curzon*. p.302. Owen. *Tempestuous Journey*. p.637–40.
48. Ronaldshay. *Life of Lord Curzon*. p.305.
49. Owen. *Text of Communiqué*. p.640. General Harrington's dispatch giving his reasons for ignoring it. p.651.
50. R. Blake. *Bonar Law. The Unknown Prime Minister*. p.455.
51. *Dictionary of National Biography*.

6.13   Germans Taunt the Allies

It was necessary for him to stay there for more than the few weeks envisaged by the Daily Express. The Germans were taunting the Allies again. On 13 November, the German government declared that the mark could only be stabilised if their country was released from all reparations' payments for the next three or four years.[52]

The Allies could not declare Germany in default on its monetary payments as Belgium had accepted paper instead of gold in the Autumn. However, on 26 December 1922 the Commission declared by a vote of three to one that Germany was in default on its deliveries of timber.[53]

On 9 January the Reparations Commission again by a vote of three to one declared Germany in default of her deliveries of coal.

On 11 January French and Belgian troops occupied the Ruhr.[54]

Many outside observers in Britain and America were to view France's invasion and long quest for surrender as an act of revenge. Had not Keynes's prediction of 'inevitable default' been accurately realised? Had not the Treaty 'reduced Germany to servitude' and 'perpetuated its economic ruin'? This was not how the *Times Financial and Commercial Review* viewed it. Under the heading RECOVERY DESPITE EXCHANGE the Times correspondent reported that 'despite continuous currency degradation, with the inconvenience to State finance and to the individual which currency degradation brings' he noted 'a general and marked recovery in all branches of industry and trade. Here 1922 was a repetition of the three preceding postwar years; but in 1922 the currency collapse was more extreme, and the general economic recovery, as shown by statistics of employment, production, foreign trade, shipping, and all other registers of movements of real values was more pronounced.'

The correspondent concluded by saying:

'To superficial students this contrast appears almost as a paradox. The theory of the German 'catastrophe' (so-called) which appears in the Press and comes from the mouths of experts during and immediately after every heavy mark-exchange decline is based on the assumption that the aggravation of currency conditions inevitably brings (or results from) an aggravation in real economic substance. But without impugning the doctrine that worse currency may, and sometimes does, accompany worse economic conditions, it must be repeated that 1922, witnessing as it did, an unexampled decline in

---

52. E. Mantoux. *The Carthaginian Peace*. p.140.
53. E. Mantoux. *The Carthaginian Peace*. p.140–1.
54. E. Mantoux. *The Carthaginian Peace*.

the foreign exchange and home purchasing power of the Reichsmark, witnessed simultaneously national recovery in every other economic domain.'[55]

Poincaré had hoped, wrongly, initially as it turned out, that many of the disaffected, socialist workers in those enormous German factories would cooperate with the French invaders to reduce the power of the industrialists. He appealed to the local population before he invaded the Ruhr, when he explained to them on 21 December 1922:

'We want these goods, and others which you have, to serve as guarantees for your unpaid debts, and also as means for bringing pressure to bear on your great manufacturers, I mean those persons who are acquiring great wealth in Germany at the expense of the people itself.'

These hopes were not realised initially. There was alarm in Britain at the prospect of quality Westphalian coal being united with France's vast stock of iron ore. Because of Britain's faith in Keynes and the equation of a strong currency with a strong nation economically, most Britons perceived Germany as no longer a power to tremble over. It was the prospect of France's vast conscript army being used in Germany (despite Poincaré's protestations to the contrary) that alarmed the British. J.R. Morgan late adjutant General on the Inter-Allied Military Commission of Control in Germany and an opponent of the French invasion however declared:

'Although my judgement is for the British point of view, my sympathy to a considerable extent is for the French' and tried to explain to the sceptical British, France's apparently aggressive insistence on her reparations' rights when the defaults on Germany's timber and coal deliveries had reportedly been so minor. 'In the course of my inspections of the Army units, I hardly ever found a strength return, a 'rank-list,' a nominal roll, an attestation form, or a pay-sheet which I could trust, and the experience of all the officers serving under me was the same.'[56]

6.14 Memorandum to Treaty of Versailles

The Allies had added a memorandum to the Treaty of Versailles in 1919:

'Only on the firm basis of justice is a settlement possible after this frightful war. The German delegates demand justice and call upon us to do justice to

55. *The Times*. (Annual and Commercial Review) 30.1.23.
56. J. R. Morgan. *The Present State of Germany*. p.82–3.

Germany. Germany shall have justice. But it must be justice towards all, to the dead, the wounded, the orphans, to all who today are wearing the garb of mourning, that Europe may be freed from the domination of Prussia. To save freedom the nations have piled up a war debt of thirty thousand million. Those who stagger beneath its burden must receive justice. So too must those millions whose lands, homes, vessels or goods have been ruined, wrecked or pillaged by German ruthlessness ...

'And for the same reason Germany must for several years be subjected to special restrictions and arrangements. Germany has destroyed her neighbours' factories, mines and industries, not in the course of fighting but in the execution of a deliberate plan aimed at securing the market of these nations before their industries can recover from the damage inflicted in cold blood. ... Someone must suffer from the results of the war. Who is it to be? Germany or the nations on whom she has brought such suffering?

'... if nations like individuals are to be made subject to law, if there is to be any possibility of reconciliation and appeasement in the near future, those responsible for making peace must have the courage to uphold justice in her austere purity and not sacrifice her for the advantage of an easy-going agreement.'[57]

So far justice had been sacrificed 'for the advantage of an easy-going agreement' but Poincaré hoped that by taking a firm line now France would escape receiving 'no reparations' and demonstrate to her former vanquished foe of October 1918 President Wilson's maxim that causing deliberate destruction, such as Germany had inflicted on France's mines and industry on her retreat in 1918, does not pay.

Bonar Law, already hoarse with throat cancer, could not allow his weak and divided party to support the French when he had been elected on the specific pledge of avoiding overseas adventures but he was too good an economist to be anything but aware of the interest Britain had in the debt situation. Britain had succeeded in balancing her Budget only by submitting her industry and population to an unprecedented load of taxation. Britain's trade, indeed, had suffered worse than both the supposedly impoverished nations, Germany and France. The French government had resolutely advanced the money to their industries to rebuild and re-equip their factories even though, as yet, they had received no reimbursement. The overtaxed British factories, labouring under an uncompetitive rate of exchange, had been spared no profits for reinvestment. Bonar Law wished the French well in their effort to bring Germany to justice.

'His Majesty's government, after giving the most urgent consideration to the French proposals, are definitely of the opinion that these proposals, if carried into effect, will not only fail in obtaining the desired results, but are likely to

57. F. W. Foerster. *Europe and the German Question.* p.255–7.

have a grave and even disastrous result upon the economic situation ii
Europe, and in these circumstances they cannot take part in or accept respon
sibility for them. His Majesty's government at the same time, desire to assun
the Government of the Republic that while they regret extremely that then
should be an irreconcilable difference of opinion on a subject so serious, th
feeling of friendship not only on the part of the British government but als
as I believe of the British people towards the Government and people o
France remains unchanged.'[58]

58. *Annual Register.* 1923. p.3.

–7–

Passive Resistance

7.1 Introduction

Spurred on by the Belgians who had accepted what turned out to be waste-paper in the form of Treasury Bonds, in August 1922, instead of demanding gold, the French who had received no money at all[1] marched into the Ruhr.

The Germans promised passive resistance. Meanwhile the Americans made haste to recover their debts from the one country apparently still solvent in Europe, Britain.

They had chosen their moment well. It is curious how a high rate of exchange makes a country's citizens feel prosperous, self-righteous, full of largesse. Up on the Clyde the ship berths might remain empty, the equipment unmodernised through excessive taxation and an uncompetitive rate of exchange, but down in London there was still money enough for a day at the races and an evening table at Claridges with champagne. Abstemious economist Bonar Law, aware of how the country had undergone a crippling experience to pay for such days of pleasure, had no wish to add extra burdens to overtaxed industry and working people: 'I am convinced that to make that payment without receiving anything from outside sources would reduce the standard of living in this country for a generation.'[2]

However, Stanley Baldwin, newly promoted Chancellor of the Exchequer of this fragile, unrated Parliament, felt that Britain was duty bound to pay her war debts. He was aware of Britain's crushing burden of internal debt and had personally donated 20% of his capital after the war to diminish its burden[3] – and yet Britain was the banking capital of the world with millions of pounds lent world wide which needed to be repaid. Small investors who had lately found gilt-edged stocks a much

1. Menscheit. 10.3.23. Director of the Darmstadt and National Bank. Berlin.
2. H. A. Taylor. *The Strange Case of Bonar Law*. p.270.
3. *Dictionary of National Biography*. 41–50. p.43.

better investment than industrial shares, agreed with him. Bonar Law threatened to defy his party or resign: 'If I sign the terms suggested at Washington I shall be the most cursed man in England.'

But he allowed himself to be over-ruled. He was visibly ailing. His voice was already nearly inaudible, cancer gripped his throat, four months later he would be compelled to retire. Meanwhile through his patronage the Conservatives clung to power, each day giving them strength. Bernard Baruch, however, viewing Britain's crippled industrial base and her unpaid debts from the war, would state that Britain's sincere efforts to pay her war debts had been made 'at a cost almost impossible for others to realise ...'[4]

Meanwhile the French who had told the Americans that they could not pay their war debts until they had received compensation from Germany, took practical steps to recover the raw materials that they were entitled to.

7.2   France Demands Compensation from Germany

Poincaré had planned a low key intervention, a small band of engineers with minimal backing (MICUM) would come like bailiffs and take productive pledges of Germany's good intent. Initially it appeared as though this approach was going to achieve results. Rumours circulated that the socialists were about to eject the new Chancellor, Herr Cuno, a man widely regarded as the industrialist's pawn, and do a deal with the French.

The *Herald Tribune* reported on 17 January:

> 'Chancellor Cuno's ministerial ship is sinking. The flag of defiance to France still flies at the masthead but the craft itself is virtually a derelict. There is every indication the Cuno Cabinet will collapse within two weeks. A Socialist-Centrist coalition, with former President Mueller, new socialist leader in the Reichstag, as its probable Chancellor, will no doubt take the helm of government. The new administration will lose no time in re-opening negotiations with France and bringing pressure to bear on the industrialists to force through a compromise acceptable to Paris.'[5]

However attitudes soon hardened when the Germans were reassured that both the British and Americans had turned their backs on Europe. German newspapers had no difficulty in whipping up the patriotism of the German nation against the invading French. Even though many

4. Sarah Gertrude Millin. *General Smuts*. Vol. 2. p.201.
5. *New York Times*. 17.1.23.

people still loathed the government which had presided over the loss of their savings, when they were asked to stop work and refuse to send iron and coal to France while still receiving their wages, they responded to the call of patriotism:

> 'Dr. Grimm who appeared as attorney for the coal barons and Herr Thyssen who came to the car window in every town ... led the crowd in the singing of Deutschland uber alles.'[6]

The German government built on this support by offering to pay the salaries of any German official who would not cooperate with the French. But coercion was also used to reinforce patriotism. Those who refused to support what came to be known as passive resistance were threatened with severe penalties. Germany did not increase her army to cope with any planned disturbances but ex-army officers, in marked contrast to British army officers, now the heroes of the republic, flocked in numbers to offer their help. Thus the so-called 'Black army' was formed[7] to ensure that 'resistance.'

7.3 France's Military Occupation

The French soon had to increase the initially small military force they had sent into the Ruhr, with the Commission of Engineers, and the military had the unenviable task of requisitioning lorries etc., from a resentful local population, to carry the precious coal to France. On 31 March a small band of soldiers, with two machine guns, occupied a garage owned by Krupps at Essen and attempted to requisition a lorry. A large group of workers gathered outside the factory to protest at this action. After some hours of impasse a machine gun opened fire on the workers killing thirteen of them and wounding thirty more. The French disclaimed all responsibility for the action, saying that the workers had been incited by the management to impede the French. Eight directors, including the volunteer, Krupp von Bolen und Halbach, himself, were put on trial and condemned to long terms of imprisonment. The workers, however, were outraged and in a collective statement accused the occupying French of massacre and of attempting to turn free labourers into slaves.[8]

Not only were they being turned into slaves by the reparations'

6. *New York Times.* 18.1.23.
7. E. Eyck. *The Weimar Republic.* p.239.
8. *New York Times.* 26.1.23.

demands, but it was claimed they were also becoming malnourished, as was vividly described by the President of the Department of Health in the Reichstag in February 1923:

'The height to which prices have climbed may be shown by the fact that as of February 15th, wholesale prices have risen on the average to 5,967 times the peacetime level, those of foodstuffs to 4,902 times, and those for industrial products to 7,958 times. Meat consumption has fallen from 52 kilograms per person in 1912 to 26 kilograms per person in 1922 ... For many people, meat has become altogether a rarity. A million and a half German families are inadequately provided with fuel ... The provision of linen and clothing becomes daily more difficult ... There are complaints of the appearance of scurvy, which is a consequence of an unbalanced and improper diet ... Now all this misery is doubly and cruelly sharpened in those parts of the Fatherland which have already been subjected to foreign occupation for four years, but more particularly for the inhabitants of the Ruhr region, which has recently been invaded by French and Belgian troops in violation of the peace treaty of Versailles.'[9]

This emotive statement struck a chord with the American farm lobby, needy for customers for its bulging grain stocks. The great war had left an indelible mark on the American people which had manifested itself in excessive nationalism. Americans had poured their money into Europe. They had come over to save the Allies from destruction, but, six years after the war had ended, Europeans were still bleating for American dollars to bale them out. Meanwhile a good customer for agricultural produce was in danger of being lost to America because of the reparations' issue. Banners of the *American Legion* blazed with the headings: 'Real American money for American people, we are not unreasonable only patriotic.' Legalists supported the right of France to enter Germany to recover her debts. But in a major article on 17 January 1923 entitled 'Hands off' will rule American policy in the Ruhr' the editor of the *New York Times* affirmed that the anti-interventionist majority were beginning to lose support:

'In point of fact much of that support has been broken up by the feeling of what the politicians call the 'church people.' Most recently an even larger defection has been caused by the farmers coming suddenly to believe that their economic salvation is dependant on a stabilised Europe.'[10]

7.4   Neutral Benevolence Towards the French

Bonar Law, the Conservative Prime Minister, had pursued a policy of

9. Tony Howarth. *20th Century History.* (BBC 1979) p.53.
10. *New York Times.* 17.1.23.

neutral benevolence towards French actions in Germany but his cancer visibly weakened him during the Spring of 1923. Lord Curzon, his heir apparent, was a great expert on the Near East but less knowledgeable about France and Germany.

Curzon had become a member of the war cabinet after Lloyd George became Secretary of State for War in July 1916. Postwar he had shared Lloyd George's political reservations over supporting France's determination to secure her reparations and showed no inclination to censure the Germans.

But his distaste for the French was personal as well as political. He had already suffered a humiliation at the hands of Poincaré over France's resolve not to become involved at Chanak. Harold Nicolson in his biography of Curzon describes the occasion:

'Lord Curzon in cutting phrases, summarised the disloyalty of the French during the last two years, of which the betrayal of their British comrades behind the wire entanglement of Chanak was but the final culmination ... M. Poincaré responded to the attack. His voice was dry, his words were clipped, his insults were lancets of steel. Curzon's wide white hands upon the green baize cloth trembled violently. He could stand it no further. Rising from his seat he muttered something about an adjournment and limped hurriedly into the adjoining room ... He collapsed upon a scarlet settee. He grasped Lord Hardinge by the arm. 'Charley', he panted, 'I can't bear that horrid little man. I can't bear him. I can't bear him.
  'He wept.'[11]

This was not a humiliation that he would easily forget. Besides he was sure that it was France's occupation of the Ruhr and general obdurance over the reparations that was ruining Britain's industry. He took advantage of Bonar Law's declining health to encourage Germany to make another offer to the Allies over the reparations' issue.

In the same debate, Lord Grey, formerly Foreign Secretary in 1914, showed his deeper understanding of the problem by stressing that French desires for reparations sprang from fears for their security:

'With a people as numerous as the Germans, and increasing, and as efficient as the Germans, the question of security in the course of ten or twenty years is a very real and anxious one for France, and must be so.'[12]

On 2 May new German proposals arrived at the Allies' desk but were summarily rejected. Even Lord Curzon felt let down by the proposals. The Germans had made a derisory unguaranteed offer, encumbered with

11. Harold Nicolson. *Curzon. The Last Phase*. p.274.
12. E. Eyck. *The Weimar Republic*. Vol. I. p.244.

Figure 7.1 Lord Curzon
'He (Curzon) grasped Lord Hardinge by the arm. 'Charley' he panted, 'I can't bear that horrid little man (Poincaré). I can't bear him.' He wept.'
Harold Nicolson. Curzon. The Last Phase.
© Hulton Deutsch

numerous conditions, all devised to further diminish its value. Furthermore the offer was not humbly offered as if by a penitent and defeated nation, but accompanied arrogantly by a threat to continue passive resistance.

> 'Until those territories which have been occupied without the authority of the Treaty of Versailles are evacuated and until conditions which are in conformity with the treaty are re-established in the Rhineland.'[13]

Poincaré pounced on this statement as evidence that the passive resistance was not spontaneous, but engineered, and could be stopped at will. There would be no dialogue with the Germans, he insisted, unless all passive resistance ceased. But he had chosen a bad moment to stand up to Germany since to be successful against such a strong country, he needed the support of his wartime Ally on the other side of the channel.

Unfortunately for Poincaré, however, the political scene in Britain was in disarray. On 21 May ill health forced Bonar Law to resign. Against all the odds, Stanley Baldwin was made Prime Minister.

7.5 Baldwin Returns as Prime Minister

On 30 May, the ubiquitous Keynes, now besides contributing to the *Manchester Guardian*, writing for the liberal organ, *The Nation*, and syndicating his articles all over the world, expressed his desire to see the new Prime Minister, explaining:

> 'I have something I want badly to ask you. I have had certain communications with Germany in the last few days.'[14]

In August 1922, when Germany had secured virtually a moratorium on the payment of reparations for the year, the *Daily Telegraph* had observed that Keynes's remarks 'are reported in the German Press at a length and with a prominence which is usually reserved for the heads of a government.'[15] So the new, inexperienced Baldwin sought the advice of the expert on the reparations.

Keynes apparently was of the opinion that the British Exchequer was a bottomless pit and he advised the Prime Minister to give more financial

13. The French and the Belgians observed of this note: 'The German note, from beginning to end, is nothing but the scarcely-veiled expression of a systematic revolt against the Treaty of Versailles.' Royal Institute of International Affairs Survey. 1924. p.326.

14. Baldwin Papers. Middlemas and Barnes. *Baldwin*. p.180–1.

15. R. Harrod. *Life of J. M. Keynes*. p.317.

Peace without Victory for the Allies

concessions to the French so they would allow the Germans to substantially reduce their reparations.

On 7 June, Germany made a new offer. Again the amount offered was derisory but this time it was, at least, not waste paper but based on the interest received on gold bonds, to be secured against state railways and property. This appealed to the British. But the main contention of the Germans in offering this sum was that they had proved that they were bankrupt and they wanted a new committee of experts to prove it. They asserted that 'the question of Germany's capacity to pay was after all a question of fact' and they offered, needless to say, 'to furnish all the materials for a trustworthy of German capacity.'[16]

The French were not impressed. One much maligned commission of experts had already investigated, at length, Germany's capacity to pay. Besides Germany had not even agreed to give up passive resistance. If Germany did that, the French declared, there might be a fresh 'constructive' attempt at a solution of the reparations' problem.[17] They were not eager to make concessions to Germany over the amount to be paid in reparations. However, they repeated a former proposition they had made to the British. The reparations had been divided into A B & C Bonds. The French were prepared to relinquish their C Bonds against their payment of war debts to Britain, if Britain wanted to let Germany off paying some of her reparations.[18]

This proposal did not go down well with the British Treasury. So far the A & B Bonds had born little fruit. As the C Bonds were only to be issued when the Reparations Commission was satisfied that German payments were sufficient to meet the interest and sinking fund on the A & B Bonds, the C Bonds had always been deemed to be of little value.[19] Britain felt that France was merely trying to wriggle out of her war debt obligations. If other Allies followed France's lead, Britain feared that she would end up paying for the whole war.

In their reply to Germany's note of 7 June the French and the Belgians had talked of making 'constructive' proposals if the Germans abandoned passive resistance. As they had not disclosed what these might be the British retorted to their war debt proposal with a 'questionnaire.'[20] Meanwhile the mark continued to plummet.

On 3 and 6 July the French and Belgians made their official replies to the questionnaire maintaining that the occupation of the Ruhr was legal

16. *Royal Institute of International Affairs Survey.* 1924. p.326–7.
17. *Royal Institute of International Affairs Survey.* 1924. p.327.
18. *Royal Institute of International Affairs Survey.* p.328.
19. Middlemas & Barnes. p.183. *Niemeyer.* 'The notion that we should cancel the Allied debts against worthless C Bonds is fantastic.'
20. *Royal Institute of International Affairs Survey.* p.328.

and that the provisions of the Treaty of Versailles remained sacrosanct.

The new premier, Baldwin, had wished to continue Bonar Law's policy of benevolent neutrality towards France but he had only managed to become Prime Minister primarily because the senior, much more experienced, favourite for the job, Lord Curzon, was a member of the House of Lords.

Lord Curzon remained Foreign Minister and resented interference. He had convinced himself of the Treasury line that France was selfishly destroying everyone's hopes of getting reparations and normal trading through her invasion.

> 'As long as the most highly developed area of German industrial life remains under military rule, and is made the scene of political agitation, it is difficult to see how the economic problem can be solved. It may be possible to break Germany's power of resistance by such means; but it will be at the price of the very recovery on which the Allied policy depends for its ultimate success.'[21]

Lord Curzon did not at this stage suggest a rupture with France, however. The Treasury team were more vociferous. The Treasury figures of Leith-Ross, Bradbury, Warren Fisher and Niemeyer comprised a formidable team. Niemeyer had had an even more illustrious academic career than Keynes, defeating the latter by over 400 points in the civil service exams.[22] The new Prime Minister, Baldwin, had only achieved a third in history at Cambridge and was much influenced by Treasury deliberations on what appeared to be a highly technical matter.[23]

Warren Fischer declared that Britain would only concur with French demands for ceasing passive resistance: '(a) in the teeth of our conviction that the French are acting illegally and madly, (b) in the certainty that it will encourage the French to further folly, (c) with the high probability of collapse in Germany (and where then would be reparations?) (d) above all, in the certainty of eventual rupture with France when the time comes for us to refuse any longer to be tied to the wheels of a chariot which is dashing towards a precipice.'[24]

The financial ramifications, however, had disguised the fact that the question was in essence not an economic one at all but a practical and moral dilemma, whether to secure the 'unconditional surrender' of Germany which the Allies had failed to demand at the end of the war, or to try and browbeat the French into a policy of appeasement.

21. Despatch from Lord Curzon to the Conte de Sainte Aulaire. Ronaldshay. *Life of Lord Curzon.* II. p.356.
22. R. Skidelsky. *J. M. Keynes*. p.175.
23. *Dictionary of National Biography*. Baldwin. p.43.
24. Baldwin Papers. Middlemas and Barnes. *Baldwin*. p.183.

The Treasury may have been afraid of the Germans but they also had a lively respect for Keynes. Keynes had been runner-up to the future Sir Otto Niemeyer in the civil service exams seventeen years previously but as a postwar economic publicist he had proved himself second to none. In *The Economics of the Peace* venom, anger, outrage, and caricature had epitomised the pages that had been read by an estimated quarter of a million people. Even tame statistics of continental coal concentrations were impregnated with emotion. His words had an international following. And he had predicted as long ago as 1919 the very state which the German people would be reduced to if the Allies persisted with their reparations' policy.

Small wonder then that Warren Fischer, speaking in a highly charged manner very reminiscent of Keynes, insisted that, if Britain allowed herself to be dictated to by the French over the matter of passive resistance, she would be treating the Treaty of Versailles as a 'scrap of paper.'[25] Keynes had declared the reparations' clauses of the Treaty to be 'impossible, unfair and disastrous.' Gradually, the Treasury and a great body of men, the Liberals, the City, the Labour party had come to agree with him. Only the 'die-hards' remained, Baldwin's Conservative right.

7.6 British Politicians Split Over Ruhr Occupation

Lord Curzon's response to the French and Belgian notes of 3 and 6 July was to try and isolate them in international opinion, by circulating a note to the four other Allied governments concerned, stating his view that if passive resistance was abandoned, a new 'impartial' body should be constituted to look into Germany's capacity to pay the reparations. As soon as this was constituted the occupation of the Ruhr should end.[26]

Much alarmed by this course of events Poincaré made a desperate plea for the British to see matters his way. He argued that there was a precedent for his action in occupying the Ruhr until France's indemnity had been paid.

France, was, after all, merely utilising the methods employed by Germany in 1871 which had produced such excellent results. Nobody then had tried to prevent the Germans from remaining in occupation of large parts of France until the indemnity was paid.

The *Daily Mail* reported Poincaré's speech:

'The French government agrees with the British government in its view that

25. Baldwin Papers. Middlemas and Barnes. *Baldwin*. p.184.
26. Ronaldshay. *Life of Lord Curzon*. III. p.357.

Germany ought to restore its credit, stabilise its currency, balance its budget and encourage its production. This is the advice that the Allies have been giving Germany since 1920 but all in vain. But Germany, on the contrary, has ... disdained all advice, and has reversed all principles of political economy consecrated by experience. Her present state of ruin is not consequent upon the occupation of the Ruhr, but is the work of Germany itself.'[27]

The British nation was dividing slowly down the middle over the issue. On the one hand was Lloyd George, Curzon with his supporters in the Treasury, Asquith, the left and the compassionate centre – and on the other hand, the 'die-hards', right-wing relics of the war, who disregarded the pleas of hardship from the Germans and supported the 'vengeful' French.

Indeed the die-hards did appear to be extreme in their views; witness, for instance, the outlook of the Earl of Pembroke and Montgomery, Chancellor of the Primrose League, the grass-root Tory organisation:

'The I.L.P. the Socialist organisation which controls the Labour Party, has organised a national campaign to strengthen the position of the Labour Party at the next election ... Yet people are apt to forget the disgraceful 'pro-Germanism' of the I.L.P. during the Great War and they do not realise the possible consequences of supporting a party led by men devoted to the promotion of German interests and aims.

'At the moment, the whole of the forces of the Socialists and Communists are ranged on the German side. The Entente with France is hated, and the Labour Party leaders would do almost anything to destroy it and to bring this country round to the support of Germany against France. They will not forgive the Allies for beating 'our German comrades' and the Labour Party is now committed to a policy which would enable Germany to escape reparation for the war, and would end in the scrapping of the Versailles Treaty.

'If the Labour Party would pay as much attention to the interests and welfare of the British workers as it pays to German interests it would be a useful instead of being, as it is at present, a mischievous party. I trust Conservatives and Primrose Leaguers will oppose the Labour Party on every possible occasion, not only on account of its Socialist aims, but because it is the enemy of our friends and the friend of our enemies.'[28]

Despite these strong words, however, Baldwin's struggling government of 'second-class' brains, as defined by Lord Birkenhead, seemed less afraid of the emerging Labour Party than of the danger represented by Lloyd George's attitude over the reparations. Lloyd George was in danger of splitting the Conservative Party, as he had previously split the Liberals. Despite right-wing suspicions of Germany, suspicions of France had lasted longer, since Napoleon, and were more deep rooted in

27. *Daily Mail.* 3.8.23.
28. *The Times.* 11.2.23.

British minds. The Conservative hierarchy did not wait to find out if Lloyd George was to be allowed an election platform for his anti-French stance on his forthcoming lecture tour of America. They disregarded their 'die-hards' and accepted the advice of the civil service who advised brow-beating the French.

In spite of Germany's gross default on her obligations, therefore, British legal experts decided to disregard precedents such as 15 November 1920 when an agreement had been signed, not only by the French but also by the then Chancellor of Germany, Herr Fehrenrenbach, his Foreign Secretary, Dr. Simons, and Lloyd George, to occupy the Ruhr if coal deliveries were not forthcoming.

7.7 Britain Bleeding to Death

On 11 August Lord Curzon made Great Britain's response to Poincaré's notes of 6 July and 30 July over the reparations' issue.[29] In a note, whose contents were published all over the world, he declared that Britain was bleeding to death from her wartime and postwar burdens; she was outraged by the French and Belgians allegedly trying to take more of the reparations than those originally allocated and refusing to pay Britain their war debts over which Britain had already been prepared to make such extensive concessions. Britain could not be more generous to France and Belgium if she had to pay such sizeable war debts. Besides his government had been told on the highest legal authority that France's occupation of the Ruhr was illegal.

His words were tinged with bitterness at the unenviable economic load that Britain was already carrying and the lack of understanding and generosity on the part of the French.

'Apart from the extensive material damages suffered by Great Britain, His Majesty's Government are now involved in heavy payments to meet unemployment in respect of which they have been compelled to spend over £400,000,000 since the armistice. They alone, among the Allies are paying interest on debts incurred abroad during the war, representing a capital sum due to the United States Government of £1000,000,000 at the present rate of exchange. They alone have been deprived in the Allied interest, of foreign

29. *Royal Institute of International Affairs Survey.* The French had answered the 'questionnaire' maintaining their refusal to parley with the Germans until passive resistance had been abandoned and then to adhere to the terms as laid down in the Treaty of Versailles. Curzon's reply to this had been to circulate a memo to the other countries involved, suggesting that if passive resistance was abandoned, a new body of experts would look into Germany's capacity to pay. Afraid of being isolated France offered Britain her C Bonds. In reply Curzon made his famous speech of August 11th.

securities estimated from £700,000,000 to £800,000,000 which would otherwise substantially assist in the payment of the British debt in America. Notwithstanding these gigantic burdens, Great Britain made an offer at the Paris Conference of January last to forego her rights to reimbursement of her damage, and expressed her readiness, by reducing the debts of the Allies, to treat her share of German Reparations as if it were a repayment by her Allies of their debts due to her. It would be inequitable, and it is impossible to ask the British taxpayer, already much more heavily burdened than his French and Belgian Allies, to make further sacrifices by modifying the Spa percentages for the benefit of France and Belgium.'[30]

Ie stated that Germany should be made to pay up to 'the maximum of er capacity' but pleaded for the French to allow an 'impartial inquiry nto the facts' (Germany had managed to discredit the Reparations ommission in his eyes) to assess Germany's capacity to pay.

But the statement in his speech which most commanded attention at ome and abroad was his assertion that the occupation of the Ruhr was illegal' under the terms of the Treaty of Versailles.

Although Lord Curzon may have pleased those on the left in England vith his speech, 'die-hard' readers of the *Daily Mail* were dismayed. hey wrote to the *Daily Mail* in droves to express their disgust:[31]

Sir,
Who are to be our friends of the future – France or Germany? The nation must choose now. If you could only get the people to realise that the next war will be settled nearly (if not quite) as soon as the average football match they would never dream of breaking with France for the sake of the 'legal' aspect. It is a great pity that our government is both shortsighted and suffering from loss of memory.
Walter Prigue,
Bow, E.3.

Sir,
I emphatically agree with you that the immense preponderance of opinion is with the French, and that the action – or rather, the 'gassing' of the Government is viewed with nothing short of dismay. In the street, in restaurants, and in the train one cannot help hearing bits of conversation, all to the same effect.
There is a recrudescence of feeling which many people share (I among them) that there is some underlying influence, in times past stigmatised as the 'hidden hand' which it is amazing has not been more fully worked out. It is absolutely impossible for any reasonable person to resist the conclusion, from overt acts and sayings, that some powerful interest – or, rather, interests – is working with potency in favour of Germany.

30. Ronaldshay. *Life of Lord Curzon*. p.359.
31. *Daily Mail*. 3.8.23.

After threatening ourselves to occupy the Ruhr ... to turn round and charge
France with illegality – it is monstrous.
Owen B. Thomas,
Chancery Lane, W.C.2.

Lord Northcliffe had died in 1922 but there is no doubt that the *Daily
Mail* was still biased in favour of France and supported his contention of
April 1919 that unless Britain was careful she would end up paying
'excess profits tax and super tax for the benefit of Germany. If we let
her, she will dodge and cheat.'

To this end he had started a tireless campaign when the 'hidden hand'
of appeasement started working in favour of Germany. But although he
became mentally and physically ill before he died in 1922 his newspaper, the *Daily Mail*, carried on his campaign after his death. It had obviously welcomed letters to support its point of view. It also produced an
impressive array of figures to support its contention that Germany was
strong, not weak economically, and that it was Britain who had been
crushed by taxation post-war not the Fatherland. Germany could easily
pay its reparations.

Under the banner headline GERMANY TAKING OUR TRADE the
Daily Mail complained that Germany was taking Britain's livelihood
with the low price of her mark. It quoted statistics from *The Times* trade
supplement to support its argument:

'Germany is dumping large quantities of crossbred cloths in all countries
adjacent to her at prices with which we cannot compete ... Consequently a
gloomy view is taken of prospects, and the Bradford worsted industry looks
like having a bad winter.'

It also quoted from the *Daily News* which the writer of the *Daily Mail*
said has never been 'over- friendly to the Entente':
'In spite of internal disturbances, Germany has been exporting to us
on a larger scale, apparently than last year.' *The Times* trade supplement
had commented on the 4 August: 'German cutlery products are now
being sold in Sheffield at prices with which the local manufacturer cannot compete, even if he sacrifices the whole of his profit.'

Before ill health forced him from Parliament, Bonar Law had made a
wry comment on the subject of German competition on 2 January 1923
which the *Daily Mail* faithfully recorded:

'It is my conviction that from a purely selfish point of view, if..an earthquake
were suddenly to swallow up the whole of Germany, we ought to gain
materially.'

7.8 Bleak Outlook for British Economy

Cancer had forced the retirement of Bonar Law in the Spring of 1923, and the weak Conservative Party, grew weaker. The *Daily Mail* was still militant, however. It quoted extracts from the City Notes of *The Times* to support its case that Germany could and should pay its reparations:

> 'The shipping of the world is greater by some 15,000,000 tons gross than it was before the war. The volume of overseas commerce is smaller.'
>
> 'It follows that somebody's shipping must be deprived of freight; and the first sufferer has been the British Mercantile Marine. It had on July 1 667,000 tons laid up in port because no work for it could be found; so that it is pretty nearly true that each German ton completed last year dislodged from business one ton of British shipping this year.'[32]

In 1920 Germany had produced 204,000 tons of shipping. In 1921 Germany produced 623,000 tons of shipping, an increase of 150%, and this against a background of a 25% drop in the world manufacture of ships.[33]

In 1922 Germany became the second largest shipbuilder in the world.[34] The *Daily Mail* commenting on the position of 'one of the most famous firms of Belfast shipbuilders – Workman, Clark, and Co.' in 1923 – announcing cruel losses because of 'the serious 'slump' in the shipbuilding industry' wrote 'It seems to us that if Germany can expend great sums of money in building ships, this money ought to be applied to payment of reparations, and not to be employed in putting more tonnage into the water at a time when so much of our tonnage is idle.'

British unemployment had fallen slightly from 16% in 1921 to 14% in 1922[35] but, despite increased activity in the coal mines in the current year on account of the Ruhr mines being out of action, the outlook for the economy as a whole remained bleak.

7.9 French Occupation of the Ruhr Illegal

Lord Curzon's declaration that France's occupation of the Ruhr was 'illegal' under the terms of the Treaty of Versailles, arrived at an oppor-

32. *Daily Mail*. 18.8.23.
33. *Annual Register*. 1921. p.79. Finance & Commerce.
34. *Annual Register*. 1922. p.92. Finance & Commerce.
35. *Annual Register*. 1922. p.91. Finance & Commerce.

tune moment in Germany. Recently people had begun to blame the government and not the French for the country's misfortunes.

They had learned to live with inflation over the last five years. Prices and wages had been indexed and, at least, just about everyone had a job.[36] It was only the upright, thrifty fixed-income folk, the backbone of society, who didn't like to cheat the system, who had really suffered. But after the present collapse of the exchange, everyone was in a state of distress.

Between December 1920 and December 1921 the value of the German currency dropped from 258 marks to the £ to 771 marks to the £. Between December 1921 and December 1922 it dropped from 771 marks to the £ to 34,125 marks to the £. After January 1923 it accelerated its headlong descent in value until by August 1923 £1 was worth 19,800,000 German paper marks.[37]

The German farmers weren't going to be paid waste paper for their produce. They barricaded their cattle sheds and kept their granaries under lock and key. Hungry groups of workers from the towns came out to the country to fight for food.

The Socialists in the Reichstag promised a reform of Germany's agriculture. The big estates would be broken up. The 7,500,000 acres of 'waste' lands which were neither mountainous nor stony should produce 3,000,000 more tons of bread grains for the population if brought into production. They held out a vision of plenty for the future. But it seemed extremely unlikely that they would be permitted to carry out their project. For right-wing Press opinion had already decided that it was not the impassioned Junker landowners who were to blame for the present state of malnutrition in the country. It was the Socialists who were given the odium by the right-wing Press for the evils besetting the nation for refusing to renounce their precious concession, won in the 'November Revolution', of the eight hour working day.

When the coalition government headed by Herr Cuno fell, the blame was directly attributed by Hugenberg's Press to the S.P.D., however, because they had refused to allow Herr Stresemann to suspend the eight hour day and grant industry the longer working hours that the Ruhr industrialists declared were imperative for the future of the Fatherland.

Herr Cuno, the industrialists' pawn, was thrown out of office, and Stresemann, who succeeded him, had to accept the Chancellorship with-

36. *Annual Register*. 1923. p.180. 114,000 (Out of a population of approximately 62,075,838 except in the occupied Ruhr territory where the workers were being paid not to work.)

37. *Annual Register*. 1921. Finance & Commerce. p.76.
Annual Register. 1922. Finance & Commerce. p.89.
Harold Nicolson. *Curzon. The Last Phase*. p.366.

out the agreement of the S.P.D. to suspend the eight hour day. It was into this unhappy atmosphere that Lord Curzon's note on the reparations arrived in the name of Great Britain, declaring that the French occupation of the Ruhr was illegal and, by inference, that all Germany's present troubles were due to France.

Stresemann pounced upon Lord Curzon's note and caused it to be printed in every newspaper in Germany. It proved invaluable in persuading the populace that it was the iniquities of the Treaty of Versailles, and not the greed of the industrialists, that was responsible for their troubles. Impoverished Germans must always blame the French for their misfortunes. It was the French who were trying 'to turn free workers into slaves' producing the necessity for the ten hour day.

Harold Nicolson in his book on Curzon, praised Stresemann for his action in publishing his note of 11 August, 'complete national hysteria was thus checked' he declared[38] 'the communist menace for the time, was averted.' Yet, with hindsight, one can see that his fears of communism in Germany were too acute. Britain would be faced with a more difficult task, in combatting left-wing propaganda, to explain away the necessity of working longer hours in British mines after the stabilisation of the mark, when 'destitute' Germany's re-introduction of an eight and a half hour day in the mines, while Britain's miners were working only seven, rendered British coal mines uncompetitive.

7.10 France Restores Devastated Province

The French nation was dismayed at Lord Curzon's proclamation on their occupation of the Ruhr. The *Daily Mail* reprinted a letter expressing the shame felt by the British residents in France:

Dear Sir,
I and mine have always held that every English man, woman and child abroad stands for England. According to the conduct of each one of us the foreigner judges our country. Thus we have taught our children. They have learnt that they have a proud heritage not only because of Britain's might but because she stands for truth, loyalty and honourable dealing.

What are our leaders doing to this England of ours? How will our children look on an England who deserts her Ally, France, to play Germany's game?

W. J. Rosse,
Avenue Carnot, Menton.

38. Harold Nicolson. *Curzon. The Last Phase*. p.267.

Poincaré, in an emotional statement, reminded the British of Lloyd George's several previous threats to occupy the Ruhr. He reiterated that he had no political or annexationist intentions in Germany. He merely wished to recover the money that was due. According to him passive resistance had not been a spontaneous gesture but had been forced upon the local population by the central government. He stated categorically: 'We know perfectly well that Germany can pay us what she owes us quite quickly, and that consequently she has it in her own hands to secure progressive evacuation. The date at which payments are made depends on Germany's will.'

In discussing further the question of legality he reminded the British that the declaration of German default had been passed by a majority of three to one without the French President's casting vote being exercised. He also declared that France and Belgium, by themselves, possessed 60% of the Allied claims against Germany.

> 'What are we to say of a company in which shareholders representing 60% of the shares can be put in a minority by others holding only 20%?' he declared.[39]

Meanwhile France continued to restore her devastated provinces. 50,000 houses were renovated in 1923, 150,000 hectares of land brought under cultivation, 15,000 kilometres of roadway restored, 5,000 tunnels and bridges reconstructed and 400 factories rebuilt. Coal output was nearly double the previous year, approaching the pre-war figure and, except for the number of cattle, reduced to nearly half the pre- war figure, the war was slowly being obliterated.[40] Nevertheless none of the costs of the restoration had yet been repaid.

7.11 Lloyd George Tours America

Lord Curzon's declaration found no favour in America either. Support for Poincaré's assertion of legality had already come from an independent source. Senator Pepper of Pennsylvania, America's 'German' state, boasting a German language newspaper selling 171,273 copies daily, had stated unequivocally in January to the American bar association that France's action was of unquestionable legality and that the United States ought not to interfere. In August the *New York Tribune* added that 'American popular opinion is overwhelmingly behind the Ruhr venture.'[41]

39. *Royal Institute of International Affairs Survey*. 1924. p.337.
40. *Annual Register*. 1923. p.160–1.
41. *New York Times*. January 1923.

The Americans were angry and resentful at Lord Curzon's note. Once again Britain was trying to drag them into the European squabbles. Even if people knew the Germans could pay their debts who would want to have the grim task of collecting them against a people who did not hesitate to use 'starvation' as a weapon?

Lloyd George was not permitted to use the huge audiences he attracted on his American tour for political purposes. At the end of his speech in Indianapolis he merely permitted himself to reflect:

'The question is often asked 'who won the war?' There are many claimants who never saw the war! Now I will tell you who won the war. The man who won the war was the humble man in the steel helmet. God bless the man in the Steel Helmet and his children.'[42]

It was an unfortunate speech to make. When the antics of the Stahlhelm, Germany's illegal organisation of aristocratic war veterans, became more reported in the late 1920s after their political link up with Herr Hugenberg and Herr Hitler over the 'Bill against the Enslavement of the German people', Americans of German extraction would ponder on Lloyd George's words. For the word 'Stahlhelm' means Steel Helmet in the English language.

7.12 Conservative Back Benches Pro-French

Even though Baldwin, the appointed leader of the Conservative Party, was pursuing a policy of appeasement towards Germany similar to Lloyd George's, the backbone of the Conservative party were the pro-French 'die- hards' of the Primrose League, restive and angry after Lord Curzon's speech in August.

However, there was one issue which began to sway the die-hard Conservative voters away from their allegiance to the French – and that was the separatist issue of the Rhineland.

Before Napoleon's time the Rhineland had been separate. So had the Palatinate, Hanover, Thuringia, Saxony and all the German states. Then their external preoccupation had been with each other. That is why each had developed such a military tradition, to preserve their small patches of German soil free from invasion by other German speaking people. The thirty years war had cost so much German blood it had taken a hundred years to recover but the individual states had managed to preserve their independence.

42. Owen. *Tempestuous Journey*. p.670.

Then Napoleon had destroyed their Commonwealth, changed boundaries and given them an outside enemy to unite against. At the Congress of Vienna in 1815 the pro-republican Rhineland had been given to reactionary Prussia to compensate the Prussians for relinquishing Eastern territory to the Russia. Later Bismarck with his philosophy of 'blood and iron' had united the German States under Prussian domination by fighting external foes. In 1914 war had come again with what Hegel called its purifying and uniting qualities. President Wilson's peace, taking away the states individual armies and branding them all with Prussia as equal culprits, had cemented the nations together. But now, in their extremity, they dreamed of the old days when they were free.

Left-wing administrations, posing a threat to central government, were reported in Saxony and Thuringia in October 1923 whilst in Bavaria the government was menaced by a right-wing separatist movement led by von Kahr, and a threat to march on Berlin on 8 November by Adolph Hitler in collusion with the prestigious General Ludendorff.

But the separatist movement which received most column space in Allied Press Correspondents' newspapers was the one, close to home, in the Rhineland.

The leaders of the two principal Rhineland independence parties had issued their declaration of independence on 15 August stating 'that Berlin has entirely Prussianised Germany and systematically ruined the Reich.' They promised that an independent Rhineland 'will endeavour honestly and seriously to solve the problem of reparations.'

This was to be achieved by ceasing to pay their taxes 'to Berlin while all that is done is to waste the public wealth of the Rhineland for nefarious ends.'[43]

7.13 Germany Abandons Passive Resistance

This proposal might have been welcomed by British, French and Americans alike. But as time went on separatist Rhineland looked more and more like becoming France's pawn. By November the *New York Times* would be complaining of events in the Rhineland:

'The French maintain a pretence of neutrality but actually give the separatists a free hand to commit any violation or illegality they like. They make it quite clear to loyal Germans that they can escape at any time from their present plight by throwing over the Reich. The Mayor of a town in the Palatinate recently sought the protection of the local French officer as the Separatists

43. *New York Times.* 11.8.23

were threatening his life. The Frenchman told him: "You must decide one way or the other. I will guarantee your safety for a fortnight. If by that time you have not made up your mind, I will not be responsible if they hang you." '[44]

The *Basler Nationalzeitung* stated its belief that the English and the Americans would oppose France's presence in the Ruhr to claim their reparations in case she remained there and claimed the valuable coal-fields.

'English and the United States are afraid that by uniting under a single control the iron ore of Lorraine and the Ruhr coke, France may secure a monopoly of the continental iron and steel manufacture.'[45]

The separatist movements in the Rhineland served to increase their suspicions. British papers in September showed how impotent their country would be if France had such plans in mind. For France had 800,000 conscripts under arms whereas Britain had only 157,000 regular soldiers.[46] Comparisons of France's expanding air force compared to Britain's few planes, swept the newspapers, sowing doubt and suspicion in British minds. Over 100 British companies had taken advantage of Germany's low exchange rate to set up in business in the British administered sector of Cologne. They were now increasingly alarmed at what they considered predatory moves by France in neighbouring Rhineland.

Baldwin planned to meet Poincaré on his way back from holiday to set British fears at rest over French ambitions in occupied territory and to try and get him to modify his stance over the reparations. However, he was criticised for a communiqué which emanated from that meeting stating that there was 'no difference of purpose or divergence of principle between them (Poincaré and Baldwin) on the reparations' question.'

Although Baldwin elucidated in return a renunciation by Poincaré of any territorial ambition in the Rhineland[47] many in Britain did not believe this pledge.

Yet it was no wonder that Britain had joined France in issuing a joint communiqué over the reparations, for on 26 September, only ten days after their meeting, Germany abandoned 'passive resistance.'

44. *New York Times*. 11.8.23.
45. Quoted in F. W. Foerster. *Europe and the German Question*. p.278.
46. *Annual Register*. 1923. p.103–5, p.159.
47. Middlemas and Barnes. *Baldwin*. p.201. 'We had won from Poincaré a renouncement of any territorial ambition in Germany.'

–8–

The Fight for the Ten-Hour Day

8.1 A Policy of Passive Resistance

Germany had focused the world's attention on the payment of the repa-rations, by adopting a policy of 'passive resistance.' This alone would not have provoked more interest than a prolonged strike. But in addition its currency had been reduced to near worthlessness. On 9 August 1923 the *Daily Mail* proclaimed GERMANY HAS NO DEBT. The currency was not yet absolutely worthless at that date. But it was soon to be so. In January there were 81,200 marks to the pound, by August 19,800,000, in September 250,000,000 while in November the number of marks to the pound reached the awesome total of 22,300,000,000.[1] The farmers naturally refused to be paid waste paper for their produce and the ensu-ing cries of hardship focused the world's attention on the reparations' issue. Keynes's prediction that the reparations levied by the Allies would degrade 'the lives of millions of human beings' seemed to be amply justified.

Yet was this suffering really due to the reparations levied by the Allies or was it self imposed? The fact remained that Germany had paid almost no monetary reparations and its deliveries in kind (coal, timber etc.) were always short. On the other hand Stresemann had told the Reichstag on 7 September that 'the present costs of passive resistance amount to 40 million gold marks every day.'[2] That meant that Germany had spent about 10,800,000,000 gold marks, about £540,000,000 – or just under a tenth of the total amount payable in reparations over a great many years, on its policy of 'passive resistance' in 1923.

On 10 July 1922 a 'well-known' banker had told the reporter from the *New York Times* that unless Germany received satisfaction on the repa-rations' issue 'the mark would go lower and lower until it became worthless' intimating that the German authorities themselves were

1. Harold Nicolson. *Curzon. The Last Phase.* p.366.
2. E. Eyck. *The Weimar Republic.* Vol. I. p.256.

manipulating and destroying Germany's currency.

Poincaré had tried to convince the Allies of this on 3 August stating that 'her present state of ruin is not consequent upon the occupation of the Ruhr, but is the work of Germany itself.'

He received confirmation of his accusation from the German Chancellor, Herr Stresemann, himself. For, when on 28 September passive resistance was finally abandoned, Stresemann reassured the angry right- wing parties in the Reichstag. 'Passive resistance was an inner German affair. When the final decision is at stake then you will see if we ever gave anything up.'[3]

Herr Stresemann was in effect telling his Parliament that 'passive resistance' had nothing to do with the reparations' problem.

8.2 Low German Labour Costs

The paper value of the mark was being wiped out. But after it was destroyed, Germany would have to start again with a new, stabilised currency. The country would then be competing on level terms with its old economic rival, Great Britain. At present, because labour cost so little, there were many cheap hands employed in German industry. When labour cost the proper price there would have to be rationalisation to cut out the dead wood. In order to really succeed Stinnes, the powerful industrialist, felt that each individual citizen had to work harder too. That meant a return to the ten hour day.

In 1922 Herr Stinnes had declared: 'I do not hesitate to say that I am convinced that the German people will have to work two extra hours per day for the next ten or fifteen years ... The preliminary condition for any successful stabilisation is, in my opinion, that wage struggles and strikes be excluded for a long period ... We must have the courage to say to the people: 'For the present and for some time to come you will have to work overtime without overtime payment.'[4]

Only when his workforce was in a truly abject state could he put such a proposition to them. For the Decree on 23 November 1918, establishing the eight hour day, had been to the S.P.D. the most important gain from the 'revolution.' However, Stinnes was in a better economic position, now, in 1923, than his workforce if it came to a lengthy confrontation to try and force changes in working hours. For Herr Stinnes had his money safely tucked away in foreign currency abroad.

3. *New York Times*. 7.10.23.
4. Stinnes to National Economic Council. Oct. 1992. S. Taylor. *Germany 1918–1933*. p.53.

Figure 8.1 Hugo Stinnes
'I do not hesitate to say that I am convinced that the German people will
have to work two extra hours per day for the next ten to fifteen years.
We must have the courage to say to the people: 'For the present and for
some time to come you will have to work overtime without payment''.
© Hulton Deutsch

People began to worry that, not content with economic power, he was going to make a bid for political power too.

8.3   Fears that Stinnes might seize Power

At the start of October there were violent political upheavals over the issue of the eight hour day. Stresemann resigned on 3 October but after three days absence he became Chancellor again. The principle of the eight hour day would not be violated but the socialists agreed to him passing a 'Special Powers Bill' which compromised the matter.[5]

His reappearance as Chancellor after three days was greeted with even more anger by those on the left than by those on the extreme right who had rebuked him over terminating passive resistance. Rumours had been circulating that Stinnes was about to install General Ludendorff as dictator. Herr Helfferich was to be Secretary of Finance and Stegerwold, Minister of Labour.[6] Stresemann, as leader of the National Liberals, had been largely instrumental in Ludendorff's rise to power in 1917 by ejecting Chancellor Bethmann Hollweg.[7] It was feared that he was preparing the ground for another dictator. He was denounced as 'Stinnes' representative' and 'Stinnes' puppet' after democrats had read with horror that Stinnes' newspaper, the *Deutsche Allegmagne Zeitung*, had recorded its conviction that parliamentarianism was dead.

With the termination of passive resistance there had been expectation overseas that Germany would start paying its reparations again. Negotiations had in fact started off relatively smoothly. On 7 October, ten days after 'passive resistance' had ceased, a comprehensive agreement was signed between France and the Phoenix mine and Stahlwerke directed by Otto Wolff, Carp, Stein and the Dutchman Vlissingen, a group which represented nearly 10% of the total output of the Ruhr.[8]12

It was to be hoped that the clauses of the agreement would serve as a model for the rest of the industrialists. Krupp appeared initially cooperative, Stinnes was not. The reason appeared to be that Germany would not be able to wipe out British industry under the terms proposed. The *New York Times* explained:

'What the Frenchmen and the Belgians wanted to know was whether the

5. *Annual Register*. 1923. p.185–6.
6. *New York Times*. 7.10.23.
7. Stresemann, H. H. Herwig and Neil M. Heymann. Biographical Dictionary of World War I.
8. *The Times*. 10.10.23.

Ruhr mine owners were willing to resume the delivery of 20% of the production of their mines for the reparations account, themselves being reimbursed by the Reich. To this Stinnes replied with a categoric no.'[9]

'The Belgian and French engineers at the head of the Control Commission tried to argue that the delivery price of coal in Düsseldorf was so greatly below the delivery price of English coal that even after delivering 20 per cent of their output to the Reparations Commission account the German mine owners could far undercut the British coal owners.

'So far as the household consumer was concerned Stinnes admitted the truth of this argument, but denied its truth from the point of view of the manufacturer who could take only a pithead price into account in making his calculations. In England the pithead price was about 90 francs, but in Stinnes's opinion that price could be lowered to 53 francs. If the Ruhr mine owners were to deliver 20% of their coal to the reparations commission at the Ruhr pithead, the price would rise to 72 francs, with the result that the German industry could not hope to contend with the English and Americas, and it would be impossible for Ruhr mine owners to consent to dig coal at that price.

'The conversation was warm and at times almost violent' The *New York Times* reporter recorded:

'But the French believe that Stinnes's arguments all served to show that coal can be obtained at a price which will allow delivery of 20% to the Allies if there is an accord between the mine owners as to hours of work and other conditions.'

The pertinent comment there was 'If there was an accord..as to hours of work and other conditions.'

Herr Stinnes did suggest to General Degoutté, the occupying French General, that he might propose the lengthening of the hours of work in the Ruhr.

The *Journal des Debats* explains that if General Degoutté had been rash enough to accept Herr Stinnes's proposal, Stresemann would have declared in the Reichstag that it was France's idea.

'He would thus have had things both ways, he would have pulled together his Coalition in an outburst of patriotism and turned against us the working men unionists of Europe and America.'[10]

As he couldn't manoeuvre the French into asking the Germans to work a ten hour day, Stinnes decided to send the government an 'Ultimatum' in his own name and that of the other mine owners. In it, he demanded

9. *New York Times*. 18.10.23.
10. *The Times*. 10.10.23.

amongst other things, compensation for all coal 'confiscated by the French during their occupation', the removal of the coal tax, an absolutely free hand for the industrialists to bargain with the French and the lengthening of the working day in the mines 'to eight and half hours under-ground and ten hours above ground.'[11]

Die Hilfe, the German democratic newspaper, declared bitterly of Herr Stinnes:

> 'That man has done more harm to Germany during the last 10 years than anybody else ... We have only to remember his fight for the iron ore deposits of Brie and Longwy during the war and his recent fight against the timely reform of German currency ... Remember his words at Spa: 'Pshaw, let the French invade the Ruhr district. They will soon see where they get to.' All our industrial magnates stand in deadly terror of socialisation and cling to Hugo Stinnes who really did more for Social Democracy than any agitator.'[12]

8.4 American Sympathy to Germany

People overseas did not understand the struggles that were going on in Germany. They could not understand why there was still uproar and distress in Germany after 'passive resistance' had ceased.

In America many people were beginning to view France's actions in the Rhineland with the same suspicion as the British. Although it is noteworthy that the American newspapers took a softer line in their reporting of the separatist movement in the Rhineland than those of France's near neighbour, Britain, no-one in America wanted a vengeful French nation upsetting the balance of power, by uniting Germany's coal with France's vast stocks of iron ore.

In addition, Americans who had thousands of acres of wheatlands surplus to home consumption, longed to succour the Germans who were so short of food. 6,430 dogs were reportedly eaten in the third quarter of 1923[13] while infant mortality exceeded the corresponding period of 1922 by 21 percent.[14] The Salvation Army reported two old ladies lying in their beds, too weak to get up, too proud to beg.[15] Many Americans were of German or Scandinavian extraction. They could not bring themselves to believe that this acute economic distress was a self-inflicted wound.

11. *The Times*. 10.10.23.
12. *New York Times*. 18.10.23.
13. Guttmann & Meehan. *The Great Inflation*. p.186.
14. *Annual Register*. 1923. p.183.
15. Guttmann & Meehan. *The Great Inflation*. p.186.

On the 9 October Germany's ex-American ambassador, Count von Bernstorff, made a speech at the Hague which attracted America's attention.

The Americans had always admired the urbane and charming Count von Bernstorff. It was only when the British had given irrefutable evidence, in 1917, that the Germans were plotting to incite the Mexicans behind America's back to invade her Southern States, besides indulging in indiscriminate submarine warfare, that Bernstorff had regretfully to pack his bags and return home in 1917. When he addressed the Americans in 1923, therefore, in his new independent position as Head of the League of Nations society, they took special notice of what he had to say.

Bernstorff quietened their fears with regard to the political aspirations of Herr Stinnes.

'Stinnes' he declared, 'confines himself to business and naturally sees everything from a business point of view.' He also encouraged the Americans to make a stabilisation loan to Germany, not out of the humanitarian reasons which had so stimulated Keynes but because it meant 'good business.'

> 'Germany and France will never come to any agreement without the League or some third person to mediate. As I have already stated my belief is that only an American loan on lines similar to those of the Austrian loan which has proved such a success will ever solve the intricate problem with which Germany is faced as the result of the war.'
>
> 'If it means good business, I am convinced that the U.S. will be ready to make this loan but it must be on some business basis.'

What he appeared to be telling his American friends was that it was safe now to make a sizeable loan to Germany because she was able to repay both interest and capital.

He went on to play on American fears as regards French intentions in the Ruhr and to introduce the notion that the ten hour day had been asked for by the French as it was the only way that adequate reparations could be paid.

> 'It is quite certain that as long as the French occupy German territory Germany cannot and will not pay. But the whole of Germany is now convinced that France, or, to be exact the French government wishes to keep the territory now occupied; so we arrive at an impasse. I believe that passive resistance will continue worse, in the Ruhr, even if the German government does not support it. German workmen already demoralised by not working for so long a time, will never work ten hours a day for the French.'[16]

16. *New York Times.* 10.10.23.

8.5 Bankrupt Germany

The day that Count von Bernstorff made his speech the Germans had given material proof to the Americans that they could repay the interest on any loan that America advanced to them. The *New York Times* of 10 October had expressed its astonishment that, despite all the suffering on the Ruhr, Germany was still America's best customer for her important cotton crop. Germany had also imported 'approximately double' the bales of cotton of either France or England in the first eight months of the year. Germany's imports of copper over the 8 months were also larger than any other country. And, astonishingly Germany was also 'one of this country's best customers for meat products.'

The *New York Times* reported:

> 'Many bankers of the financial district, thoroughly familiar with international trade conditions, admit their inability to ascertain just how these large ship-ments of American raw materials have been financed. They know, of course, that Germany has had an opportunity of building her balances to a tremendous size in this country by the sale of marks over a long period, through shipments of gold, through American cash now in Germany, through balances in other countries, drawn on by her importers. But these bankers believe that some light might be thrown on this problem if the exact figures on imports and exports, representing Germany's foreign trade could be ascertained.
>
> 'Figures on Germany's exports are practically impossible to ascertain because of the cloak of secrecy thrown about them, but it is admitted not only by the Department of Commerce, but by international bankers in touch with the situation, that her exports probably are greatly in excess of her imports.'[17]

In commenting on these figures the next days the New York Times had these words to say under the heading:

BANKRUPT GERMANY

> 'It is clear that we must sharply distinguish between the severe financial embarrassments from which Germany is undoubtedly suffering, and her assured economic strength. Her currency has fallen into hopeless chaos. The result of the frightful depreciation of the mark has unquestionably been to ruin many middle-class Germans, and has been tantamount to levying upon them a capital tax more crushing than was ever dreamed of in the Socialist philosophy. German public finance is also undeniably in a bad way.... But all this apart from the question what the real worth of the country may be and what sort of a boom in manufacture, together with a roaring foreign trade, Germany is making preparations for as soon as her finances are set to order her foreign relations stabilised.

17. *New York Times*. 10.10.23.

'It is easy to talk about national bankruptcy. But nations do not in reality go bankrupt unless the great mass of their citizens are left without property or income and unless all the sources of industry and of the creation of new wealth are dried up. It may be true that today Germany is not able to pay appreciable sums on her reparations' account, except for deliveries in kind, but what she may be able to pay in five or ten years time is significantly indicated by what she is doing now through putting her hand upon great supplies of the raw materials of manufacture to make ready for an immense economic expansion in the near future.'[18]

8.6 The Imperial Conference

President Harding died suddenly of ptomaine poisoning on 2 August 1923.[19] The new President, Coolidge, was so impressed by the figures showing Germany's value as a trading partner that he rewarded Germany with Most Favoured Nation status.[20]

Lloyd George was credited with having now revived in America, Secretary Hughes's offer of the previous December, that America should join in an enquiry into Germany's capacity to pay reparations provided that all of the Allies approached him in unison.[21]

Britain had agreed to pay her war debts without receiving reparations. But Finland was the only other country prepared to face up to her responsibilities.[22] American financiers reasoned that if Germany was presented with an amount of reparations to pay which she considered 'reasonable', she could be persuaded to stop her feud with France, and her reparations could fuel the economies of other nations, enabling them to pay their war debts.

M. Poincaré, however, did not want the total charged to Germany to be reduced, just because she had made herself financially insolvent in the short term.

'I don't know what Germany can pay twenty years from now. Neither does Mr. Morgan.' asserted the French Premier. 'Any sum Mr. Morgan and other bankers fixed would be a guess. When it comes to money due to us we prefer to do our own guessing.'[23] 'Two things may happen depending entirely on German goodwill' he continued grimly – 'either Germany may recover and pay or she may not recover and not pay. But what shall not happen is that Germany shall recover and not pay.'

18. *New York Times*. 11.10.23.
19. *Annual Register*. 1923. p.298.
20. *New York Times*. 10.10.23.
21. 12.10.23. For plan see E. Mantoux. *The Carthaginian Peace*. p.144.
22. *Annual Register*. 1923. Note at the foot of page 293.
23. *New York Times*. 12.10.23.

Ex-President Woodrow Wilson was worried about a new resurgent Germany spinning a tale of poverty and then devastating the world's trade. It was not what he had envisaged when he had saved Germany from defeat at the end of World War I. Instead of Baldwin, the British Prime minister, building on the communiqué that he had issued in France with the French Premier, Poincaré, at the end of September, by taking an active part in the negotiations with the German industrialists, the British Premier had seemed unwilling to make a statement on the reparations' issue at all. Meanwhile Lord Curzon was making hostile noises.[24] Ramsay Macdonald, the Labour opposition leader, had maintained that the French success in the Ruhr was important for 'evil not good', while Lloyd George's endeavours in the U.S.A. could have been construed as an attempt to persuade America to come over to Europe to save the Germans again from the consequences of their military defeat in 1918.

In the face of this sympathetic attitude towards Germany's protestations that she could not pay her reparations, Woodrow Wilson, who had not held a very high opinion of the British leaders at the Peace Conference, became worried at the drift of public opinion in the British Isles. against France.

The Imperial Conference was in session in Britain in October and at that Conference was the one man whom Wilson had held in high esteem at the Versailles Peace Conference in 1919. His name was General Smuts.

The integrity of General Smuts had so impressed President Wilson at the Peace Conference that he had allowed himself to be persuaded into changing his mind over the issue of 'pensions and separations' being included in the reparations' charges.

The General had reaped much prestige from the other delegates at the Peace Conference for managing to persuade the President to change his mind over the pensions issue. He was a senior respected figure at the Imperial Conference now. His speeches achieved press space. So far they had condemned France. Yet the ex- President hoped that if he and his former financial adviser, Bernard Baruch, acquainted Smuts of the true facts regarding the reparations and Germany's economic strength, Smuts could enlighten the world as to the dangers of letting Germany off its reparations too lightly.

Bernard Baruch, President Wilson's former economic adviser, sent Smuts a 1760 word telegram acquainting him with the economic facts of the situation. He disclosed that:

24. Middlemas and Barnes. *Baldwin*. p.202.

'We (the Allies and America) have a real interest in seeing that Germany pays her just reparations. There seems little realisation in England and America of what it would mean to them if Germany should escape too lightly. In the United States of America the increased borrowing of the Federal Government as well as those of the States continues; industries and individual dues to the war have piled up and added tax burdens; our Federal budget has risen from one billion to four billion dollars annually. While the amount of money we have to raise in taxes because of these increased expenses and borrowings has risen so greatly the taxes of the German government and fixed charge on German industries have been practically wiped out owing to the use of the printing press. That means that there must be taken from the efforts of our people in taxes for the Federal Government alone four billion dollars in taxes and nothing from the Germans unless they are compelled to pay some fixed tax in the way of reparations. 'Unless this is done Germany will conquer the world in dustrially.'[25]

Wilson had been a great believer in the 'dumb force' of public opinion before World War I had ended. He knew it could be manipulated by rhetoric and eloquent speech. He was worried that prestigious Smuts had, himself, been deceived into believing that Germany was weak, not strong, after the war and had been innocently promoting a wrong view of the reparations' issue to the world at large at the Imperial Conference. He hoped that Baruch's telegram would open his eyes to the true facts so that Smuts could relay them to the rest of the world and strengthen the resolve of the British.

'I beg leave to associate myself with the appeal Baruch is making to you.' He wrote. 'I hope with all my heart that you will do what he suggested.'[26]

Smuts did use the forum provided by the Imperial Conference to promote a view of the reparations' issue to the rest of the world. But it was not the view of President Wilson and Bernard Baruch that he promoted. South Africa had another general election coming up shortly. Smuts's angry, anti-British opposition had been swelled by immigrants from the neighbouring ex-German colony of South West Africa. The tide of public opinion back home had turned against close links with a weakened Britain.

Thus, having checked with Baruch that President Coolidge had made an offer of an initiative over the reparations, provided that there was 'unanimity among the Allies', and hearing that a response had been made 'in the name of the whole British Empire', Smuts decided to pre-empt the proceedings by putting his own message across.

25. Sarah Gertrude Millin. *General Smuts*. Vol. 2. p.262.
26. Sarah Gertrude Millin. *General Smuts*. Vol. 2. p.263.

Figure 8.2 General Smuts
'Defeated, broken, utterly exhausted, my little people also had to bow to the will of a conqueror.' Smuts 23rd October 1923.
© Hulton Deutsch

His speech was given at a dinner in his honour on 23 October. Moreover it was broadcast on the 'wireless,' the novelty of the age. Thus it was heard by 'vast numbers of people in all parts of the country, many of whom otherwise would have taken no heed of it.'[27] Its message was relayed by newspapers to the rest of the world. Smuts words were characterised by their high moral tone. Their message was that Germany was weak and defenceless and France, strong and filled with thoughts of revenge.

It is partly from General Smuts's comparisons in this speech of the little Boer nation, being subdued by the mighty British Empire after the Boer War, that many have come to regard post World War I Germany as a tiny, severely treated, defenceless country, pillaged by the 'conqueror' and the 'spoils of war.'

'Defeated, broken, utterly exhausted, my little people also had to bow to the will of the conqueror' he began.

He went on to call for the French occupation of the Ruhr to cease or at least to become 'invisible.' He questioned France's right to take 'productive pledges' from the Ruhr because they had not received their reparations and he declared that General Degoutté's negotiations with the German industrialists over the head of the German government comprised a 'revision of the Treaty.' The British government had called the occupation of the Ruhr 'illegal.' It was a position which he appeared to agree with. He even went as far as to compare France's occupation of the Ruhr with the invasion of Belgium in 1914, when the Allies had gone to war especially to prevent treaties being treated like 'scraps of paper.' He called for a great Conference of all interested powers on the question of the reparations and he warned the world of French 'militarism.'

'The British people will no doubt be invited to share in the spoils of the Ruhr, our hard-pressed industrialists may feel tempted to accept the invitation. My advice is to have nothing to do with the Ruhr.'

And in a reference to the separatist movement on the Rhine he concluded: 'There is a serious danger lest a policy of excessive generosity on our part, or on the part of America, may simply enable France still more effectively to subsidise and foster militarism on the Continent.'[28]

His speech attracted enormous Press comment both in Britain and overseas. The *New York Times* commented that the speech must have

27. *Annual Register.* 1923. p.111.
28. S. G. Millin. *General Smuts.* Vol. 2. p.266.

been made with the approval of the British Prime Minister.[29]

> 'A good deal of interest lies in the question of how far General Smuts can be taken as a spokesman for the British government. The most probable answer is that Premier Baldwin knew and agreed, in a general way to what he was going to say but that he did not censor it in detail. Indeed General Smuts emphasised his personal right to speak as one of the signatories of the Treaty of Versailles and never suggested that he was a spokesman for Downing Street. But it is incredible that he should have made such utterances in the midst of the Imperial Conference without the knowledge of the Prime Minister.'

The *New York Times* contained a summary of most British newspapers attitude to the speech. Nearly all were complimentary with the exception of the *Morning Post* and the *Daily Mail*. The *Daily Mail* contended that Smuts 'wishes England to quarrel with France.' While the *Morning Post* declared that Smuts's 'inability to understand that preliminary to the Conference which he suggests is an understanding between Britain and France – an understanding which we do not think is made any easier by his speech of Tuesday night. America, as Mr. Harvey made perfectly clear, will attend an international conference only when invited by all the Allies.'[30]

The main purpose of General Smuts's speech appeared to be to canvass support for the new President Coolidge's offer of a Conference on the reparations. However, many Americans were annoyed at the thought of being embroiled in the affairs of Europe again. Senator Johnson of California charged that it was the ex-British Premier Lloyd George who had revived the issue.

> 'The former British Premier took advantage of a 'forgotten speech of our Secretary of State, made a year ago at New Haven, and gently flatters us by insinuating that through our distinguished Secretary we were the very first to discover how to avert European chaos.'

The purpose of the proposed Conference appeared to be to reassess the reparations' figure to see if Germany had been overcharged. Senator Johnson declared of the proposed new body of experts:

> 'We have had a hotel full of experts in Paris, who, described as 'observers' have really been a part of the reparations muddle. Is it possible that they do not know what Germany can pay? If they do not, then our Government has a fair conception of it. And if we know, why not say it?'
> 'Lloyd George has made it clear what we must do for he said at Chicago:

29. *New York Times*. 25.10.23.
30. *New York Times*. 25.10.23.

'Once this committee has concluded its task and Germany has refused to pay, the Allies could then march together to deal with her recalcitrance.'[31]

However, the Senator from California hardly relished the thought of Americans becoming either 'policemen' or 'collectors.' He shared Americans distaste for any more messy involvements in Europe.

8.7 Ruhr Work Hangs on the Ten-Hour Day

Count Bernstorff had not encouraged the Americans to come over to Europe as 'policemen' or 'collectors', however, but to give Germany a loan. The German leadership were confident that any new body of experts would decide that the figure for reparations, decided just two years ago, was unrealistic and would also advocate Germany being given a large stabilisation loan. Then the economic life of Europe could get back to normal again and countries could start paying their war debts back to America. At the moment people were suffering from unemployment all over Europe. But the material conditions in Germany were much the worst. The *New York Times* reported on the food riots in Berlin and how, in their desperation, the rioters turned against the Jews.

'Mass food riots and plunderings all over the place occurred today in Berlin and they continue tonight in all sections of the greater city. A mass mob attack on the Bourse was one feature of the outbreak, and for the first time a pogrom spirit manifested itself in brutal treatment of Jews and others who looked like Jews ... Many bakeries, butcher shops, groceries and delicatessens in all parts of Greater Berlin were stormed and plundered.'

The *New York Times* did give a reason for the Berlin food riot, however. The price of bread had been put up overnight by 600%. 'This sudden increase in food cost set the masses in motion early this morning, for a skilled worker's pay for last week hardly sufficed to pay for a loaf today ... unable to buy bread, thousands of men and women paraded the streets, plundering the bakeries and other food shops as they went.'[32]

There was one way in which the industrialists indicated that the shop floor could get back to work and receive proper remuneration and not just waste paper. Under the heading: RUHR WORK HANGS ON THE TEN-HOUR DAY the *New York Times* of 8 November described the negotiations going on in the Ruhr.

31. *New York Times*. 2.11.23.
32. *New York Times*. 6.11.23.

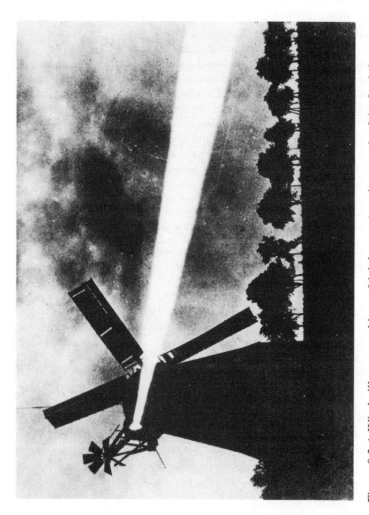

Figure 8.3 A Windmill converted into a Lighthouse. A curious result of the food shortage.
© The Illustrated London News Picture Library

'The German industrialists told their workforce that they could only afford to make reparations deliveries to the French and what they called 'the resumption of economic life' provided that the workforce worked a ten hour day above ground and eight and a half below.'

The reporter continued:

'If the workers refuse, the industrialists will probably carry out their threat and close down, throwing all their workers on the mercy of the unemployment doles. On the question of increasing the working day ... the workers have remained adamant and undoubtedly this will be one of the possibly insuperable obstacles to finding a solution to the Ruhr stagnation with the French.

'The workers attitude seems to be ... that they are caught between the upper millstone of the industrialists pressure and the nether millstone of wholesale unemployment, with danger of starvation.. From their conversations they appear to be equally acrimonious against the French for manoeuvring the employers into a position where it is impossible to compete in the world markets, and the employers whom they blame for using threats of unemployment to work the longer hours.'

'Already grim starvation is staring several hundred thousand workmen in the face with the cold, dark winter nights creeping in. On the question of increasing the working day, which was fixed by law after the 1918 revolution, the workers have remained adamant, and undoubtedly this will be one of the possibly insuperable obstacles to finding a satisfactory solution of the Ruhr stagnation with the French.

'If all the industrial plants close as threatened the total unemployed will reach from 700,000 to 800,000. The Bochum Verein has already turned out 20,000 men and the Thyssen works at Mulhelm and Hamborn expect to drop 40,000 on Saturday. Even the Krupp company expects to shut out 10% of its workforce on November 15th and an additional 10% a few days later.'[33]

8.8 Propaganda of Revenge

The French Premier Poincaré was not at all enamoured of the idea of a Conference to help Germany escape her responsibilities. He had come to power because Conferences had not worked in the past. The entire French nation, with the exception of the Communists and Radical Socialists,[34] had supported his intervention in the Ruhr. At that time the correspondent of the German *Basler Nationalzeitung* sent the following report to his paper:

33. *New York Times.* 8.11.23.
34. *Annual Register.* 1923. p.158. 'The only active opponents of his policy were the Communists. These made active cause with the Germans and many of them were arrested on the day of the occupation.'

'The German heavy industrialists think they are sufficiently strong to hold out ... Their objects are to mobilise public opinion everywhere against the French action and compel the French to take increasingly severe measure, then to increase the French coal famine, and finally to reduce the exchange value of the franc and thus make the French weary of the conflict.'[35]

They had managed to 'compel the French to take increasingly severe measures' in the Ruhr helping them to 'mobilise public opinion' practically everywhere against France. They had also managed to 'reduce the exchange value of the franc.' By December it would be 30% lower in value than at the start of the year.[36] But except for the far left, the French people remained solidly in support of the action of their Prime Minister. France's actions in the Ruhr, however, had 'estranged public sympathy from France throughout the world..even in the United States where it was strongest.'[37]

So when America intervened France had to respond, for it was not only the non-payment of the money due for the restoration of her devastated provinces that bothered France, it was also the problem of 'security.'

Poincaré knew the extreme 'propaganda of revenge and hate which is carried on against France in the schools and colleges; the Reichswehr and Security Police which defy the central authority and which, united in secret societies and Black Reichswehr, constitute throughout Germany an independent and redoubtable power.'[38] So France could not afford to flout American public opinion. She needed America's support in case she was invaded again. Poincaré bowed to international pressure to allow another evaluation of Germany's economy. But as he was in control of the Ruhr he was in a position to make conditions; first that no expert enquiry should be undertaken into Germany's capacity to pay unless it was coupled with discussions into inter-Allied debt. In addition it was only to be allowed to look into Germany's 'present capacity' to pay reparations, not fix a new total amount payable. Bankers might look at the matter from a different point of view to those with other preoccupations. They were used to making deals. They would argue, therefore, that there must be some sum for reparations which the German hierarchy would agree was 'reasonable.' Then Europe could get back to business

35. F. W. Foerster. *Europe and the German Question.* p.278. 'The belief is still strong that German patience and German marks can outlast French patience and French francs.' *New York Times.* 2.2.23. Estimates suggest that Germany lost some 400 million marks speculating against the franc before March 1924. Austria even more. Charles P. Kindleberger. *A Financial History of Western Europe.* p.354–5. After Poincaré fell from power, however, the franc's fall could have been an internal affair.

36. December 1922 – 63.50. December 1923 – 84.65.

37. *Annual Register.* 1923. p.160.

38. *New York Times.* 2.11.23. Bruno Buchrucker: *Im Schatten Seeckts; die Geschichte der 'Schwarzen Reichswehr.*

again. Poincaré, however, looked at the matter from the aspect of security. He envisaged a resurgent Germany, controlled by powerful industrialists, menacing France.

Elon Huntingdon Hooker, Chairman of the American Defence Society was equally worried. Under the heading GERMANY CAN PAY 33 BILLIONS he stated

> 'For the industrial safety of England and the United States, and for the physical safety of France, Germany must be forced to pay from her surplus and current receipts heavily and for a long period of years, otherwise the commercial advantage, without overhead, at which she will work, will constitute an insuperable barrier to possible competition or peace of reasonable duration.'[39]

Poincaré was also concerned to repatriate Germany's external balances so that it would be unable to finance another hyperinflation. So it was decided to create two Committees of Experts. The first one was to consider the means of balancing the budget and ensure the permanent stabilisation of the currency.

Another committee of experts would attempt to assess, locate and repatriate German money abroad to deter it from debasing its currency again. According to the Annual Register the Committee of Experts estimated that Germany's external balances 'amounted to nearly seven milliard marks though it could hardly arrive at precise figures.'[40] *The New York Times* assessed the figure somewhat higher at 2 billion dollars.[41] While France assessed it still higher at 15 milliard marks.

While the interested powers mulled over his terms Poincaré continued his efforts to secure an agreement over coal deliveries with the German industrialists. He reassured his workers:

> 'We do not treat with those who try to make agreements detrimental to the workers. General Degoutté has clearly explained that the conditions laid down by the Inter-Allied Commission were carefully prepared and that it is a question simply of obliging the German industrialists to assume part of the reparations out of the enormous profits they have made since 1919.'[42]

Finally on 23 November the Ruhr industrialists agreed to French terms for resuming reparations deliveries to France. They were: payment of 15,000,000 dollars within six months, 18% of the output of the mines as

39. *New York Times*. 2.11.23.
40. *Annual Register*. 1924. p.155.
41. *New York Times*. Feb. 1924.
42. *New York Times*. 2.11.23.

reparations' deliveries to France and Belgium and an additional tax of 10 francs a ton on the rest of the coal they sold, the money to go towards the costs of the Ruhr Occupation and the payment of the reparations. The French had finally confounded those who said that they didn't want reparations, they just wanted revenge.

Sadly for France, however, the agreement had come too late. The tide of public opinion, world wide had turned against them. German misery was too palpable. Even the French swung left in 1924 as the franc continued to fall. On 11 May 1924 Poincaré lost the general election. Throughout 1925 the franc continued to fall. Gordon Wright in his *France in Modern Times*, takes up the story:

> 'This state of almost permanent crisis with the franc down to less than one-tenth of its pre-war value and threatening to collapse entirely, forced the Radical leadership to make a decisive choice; either to adopt the Socialists drastic program, or to abdicate power to the Moderates. Most of them preferred the second alternative; Raymond Poincaré was called back to the premiership in 1926, and the Radicals assured him of their support. Poincaré they trusted as scrupulously honest, a dedicated republican, and a lifelong anticlerical. His broadly-based cabinet checked the crisis with remarkable ease, and without either foreign borrowing or really fundamental reforms at home ... The Paris Daily *Le Temps* (which reflected the outlook of its industrialist owners) labelled the premier 'Poincaré the Well-Beloved' and asserted that 'one would have to go back to Saint Louis to find such popular enthusiasm for a sovereign.'

Gordon Wright concluded of France's Great Inflation:

> 'The French solution to the war's financial burden – an inflation that was checked short of disaster – fell midway between that of the Germans and that of the British and was probably healthier than either. It was, however a solution more empirical than planned.'[43]

8.9 Injustice to Germany

By the middle of October 1923 the British had come round to the idea that a terrible injustice had been done to Germany. True, the 'die-hards' clung to sympathy for France, but they were a dwindling band. Lloyd George, Curzon, Asquith, Ramsay Macdonald, all supported the financial experts in the Treasury who declared that trying to make Germany pay was merely extinguishing the embers of her economic life. Finally

43. Gordon Wright. *France in Modern Times*. 1962. p.456–7.

General Smuts, the independent witness, had told the country that ungrateful France had been trying to grab the 'spoils of war' when Britain had spent so many lives and so much of her national treasure trying to save her from destruction in the Great War.

The Times had reported Herr Stinnes's ultimatum on 10 October, commenting:

> 'This action of the industrialists is generally condemned as a high-handed proceeding.'[44]

But sentiment generally had swung to the opinion that victorious France was the wrong-doer in Germany. The misery of the German population in the Ruhr persuaded sentiment in England that all Germany must be destitute.

The desperate straights to which the German population had been reduced were graphically described by the British General in charge of the Allied occupationary force, General Morgan:

> 'I know personally of a case' he said 'in which a German, who had advanced the equivalent of £7,000 on a mortgage in 1914, was paid back by way of redemption and in full discharge of the debt, the equivalent of less than £1.
> 'I know also of a judge of a high court, receiving a salary equivalent to barely £100 a year, who was turned away from the door of his own court by a new usher who mistook him for a beggar.' He was full of censure for the rich and powerful in Germany.
> 'It is idle and indeed mischievous' he declared 'to blame French imperialism for this state of political decay ... the origins ... are rooted in the financial policy of the German government during the war, a policy which, by its neglect to tax war profits, played directly into the hands of the big industrialists ... By their policy of inflation they hoped to conquer the markets of the world, to renew and extend their plant and to 'reconstruct' the whole of industrial Germany. The result was a 'boom' of such prosperity as Germany had never known. But it is at an end – virtue is gone out of it, and Germany is faced with the prospect of having to number her unemployed not, as hitherto, by thousands but by millions.'[45]

8.10 First Labour Government

Stories of the distress of the German people touched the hearts of the British, not least because there had been dreadful rumours, 'categorically' denied, that Great Britain, to its inhabitants the most powerful

44. *New York Times.* 10.10.23.
45. J. H. Morgan. *The Present State of Germany.* p.72–3, p.81–2, p.92.

industrial nation in the world, was also contemplating the necessity of having a 'great inflation'[46] because of the straights to which competition from Germany's unfairly priced mark had reduced her industry. Now France's franc was being debased to the further distress of British industry. The only way her leaders could envisage, to stem the flood of imports, was to erect more tariffs.

Baldwin decided to turn his back on the reparations' issue and rally the party faithful on the issue of protection before Lloyd George came home from America. Thus he hoped to prevent 'the goat' from seizing 'protection' as an issue himself and dividing if not completely destroying the Conservative Party. The economic situation in Britain before the promise of stabilisation of the German mark, was desperate:

> 'Nearly all the great trades of the country were suffering as acutely as agriculture. The cotton trade was passing through the worst period it had ever known owing to the difficulty of obtaining American cotton at a sufficiently low price. The woollen manufacturers of Bradford found themselves so hard hit by French competition, due to the depreciation of the franc – that, in spite of their Free Trade traditions, they began to consider seriously the advisability of asking for protection. The lace industry of Nottingham was perishing from a similar cause. The shipbuilding returns of Lloyd's Register for the quarter ending 30 September, showed a decrease of about 67,000 tons as compared with the figures for June, and of about 346,000 tons as compared with the figures of a year previous. The number of unemployed and partially employed had commenced to increase ominously after the end of August.'[47]

Ordinary British people no longer blamed the Germans for their desperate economic plight. They blamed their own industrialists. They identified with the poor German worker whose present sufferings seemed even worse than their own, and they turned to Ramsay Macdonald, who had resigned as leader of the Labour Party in 1914 over his opposition to Britain joining World War I.

On 7 August 1914, Ramsay Macdonald had asserted:

> 'We are not really fighting for the independence of Belgium..we are fighting because we belong to the Triple Entente, because our foreign policy has been conducted on the lines of alliances to preserve the balance of power, and because we have prejudices against a very strong commercial rival. We are in it and must see it through. It is a sad thing that we, loving our country best, and hoping and striving that we shall not be defeated or worsened or disgraced, should have as a counterpart to that the desire that this great nation of Germany should be worsened, defeated, and disgraced. How one almost hates the diplomacy that has brought us to this.'

46. *The Times.* 20.10.23.
47. *Annual Register.* 1923. p.118.

The British nation had vilified Ramsay Macdonald after he had made this speech. But now the anti- French undertones struck a chord with the British people. When the nation went to the polls again on 6 December 1923, just a year and day after it had voted before, there was a massive desertion from the Conservative Party with their uncaring 'die-hard' wing. The *Annual Register* recorded:

> 'So ended a year which for the mass of the British public completed the process of disillusionment over the Lloyd George regime of the post-war period and its promises of a better world.'

The Labour Party formed its first administration.

By equating Germany's crime, in allegedly starting the First World War, with Britain's crime in not honouring the agreements made at the end, the left felt that Great Britain had shared in the guilt of 1914–18. But as Britain's lack of humanity involved hardship to women and children, whereas Germany's alleged actions merely involved the manly occupation of battle, their own country had somehow sunk to greater depths of depravity.

8.11 Stabilisation of the Mark

The German Economist. Dr. Schacht, became an internationally acclaimed 'economic wizard' after he achieved the stabilisation of the mark on 15 November 1923. Suddenly the whole world could breathe again and, hopefully, their trade could get back to normal. But in the inner circles of the German banking world, Herr Helfferich, the man responsible for Herr Erzberger's fall from public favour, and even accused of complicity in Herr Rathenau's murder, received the accolade for his brilliant innovation of adopting the economic policy of hyperinflation to remove the insurmountable debts of war.[48]

Herr Helfferich had been the wartime finance minister and, rather than resorting to taxation like the British, had encouraged the nation to invest in his 'mammoth loans.' But now that those 'mammoth loans' were worthless, he proposed a new currency backed up by the value of Germany's staple commodity, rye. In the end, the 'rentenmark' as it came to be called, was backed up by a charge, half on the forests and agricultural land of Germany and half on its industry and commerce.[49] It

---

48. *Helfferich. Biographical Dictionary of World War I.* H. H. Herwig and Neil Heyman.
49. Guttmann and Meehan. *The Great Inflation.* p.207.

was a good concept, encouraging Germans to have faith in their currency again. However, although the directors of the Reichsbank, (Germany's central bank) unanimously endorsed Helfferich's candidacy for the Presidency in recognition of his outstanding financial genius, in deference to President Ebert and Chancellor Stresemann's fears of Allied susceptibilities, Hjalmar Schacht was given the appointment of the Reichsbank's Presidency.[50]

Meanwhile the turbulent life of Herr Helfferich was shortly to come to a close. He died in a train accident at Bellizona in Switzerland, in the Spring of 1924. He was still only 52 years old.

The plans for the rentenmark had been published as early as 19 September, 1923, seven days before the government-backed passive resistance was abandoned.[51] It would not have been realistic to have negotiated with Poincaré without this earnest of good faith. But the rentenmark did not become currency until 15 November, one week before the industrialists finally agreed terms with Poincaré on the 23 November,[52] when the industrial workers on the Ruhr finally gave up hope of being able to defy their bosses. It was perhaps inevitable that the industrialists should wait until after stabilisation before agreeing to renewed reparations' deliveries. The workers must be made to realise that the meagre size of their post-stabilisation pay packet was due to the extortionate reparation demands of the French and not to renewed German greed and ambition.[53]

The German industrialists must have felt elated at the turn of events. They now had a compliant workforce, a fully modernised industrial base, no debt – and on top of it all the Americans were offering them a large loan, of 800 million gold marks, so that they would not have to dip deep into their pockets to pay the reparations.

How cruel were the German industrialists to the rest of the German population in those post-war years? The middle classes, pensioners and all those on fixed incomes, with small savings in the bank, suffered dreadfully after World War I. But the ordinary German worker had been better off in the years 1920–22 than his counterpart in Great Britain during the same period. This was because, by dint of unfair competition, practically every single German was ensured a job. But in the last

50. H. H. Herwig and Neil Heyman. *Helfferich. Biographical Dictionary of World War I.*

51. Bergmann. *The History of the Reparations.* p.210.

52. *Statesman's Yearbook.* (1926) p.920.

53. *Annual Register.* p.142. 'Owing to the stringent conditions of this agreement, the employers laid down for the workers exceedingly harsh regulations in the matter of the hours of work and amount of wages which involved the sacrifice by the latter of the gains of the revolution.'

eighteen months of the Great Inflation even German workers began to suffer. The harvest in 1922 had not been good. And in the last quarter of 1923 incomes evaporated but there were no savings left to exist on. The needs of industry had been paramount.

Whether Germany actually starved, however, is a different matter. Although there were many less births in 1923 and infant mortality was especially high in the last quarter of the year, taken as a whole, there were less deaths per head of population in 1923 than in 1922.[54]

Sometimes, however, the injury to one's pride of losing one's place in society is almost worse than death. Britain averaged 14% of its work-force unemployed in 1923, a gruesome total, while in Germany, except for the occupied areas of the Ruhr there were still only 114,000 people unemployed on 1 August. But after 1 August the situation rapidly deteriorated. Unemployment increased dramatically. In October there were 530,000 unemployed, by November 880,000 and by December there were 1,450,000 unemployed and 1,800,000 on short time. In the great industrial, occupied areas of the Ruhr there was hardship already by the end of September with 800,000 on short time and hundreds of thousands out of work. The unemployed had to exist on 10 to 15% of their pre-war wages, while all had to pay exorbitant prices for their foodstuffs which were sold at between 30 and 100% above the world price.[55]

It was no wonder that Poincaré, in commenting on German hardship on 2 November 1923, spoke of the 'real misery of the intellectuals, of the little tradespeople and of the workers.' But he declared that 'the German peasant is not so unhappy. He lives well; he has agricultural equipment and supplies of cattle far superior to those of the French farmers.'

'As for the great landed proprietors, they have enriched themselves like the industrialists, have drawn enormous profits from inflation and are the most ardent supporters of Prussian militarism.'[56]

'What an injustice and what a danger' he declared at his speech at Nevers 'if Germany were freed of part of her debt tomorrow and if in a few years she appeared before us restrengthened and enriched to humiliate us by the recovery of her power and to crush us by her supremacy. We do not wish to be caught in that trap.'

It was ominous that on 26 January 1924 the Chief Editor of the socialist newspaper, the *Vossiche Zeitung* should comment with foreboding: 'in the mental semi-darkness created by the reactionary right with its

54. *Statesman's Yearbook*. 1926. p.920.
55. *Annual Register*. 1923. p.180. Price of food. p.187.
56. *New York Times*. 2.11.23.

pretensions of false nationalism the German people still have the idea that they have not lost the war.'[57]

8.12 Rise of Opposition Parties in Germany

The German Nationalists had won a great propaganda victory in 1923. They lost no time in humiliating the socialists whose policy of fulfilment over the reparations had seemingly brought the country to the verge of bankruptcy and chaos. A newspaper at Madgeburg accused President Ebert of treason for heading the German munitions strike of January 1918. This prompted a libel trial, at a critical time, just before the forthcoming Presidential elections. Although witnesses against the President were discredited, and the newspaper was found technically guilty of libel, President Ebert was found guilty of treason in taking any part in the strike. The judge 'distinguished between the moral, political, and historical aspect of the case and its criminal aspect. The latter he held to be proved.'[58]

The success of the German far right in putting their propaganda message across was recorded in the polls. The avowed enemies of the Republic, the German Nationalists or DNVP celebrated their propaganda success of 1923, by gaining 96 seats in Parliament in the Spring elections of 1924. With their friends, Hitler's NSDAP, currently calling themselves The Racialists, who achieved 36 seats in Parliament and the National Liberals, the landowners' party, which gained 9, they could have formed an administration. But they preferred to remain in opposition.

The Nationalist Party declined to take office in order to avoid the stigma of agreeing to the new Dawes Plan proposal for paying the reparations, preferring to ensure the Dawes Plan's success through Parliament[59] while instigating a virulent personal campaign against Stresemann as Foreign Minister for agreeing to its proposals. Their main condition to any form of acceptance to the Dawes Plan was that the Government should include a protest against the so-called 'war-guilt lie.'

The resurrecting of this moral issue would have a great impact on the

57. *New York Times*. 27.1.24.
58. *The Times*. 24.12.24. Although Ebert had accepted to be head of the strike, he had done so reluctantly, to defuse the situation. During the trial a letter had been read out, returned unopened from one of his two sons killed in action. It declared: 'During the last few days some useless strikes have broken out ... Such fool's tricks do not serve the cause of peace, but only strengthen the fighting spirit of the enemy.' *The Times*. 15.12.24.
59. E. Eyck. *The Weimar Republic*. p.300, p.307.

German people in future years. For in the future the necessity of working longer hours and future economic hardship would increasingly be
associated with the burden of paying those 'unfair' reparations.

The National Socialist seats in the Reichstag shrunk from 36 to 14 in
the subsequent elections in December but the DNVP's Press Campaign
against the new Dawes Plan reparations' agreement bore fruit. The anti-
Republican Party secured 103 seats in the Reichstag. The Reichstag was
polarised. Socialist voters flocked in even greater numbers to give the
SPD 131 seats, but impotent socialism had demonstrated that it had been
unable to defend workers' rights or prevent German distress in 1923. On
23.12.24, a law court in Magdeburg upheld a journalist's accusation that
the socialist President of the Republic, Ebert, was guilty of treason for
having taking any part in the great armament workers' strike of 1918.
He died two months later, his reputation besmirched. On 6.4.25 that
symbol of Prussian militarism, Paul von Hindenburg, was elected
President in his place. President Hindenburg had misled the nation as to
how the war had ended in 1918. He did not regret his decision. On the
contrary, now that the moment of crisis was over, and the terror of
defeat had slipped by, his one regret was in having forced the Emperor
to comply with President Woodrow Wilson's edict to abdicate, in those
fateful days of November 1918. He would never be allowed to forget
this mistake from those to whom he owed his election, on the right.

His words on accepting the Presidency showed his distaste for the
form of Government over which he was forced to preside.

'As a soldier I have always had the whole nation before my eyes, and not its
parties. Parties are necessary in a parliamentary state, but the Chief of the
State must stand above them ... Just as the first German President, even as
Protector of the Constitution, never concealed his origin from the ranks of
labour, no one will be able to expect of me that I should surrender my political convictions.'[60]

8.13 The Bloomsbury Group

While the intellectuals in Germany were rendered destitute and unes-
teemed by the 'great inflations' the intellectuals in England reaped
rewards from the affair. The *Economics of the Peace* had been republished in 1923. By 1924 some 140,000 copies had been sold and it had
been translated into eleven languages.[61] Keynes's thesis that the Allies

60. J. Wheeler Bennet. *Hindenburg. The Wooden Titan*. p.242.
61. Etienne Mantoux. *The Carthaginian Peace*. p.6.

had been drumming the economic life out of Germany after the war, impoverishing them in the process, was widely believed. His values and those of his pacifist friends, the Bloomsbury Group, suddenly came into fashion. By the same token, now that Germany had been shown to be weak and starving, all those large, red-corpuscled folk who had fought so long and hard to subdue Germany in the Great War, wondered what they had been fighting for and why they had fought so long.

The word 'reparation' is an emotive one, meaning the atonement of sin. The right were now taxed with guilt, not only for driving Germany into penury and starvation but also for grinding the faces of the poor in satanic mills in England and raping her Empire overseas. It was no good remembering that Germany had 'serfdom' in its colonies right up to the First World War or that children under the age of 14 had been sent down German mines in 1922.[62] Great Britain could no longer talk of its civilising mission in the world, when it had behaved in such a seemingly barbaric fashion in Europe.

The Bloomsbury Group considered themselves an elite – cultured, intellectual and vastly superior to the general run of man and womankind. The concept of such an elite had been brought down to them from Cambridge by Keynes and Lytton Strachey who had gained their first taste of superiority as members of the 'Apostles.' Whereas ancient Prussia had been likened to the soldier state of Sparta,[63] Lytton Strachey had, perhaps tongue in cheek, envisaged the 'Apostles' as Athenians.

> 'I sometimes feel as if it were not only we ourselves who are concerned, but that the destinies of the whole world are somehow involved in ours. We are – Oh! in more ways than one – Athenians of the Periclean age. We are the mysterious priests of a new and amazing civilisation ... What is hidden from us? We have mastered all. We have abolished religion, we have founded ethics, we have established philosophy, we have sown our strange illumination in every province of thought, we have conquered art, we have liberated love. It would be pleasant to spend our days in a perpetual proclamation of our magnificence.'

In 1924 Keynes and Lytton Strachey could congratulate themselves. They had been in the forefront of those who exclaimed against reparations from Germany and now felt they had been vindicated by events.

---

62. *Statesman's Yearbook*. Statistics for German coal industry in 1922. p.929.
63. F. W. Foerster. *Europe and the German Question*. p.53. 'What Plato said of Sparta, that there was more genuine philosophy there than elsewhere – and he had in mind the unifying power of a political principle logically applied in every sphere – is equally applicable to this (Prussian) religious and military state.'

Figure 8.4 Lytton Strachey
'... when I hear people called 'Victorians' I suspect then. But when I hear them called 'Eminent Victorians' I write their lives.'
© Hulton Deutsch

They had proved that the 'Eminent Victorians'[64] who had built the United Kingdom into one of the most envied nations in the world, were not 'Eminent' at all, but greedy, self-seeking, imperialistic and uncaring. It was a devastating indictment.

The Bloomsburys had a new dogma to offer – 'self-determination.' Even President Wilson had endorsed it. It was a heady philosophy. The Bloomsburys became the darlings of the age.

64. Cyril Connolly: '*Eminent Victorians* is the work of a great anarch, a revolutionary textbook on bourgeois society written in the language through which the bourgeois ear could be lulled and beguiled, the Mandarin style.' (Enemies of Promise.)
Lytton Strachey: 'Similarly when I hear people called "Victorians", I suspect them. But when I hear them called "Eminent Victorians" I write their lives.' Speech to the Apostles. Quotes from Lytton Strachey. *The years of Achievement. 1910–1932*. p.260. Michael Holroyd.

–9–

The Logic Behind Locarno

9.1 The Dawes Report

The Dawes Report on the future payment of the reparations, published in April 1924, was initially welcomed by Keynes. 'Germany' he wrote 'can scarcely expect better terms than these.' It confirmed under Article VIII b.1. the observation made by the editor of the *Daily Mail* six months earlier.

> 'Government Internal Debt has been practically extinguished by the depreciation of the currency.'

It also declared under Article V (b) that in contrast to British industry:

> 'Plant capacity has been increased and improved since the war.'

The Dawes Plan did not attempt to alter the decision made in 1921 as to what figure Germany was to pay in total but it did try and agree what had already been paid in cash and 'deliveries in kind' and set a smooth framework for future payments.

It is true that there was a large discrepancy between the amount that the German government claimed had been paid in reparations and what the Reparations Commission claimed had been received. Strident noises were made in Germany and the Allies and America were fearful that the German mark might start to tumble in value again. It was an unfortunate fact that the far right DNVP and other like-minded parties in the German Reichstag could muster sufficient votes to defeat the ratification of any reparations' deal produced by the Allies and America. The Washington Institute of Economics was perturbed by the differences in the figures produced by the German government and those produced by the Reparations Commission and decided to look into the matter independently. It produced a tactful report which adjudged the correct amount payable to be roughly half way between the two sets of figures.

REPARATIONS TO 1924

	1 Reparations Commission	2 German Figures	3 W. Institute of Economics
1 Cash payments under London Agreement of 1921 and 22	1,690.7	1,700	1,580
2 Rhineland Customs duties	3.3	3	3.3
3 Other cash payments	16.0	51	1.4
4 Payments under the Rep. Rec. Act (Mainly to England)	372.6	373	172.2
5 Coal and Coke	959.2	2,334	929.7
6 By-products of coal	30.7	40	.
7 Dyes and Pharmaceutical Mats.	115.3	250	71.7
8 Deliveries of Livestock	146.9	204	273.3
9 Agricultural Machinery & Tools	20.8	21	.
10 Other deliveries in kind	395.1	385	159.3
11 Belgian works of art and the Louvain Library	2.2	16	1.0
12 Ocean-going ships: (a) Handed over (b) Seized during the War	711.5	3,426 1,060	3,650.0 .
13 Inland water craft	50.0	56	106.4
14 Dock and harbour works (Compensation demand for the fleet sunk at Scapa Flow)	.	80	.
15 Railway rolling stock	1,102.5	1,803	1,011.6
16 Lorries	32.2	59	.
17 Non-military property left in occupied areas	140.0	5,041	1,200
18 Private cables	53.2	78	77.8
19 German private property abroad	13.2	10,080	10,000
20 Settlements	.	617	.
21 Railway and coal mines in Shantung, schools in Shanghai Share of the State Bank of Morocco	2.5	95	. 0.6
22 Value of share of Reich and State Debt apportioned to ceded territories	25.6	657	
23 Ceded property of Reich & States Saar Coal mines Railroad equipment in ceded territory Value of securities delivered	2,480.5 300.0 . .	8,652 1,018 . .	5,000 651.1 400 303
24 Labour of German Prisoners of war	.	1,200	.
25 Scrap Metal for war material	52.8	52	200
26 Surrendered war fleet	.	1,338	.
27 Enforced payments and deliveries during the Ruhr occupation	921.2	1,370	
28 Cost of occupation	778.9	2,012	
29 Sundries: (a) Cost of Interallied Commissions (b) Destruction of War Material, including scuttling of the fleet (c) Industrial disarmament (d) Cost of plebiscites		106 8,500 3,500 400	
	10,416.9	56,577	25,791

20.43 Gold Marks to £. Data from Borsky's Greatest Swindle in the World. In a footnote he declares that the data given by the Washington Institute of Economics are incomplete as regards points 1,3,4,6,7,27 and 28, since the data only cover the period up to September 31st 1922. Up to the outbreak of the Ruhr conflict on January 11th 1923 Germany had made a number of further small payments in cash and deliveries in kind which are not taken into consideration in this statement, which neither includes the compulsory deliveries made during the Ruhr occupation (point 27) not the cost of the occupation of the Rhineland referred to under point 28. Another 2,000 million gold marks should be added under these headlines.

Figure 9.1 Differing Estimates of Reparations paid by Germany by 1924

It backed German claims that any private property abroad, appropriated by the Allies, should be credited in full against the reparations by the Allies, whereas in making its assessment the Reparations Commission had only taken into account the 'balance resulting from the proceeds of the liquidation of German property abroad and compensation to the owners of Allied investments in Germany, also liquidated in the war.'[1]

Whereas the fate of the pre-war Allied investments in Germany was allowed to pass into oblivion in the rapprochement of the 1920s, Germany never forgot the value of its citizens'appropriated property and investments abroad, which had been credited against the reparations. In February 1930, as part of the Young Plan settlement, Germany secured a further concession over the reparations that 'the Allied Governments should make no further use of their rights to seize, retain or liquidate German property abroad.' *The Economist* got hot under the collar about the settlement and regarded the whole saga as 'unfortunate.'[2]

The Washington Institute was also generous to Germany over the amount it credited for the loss of the German merchant fleet, as the magnificent new fleet which Germany produced between 1921 and 1923 cost far less than the amount which the Washington Institute had credited for the loss of its aged merchant fleet.[3]

Other items, which inflated the German figures, included the destruction of war material. Germany even included the fleet which it had itself scuttled at Scapa Flow!

It is astonishing that the German government had the audacity to include this item in its list of reparations, or that America took the German government's figures at all seriously after noting its inclusion. Germany also included in its figures the value of the work done by the German prisoners of war, without any mention being made, of the labour performed, often under inhuman conditions, of the Allied prisoners of war in World War I.

The Czech economist, Borsky, would complain bitterly of comparisons between the war indemnity paid by France to Germany after the Franco-Prussian war with the sums extracted from Germany in reparations after World War I, because he stated that the French had not had

1. Official statement of the Reparations Commission, published by Havas on 11 February 1931. G. Borsky. *The Greatest Swindle in the World.* p.50.

2. *The Economist.* 22.2.30.

3. The German government compensated the German shipowners in 1921 for the loss of their ships in 1921 by paying them 550 million marks (Report of the Schiffbau-Treuhand-Bank quoted by Minister of State Count Roedern in 10 Jahre Deutsche Geschichte 1918–28) but it claimed they had been worth more in 1919 due to the acute shortage of ships at that time.

the value of non-military property left behind at Sedan in 1870 credited against their indemnity at all, nor the value of 'state property' in Alsace-Lorraine, whereas even the Reparations Commission had credited Germany with having paid 2,480.5 million marks (£124 million approx) in respect of property ceded by Germany in areas it had occupied in Alsace and Lorraine between 1870 and 1918. Germany had blithely valued the property it had erected in the ceded territories at £483 million and received sympathy at home and abroad for having its valuation questioned.

The Dawes Report proposed stabilising German currency on a gold basis. The annuities payable in reparations would rise gradually according to an index which would vary according to the nation's prosperity. A transfer committee was to be set up to ease currency exchange problems and Germany was to receive 800 million gold marks initially to set up the system and ease its teething problems.[4]

The strident opposition of the largest party[5] in the German Reichstag, the DNVP, to the Dawes Plan persuaded the Allies and America to give Germany sweeteners to accept the deal. If Germany agreed to stabilise its currency on the basis of a 'gold-exchange in effect' the American Federal Reserve Bank agreed to consider as eligible for their open market purchases certain German dollar trade bills payable in the United States, if endorsed by the recently established German Gold Rediscount Bank, the so-called Schacht Bank.'[6]

The weakness of the American negotiators in believing that they had to bribe Germany to accept the Dawes Plan was greeted with delight by Stresemann. He declared to the Reichstag ecstatically,

> 'This marks the beginning of the great changes in the constellation of world powers which are necessary to bring about the revision of the Versailles Treaty.'[7]

On the insistence of Poincaré, a second Commission was set up to locate and repatriate the German money the Allies had located overseas, to stop

---

4. *Royal Institute of International Affairs Survey*. 1924. p.352.

5. In the elections of May 1924 the German Nationalists (DNVP) had made great gains and become the largest single party in the Reichstag with 10 extra seats added to their 96 under Germany's proportional representation system. Refusing to take office they had made a howl of protest against the Dawes Plan.

6. *New York Times*. 17.5.24.

7. 6.6.24. Reproduced in G. Borsky. *The Greatest Swindle in the World*.

8. *Annual Register*. 1924. 7 milliard marks

New York Times. $2,000,000,000 dollars. Feb. 1924.

New York Times. Said France assessed German marks abroad at between 8 and 15 milliard marks.

the country financing another 'great inflation.' Estimates of the amount of money Germany had abroad varied from 7 to 15 milliard marks[8] but it is difficult to discover how much money was actually repatriated.

With the knowledge gained after World War II one can say that the Dawes Plan was a generous plan. France, after all, never got a loan to stabilise her currency after her hyperinflation in 1926. Germany received 800,000 gold marks. While figures, which emerged after 1945, show that although Germany paid 8 milliard gold marks (approximately £400 million at 20.43 marks to the £) in reparations by 1924, only about £80 million was in cash, the rest being old ships, property etc. from the French territory that Germany had occupied since 1870.[9] Germany had also netted a useful influx of hard currency of some £400 million during the hyper-inflationary period.

So Germany had actually received substantially more hard currency during the 'Great Inflation' than it had paid back in monetary reparations.[10]

Germany was now in a most favourable position to compete with foreign industry as its workers were now mostly working a ten hour working day, and its real wages had dropped to 74% of the average level in 1913.[11]

Unfortunately, however, Keynes had changed his mind about the terms of the Dawes Plan by October 1924. Perhaps he was influenced by the distress emanating from Germany. Those who had been forced to sell goods and property for what turned out to be waste paper in the hyper-inflationary years had been allowed no compensation. Inevitably the necessity for paying reparations was used to excuse the inequity involved. Perhaps it was listening to the hardship of individual citizens which persuaded Keynes to change his mind about the Dawes Plan. For in the Autumn he mustered up all his invective to protest against it:

'The Dawes Plan pretends to erect a system which is not compatible with civilisation or with human nature. It sets up foreign control over the banking, the transport, and the fiscal systems of Germany, the object of which will be to extract the last drop of sweat ... No reparations will ever be obtained from Germany except such moderate sums, well within her powers, as she will voluntarily pay. The Dawes Scheme pretends to attempt more than this. Therefore it will fail.'[12]

9. G. Borsky. *The Greatest Swindle in the World.* Table on page 45 and 46 shows the different values which the Allies, their associate America and Germany put upon the value of the property etc. surrendered to the Allies in reparations.

10. *Financial News.* 9.4.45. Figures taken from the April issue of *The Banker.*

11. S. Taylor. *Germany. 1918–1933.*

12. The Nation and the Athenaeum. 4.10.24. Quoted in *The Carthaginian Peace.* E. Mantoux. p.146.

Such words seem to have been influenced by German propaganda. Looking at Germany in an unbiased light one can see that country was in a position to make a great fortune. It had no debt, a large, fully modernised industrial base, plenty of raw materials and an impoverished workforce, desperate for work.[13] In contrast the British working man unfortunately still laboured under the delusion that the world owed him a living. The disaffected British miner was still working a seven hour day, competing against the miners in the Ruhr, working an eight and a half hour day underground and a ten hour day above. During the great strike of 1926, therefore, the British miners were, to a very real extent, fighting the German mine owners rather than their own[14] and that was a fight they could not win.

In 1919 Keynes had predicted that Germany 'cannot export coal in the near future ... if she is to continue as an industrial nation.'

But in 1926 Germany exported (net) 35 million tons, or twice the amount of average pre-World War I exports (including the parts of Silesia which had been ceded to Poland).[15] As no-one had told the British miners the truth about Germany's 'great inflation' however they could not believe that German coal could pose a threat to their own livelihood. Their simmering sense of injustice over an, impossible to believe, request to accept longer hours and lower wages, because of competition from 'destitute' Germany, has lasted nearly to this day.

The reason that the Allies had decided to set up 'foreign control over the banking, transport and the fiscal systems of Germany' was because, after their experience before the stablisation of the mark, they did not trust Germany to maintain the value of the mark and pay the reparations without foreign supervision.

The 'gold-exchange standard in effect' would mean that countries, like Britain, which had to compete on level terms with Germany, would find its high interest rates increasingly constricting.

The Allies hoped that with all the controls that they proposed to create to ensure payment of the reparations that the stability of the mark would not be threatened. But perhaps because of the powerful DNVP's agitation against the Dawes Plan and their determination to secure an

13. *Royal Institute of International Affairs Survey*. 1930. p.544. The economist, Menkin, testified to the great increase in the workforce in this period, presumably from those who had been living on unearned incomes before.

14. *Economic Organisation of the British Coal Industry*. A. M. Neuman. 1934. Appendix A. p.475 – After the coal strike 'Most of the districts made arrangements on the basis of an eight hours' working day: only Yorkshire, Nottinghamshire, Derbyshire and Kent agreed on a 7 and a half hour basis, whilst the North East coast introduced 7 and a half hours for hewers only.'

15. E. Mantoux. *The Carthaginian Peace*. p.163. R. C. Long. *The Mythology of Reparations*. 1928. p.103–4.

agreement they did promise to give Germany 'transfer protection' over its reparations' payments.

'Transfer protection' promised that if Germany was ever faced with an economic depression and the stability of the mark was threatened by the need to make large reparations' payments overseas, these could be suspended in order to ensure the stability of the mark. Carl Bergmann, the German reparations expert, looking at this concession from a German point of view, declared it to be 'the fundamental innovation, the decisive forward step, in dealing with the reparation problem.'

The American economist, Stephen A. Schuker,[16] in his study of the period, *The End of French Predominance in Europe*, declared of the issue of 'transfer protection'.

> 'When the Germans accepted the Dawes Plan, they fully intended to ask for another reduction in reparations within three or four years. The outcome at London, by tying France's hands in the event of default, made it virtually certain that the next German bid for downward revision would meet with success. Meanwhile, French troops were unconditionally bound to leave the Ruhr – as they did on schedule in August 1925. Germany remained free to take advantage of its industrial superiority in subsequent trade and metallurgical negotiations. In the following years German businessmen would often demonstrate greater willingness to work toward the creation of what Sydoux described as a 'West European Zollverein' than their protectionist-minded French counterparts. But this very fact bore eloquent witness to the Germans' confidence that the formidable economic organisation of the Reich would enable them to dominate any such precursor of the Common Market.'

In accordance with the agreement it had made after Stinnes's ultimatum in October 1923, the German government paid the Ruhr industrialists 706 million gold marks (roughly £35 million) in 1925 as compensation for the effects of the Ruhr conflict.[17]

'Cash transfers' in reparations for 1925 totalled 65 million gold marks (roughly £3 million).[18]

9.2 Germany Undertakes not to Launch an Aggressive War Across the Rhine

As the Allies' economic hold over Germany was tenuous, France tried to ensure her country's protection by political means. The fruit of this

---

16. Stephen A. Schuker. *American 'Reparations' to Germany*. p.87.

17. Report of Reichsfinanzministerium to the Reichstag. 1925.

18. *Royal Institute of International Affairs Survey*. 1929. p.116. note.1.

activity was the Geneva Protocol – a proposal by which all signatories to the League of Nations would be bound to come to each other's defence if they were subjected to an unprovoked attack. The Protocol was couched in Olympian language but the message was plain. France did not feel that she had won the war.

She felt that Germany still posed a danger to France. The Allied troops were due soon to leave the Ruhr. Then Germany would ask for more concessions. France pleaded for Britain to pledge help for her defence. Naturally weakened Britain could not give that assurance. The Geneva Protocol, designed to give her that protection, failed.[19]

It was into this climate of international unease that Herr Stresemann's Foreign Policy initiative came, like a shaft of sunlight. Stresemann proposed a memorandum that would give France her peace of mind, an undertaking not to launch an aggressive war against France across the Rhine.[20] Stresemann was later awarded the Nobel Peace prize for this pledge.[21] Germany had confounded all the doubters, showing 'proof' of good intent.

Briand for France's positive response to his proposal delighted Stresemann. The reassured French left the Ruhr on 31 July as agreed under the terms of the Dawes Plan and on 25 August the last French soldier evacuated the towns of Duisberg and Düsseldorf.

It has been argued that the impetus for Stresemann's promise to guarantee the status quo along the Rhine did not come from purely altruistic motives, however. Partly perhaps he feared a renewed British/French entente. But there was another more potent reason for his action. Now that France had withdrawn from the Ruhr, and were scheduled to leave the Cologne area soon, he looked forward to the day when they would evacuate the Rhineland altogether. In a message he had his ambassador, Count Brockforff- Rantzau deliver to the Russian Commissar Litvinov on 7 April Stresemann had written:

'From the start the German government has presumed that the French government will not be persuaded to withdraw its forces (from the Rhine) unless France's so-called need for security is satisfied in some manner.'[22]

On 7 September he was more explicit. In a letter to the Crown Prince, written just before his invitation to Locarno he wrote: 'The most

19. 'the signatory states assume the obligation, individually and collectively, of coming to the assistance of the attacked or threatened State.' (Article XI, paragraph 3.)

20. E. Eyck. *The Weimar Republic*. Vol. II. 20.1.25. Memo to Britain. p.5.

21. 1926 Nobel Peace Prize went to Stresemann and Briand. p.83.

22. *Stresemann Papers*. 7415H. *Stresemann Vermachtnis*. II. p.553. See also Annelise Thimme. *Gustav Stresemann: Legende und Wirklichkeit. Historische Zeitscrift*, April 1956. pp.287, pp.320ff.

important task with respect to question Number One (that is the reparations) is the liberation of German soil from French occupation. First we must get the throttler from our throat.'[23]

Now that the German hierarchy had defeated the forces from 'within' in their country they were eager to go on the offensive in foreign affairs. In order to encourage the French to complete the evacuation of German soil, Germany had to make a political gesture of goodwill. Then many of the military and industrial hierarchy looked to achieving political triumphs: 'the correction of the eastern boundary: regaining Danzig and the Polish Corridor and revising the border in Upper Silesia. A German-Austrian union stands in the further future.'

9.3 Allies Make Concessions to Germany

Stresemann's offer not to launch a war across the Rhine against France, however, did not come without strings. The Allies made several concessions for Germany's pledge.

Firstly, although Germany expressly refused to recognise her Eastern borders, the treaty was still ratified.

Stresemann had made his views plain on Poland.

'Naturally we refuse to see any justification for the continued existence of the present Polish state; we shall therefore never recognise the Polish borders of our own free will.'[24] And it was amply apparent that no one felt strong enough to make him. But although he would not guarantee Poland's border, and publicly stated Germany's desire for the return of her Eastern territory, Stresemann personally vouched for Germany's peaceful intent, and declared that Germany hoped to revise its Eastern border merely by 'friendly negotiation, diplomatic procedure or ... by recourse to the good offices of the League of Nations.'

Such was his prestige with the peace-yearning Allies that, when the legislation lay on the statute book all mention of the eastern border was omitted.

---

23. Stresemann wrote of his policy 'our policy in this respect will have to consist principally of being artful' (finassieren) which the Grosse Meyer of 1908 gives as 'to use tricks, to employ artifice.'
General von Seeckt, Chief of the General Staff by Stresemann's desire to use diplomacy for political ends:
'It is not desirable to induce a crisis at this time – one doesn't change jockeys in the middle of a race – but the question does remain whether it is not even more important to get that man (Stresemann) out of the way in order to open a path for a different foreign policy.' Rabnau. Seeckt. p.418.
24. *Stresemann Papers*. 7129H.

Secondly, in order to get Germany's signature on the Locarno Treaty, the Allies agreed to evacuate the Cologne zone, one year after the signing of the Treaty, on 12 December 1926.

Their signatures, already dry on the Treaty, must have made them feel obliged to carry out this promise when the date arrived because prudence dictated otherwise. Only nine days before they were due to commence their withdrawal the Manchester Guardian published an article,[25] verified by the German paper Voerwerts, on the extent of clandestine German arms manufacture outside Germany and the connection between the German army and the communist regime in Russia, a connection which violated both the letter and the spirit of the Treaty of Versailles.

As early as 1924 Rabenau discloses in his biography of Germany's military leader, Seekt, 'it was not at all easy for Seekt to conceal from the Allies the increasingly evident signs of the Army's illegal growth.'[26]

They had ample evidence now if they felt strong enough to act on it.

The Allies were also anxious for Germany to become a member of the League of Nations to tie the country in with other responsible nations, in the cause of peace. However, Article 16 of the charter required every member of the League of Nations to co-operate in sanctions, military ones if necessary, if agreed by the League. Germany protested that, as the provisions of the Treaty of Versailles had left its country with so few troops, it would have to be released from the terms of this all important provision. Whereupon the Allies changed the wording of Article 16 so that every member would only have to cooperate in applying sanctions 'to an extent which is compatible with its military situation and takes its geographical position into account.'[27]

As Germany had promised not to launch an aggressive war to retake Alsace/Lorraine Britain guaranteed her signature. It was a measure of Britain's extreme unease over Germany's previous postwar intentions that Stresemann's solemn undertaking not to wage war against France now should have been greeted with such euphoria. It seemed that peace at last had returned to the world. Paul Schmidt recalls the atmosphere outside the Conference.

'As we descended the few steps of the little stairway with Stresemann and Luther, the crowd exploded in another roar of acclaim. Then suddenly everyone was still. All the men in the crowd removed their hats and formed a silent, immobile double row through which we, doubly moved, proceeded to our carriage.'[28] This was the sentiment with which

---

25. *Manchester Guardian.* December 3rd 1926.
26. E. Eyck. *The Weimar Republic.* Vol. II. p.46.
27. *Royal Institute of International Affairs Survey.* 1925. II. p.51.
28. Paul Schmidt. *Statist auf diplomatischer Buhne. 1923–45.* p.92.

the aching, war-weary democratic world had greeted the initiative of the representative of what they had previously considered an autocratic bellicose nation. At last, it seemed that Germany had produced a democrat and a man of peace. Austen Chamberlain, British Foreign Secretary, regarded Stresemann as a hard negotiator but a fair man. When he put his signature to an international agreement on behalf of his country Chamberlain believed his word and guaranteed his signature with a light heart.

Britain had always placed great importance in 'scraps of paper' as an earnest of one's intentions. The British Empire was a civilised one, founded on the rule of law and written guarantees between nations, scrupulously kept. Such a far flung Empire, encompassing so many different nations, could not operate otherwise. This was why Britain had experienced such agonies over Keynes's allegations that the Allies had not fulfilled their obligations embodied in the loosely worded provisions of the Treaty of Versailles. To a punctilious man like Chamberlain, agreements were particularly important. The Times wrote of him on his promotion: 'The shortcomings in leadership which have been attributed to him in his long political career – that he is aloof from his younger colleagues, rather wooden in his outlook on domestic problems, punctilious to the point of rigidity where there is any question of fulfilling even a supposed obligation –are none of them serious faults, may some of them be positive virtues in a Foreign Secretary.'[29]

It was a matter of honour for him to keep his word and he expected the same from Germany.

9.4 Locarno Negotiations

Stresemann's negotiations with men such as Chamberlain, and the French Foreign Minister, Briand, at Locarno, had convinced him that almost everything that Germany desired could be achieved by negotiation. One didn't have to wave a big stick, or deceive. Many in Germany, however, viewed treaties differently, through the eyes of 'real politik.' It was long before Bismarck's time that Frederick the Great had laid down the laws for German diplomacy.

'A sovereign must be guided by the interest of the State.

In the following cases alliances may be broken:

---

29. Austen Chamberlain. *Gentleman in Politics*. p.233. Chamberlain had written to the British Ambassador in Paris: 'no British government ever will or ever can risk the bones of one British grenadier (in defense of the Polish Corridor.)'

(1) When one's ally does not fulfil his engagements;
(2) When one's ally wishes to deceive one and when one cannot by any other means prevent him.
(3) When necessity (force majeure) compels one;
(4) When one lacks means to continue the war.

By the will of Fate wealth influences everything. Rulers are slaves of their means. To promote the interest of their State is a law, to them a law which is inviolable. If a ruler must be ready to sacrifice his life for the welfare of his subjects, he must be still more ready to sacrifice, for the benefit of his subjects, solemn engagements which he has undertaken if their observance would be harmful to his people.'[30]

Frederick the Great had another principle with which to guide his nation. Always negotiate from a position of strength behind which there is always a latent threat of force.

'Royal crowns are won only by means of big guns' he had declared a hundred years before Bismarck had spoken of 'blood and iron.' Germany had the economic strength now to give her political power. Even Stresemann knew that it had been the uncomfortable awareness of Germany's previous intransigence which had persuaded the Allies to treat Germany's promises at Locarno with such solemnity.

In writing *The Economic Consequences of the Peace* Keynes had sat in judgement on Clemenceau for his attitude to the Germans as negotiators:

> 'In the first place he (Clemenceau) was a foremost believer in the view of German psychology that the German understands and can understand nothing but intimidation, that he is without generosity or remorse in negotiation, that there is no advantage he will not take of you and no extent to which he will not demean himself for profit, that he is without honour, pride or mercy. Therefore you must never negotiate with a German or conciliate him; you must dictate to him. On no other terms will he respect you or will you prevent him from cheating you.'[31]

Certainly Hugenberg's and Stinnes's newspapers appeared to confirm Clemenceau's view of the Prussians. Stresemann had won every single object that he had set out to achieve at Locarno. Yet despite the acclaim that resounded around the world, there was no rejoicing in Germany. On the contrary Stinnes's paper declared: 'Warning, if our enemies are rejoicing – and despite, Locarno and the League of Nations they are our enemies so long as they stand on German soil – it is a bad sign for Germany.' Slogans appeared: 'Stresemann, verse man, the pig must be

---

30. J. Ellis Barker. *The Foundations of Germany*. p.85.
31. J. M. Keynes. *The Economic Consequences of the Peace*. p.29.

slaughtered.'[32] A member of the far right in the Reichstag even called the German signatories of the Treaty 'Assassins of their own people.'

The French Foreign minister, Briand, was a great man with a warm heart. Upon the signing of the Treaty Briand said to Stresemann: 'Between our two nations there are still areas of friction and points of pain. May the pact which we have just signed serve as balsam to these wounds ... Then we shall be able to work together toward the realisation in every area of life of the ideal we all bear in our hearts, a Europe that will fulfil its destiny by remaining true to its tradition of civilised and generous spirits.'[33] Then he rushed up to Stresemann with open arms.

'I seized his right hand' Stresemann recalled 'and told him I was sincerely grateful for the words which he had spoken.' Whereupon Briand replied: 'No do not speak of words. I shall give you proof that those were not just words, but rather deeds.'

One likes to think that Stresemann was impressed by such sentiment. In Germany the Hugenberg's newspapers, organ of the prominent German Nationalist Party, the DNVP, dropped their agitation against him. Herr Hugenberg argued that one should not make a martyr out of someone 'whose political star was failing anyway.' For 'Stresemann was an example of the errors of the post-Bismarck, ante-bellum generation, which had ripened from its pre-war blossoms to its present harvest and therefore – one has reason to hope – would soon fade away.'[34]

9.5 Germany Joins League of Nations

After all the euphoria engendered by the Treaty of Locarno the evacuation of Allied troops from the Cologne Zone was completed on 1 February 1926, despite revelations of illegal arms imports. Germany was welcomed with open arms into the League of Nations. No doubt prompted by the DNVP, Stresemann chose to sour this atmosphere by misconstruing the Allies' well-intentioned applause into an admission by them that they had been wrong over the war-guilt issue.

Poincaré had returned to power in France in the Summer of 1926. One can imagine his ire at this topic being brought up again. On the 26 and 27 September 1926 he repeated, yet again, his premise that Imperial Germany was responsible for starting the war. The French government

32. For abuse of Stresemann. E. Eyck. *A History of the Weimar Republic.* p.53. *Stresemann. Vermachtnis.* II. 80. For Newspaper comment from *Deutsche Allemeine Zeitung.* E. Eyck. *The Weimar Republic.* Vol. II. p.38.

33. Suarez. *Briand. L'Artizan de la Paix.* p.129.

34. Hugenberg. *Streiflichter.* p.83.

further issued an official declaration that this was the 'opinion constant' (unaltered view) of the entire administration. In England, *The Times* newspaper supported his view, by declaring that public sentiment in Britain, as in all Allied countries, was in accord with France.

The economic position of Britain and France by 1926, however, was very different to that of Germany. Britain was still enduring the miners' strike which was causing physical and moral suffering to the nation. France, having just endured her own Great Inflation, had been knocking on Germany's door asking for money. Under the stream of German accusations, politicians on all sides of the divide, wrote their memoirs, justifying their actions in the Great War.

9.6   German Propaganda over War Guilt Issue

The first essential to Nationalist leaders, like Herr Hugenberg, was that the slightest slur of guilt should never be placed upon the leaders of German society who had so magnificently wiped out the nation's debts and put it in a position to compete advantageously again in world markets. A foreign scapegoat, therefore, was essential. At the start of World War I Germany had secured the support of the pacifist-minded Social Democrats by accusing Russia of starting the war.[35]

Later Germany then turned the full fury of its propaganda machine on the British whom it had believed would remain neutral in the conflict.

Ramsay Macdonald, who had resigned as leader of the minority Labour Party over his opposition to the war, had unwittingly handed them a fabulous propaganda weapon. A pacifist himself, he had initially blamed the navy for dragging Britain into World War I and then printed an article in the newspaper, *The Labour Leader*, on 13 August 1914, entitled: 'Why we are at War' subtitling it, 'A reply to Sir Edward Grey.'

In the article Ramsay Macdonald, accused Sir Edward Grey, not of going to war over the invasion of neutral Belgium, but because of Britain's entangling Entente with France.

Firstly he charged that:

> 'When Sir Edward Grey failed to secure peace between Germany and Russia, he worked deliberately to involve us in the war, using Belgium as his chief excuse.'

---

35. Fritz Fischer. *War of Illusions.* p.469–70.
'But behind Bethmann Hollweg's hostility to Russia there was a domestic factor which cannot be over-estimated; the German Social Democrats were prepared to accept a foreign policy which treated Russia as the enemy ...'

Secondly he charged in heavy type:

'If France had decided to attack Germany through Belgium, Sir Edward Grey would not have objected.'

Thirdly he charged that both the Prime Minister and Sir Edward Grey had 'withheld the full truth from us.'

These were very grave accusations but they struck no echo in Britain in 1914, even though, ever since Napoleon's time, the British had had an antipathy towards the French. The emergent Labour Party distanced itself from Macdonald and rallied to the government.

However one outraged observer, Sir Valentine Chirol, wrote a letter to *The Times*, complaining of the disastrous impact of Ramsay Macdonald's pamphlet in Germany:

'Is it mere coincidence that the German Chancellor himself, in framing his appeals for sympathy with a peace-loving Germany reluctantly dragged into war by the machinations of her enemies, invariably bases his denunciations of Great Britain's perfidy on just the same arguments which Mr. Macdonald employs? Is it mere coincidence that following Mr. Macdonald's lead, the whole German Press has concentrated the worst venom upon Sir Edward Grey as the embodiment of British bad faith, with peace always on his lips and war in his heart? It has been my business, though no longer in a journalistic capacity, to study the German Press and the Press of some of neutral States, very carefully during the last seven weeks. There is scarcely an important German paper which has not reproduced Mr. Macdonald's manifesto, in part or in whole, to justify his own diatribes against England. So much value is, indeed, attached to it for the purpose of German propaganda that it has evidently been imported in considerable quantities into Germany in the leaflet shape, as it is being actually distributed from there to neutral countries with a view to 'spreading the truth.'[36]

Ramsay Macdonald was a sincere man who later became widely respected. He could not have understood the impact his words would have in a country, like Germany in 1914, where freedom of speech was much more proscribed than in Britain, even in peacetime, and where individuals promoting an unpatriotic point of view in a popular war would almost certainly have been interned, if not tried for treason. He might have written in a completely different vein anyway had he known that Poincaré had withdrawn France's troops 10 kilometres behind her borders, after the murder of the Archduke Ferdinand at Sarajevo and Austria's strongly worded ultimatum to the Serbs, in order to avoid giving Germany the slightest excuse to invade. He wrote a robust letter to

36. *The Times*. 1 October 1914.

The Times in answer to Sir Valentine Chirol's letter maintaining that the Kaiser had accused the British of 'treachery' before the publication of his leaflet and that his was merely one of many British letters published in Germany, written in a similar vein.

However Sir Valentine Chirol had a more profound insight than Ramsay Macdonald of the impact of 'Why we are at War' in Germany in 1914, and in the years to come.

In his letter Sir Valentine Chirol disclosed that,

> 'The fact is never mentioned in Germany that Mr. Macdonald can no longer be recognised as the mouthpiece of the political party which he is supposed to lead; that the *Labour Leader* ... is the only one of the socialist organs which still follows him; that the British public as a whole ... treat him with contemptuous indifference. No: abroad his name is still good enough to represent an important and recognised political party; he is the spokesman of the guilty conscience of England.'

In the Spring of 1915 The Times disclosed that Ramsay Macdonald's name was again being used by the Germans in the Spanish edition of the *Hamburger Nachtrichten* to justify Germany's involvement in the war and persuade firms in the neutral countries to continue to do business with Germany. It was inevitable that there would be many newspapers in Germany as well as the British *Morning Post*, which stated that Ramsay Macdonald had 'attributed the cataclysm of Europe to the Machiavellism of Sir Edward Grey.'[37]

In August 1914 Bethmann Hollweg, the incumbent German Chancellor, had declared to the Reichstag:

> 'Russia has hurled a firebrand into our house. A war with Russia and France has been forced upon us.'[38]

However after Ramsay Macdonald's outburst had been disseminated in Germany and gained widespread acceptance, Bethmann Hollweg publicly changed his views on the origins of the war. Herr Erzberger commentated admiringly on Bethmann Hollweg's speech to the Reichstag on 2 December 1914 in his article in *Der Tag* a few days later:

> 'It expressed the heartfelt convictions of the whole nation. It touched on France, referred briefly to Russia and then with the full force of irrefutable facts gave historic proof that this is England's war and England wanted the war. This is what Germany believes today.'[39]

37. H. Hessell Tiltman. *James Ramsey Macdonald. Labour's Man of Destiny.* (1929) p.95.
38. *Geiss.* II. No. 1146. Bethmann Hollweg's declaration to the Reichstag. 4.8.14. 3.30 pm. F. Fischer. *War of Illusions.* p.511.
39. M. Erzberger. *Der Tag.* 6.12.12. Fritz Fischer. *War of Illusions.* p.548.

One does not know to what extent the German public as a whole became imbued with the conviction that 'England' was the originator of the war during the conflict. Certainly not all people retained that conviction. For on 24 June 1918, after victory had been won against Russia but was beginning to look uncertain on the western front, Richard von Kuhlmann, Germany's Foreign minister, and an advocate of coexistence with Britain before the war, decided to pursue a more tactful course in case overall victory should prove impossible. It had been fear of the Russian mobilisation which had rallied the German socialists in 1914. Kuhlmann blamed defeated Russia in 1918 for starting the Great War.

> 'I believe one can say, without fear of being contradicted by the result of further revelations and investigations, that the deeper we penetrate into the antecedents of the war the clearer it becomes that the Power which planned and desired the war was Russia.'[40]

Communists were happy to subscribe to this theory. Any propaganda detrimental to Imperial Russia could not but strengthen their tenuous hold on power. However, they decided to enlarge on the theme. They accused all leaders of society, everywhere, of imperialism. The Allies had different ideas however.

The Austrian and Prussian State Archives were not opened until after World War II, but the delegates to the Peace Conference at Versailles felt sufficiently confident of their facts to demand that the Socialist German Government admit Germany's responsibility for the war in 1919. The German Socialists, however, managed to salvage some honour from the admission by asserting stoutly that Germany was not 'alone' responsible.[41]

By the mid 1920s the German right-wing Press wished to retreat from this position. The DNVP and the NSDAP went still farther.

Hitler in *Mein Kampf* was representative of extreme right opinion over the war-guilt issue:

> 'To make Germany alone responsible for the war is pure falsehood. On the contrary, we should place the entire guilt on our opponents, even if this were not, as in fact it is, the strict truth.
>
> 'The vast mass of a nation consists of men who are disposed to doubt and uncertainty. If its propaganda admits the least shadow of right on the enemy's side, the way has been paved for doubting its own right.'[42]

40. *Annual Register*. 1918. p.198.
41. Count V. Brockdorff-Rantzau at the Peace Conference: 'It is demanded of us that we shall confess to ourselves to be the only ones guilty of the war. Such a confession in my mouth would be a lie ... We energetically deny that Germany and its people, who were convinced that they were waging a war of defense, were alone guilty.'
42. *Mein Kampf*. Quoted by F. W. Foerster in *Europe and the German Question*. p.82.

Some of the people on the Government Committee set up to investigate the 'war-guilt' problem seemed to be of a like mind to Hitler. Professor Fischer-Baling who took part in the proceedings explains his frustrations:

> 'It has often been said that the Committee should have come to some valid conclusions after ten years' time. And it would have if some of the experts had not deliberately impeded progress. Anybody who actually watched these men operate still explodes with rage at the way they used marked cards in this game of making their own notion of the national interest prevail. It is true that some responsible members sought to present ... a view of events which emphasised the interrelationship of the power struggles of all countries. Such members concluded that they had to assign joint responsibility for what had ensued; nevertheless they regarded the policies of Russia and Germany as the chief causes of European unrest. Other members of the Committee, however, flatly refused to admit that Germany had made any mistakes whatever or had even caused any provocations. They were adamant on this point because they thought any admission from Germans would foul their own nest and weaken their front in their battle against the Treaty of Versailles.'[43]

In the end the German extreme right reverted to their old accusations. The country which had started the war had been their old economic rival Great Britain. The British people had actually elected as Prime Minister in 1923, the man who, in 1914, in Sir Valentine Chirol's words, had 'sought to besmirch the reputation of his country', Ramsay Macdonald. No one would have surely elevated someone to run their country unless they shared his political views.

This was however not the case. Although they shared his anti-French sentiment in 1923, working class Britons had elected Ramsay Macdonald leader of the country primarily because of his concern over unemployment and deprivation in their own country, not because of his little publicised views (in Britain) as to who started World War I. Patriotic Germans and their friends however who had received the full blast of publicity over his leaflet 'Why we are at War', felt that Ramsay Macdonald could not have been elected, ever, to the leadership, if the British nation had not agreed with his wartime views. It was only one short step from saying that Britain was partly responsible for the war to saying that Britain was the prime mover. It had been asserted before and would soon be asserted again, with devastating timing, by Herr Hugenberg's vast publicity machine.

43. Eugen Fischer-Baling. *Der Untersuchungsausschuss fur die Schuldfrage des ersten Weltkrieges* in Alfred Herrmann. ed., Aus Geschichte und Politik. *Feschrift zum 70.* Geburtstag von Ludwig Bergstrasser. p.136. E. Eyck. *The Weimar Republic*. Vol. II. p.80–1.

The German Nationalists and their friends on the extreme right, however, had to wait until they managed to persuade the Americans that the system of payment for the reparations needed revising before they could utilise the war guilt issue to their own advantage. It would be extremely felicitous for them that when they chose to make their protest against the so-called 'war guilt' clause, in the Autumn of 1929, Ramsay Macdonald would be Prime Minister of England again.

9.7 Germany Begins Programme of Public Works

Stresemann had heralded the opening up of the American banking system to Germany with the words:

> 'This marks the beginning of the great changes in the constellation of world powers which are necessary to bring about the revision of the Treaty of Versailles.'

As Germany decided upon a high interest rate policy,[44] cash which might have gone to weak, new Republics in Eastern Europe went to Germany. Germany hoped to encourage America to become its friend by encouraging her to make loans and become financially involved in the country's wellbeing, as Stresemann wrote in his diary on 25 September 1924:

> 'The thing to do now is to win over the individual subscriber to the idea of a German loan. The granting of a loan would give us an army of 300,000 people in America who would make propaganda for Germany because they would be interested in her welfare.'[45]

The first 'private' or commercial loan for 10 million dollars was issued to the Krupp Works in Essen on 24 December 1924, closely followed by one for 12 million dollars to the Thyssen undertaking.[46]

---

44. 9% – 1925, 6¹/2% – 1926, 7% – 1927, 7% – 1928.
45. Stresemann's Diary. (1/591) G. Borsky. *The Greatest Swindle in the World.* p.63. F. W. Foerster. *Europe and the German Question.* p.276–7 – printed the following extract from the *American Saturday Evening Post* on the assertion made in Germany regarding how lending money forced countries with basically different interests and viewpoints into friendship.
'America joined the Allies in 1917 because she had lent them her money. In international intercourse the debtor is supported by the creditor. The object of the Hoover Plan of 1931 for paying reparations is to protect the two billions of American money invested in Germany. For the debt obliges America to be Germany's political friend.'
46. G. Borsky. *The Greatest Swindle in the World.* Prefaced by Lord Vansittart. 64.

Millions more money was poured into Germany. It seemed a wonderful investment opportunity. Germany now had a stable, low cost economy and the Dawes Plan mechanism worked well enough in gathering the reparations. America had failed to prosecute the war to its finish and since then propaganda had flourished on both sides. Now however America felt that, if she lent Germany sufficient money to enable industry to generate the profits to pay its reparations without pain, old passions from the war might die down and Germany become the friend of its ex-enemies. Under the new Dawes Plan the reparations were to be looked upon as a 'business rather than a political problem'[47] The framers of the plan knew that the cumbersome machinery was not a final solution to the reparations 'problem' so there was no new finite amount that Germany might be required to pay. The payments were scheduled to be paid on a sliding scale rising to 2,500,000,000 marks (£125,000,000 a year) after five years. They were made principally by means of 'deliveries in kind' tariffs, railway bonds and the proceeds of a transport tax, the money raised being used not only to pay the reparations, but also to pay the costs, amongst other items, of the interest on the Dawes Loan.

A major consideration with the Allies was the fear that Germany might 'collapse' its currency again. In order to make certain that the value of the German mark remained constant the Allies declared that Germany would be allowed to 'suspend' reparations' payments if the stability of the German mark was ever threatened. Germany stressed repeatedly the problem it would have in paying money overseas. It needed export outlets for its industry to generate the cash to pay the Allies. So the Allies and America lent Germany copious sums to modernise its industry and decided that they would be responsible for the 'transfer problem' by instituting controls to ensure payment.

The French excuse for occupying the Ruhr had been because France had not received her precious coal deliveries and other 'deliveries in kind' specified by the Treaty of Versailles. Elaborate arrangements were now made to ensure that the 'deliveries in kind' would be made, and funded by Germany. By 1929 the French supervised railways' bonds were producing the magnificent sum of £32, and the industrial debentures and transport tax, almost another £30 million with which to reimburse the German exporters. The Royal Institute of International Affairs' Survey for 1929 gives the tortuous route through which the reparations came, a method by which the French coal merchant's payment for German coal was used to fund France's reparations, while the German coal owner was paid for his produce from the tax levied on the German railways etc.

47. *Royal Institute of International Affairs Survey.* 1929. p.112.

'A French importer would contract with a German manufacturer for the delivery of machinery; the actual contract followed ordinary commercial practice, except that the German exporter agreed to accept his price from the office of the Agent-General for Reparation Payments and the French buyer agreed not to re-export his purchase. The contract was then sent to the Paris office of the Reparations Commission for approval and afterwards to the Transfer Committee. When the date of payment arrived, the French Government made out a draft upon their credit with the Agent-General, and handed over this draft to the French buyer who paid the French government according to agreed terms. The buyer then endorsed the draft and forwarded it to his German creditor, who had it collected in the ordinary way through his bank; and the final payment was then made by the Agent- General out of the general funds provided by the German government's Reparations account.'

Though coal, coke, lignite, dyestuffs and fertilisers and other heavy materials consisted the major part of 'deliveries in kind', 'practically any commodity or service could be sold under a delivery in kind contract.'

Most of the reparations to Britain however were counted as 'cash transfers' and were made by means of a somewhat simpler system of a tariff of 30% on exports. In March 1924, after the stabilisation of the German mark, the British government government, listening to pleas from German exporters that they had not been reimbursed by their government, had reduced its tariff on German goods to 5%, confident that Britain could compete with Germany on those terms. But in August 1924 the tariff had been raised again to 26%, collectable by British customs.

After securing Germany's return to a 'gold-exchange standard in effect' America had put pressure on other countries to set a good example of stable currencies and return to the gold standard. Before Britain returned to the gold standard in May 1925, however, Germany and Britain came to a new arrangement over the tariff collection of reparations by which, instead of the tariff being collected by British customs and Germany reimbursing it to its exporters, Germany declared that it would collect a higher tariff of 30% and deliver it direct into the hands of the Agent-General for reparations.

T*he Royal Institute Survey* explains how it worked:

'This new scheme was based on the voluntary surrender by the German exporters of part of the sterling proceeds accruing to them from their shipments to Great Britain. By the end of May 1925, 1,200 German exporting firms, representing 90 per cent of the trade with Great Britain had fallen in with the scheme and had agreed to surrender 30% of their sterling proceeds. This percentage was delivered to the Reichsbank; and out of the amount thus acquired the Reichsbank made payments each month into the account of the

Agent-General for Reparation Payments with the Bank of England, these sums representing the sterling equivalent of the Reichsmark credits held by him for the British government. As soon as he was notified of the deposits thus made, the Agent-General reimbursed the German exporters against the appropriate documents, and, subject to the approval of the Transfer Committee, paid over his sterling credits to the British government.'[48]

German exporters were reimbursed for the 30% deducted in reparations and the burden of paying the tax was divided amongst the whole of German industry, burdening it with some 15% more onerous taxes than British industry[49] while the Dawes Plan was in force. Despite this German industry prospered because practically all its previous burden of debt had been washed away in the Great Inflation and, under the agreement made in November 1923, its employees were working longer hours for lower wages than those in Britain.

Although the 'cash' balance sheet was swelled by the proceeds of tariffs, including them as cash was slightly a misnomer.[50] Churchill promised his British audience, that if the German government failed to hand over the sums paid to them by the German exporters, Britain would revert to levying the tariff herself.[51]

After Locarno, though, suspicions of German intentions over the reparations subsided. In the 'forgive and forget' atmosphere of the mid 1920s people were disposed to believe that any shortage of cash remittances would be due to an inability to pay, rather than an unwillingness to adapt the German economy to fulfil its international obligations. Sentiment waxed pro-German and anti-French, especially after foreigners had stretched out their hand in friendship to Germany by lending it money. Much of the reparations had been secured through the Allied controls on tariffs and 'deliveries in kind.' But tedious form filling had to be undertaken for both methods of collection. How much easier it would be, Germany inferred, if it just received a bill twice a year for the reparations and paid it, without an army of civil servants to supervise. After the events of 1923 majority opinion in Great Britain was already firmly of the opinion that Germany had been harshly treated under the terms of the Treaty of Versailles. Besides Germany's coal 'deliveries in kind' were hurting Britain's mining industry. As soon as everyone was equally satisfied that Germany was a responsible power, the time-con-

48. *Royal Institute of International Affairs Survey.* 1929. pp.115–23.

49. Stephen A. Schuker. *American 'Reparations' to Germany.* p.32.

50. G. Borsky. *The Greatest Swindle in the World.* (1942) Preface by Lord Vansittart. p.57. According to Borsky they should have been labelled 'deliveries in kind' as the 'German government had neither to pay this amount in foreign currency nor to transfer it.'

51. *Annual Register.* 1925. p.37.

suming paper checks designed to ensure payment should be removed.[52]

In Germany it was felt that this should happen sooner, rather than later, provided that Germany was given a smaller reparation bill to bear. In March 1927 there was a popular debate by all parties in the Reichstag in favour of a revision of the Dawes Plan. Herr Dessauer of the Centre Party declared that the fact that reparations had been made 'with comparative ease' every year was due to the large loans which Germany could not expect to continue indefinitely. His chief argument in favour of revision was that the 'artificial stimulation of German exports caused by the Plan would, in the long run, do considerable harm to the rest of the world.'[53]

Germany's coal imports had indeed so flooded Britain in 1926 that some of the tariff money had been used to help swell France's reparations. Coal 'deliveries in kind' to France and Italy represented a continual lost market to Britain's coal mines. 'Deliveries in kind' were hurting French manufacturers too, not only in export markets but also on the home market. But Germany had declared that after its hyper- inflation its citizens were too poor to be taxed to pay reparations. Only by exporting could the country raise the reparations sums due.

None of the Allies liked to dwell in public on this aspect of the reparations however. America began to get worried by Germany's insatiable demand for money and whether the return of her loans would rate equally with reparations dues. American newspapers did not linger on the impressive 'technical rationalisation' which German industry was carrying out with the aid of their funds. The American public however grew increasingly restive with the stories of the misappropriation of American loans by German socialist spending agencies.

9.8 Americans Worried over their Loans to Germany

After their humiliation over the suspension of the eight hour day in 1923 the German Social Democrat Party, the SPD had preferred to remain in opposition but in May 1928 they won a victory at the polls and the President asked them to form a coalition government. They had campaigned for the evacuation of the Rhineland and had told their electorate that their party would be the most likely to achieve this because Poincaré trusted them, provided of course, that the payment

---

52. *Royal Institute of International Affairs Survey.* 1929. History of German reparations. Germany's payments. pp.115–22.

53. *Royal Institute of International Affairs Survey.* 1929. p.126.

of the reparations was 'put on a secure basis.'[54]

The arrival of the socialists in power persuaded both the Americans and the French into believing that democracy had finally dawned in the ex-Prussian Empire. In the relatively prosperous May of 1928 Hitler's party, the NSDAP, polled only 810,000 votes in the Reichstag elections and the militant opposers of the Weimar Republic in high places, the German Nationalists or DNVP, 4.3 millions, compared to 9.1 million for the SPD socialists. Now at last the Americans felt that Germany could be trusted to pay the reparations 'under her own responsibility without foreign supervision and without transfer protection.'

Parker Gilbert, the young American reparations agent, had been critical of the lax way Germany had been managing the American money lent to Germany.

The internal situation in Germany when the socialist SPD came to power however was not stable. The SPD administration was not a strong one as it had less than a third of the vote and had to depend on other parties for support. The hefty salary increases given to the civil servants by the previous right wing administration in 1927 had given the shop floor the ambition to achieve high wage increases too. The endorsement that the socialists had received from the nation was undermined almost immediately by a strike of 50,000 dock workers which lasted several months.[55] Wages rose 7% under this apparently weak government when inflation only increased by 1%.[56]

The ironmasters of the Ruhr felt obliged to lock out their 225,000 workers for four weeks rather than permit the elected government to force them to shorten the working week and allow an increase in wages.[57] Dr. Schacht, who was held in such high esteem by the Allies, made much of the government's inadequacies to his opposite numbers in England and America. Solid citizens in those countries shuddered at the thought of the equivalent of the British Labour Party so mismanaging Germany's economy. But other observers wondered where the power resided in Germany, within or without Parliament, if the great industrialists could defy both its workers and their government.

It was when the reparations agent, Parker Gilbert, asked where all the money that had been poured into Germany to make it a viable economy, had gone to, that Dr. Schacht waxed most lyrical. It appeared that the cities had wantonly thrown it away on 'swimming pools, parks, libraries

54. Bruce Kent. *The Spoils of War*. p.278.
55. *Annual Register*. 1928. p.153.
56. *Annual Register*. 1928. p.152.
57. *Annual Register*. 1928. p.153.

and playgrounds.'[58] In 1955 the German Municipal Congress, in its Festschrift, would refute this charge, insisting that they had been made 'public scapegoats on this issue of their alleged luxury projects.' They declared that even in 1925 demands for foreign funding of civic projects had been most rigorously scrutinised.

In 1928 the mayor of Frankfurt am Main, at a meeting of the Congress for Social Welfare in Zurich, had tried to argue that there was no difference between using foreign capital to build a factory or a hospital. But his argument was refuted on the grounds that the use of foreign funds to fight German unemployment amounted to 'semi-inflation.'[59]

Loans to public corporations peaked at 1.6 billion marks in 1926, interestingly at a time when the extreme nationalists, the DNVP, shared power.

It had been indeed basically the profligacy of the right wing administration dominated by the DNVP, with its four members in the cabinet, which was to cause so many problems for the subsequent socialist administration. And yet the socialists were the ones who would take the blame for the growing chasm in the budget they inherited and the refusal of the right to help sort it out.

After the rationalisation of industry and the severe Winter of 1926 had led to over 2,000,000 people being thrown out of work, Chancellor Marx's rightist administration had brought in unemployment benefit but this had only been funded for 1.1 million people despite the fact that there had never been less than 1.3 million people unemployed in Germany even in the height of Summer in 1926.[60] In addition civil servants wages were increased by between 21% and 25%, 'legislation was passed for the benefit of agriculture' and 9 million marks was set aside for the construction of a 'pocket battleship.' It was no wonder that the subsequent socialist administration inherited a budget deficit which grew by leaps and bounds with all the demands made upon it, especially as the cold January of 1929 would cause over 2,000,000 to be unemployed again, demanding benefits.

Naturally the Americans were worried at the fate of their overseas loans. Had they been guilty of throwing more good money after bad?

58. Otto Ziebill. *Geschte des Deutschen Stadbetags*. Funfzig Jahre Deutsche Kommonalpolitik. (Stuttgart und Cologne 1955) p.257. E. Eyck. *The Weimar Republic*. Vol. II. p.118.

59. E. Eyck. *The Weimar Republic*. Vol. II. p.119.

60. E. Eyck. *The Weimar Republic*. Vol. II. p.197–8. Although led by Marx of the Centre Party (69 seats in Parliament) the DNVP with 103 seats must have had the major say by virtue of their superior numbers, and they could count on many friends in the DVP. The inclusion of the DNVP member, von Keudell, in the administration caused an uproar both in and out of Parliament because he had been alleged to have been implicated in the Kapp putsch.

Could they trust the incompetent German socialists to manage the economy sufficiently well for the reparations to be paid. We can be sure that Dr. Schacht soothed their fears. It was indeed all the fault of the reparations' provisions. If only Germany knew exactly how much money they could be expected finally to pay, and could plan for it, all would be well. Naturally in view of the state of the country Germany's liability could not be too onerous. But if the country was treated like a responsible adult without the big stick of the Rhine occupation constantly hanging over its head, the trusted financial establishment would ensure that Germany's economy was put in order. After all Germany was now a respected member of the League of Nations. The dreadful dip in the exchange rate after the socialists got into power seemed to support Schacht's view that a new deal was necessary. Money rushed from Germany into the safe haven of the United States and America promised to help.

One would be surprised if the French had not viewed an alteration to the Dawes Plan with apprehension. Despite its cumbersome nature the Dawes Plan had worked without a hitch.

But Poincaré was much reassured by the presence of a socialist government in Germany. Moreover the Lorraine ore owners, with whom he had worked in his youth, had been prospering in a cartel with the German iron and steel barons. Old wounds from the war were healing. Many Frenchmen complained that Germany's 'deliveries in kind' reduced 'French selling to other countries.' France would far prefer more cash. Besides the country was not in a strong position to bargain over the reparations. While she had been proceeding with her own great inflation she had declared France to be unable to pay American war debts. Now she had stabilised her currency she had to display her responsibility by starting the payment of her war debt annuities. Unless France agreed to ratify the Mellon-Berenger agreement on the payment of the war debts by 1 August 1929 she would be liable for an extra $407,000,000. (over 2,000,000,000 marks.) It was against this background that the Young Committee met on the 11 February 1929 to agree on a new arrangement for the payment of the reparations.

9.9   The Transfer Problem

In March 1929 Keynes would write an article campaigning for a generosity to Germany in the forthcoming negotiations. In the article Keynes asserted that there were two impediments to the Allies receiving satisfactory reparations from Germany, the Budgetary Problem and the Transfer Problem.

Keynes's main concern was the Transfer Problem but he declared that there was a 'school' who believed that 'the real question is, how much money can the German government raise by sound financial methods and pay over to the Agent-General.' Once this was settled, 'a way would be found of looking after the Transfer Problem.'[61]

It was surprising that Keynes took so little interest in the Budgetary Problem. He must have surmised that Poincaré would be unhappy to leave payment of France's reparations to the whim of the German government or the largesse of the Americans, after the trials and tribulations of the occupation of the Ruhr. By applying 'sound financial methods,' France had been able to secure the funding for its 'deliveries in kind,' relatively painlessly, by netting £32 million a year from the German railway bonds, £15 million a year by 1929 from German industrial debentures, and nearly the same amount from a German transport tax, giving hope that an extension of such taxes could secure most of the reparations for all claimant countries.

It is true that many Germans, on fixed incomes, had lost all their savings during the Great Inflation but the hard-working nation's savings had recovered fast and, by 1928, had risen to about £1,700 million.[62] By 1929, the real income of the German people had risen some 77% above pre-war levels, from 43,000 gold marks in 1913 to 75,900 million gold marks in 1929.[63] Germany was a prosperous country. With four per cent more Germans in work than in Great Britain, and relatively few private cars being in use, enterprises such as the railways were able to make a real contribution towards the payment of the reparations.

Unfortunately, however, Poincaré was no longer in a position to impose his will on Germany, as had been the case in 1924. In the Spring of 1927, Nationalist newspapers got wind of proposals to extend reparation taxation to other spheres. The Deutsche Zeitung declared that it was proposed to transform the postal service into a limited company, to create a tobacco monopoly, to extend the spirits' monopoly, and to use the German sugar industry as a part guarantee of the Dawes annuities. The opposition parties vilified Herr Stresemann as conniving in these schemes 'for the economic enslavement of Germany.'[64] And so any plans the Allies may have envisaged for putting such sensible ideas into operation, (envisaged under the terms of the Dawes Plan) were scrapped.

When Herr Dessauer of the Centre Party had made his remarks, in March 1927, about Germany only being able to pay its reparations

61. *The Economic Journal.* March 1929. p.1.
62. G. Borsky. *The Greatest Swindle in the World.* p.58.
63. *German Statistical Year Book.*
64. *Royal Institute of International Affairs Survey.* 1929. p.127.

because it was in receipt of overseas loans which 'could not be expected to continue indefinitely', he was voicing exactly Keynes's own sentiments.

Keynes did seem to differ from Herr Dessauer in his assessment of Germany's export potential however. Whereas Herr Dessauer seemed to imply that the volume of exports could be adjusted at will to impose pain on the Allies, in Keynes's estimation the German economy, itself, would have to face a painful adjustment in order to increase its exports sufficiently[65] to fund the reparations' payments without recourse to foreign loans.

There was no dispute that a substantial proportion of the reparations were already being paid by means of 'deliveries in kind.' There was no transfer problem for Germany in paying by this method, although the Economist, Bertil Ohlin, did comment that there would have to be a 'readjustment of production in the countries which are to receive the indemnity payments',[66] principally France. The French, indeed, by the late 1920s, were in favour of receiving a larger part of their reparations by the means by which the British had always been paid, tariff.

It seems that the British had been very, very quiet about the reparations' tariffs they had imposed on German goods in the 1920s because Keynes would surely have commented on them, had he known of their existence. Up to 1924, as a matter of fact, Winston Churchill had declared that Britain had received no reparations except by means of tariff, and it could have been the comfort of the tariff which allowed him to be persuaded, against his better judgement, to return to the gold standard in 1925. Between 1925 and 1929 the Allies raised 1,510 million gold marks for reparation by means of tariff, some 20% of the total.[67] But the Germans were allowed to organise matters so that they could levy the whole of German industry to pay the tariff, rather than allowing the individual exporter to suffer the heavy charge of 30% alone.

The imposition of the tariff, in essence, was a budgetary exercise, like the levy on Germany's railways. The proceeds were sometimes regarded as 'payments in cash' which gave the cash balance sheet a fleshier look than it really deserved. In the year ending 31 August 1926 it was revealed that 'actual cash' transfers, including tariffs, totalled only just over £3 million out of the approximately £60 reparations raised

65. 'Yet – on the assumption that Germany will have to increase her exports of finished goods by more than 40 per cent to pay reparations without borrowing – this is to me the kernel of the problem.' A Reply by Mr. Keynes to M. Jacques Rueff. The *Economic Journal*. p.408.
66. The *Economic Journal*. June 1929. p.178.
67. G. Borsky. *The Greatest Swindle in the World*. p.57.

through the Allied controls.[68] It was unfortunate when the Dawes Plan controls were producing practically all the revenue, that Keynes would imply, on 11 September 1926, that without the American loans hardly any reparations would have been forthcoming:

> 'Reparations and inter-Allied debts are being mainly in paper and not in goods. The United States lends money to Germany, Germany transfers its equivalent to the Allies, the Allies pay it back to the United States government.'[69]

If we look at Germany's payments of 7,949 gold marks, made under the terms of the French supervised Dawes Plan, roughly 55% had been secured by means of the railway bonds, the transport tax and the industrial debentures, which underpinned the 'deliveries in kind.' An estimated 20% had been paid by tariff. So 75% of the nearly £400 million received had been subject to no Transfer Problems at all. Just over 10% of the remaining 'cash' received had been lent to Germany by the Allies and America as a stabilisation loan, 'the Dawes Loan', in 1924. The servicing of this loan was paid through the reparations' controls. After the deduction of the initial Dawes Plan loan from the total 'cash' received, according to the Czech economist Borsky's, estimation, Germany only paid over £47 million in 'actual cash'[70] during the five years the Dawes Plan was in force, much of this being in the final year. There remained the very real problem of servicing Germany's ever mushrooming foreign loans. It could easily have been worries over these that persuaded overseas opinion to give ear to Keynes's pre-occupations with 'transfer.'

Germany had many friends and relations abroad who had harkened to pleas from the old country in 1923. After the German currency was stabilised in 1924, it was given valuable transfer protection. Now, the 10% plus Americans of German extraction felt that it would be both safe and profitable to help the old country, especially as German interest rates were standing at 9% in 1925. Although German interest rates fell to 7% in the mid-twenties, German Bonds still represented an outstanding opportunity compared to other European investments. By 31 July 1931 loans and credits from abroad would amount to no less than £1,190 million.

To service such an awesome amount, however, almost £100 million a

---

68. *Royal Institute of International Affairs Survey.* 1929. p.116.

69. *The Nation and Athenaeum.* 11 September 1926.

70. G. Borsky.*.The Greatest Swindle in the World.* p.57. Of the total of 3,834 million gold marks entered by the Reparations' agent as 'payment in gold and foreign currency' Borsky declared that only 1,737 million was paid in cash (including the 800 million Dawes Loan). The remaining 1,510 was revenue from tariffs paid through the Reparations' Recovery Acts.

HOW THE DAWES PLAN PAYMENTS WERE FUNDED

	1924-5	1925-6	1926-7	1927-8	1928-9
Dawes Loan	800				
Railway Bonds	200	595	550	660	660
Industrial Debentures	-	125	250	300	300
Transport Tax	-	250	290	290	290
Reich's Budget	-	250	410	500	1250
Total, according to Plan	1000	1220	1500	1750	2500
Actual Payments	893	1176	1382	1739	2453

(20.43 Marks to £. Figs. in Millions of Gold Marks)

Figure 9.2 How the Dawes Plan payments were funded.

year would be needed, nearly as much as the reparations' demands. By 1927, the Americans became alarmed that their loans were being squandered over civic projects. They could also have suspected that Germany was merely trying to raise new loans to service former loans, instead of husbanding the precious resources it had been lent. It was an unpalatable fact that, although the socialists would receive the blame, it had been the right which had ushered in the era of borrow and spend, a philosophy traditionally so alien to Conservatives.

By 1929/30, with less cash around, there would be a clear conflict of interest between the many Americans of German origin, who had supported America during the war, but had been horrified by tales of German suffering in 1923 and had showered the old country with funds to help since,[71] and the Allies demanding reparations. Until the Young Plan was in place, the Allies, with their army of controls, would always secure first charge over Germany's spare cash. But after the 'Poincaré' controls were abandoned, Dr. Schacht's words to the Bremen Chamber of Commerce on 3 December 1930, would have more impact abroad:

> 'I emphasised the fact that Germany has the most absolute and earnest wish to fulfil all her obligations to private persons.
> 'The only thing which will ruin German credit in the long run is if we continue the political payments (reparations) ... For my part, I have repeatedly pointed out that inter-Allied debts have no legal connections with reparations. I have further pointed out that England and France are very well able to pay these debts to America out of their substance, even if they do not receive a farthing from Germany.'

It is conceivable that a country with such a strong industrial base as Germany could have been able to spend nearly £200 million annually servicing its reparations and overseas loans, because, after its Great Inflation, Germany had far less internal debt than other nations. France had a debt of 475,000 million francs, Britain had a debt of £7,500 million, whilst 'poor Germany' had only £450 million of internal obligations.[72]

It was misleading to quote, as Germany's exports, such rarefied goods as 'platinum and caviare', the examples Keynes used in his article to show that exports were inelastic and subject to price falls if the market was flooded ...

---

71. Stephen A. Schuker in *American 'Reparations' to Germany* commented on the differing experience of those American loans to its kith and kin in Germany, and Britain's loans to her kith and kin in Australia, New Zealand and Canada. 'Australia and New Zealand, along with Canada, labored under the highest per capita debt burden in the world, six times greater than that of Germany. Still, imperial relationships remained ... No breakdown in debt servicing took place.' p.128–9.

72. G. Borsky. *The Greatest Swindle in the World.* p.67.

'In this case the more she exports, the smaller will be the aggregate proceeds ... The Transfer Problem will be a hopeless business.'[73]

As will be seen in later pages, Germany's industrial strength lay in goods more resilient to market forces, like chemicals, where Germany was the world market leader, and steel. German goods were already highly competitive on world markets, witness the fact that Germany would export 50% more goods to Britain than it imported from her in 1929.[74]

Keynes had made his assumption that Germany's goods were not very competitive on world markets from a statistic given to him by Parker Gilbert that German 'money wages had risen by 40% since 1924 and real wages by 23%.'[75] He did not therefore believe that an increase in Germany's export trade could be achieved without extreme internal difficulties.

'Those who see no difficulty in this – like those who saw no difficulty in Great Britain's return to the gold standard – are applying the theory of liquids to what is, if not a solid, at least a sticky mess with strong internal resistances.'

Parker Gilbert, however, had given Keynes misleading statistics on which to base his economic theories. In contrast to Britain, German organised labour had suffered a humiliating political and economic reverse in 1923, from which it never fully recovered. When the currency was stabilised after the Great Inflation, not only did the workers have to labour for longer hours than their British counterparts, but for very low wages. According to the Historian, S. Taylor, in his *Germany 1918–33*: 'By 1924 real wages had dropped to 74% of the average level in 1913.' If therefore, German wages had risen 40% between 1924 and 1929, they were still not greatly above pre-war levels. In fact in his study of the subject in 1932, J.W. Angell gave the national income per head of population in Germany, Britain and France in 1928 as follows:

$435 – Great Britain;
$231 – Germany;
$218 – France.[76]

73. The *Economic Journal*. March 1929. p.2.
74. German exports to Britain – 1,305 million marks. 1929. German imports from Britain – 805 million marks. Germany had exported substantially more goods to Britain in 1928 before Keynes wrote his article but the figures only appeared in *Whitacker's Almanack* in 1931.
75. The *Economic Journal*. March 1929. p.6.
76. Committee on Foreign Relations: J. W. Angell. *The Recovery of Germany*. 1932. p.320.

So German wages were highly competitive on World markets. Indeed, as will be seen later on in the narrative, when Keynes, as a member of the Macmillan Committee in May 1930, was to look into the wage rate issue more closely, he became alarmed that, because of Britain's uncompetitive wage rates, British capital was investing in German, rather than British industry, attracted by its profitability and the higher rate of return paid to investors.[77]

In 1930, Germany would export twice as many goods to Britain that it received in return.[78] Germany's transfer of reparations, to repair the deficit in the British Exchequer caused by the influx of German goods, would be less forthcoming.

In 1945 the economist, Etienne Mantoux, maintained that, before the Treaty of Versailles, the difficulties of transfer were little commented on. If countries wished to fulfil obligations they adapted their economies to the payment. Thus in 1871:

'Thiers, the French Prime Minister, who was a recognised authority on financial matters, did not at first believe that it (the French indemnity) could ever be paid: 'Generals, not financiers, must have suggested to you this figure' he had complained to Bismarck. Yet the sum was paid within the next four years. Before 1871, France's balance of trade was continually passive. As soon as payments started, the debt was transformed into a surplus, which disappeared as soon as the payments ceased.'[79]

However, the question in the 1920s, and still more after the Poincaré controls were removed, would be: Did Germany want to adjust its economy to fulfil its reparations, or had it merely been using its external loans to weaken the resolve of creditors overseas, those army of '300,000 people in America who would make propaganda for Germany because they would be interested in her welfare' that Stresemann had talked of on 25 September 1924?

Once more, in answer, as in 1919, Keynes would come up with a prophecy:

'In fact where a country's difficulties are due to its owing a burdensome sum, readjustment is often brought about by its just not paying it. These are the precedents relevant to the German case ... When the debt is owed in terms of the home currency, the relief comes by depreciating the currency; when it is owed in terms of a foreign currency, the relief comes by default.'[80]

77. R. Skidelsky. *John Maynard Keynes.* Vol. II. (1992) p.355.
78. German exports to Britain – 1,219,000. German imports from Britain – 630,000.
79. Etienne Mantoux. *The Carthaginian Peace.* p.120.
80. The *Economic Journal.* p.406. A rejoinder to Professor Ohlin and M. Jacques Rueff.

Keynes had made a prophecy in 1919 which had received much attention in Germany. You could almost say it became a self-fulfilling prophecy. It was a shame that Keynes should have made another such prophecy now, when there was so much expectation, on all sides, of a better world in 1929.

–10–

1929 – The Young Plan and the Stock Market Crash

10.1 Stock Market Fever

The year 1929 opened with the American stock market in a ferment. It gave a feeling of wealth to the rich in many countries as they saw the meteoric rise of the American stock market reflected in a rise in stocks on their side of the Atlantic. America was feeling in a particularly ebullient mood. Her stock market had risen greatly since July 1928. If it continued at this rate it would rise by 50% in a year. America was unquestionably taking over from Great Britain as the world's financial centre. Meanwhile America's young reparations' agent, Parker Gilbert, had brought off a brilliant coup in Germany before hurrying back to a big new job on Wall Street. There had been irritation in the U.S. lately at reports of how the German Socialist government had been squandering American loans on swimming pools and lavish parks instead of restructuring German industry to enable it to pay the reparations. In contrast to those well-endowed German cities, the city of Chicago, for instance, was pinched for funds. However, in return for Parker Gilbert promising to instigate a new initiative on the reparations – getting the Allies to agree to remove the irksome, untrustful Dawes Plan controls over the German economy and giving the country a slightly less onerous bill to pay – Dr. Schacht, who had performed such miracles with the mark in 1923, had promised to force the socialist coalition to use America's loans responsibly and structure the German economy so that the country could meet its responsibilities without recourse to American funds.

The Allies were none too pleased to re-open the reparations question. Under the strictures of the Dawes Plan, Germany had made its reparations' payments promptly. Yet Austen Chamberlain responded to the appeal to forget the war and treat the debt just like an ordinary commercial debt, as it seemed to be framed in the altruistic, forgiving and forgetting spirit of Locarno. In September 1928, at Geneva, the Allies decided to 'liquidate' the war and on 11 February 1929 they sat down round the table at the George V hotel in Paris, with Germany and

America, to thrash out the technical details involved.[1] Naturally the Allies realised that the reparations' demands might have to be scaled down slightly. There was expectation on the German side, however, that re-negotiation meant a much smaller bill to pay and this spelt trouble for the future.

Although the British and French Empires straddled the globe they looked at that time to their rich creditor, America, to be the arbiter in the forthcoming proceedings. While the delegates talked in Paris, the American stock market boom continued unabated, giving witness to all of America's wealth and power.

So violent, however, was the rise in shares that by March the *New York Times* was registering its alarm. America appeared immensely rich to the rest of the world. Yet much of its stock market boom was being fuelled by borrowed money and related little to the true value of the companies quoted. On 2 March, after the stock market rose again in the second largest day on record, the *New York Times* commented: 'There were times yesterday when even Wall Street began to think that the stock market was running absolutely wild ... The impression was based partly on the violent advance in some of the highly speculative shares ... Stocks like United States Steel and General Motors rose only a point or two.'[2]

The *New York Times* sympathised with President Hoover on the eve of his inauguration on 4 March: 'He is hardly likely to have watched with pleasure the tightening of credit under the strain of the speculative market's requisitions, until money rates now prevailing are such as have never been equalled in any new administration.'

On 7 March, after a huge net increase in brokers loans, $556,000,000 since the end of December, was revealed, the *New York Times* demanded to know what was happening:

'The time has come when financiers of knowledge and repute will be forced to come into the open, to tell deluded Wall Street what situation it had actually created.'

The financial editor of the *New York Times* seemed to feel that some hidden force behind the scenes was manipulating the stock market. But the question was, who could it be? And what could be done to quell the speculation?

The banker, Paul Warburg, who had previously been on the Federal Reserve Board himself, pleaded with the unwieldy organisation to act fast to make it more difficult, and expensive, for individuals to borrow

1. *Royal Institute of International Affairs Survey.* 1929. p.176.
2. *New York Times.* 2.3.29.

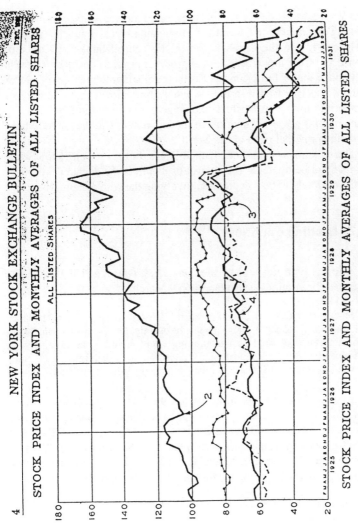

Figure 10.1 Stock price index and monthly averages of all listed shares

money and gamble with it on the stock exchange. He complained that over the last year the Federal Reserve Board had lost control of the system.

> 'History, which has a painful way of repeating itself, has taught mankind that speculative over- expansion invariably ends in over-contraction and distress ... If orgies of unrestrained speculation were permitted to spread too far, the ultimate collapse was certain not only to affect the speculators themselves, but also to bring about a general depression involving the whole country.'[3]

Paul Warburg was one of the most respected members of the New York banking community so his words were bound to receive much publicity.

He contrasted the organisation of the central banks of England, France and Germany where a small group of officials decided what was to be done and acted promptly, to the cumbersome machinery of the Federal Reserve Board in the US where he claimed that control had passed into the hands of stock exchange operators 'who have now for many months governed the flow of money, not only in the United States but in the principal parts of the world.'

'The banking system of the United States today is tossing about without its helm being under the control of its pilots' he declared. Its aftermath was likely to be a depression involving the whole country.

10.2 Lending Continues

Despite his warning words, the *New York Times* still registered its unease at the continual speculation on 9 March:

> 'Stocks continued to rise briskly, sometimes violently yesterday on the Stock Exchange ... despite the development of overnight news which could hardly have been construed as encouraging. This included an expansion of $140,000,000 in brokers loans and criticisms of the Federal Reserve Board's policies by one of the leaders of the international banking fraternity.'

There were solid reasons, however, for the Market to feel joyful. Gold was pouring into the country boosting the nation's confidence. The trade figures for January and February showed a 20% gain on 1928.[4] They were followed by a sparkling performance for March, over 100% up on a year earlier. The price of cotton, an important economic indicator, rose to a height not achieved since the previous July. Particularly gratifying

3. *New York Times*. 8.3.29.
4. *New York Times*. 2.4.29.

had been the large contribution made by finished manufactures, particularly cars, to the positive balance of trade in January and February. Argentina remained America's best customer.[5] In Europe America cast her eyes on Germany, already her largest customer after Canada and Great Britain. It appeared that for Germany to be on a parity with France in the ratio of cars to inhabitants it would be necessary to provide a million more cars immediately.[6]

Germany's citizens had lost all their savings in the Great Inflation, whereas France's had lost only 80% in their subsequent Great Inflation. But the good German burgers must have been busy working and saving since then. On 10 March it was reported that savings per capita now amounted to 105 marks per head in the Fatherland.[7] Surely they would like to see the results of their labours represented by a gleaming Model T Ford outside their front door. In contrast to the 'slums of London' where, it was claimed '680,000' were 'living in squalor.'[8] Germany seemed to be an affluent, positive place. 'Germans aim to be 'Yanks of Europe'' bannerheaded the *New York Times*.[9]

10.3   Allies Reduce Their Reparations' Bill

Germany had been laggardly in pandering to popular aspirations for a motor car. It was not that Germany didn't know how to make motor cars. The Mercedes-Benz was an exquisite piece of engineering. Opel was also making quality cars. Nor did Germany lack an efficient steel industry, capable of supplying the parts. The *New York Times* published figures showing that Germany produced 16,245,921 tons in 1929,[10] a figure which compared favourably with Great Britain's production of only 9,654,700 tons for the same period. But Germany had concentrated on its luxury market. America, the land of democracy, had majored on mass production and felt that the ordinary man in the street in Germany, now that he had money in his pocket again, would also want to enjoy the pleasures of the open road if he were presented with the opportunity to buy a low priced car.

The new reparations' plan was to be agreed by independent experts, two from each country, and then ratified by each participating nation's

5. *New York Times*. 9.4.29.
6. *New York Times*. 21.4.9.
7. *New York Times*. 10.3.29.
8. *New York Times*. 10.3.29.
9. *New York Times*. 10.3.29.
10. *New York Times*. 20.1.30.

government afterwards. Dr. Schacht, head of the Reichsbank, was unanimously chosen to be Germany's principal negotiator, and he was
backed up by Dr. Vögler, heavy industry's representative.

By virtue of his international acclaim in stabilising the mark in 1923,
and his close friendship with Parker Gilbert, the American reparations'
agent, Dr. Schacht held a position of immense power in Germany and
abroad.[11] He now had an exalted idea of his own importance and was
determined to use the current negotiations to pursue his own aims in the
reparations' negotiations, as he wrote excitedly in a letter to Stresemann
on 20 September 1928:

'The psychological moment has now come to strike for everything. Almost
more important than the sums at stake, is the opportunity to regain our
absolute international freedom. Every remnant of obligations, controls, and
unresolved questions must disappear.'[12]

The Allies, in their resolve to abide by the spirit of Locarno, had offered
Germany a generous package so that the war could be finally forgotten.
The sum that they asked for roughly compared with what they owed the
United States in War Debts.

This proposal was not good enough for Dr. Schacht, however.
Confident of America's friendship because of the many loans that
America had been encouraged to make to Germany, he was sure that he
held the whip hand in the negotiations.[13]

On 17 April he offered £82,000,000 a year. On 18 April the Allies
found that his offer was not to be considered negotiable. And even this
figure appeared to be conditional on the Allies returning some of the
land taken from Germany under the terms of the Treaty of
Versailles.[14] The astonishing demand for the return of the Saar and
Upper Silesia was given front page mention in the *New York Times*,
the paucity of the monetary offer coupled with the request for territory

11. Parker Gilbert had not had a close relationship with the high spending Ministry of
Finance in 'Marx's rightist cabinet.' He was so incensed at the right-wing administration's
increased finance to 'lands and local government' that he asked for a special meeting and
insisted on the presence at it of the trusted President of the Reichsbank, Dr. Schacht.
Vermachtniz. III. p.257.

12. *Stresemann Papers.* 7349.H. E. Eyck. *The Weimar Republic.* Vol. II. p.1752.
Curtis. Young Plan. p.29.

13. *Daily Telegraph.* 20.4.29. 'In a call to the Harris Forbes Company, the Wall Street
bankers who have taken a prominent part in German financing, Dr. Schacht said his greatest concern had been to protect German Credit ... £82,000,000 was the maximum
Germany could pay as a political debt and still continue to fulfil her commercial obligations. The explanation is regarded here as an appeal for a sympathetic attitude from
American investors, who had bought millions of dollars' worth of German securities.'

14. *Royal Institute of International Affairs Survey.* 1929. p.146.

being described by the Americans as absolutely 'outrageous.'[15]

Dr. Schacht, however, explained soothingly that Germany needed the extra land for the provision of raw materials in order that it could create a sufficiently profitable manufacturing base for the ready payment of the reparations. He had even had the audacity to declare to the Allied negotiators that Germany could pay more reparations if the Allies would be prepared to relinquish the Polish Corridor. He had always had an obsession with the colonial question and had even suggested to friends, in private conversation, that if the Allies so wished Germany might accept a 'part of British Australia in lieu of paying less reparations.'[16]

Britain and France both tartly declared that they were happy with the present political and economic arrangements, embodied in the Dawes Plan, and if Dr. Schacht didn't like the new economic proposals for the payment of the reparations they were quite happy to stick to the old deal. Dr. Schacht responded by predicting another collapse in the German mark if matters weren't settled to his satisfaction, while Herr Hugenberg, formerly of Krupps and leader of the second largest party in the Reichstag, wrote a letter to prominent American businessmen asserting that the American credits, granted to Germany, had benefitted only German socialism, not German business.[17]

It was interesting that Herr Hugenberg intervened at this crucial time in negotiations between Germany and America, especially, as will be recorded later in the narrative, his party had just been creating much-publicised mayhem in the German Reichstag, by refusing to vote funds for the budgetary overhang caused by his own party's legislation in 1927. Unfortunately his letter was believed. Foreigners railed at the deficiencies of the German socialists. The value of the mark slumped. The success of the letter in the Spring boded ill for when Herr Hugenberg next decided to try and influence the future of the reparations with his 'Freedom from the Enslavement of the German People' petition in the Autumn.

However The *New York Times* reported from London:

> 'No great stock is taken here of Dr. Schacht's threat of another German financial crisis. In the first place the British believe Germany can pay under the Dawes Plan because it puts upon her taxpayers a lesser burden than the British bear for liquidating the war, and in the second place they do not believe Germany would sacrifice the great progress she has made in the past five years by permitting another financial crisis to arise if she could prevent it, and London believes she could.

15. *New York Times.* 19.4.29.
16. *New York Times.* 22.4.29.
17. *Annual Register.* 1929. p.193.

'The general opinion here of Dr. Schacht's talk about another Reich failure is that it is intended to influence the American investors of $2,000,000,000 in Germany and thus indirectly to bring pressure to bear on the experts in the direction of a favourable German case.'[18]

When Dr. Schacht travelled back to Germany in the recess on 21 April Stresemann declared that, in his opinion, Dr. Schacht and his fellow negotiator, Dr. Vögler, had overstepped their mandate in making territorial demands at the Conference and that 'in a more objective sense, they had acted most unwisely.'[19]

Dr. Schacht dropped his territorial ambitions but secured the public promise from his government to give him and Dr. Vögler 'complete discretion' in conducting the negotiations. He intensified the pressure for the Allies to reduce their reparations' bill.[20]

10.4 Gold Fluctuations in European Economies

The French had been accused of financial manipulations that Spring in order to secure a favourable outcome of the reparations' negotiations. But the French denied this, stating that the 'somewhat alarming' withdrawals of gold from the Reichsbank were due to (German) 'financial manoeuvering.'[21] The French Press accused Dr. Schacht of trying to 'sabotage' the Conference. The Americans also commented on the 'actions of German financial houses, which had been taking advantage of New York's high call money rates to engage in the 'arbitrage business.'[22]

The French had stopped money ebbing to the American stock market in the Spring and the British had done likewise. After its own hyperinflation France had initially lacked cash. But its hyperinflation, though costing anguish to its people, had enabled it to pay for the reconstruction of its devastated provinces, while pricing its goods into competitiveness. By 1929 France was a rich country again. To deter speculation against the country France demonstrated that it possessed 34,190 billion francs of gold, representing 53% of note issue against a legal requirement of 35%, an enviable total.

Britain had also seemed rich in 1928. It had received a huge influx of gold. So much gold had come in, indeed, that the Bank of England had sold 'earning assets' in order to keep the nation's credit at a constant

18. *New York Times.* 21.4.29.
19. *Stresemann Papers.* 7386H2. E. Eyck. *The Weimar Republic.* Vol. II. p.187.
20. *New York Times.* 20.4.29.
21. *New York Times.* 26.4.29.
22. *New York Times.* 21.4.29.

level,' even though, to accomplish this, it had temporarily diminished those 'earning assets' below what would normally have been considered a prudent level in 'the general interest of the financial world.' So much of Britain's Empire depended on a stable economic climate. But in the Autumn of 1928 the gold started to depart in the same dramatic fashion as it had arrived. *The Economist* observed:

'All through the Autumn, even when the outflow of gold from the Bank was at its height, we, in common with other observers, hoped that the Bank would weather the storm.' In February, however, gold losses forced the bank to put up its interest rate from 4¹/2% to 5¹/2%. The bank hoped that the rise would not be longlived.[23]

Unlike Britain and France the German Reichsbank had not tried to halt any ebb of money from its country. The Reichsbank had experienced a fall of 745,000,000 marks since the beginning of 1929, 200,000,000 in April. Most of the gold seemed to be arriving in America, despite the fact that the American stock market had quietened after the Federal Reserve Board's intervention in March. But many observers did not believe that Germany, had been a victim of circumstance. The ensuing slide in the value of the German mark was attributed by the financial editor of the *New York Times*, as a ruse by Germany to secure better terms in the current reparation negotiations:

'No one could doubt, when the Reichsbank was drawing gold in quantity from the Bank of England and elsewhere between last June and the end of 1928, that its aspirations were certain to drive down German money rates; yet every observant financier knew also that Germany's position made high rates a prime necessity, in order to retain command of the foreign exchanges with a view commanding foreign capital and transferring reparation money. Instead of this, the Reichsbank turned its foreign credits into cash, nearly exhausted its own holdings of foreign exchange (which were very large in the middle of 1928) and forced down the Berlin market's rate for money at the moment when Wall Street was bidding 9 and 10 per cent for European credits.'

'There will doubtless be talk of the Reichsbank's past or present action being a part of a concerted program to influence the reparations' controversy.'

Over the last week of April the German mark slipped to its lowest level since 1924 bringing a chill to all those Americans who had poured money into German Bonds since the mark's stabilisation.

Many more than the 300,000 Americans Stresemann had hoped to interest in buying bonds in 1924 had invested in Germany. It was a relief

23. *The Economist*. 9.2.29.

for the Bond holders that Germany raised its interest rates by a full 1% to 7% on 25 April, although this large rise was not calculated to promote anything but deflation on the home front and was to usher in a period of higher interest rates among the Eastern European currencies within its orbit. Vienna and Warsaw, alerted by talk of an imminent German rate rise, had raised their rates a day or two earlier.[24] The Hungarians, by 1930 definitely considered in Germany's sphere of influence, raised theirs on the same day. Bucharest raised hers in May, Brussels in June and Belgrade in July. Britain and America were to raise their interest rates later in the year. But France, with a strong economy, buttressed by gold, managed to keep her interest rates low at 3%

Notwithstanding Germany's hike in interest rates, however, the value of the mark remained under pressure in those closing April days. Over the final weekend Owen D. Young, the American Chairman of the Reparations Review Committee, produced a new scheme for the payment of the reparations. The details were disclosed to the Allies the following Monday.

10.5 Young Plan Proposals

Under the Young Plan it was proposed that Germany should pay an average of £103,000,000, about $7^{1}/2$% less than what the Allies had asked for in their proposals.[25] Of this amount £32,500,000 a year was to be made unconditional so that the debt could be commercialised and private investors given the chance to buy a reparations bond, just like any other gilt-edged investment.

The success which Dr. Schacht had won over the Allies, was the right to pay less in reparations, than the Allies owed in war debts to America. As the British had decided to swallow their claim of approximately £200,000,000 for arrears paid to the United States it was only the annual sum of roughly £2,500,000 for the share of British Empire Reparation which was to cause all the trouble. Indeed the German Minister of Economics, Curtius, could not really understand why the Allied negotiators had not forced Germany to pay it.

'If 1.65 billion marks did not exceed Germany's productive capacity who could seriously argue that 300 million more would break its back?'[26]

24. Warsaw – 19.4.29 – 9%.
    Vienna   – 23.4.29 – $7^{1}/2$%.
    Budapest – 25.4.29 – 8%.
25. *Royal Institute of International Affairs Survey.* 1929.
26. E. Eyck. *The Weimar Republic.* Vol. II. p.189. Curtius. Young Plan. p.43.

But it was the vexed question of who would pay this relatively small amount that was to provide such a propaganda issue for Germany.

Britain had lent approximately £3.5 billion to her Allies during the war, little of which had been repaid. When her own money ran out she had borrowed nearly £1 billion more from America to keep their armies supplied.[27] British factories had been so busy making shells for Russia in 1915[28] that her own ships, lacking spares and replacements, became vulnerable to the threat of unrestricted submarine warfare in 1916. The construction of destroyers for Britain's navy was neglected, so was the protection of her merchant shipping,[29] in order that she could help her friends. But Russia had never repaid Britain for this assistance. Communist Russia refused to honour the debts incurred by the former Imperial regime. Even France had been tardy about making debt repayments. Now Great Britain had been asked to make the major sacrifice in the current negotiations. It rankled. As the *Sunday Dispatch* declared:

'Why should we add to our load by meeting other people's obligations?'[30]

It was a painful decision for Britain to have to take, whether to embark on one extra ill-afforded financial sacrifice so that (the British politicians hoped) the war could be eliminated everywhere from public consciousness and the French war debts finally be repaid, or whether to make a fuss and risk the whole deal foundering. The situation was very different now than in 1922/23 because then a large proportion of the British public would have been behind the government if it had taken a strong line with Germany over the reparations' issue, whereas now the average Briton was convinced that the French had been merely greedy and vengeful in 1923 and that Germany bore an onerous financial reparations' burden now. The troops on the Rhine were largely symbolic to the British. There would have been uproar had France tried to use them again. The new deal, therefore, would have to depend largely on Germany's good will, its desire to be a happy and esteemed member of the international community, and the perception of the German people that the new deal was fair. It was precisely for this last reason that the new deal needed a smooth passage.

A decision to accept a more onerous financial load was a doubly difficult one for Britain because a General Election was looming on 30 May 1929. Britain had been prepared to swallow, unwillingly, some

27. *New York Times.* 21.4.29.
28. Norman Stone. *The Eastern Front. 1914–1917.* pp.150–4.
29. A. Temple Patterson. *The Eastern Front. 1914–1917.* pp.150–4.
30. Reported in the *New York Times.* 21.4.29.

sacrifice on her own behalf, but not on behalf of her Empire. The British Socialist Party had scored its one and only success in the polls so far on the backs of anti-French sentiment over the reparations in 1923. Philip Snowden, Labour's Shadow Chancellor, had already asserted his conviction that Balfour's expansive gesture over the war debts owed to Britain[31] had been ill-considered in 1922. He did not think it right that Britain's erstwhile Allies should batter the life out of Germany with vengeful reparations and he was determined that Britain's erstwhile Allies should not connive with America to shortchange Britain either. By general agreement, however, the matter was not argued over on the election hustings. So the knotty problem of which of the Allies should pay more, net, in war debts, so that the Germans could pay less, in reparations, was left until after the General Election. Although the general figures had been concluded there was still much to be decided.

It was ominous that when Dr. Schacht returned to Germany, after agreeing terms with Owen Young, he tried to 'force sole responsibility' onto the socialist government for accepting the Young Plan proposals and state that the German delegation would only sign the Young Plan if the cabinet 'so-directed.'

The SPD had learned a little, however, since agreeing to accept the armistice in 1918. They had been encouraged to make peace with the Allies in 1918, and had subsequently been denounced. Later their prestige had been further diminished when the ten hour day had been reinstated after 'passive resistance' in 1923. This moral defeat and the voters' swing to the right in 1924, meant that, despite the fact that they gained more seats than the DNVP in the Spring elections, 100 as compared with 96, they had felt too impotent to participate in government. However they had been encouraged to take office after their great election victory in 1928 as they had been led to believe that they could get a better deal over the reparations because of Poincaré's faith in the word of socialist politicians.

However, just in case DNVP politicians, such as Herr Hugenberg, tried to make political capital out of the agreement, the socialists had insisted that the negotiations should be undertaken by independent experts. Dr. Schacht and Herr Vögler, they now firmly maintained, must take responsibility for the agreement they had negotiated.

---

31. The Balfour note 3.8.22 – stated that Britain was owed about £3,400,000,000 war debts, exclusive of interest. It also stated that Britain owed America 'about a quarter of this sum' – £850,000,000. *Annual Register*. August 1922. p.93. 'The Balfour note formally proposed the cancellation of inter-Allied debts, and announced that Great Britain would collect from her former Allies only enough to pay her own debt to America. This was no doubt a wise initiative even though it involved a loss on paper of £500 million or more.' A. J. P. Taylor. *1914–45*. p247–8.

It was a wise precaution to take. People were already worried at what they considered the politically immature socialist coalition government's lack of control over the economy. The harsh Winter of 1928–9 had produced 2,600,000 unemployed but the DNVP, and its friends in the DVP, Stresemann's own party, had refused to support socialist measures to fund the unemployment insurance that the DNVP had, itself, brought in when it was the majority party in the previous coalition.[32]

Stresemann was sickened by his own party's subservience to the Hard Right. The disruption over the German budget that Spring seemed timed to perfection to put pressure on foreign opinion over the Young Plan proposals. He declared of his party, the D.V.P:

'Today our Reichstag delegation simply no longer has the courage to oppose the great employers and manufacturers' associations.

'They let fly with all the phrases that they learned from the Stahlhelm and Hugenberg. You know me well enough to know that I cannot go along with such a crowd.'[33]

The coalition government was very much on the defensive. The Iron and Steel Federation had just successfully defied the law of the land by refusing to accept a majority ruling over how much money it should pay its employees. Rumours abounded that Herr Hugenberg, formerly of Krupps, planned to use the conflict over the budget deficit to pave the way for a 'Directorate' with him running the show behind the scenes. Certain prominent members of the former 'black army' had been told to stand ready to help carry out his plan.

Weary Stresemann made an impassioned address to the Reichstag to fight off this 'crisis for parliamentary government in Germany.'

But although the government was allowed funds to build an armoured cruiser[34] it was voted only a third of the funds necessary to balance the budget and fund the previous winter's unemployed. This heavy overhang of debt was bound to have repercussions at home and abroad, coming as it did at a critical time in the Young Plan reparations' negotiations. People quickly forgot that it had been the right who had brought in the measures which had created the mountain of

---

32. E. Eyck. *The Weimar Republic*. Vol. II. p.135. 'The increase of the salaries to civil servants had been promised by all parties in the Presidential contest of 1925, and particularly the DNVP in the name of Hindenburg. J. Wheeler-Bennett. *Hindenburg. The Wooden Titan*. p.319.

33. *Stresemann Papers*. 7383. (January 1929).

34. Armed with 11 inch guns it would have 'a greater radius of action' than the British battle-cruisers, and would fire 'a heavier weight of shell per minute' Churchill. M. Gilbert. vol.5. 1922–39. p.313. Extracts from a secret memo of General Gröner.

debt. The slide in the German stock exchange and Hugenberg's talk of a return to hyper-inflation had added to ordinary conservative worries over the present Government's lack of control over the country. Money in bank deposits in Germany contracted by 5% from the end of March to the end of May[35] and much of it was deposited in America.

Despite being forbidden to hold a public May Day parade, the Communists insisted on a rampant public demonstration, with the result that the beleaguered police opened fire. Seven people died and more than 100 were wounded in the disturbances. In previous years Social Democrats and Communists had marched peacefully, side by side, on May Day. But since the World Congress in the Summer of 1928 the Communists had refused to collaborate any longer with the Social Democrats.[36] Henceforth they mocked the SPD as 'Social Fascists.'

They declared that the country had been sold out by the 'Social Fascists' to 'international capital' over the terms for the new reparations' agreement.

A Norwegian paper, the *Oslo Aftenavis*, alleged that it was Stresemann who had forged the accord with Russia with the object of bringing pressure to bear over the reparations.[37] However Stresemann is on record as having to be restrained from causing a 'real crisis' with Russia in his anger over the German Communists' antics on May Day.[38] It was significant that the German Communists staged their protests against the Young Plan with the German extreme right. The resulting fear and confusion in Germany and the exodus of money abroad gave weight to the German right's claim that the Dawes Plan was preferable to the Young Plan proposals because the Dawes Plan provided that the reparations could be suspended if the stability of the mark was threatened.

If the Communist campaign against the Young Plan was part of an organised campaign as the SPD also alleged[39] it proved successful. America and Britain had an exaggerated fear of Bolshevism and were likely to make more concessions over the reparations in the noble cause keeping Germany's democracy intact.

---

35. H. James. *The German Slump.* 1986. p.284. For figures 298–300 see below.

Statistisches Reichsamt estimated capital flight at 3.9 billion RM short-term money and 4.9 billion RM long-term. (£490 million at £20.43 to £.) Severing in June 1930 estimated capital flight to Switzerland at 7 billion RM.

36. Alan Bullock. *The German Communists and the Rise of Hitler in the Third Reich.* (New York 1955) p.504–6. A. Rosenberg. *A History of Bolshevism.* From Marx to the First Five Year's Plan. p.224. E. Eyck. *The Weimar Republic.* Vol. II. p.169.

37. *Oslo Aftenavis.* 12.2.29. Weimar Germany and Soviet Russia. p.150.

38. Harvey Leonard Dick. Weimar Germany and Soviet Russia. 1966. p.154.

39. *Hamburger Echo.* 26.1.29.

10.6 Mini-Collapse of American Stock Market

It was perhaps inevitable that Germany's heavy industry representative at the Young Plan Conference, Dr. Vögler, should feel the necessity of resigning on 24 May. Herr Georg Bernhard, editor in chief of the *Vossiche Zeitung*, traced his resignation directly to the banquet given in his and Dr. Schacht's honour by the coal and steel barons at the Krupp Palace in Essen. According to Herr Bernhard:

> 'These circles know quite well that, hard as the Paris agreements would be for the German nation to bear, the relief which they would involve for the German budget would be used for the restoration of ordered economic conditions in Germany ... This tranquillisation, under the rule of a cabinet of the big Coalition, was to be prevented at any cost, and that is also the deeper reason for the fresh attempts by working on Herr Vögler to blow the plan to pieces at the last moment.'

The American stock market staged a mini-collapse while the *Berliner Tageblatt* concluded gloomily:

> '... that this political push had had success against Herr Vögler is all the more deplorable because he belongs to the People's Party which is also that of the Foreign Minister.'[40]

Dr. Schacht did not follow Herr Vögler's example in resigning from the Young Plan delegation. However, in remaining at the delegation, he aroused mistrust from his government by publicly seeking and receiving 'repeated attestations of his freedom of action.'

Stresemann's suspicions of Dr. Schacht were thoroughly aroused. He even noted in his diary an observation that Schacht's close relative had made:

> 'If I can warn you of any man, let it be of Hjalmar Schacht. Nothing about the man is honest. His ambitions are boundless. He walks over anything that blocks his way.'[41]

Indeed it became apparent that Herr Vögler and Dr. Schacht's brinkmanship had paid off. The collapse of the American stock market precipitated a rush to meet German demands.

In the last days of the negotiations Schacht obtained valuable new

---

40. Chatham House newspaper cuttings. Extracts from German newspapers printed in *Daily Telegraph*. 24.5.29.

41. *Stresemann Papers*. 7386ff.

Figure 10.2 Dr. Schacht at a meeting in the City of Brunswick 1934.
Stresemann on Dr. Schacht, 1929: 'If I can warn you of any man, let it be of Hjalmar Schacht. Nothing about the man is honest. His ambitions are boundless. He walks over anything that blocks his way'.
© Hulton Deutsch

concessions. Although the concession over 'transfer protection' had been a major cause of anxieties over the Dawes Plan, it was proposed to establish the machinery for 'moratoria on internal collection and external transfers' if there was a severe recession and the stability of the mark was threatened by the payments. Even more alarming, all the controls which the Allies had so carefully put in place to secure the reparations by means of tariff and 'deliveries in kind' were to be removed.

The New York Times commented on the triumph of Dr. Schacht's negotiations:

> 'Final and definite settlement of the reparations problem which has vexed the whole world for ten years, has at last been reached ... .
> 'As was promised yesterday, by today at noon a reconciliation had been found to the last conditions which Germany had attached to her acceptance of the annuity schedule proposed by Owen D. Young, the American chairman, when both creditor and debtor proposals had been perforce discarded. 'Reconciliation' is the word used officially to describe these last transactions. What happened was that in their desire to reach a settlement, and with the same goodwill which they have shown all along, Germany's European creditors abandoned practically all their reservations. They accepted the figure offered by Dr. Hjalmar Schacht, chief German delegate, of 660,000,000 marks as the unconditional part of each annuity. They abandoned the recovery system which Great Britain and Belgium have profitably used. They promised restoration of German property held abroad.'[42]

There was only one issue undecided and that was one which the Belgians felt most strongly about.

The *New York Times* explained the History of the matter.

> 'When they occupied Belgium (in 1914) the Germans removed all the Belgian gold and money and 'planted' marks in the banks in place of Belgian currency. Neither the facts nor the justice of the Belgian claim for restitution has ever been denied by Berlin. Yet, for one reason or another a settlement has always been postponed ... Emile Francqui, chief Belgian delegate, ... has gone so far as to accuse Dr. Schacht of having been party to the wholesale pillage of the Belgian banks when he was on von Bissing's staff during the occupation, and such an accusation has already envenomed the already delicate question.'[43]

The next day the *New York Times* commented:

> 'The weakest of the Allies seems still doomed to pay for defending that neu-

42. *New York Times*. 2.6.92.
43. *New York Times*. 31.5.29.

trality of which Germany was at the same time the guarantor and the violator. The only hope of settlement seems to lie in a continued refusal of the other delegates to sign the report so long as no arrangement is made.'

But, in the end, the delegates decided that they would have to sign the Young Plan agreement without agreement being settled on Belgium's claim.[44]

10.7 Ratification of Young Plan

After the Young Plan had been signed by the experts on 7 June it had to be ratified by each one of the individual governments concerned. The capital sum to be demanded from Germany in settlement of the war was reduced to £1,900,000 of which £898,000,000 had already been paid thanks principally to the material delivered after the war and the success of the Dawes Plan.

German payments were to be 'retrospectively effective' from 1 September 1929. They were to start with a payment of 1,041 million gold marks (£52 million) rising to a maximum of 2,352 million marks in 1965. Half the sums due would be raised from the German budget and the remainder, £33 million a year, from railway bonds.

The figure of £33,000,000 represented the amount that the Allies had secured from the Bonds on the extremely profitable German railways during the years of the Dawes Plan, so the authorities were confident that the sum could be collected in the future and represented a secure investment for the general public.[45] Germany was to receive a loan of £60 million to enable the new arrangement to get off to a smooth start.

The new reparations' demands had to present a great victory for Schacht's negotiating ability, for, not only was the total sum demanded from Germany 'substantially' reduced but the 'absolute international freedom' over Germany's finances, that Schacht had written about so excitedly in September 1928, was regained. Under the new Young Plan, the annual payments could only be reduced and, indeed, some could be suspended altogether if the state of the nation warranted it.

Practically 'every remnant of obligations, controls, and unresolved questions' had disappeared under the new agreement and this Schacht

---

44. The Germans counter-claimed the return of the province of Eupen-Malmedy, ceded to Belgium under the terms of the Treaty of Versailles. In the end Stresemann personally intervened to break the deadlock by dropping Germany's territorial claims and undertaking to negotiate a settlement with Belgium before the Young Plan was put into operation. Bruce Kent. *The Spoils of War*. p.301.

45. *Royal Institute of International Affairs Survey*. p.148, p.155.

had deemed 'more important than the sums at stake.'

Regarding these said 'sums at stake' the Young Plan Committee, consisting of eight nations, including America, and Japan, expressed themselves satisfied that 'the total amount of the annuity is one which they have every reason to believe can in fact be both paid and transferred by Germany.'[46]

10.8 French Ratification of Young Plan

It was a different Poincaré, weary and sick, who worked for reconciliation with France's former enemy, Germany, now. His association with the iron ore owners of Lorraine before the war had convinced him that Germany meant to crush France in battle in order to obtain France's iron ore fields in 1914. The later publication of Germany's war aims gives some credence to his conviction. The giant orefield of Longwy-Brie figured in every one of Germany's multitudinous discussions of war aims on the western front. After the war, seeing France's devastated provinces, Poincaré had demanded justice and compensation from the Germans and occupied their territory when France did not receive it.

However times had changed since then. The reparations had been paid without incident for the last five years. Stresemann had observed in his discussions with Poincaré in 1928 how important the presence of a socialist government in Germany was to the democratic Frenchman. Besides if the reparations were treated like an ordinary bond France could also commercialise part of her debt. Hopefully the reparations agreement would usher in a new era of cooperation between the two democratic countries. Germany and France were now cooperating closely on the production of iron and steel. It was hoped that this would be the precursor of rapprochement on other economic and political matters. At last the old enmities could be forgotten.

Yet Poincaré was a practical politician not a dewy-eyed idealist. He had secured the private assurance that France's enormous war debt payments to the U.S. (6,847,647,105 dollars including interest[47]) would be conditional on Germany continuing to pay reparations to France.[48] This agreed he was determined that his suspicious parliament, ever mindful of France's sufferings in the war, would accept the agreement. Refusal would only mean the French government saddling itself unnecessarily

---

46. Hugenberg. *Streiflichter*. p.83. E. Eyck. *The Weimar Republic*. Vol. II. p.37.
47. *Annual Register*. 1929. p.315. Roughly £1,300,000,000 including interest. exact rate $4.86 to the £. Original borrowings – 4,230,000,000 dollars.
48. G. Borsky. *The Greatest Swindle in the World*. p.60.

with the 407,000,000 dollars of post-war obligations in full on 1 August instead of spreading the payments over decades as with the war debts.[49] He felt that it was time for France to accept her responsibilities. Before his departure into hospital, therefore, he summoned up all his strength and gave one of the most brilliant speeches of his career. It lasted for three sessions of Parliament. It was his personal achievement that the French decided on 21 July 1929 to endorse the aims of the Young Plan to forget the war, remove the untrustful controls on the German economy and commercialise the debt. The majority for ratification by the French Parliament in July 1929 was just eight votes.[50]

10.9   Socialists Return to Power in Britain

Sentiment in England at this time was very different to that of France. In Britain a new socialist government had swept to power on 30 May with the help of Lloyd George's Liberals. It was led by Ramsay Macdonald, a man of conviction unfortunately filled with anti-French prejudice. He had felt that Britain had been dragged into the war in 1914 because of her entangling alliance with France and jealousy of her great commercial rival, Germany. Although he and the new members of the cabinet agreed with alleviating Germany's reparations under the terms of the Young Plan, they were not at all happy that it should be Britain who should foot the bill for this generosity. Nor indeed did they feel it should be the responsibility of the Germans. Their enmity was now reserved for the 'vengeful' French.

The British people, as a whole, in 1929 did not feel their country to be rich. Indeed it had been precisely the depressed state of the economy which had led to a change of government. Already in 1923 the Chairman of one of Britain's largest companies had declared that local rates, direct charges and Imperial taxes, other than income taxes, imposed on every ton of steel a charge of nearly 18s. 6d. (92p.) an increase of nearly 16s. (80p) compared with the burden of 1914.[51]

The burden of debt had not been reduced much since then. 'The great export trades – coal, textiles, steel and iron and ship-building – were still suffering from severe depression.'[52] Although her citizens were largely

49. *Annual Register*. 1929. p.194.
50. *Annual Register*. 1929. p.174. The Senate waited until after German ratification in 1930 before they endorsed it by a large majority.
51. *The Times*. 30.1.23.
52. *Annual Register*. 1929. p.1. 'In spite of inventions, reconstructions, and reorganisations, British industry is still unable to hold its markets, and this is very largely due to the enormous overhead charges imposed by Government.' *Annual Register*. Finance & Commerce. p.68..

unaware of it, indebted Britain was finding it almost impossible to compete with a rejuvenated Germany. But it was the poorer labourers who had to suffer the consequences as British industry, overburdened with debt, was forced to work the longer hours that the Germans worked, or throw their labourers out of work – unemployment stood at nearly 1,500,000 out of a working population of some 12,000,000.[53] In response to the horrors of World War I Keynes had labelled Britain's traditional leaders 'wicked and incompetent' in 1917. Men like Snowden, Britain's new socialist Finance Minister, felt similar anger and frustration now.

Snowden, like his Premier, Ramsay Macdonald, had been one of the few to oppose Britain going to war over Germany's invasion of neutral Belgium in 1914. There seemed no other explanation to him, and an ever increasing swell of popular opinion, than that Britain's old guard, her industrialists and generals, had been ineffectual and incompetent in the past to an extent that was almost criminal. The British public now firmly supported him in his belief that Germany had been driven destitute in 1923 by those enormous reparations' charges, imposed on her by Britain's imperialistic old guard, and the iniquitous French.

A sharp-tongued Yorkshireman, Snowden, was a man of the people, a man with the fire in his belly that the elite seemed to lack, one who could tell Britain's pre-World War I traditional enemy, France, that Great Britain would be pushed around no longer.

It was understandable, therefore, that Snowden should approach the forthcoming Hague Conference to settle the outstanding issues on the Young Plan full of righteous indignation. He felt a natural affinity with the Germans whose country he considered to be in a similar threadbare economic state as Great Britain, practically submerged in a sea of debt.

Snowden had hoped that the forthcoming Conference would be held in London, a venue which both he and the Germans strongly favoured. But France had disagreed. However, Snowden was determined that Britain, at the Hague, should not ask the Germans to pay one penny more to bridge that £2,000,000 a year gap between what the Allies owed the U.S. and what they were due to receive from Germany but that France and Italy should make the sacrifices. The debate raged on for days and weeks. Snowden called the French delegate, Cheron's interpretation of Balfour's note 'ridiculous and grotesque' while the exasperated Cheron muttered to his associate 'There sits the man who burned Joan of Arc!'[54] Finally Snowden threatened a walkout if his demands were not met.

53. *Annual Register.* Finance & Commerce. 1929. p.68.
54. E. Eyck. *The Weimar Republic.* Vol. II. p.206.

The German delegation had remained on the sidelines while their erstwhile enemies fought between themselves over who should pay a little bit more, to pay for the war, so that they could pay a little bit less. But eventually they offered, unsolicited, to pay more than the terms agreed, to accommodate the British. They had only one condition, that the occupation troops, 'the throttler' as Stresemann had called them, just four years before, would leave the Rhineland the following year, five years ahead of schedule. The Allies agreed. The sunlight streamed in from the North Sea onto the balcony of the hotel where Stresemann lay near to death as Briand personally came to tell him that the Allies had agreed to Germany's condition. Paul Schmidt, Stresemann's interpreter, recorded this 'unforgettable afternoon.'

'And now, at this moment, both hoped that a new age had come, one in which France and Germany would truly become good neighbours.'[55] But alas this was not to be.

For the concession over letting the troops be removed from the Rhine five years ahead of schedule, Britain was to receive an extra £2,100,000 a year more than envisaged under the original Young Plan scheme. In addition the Italian state railways undertook to buy 1,000,000 tons of British coal every year for three years 'at the best British freemarket export price ruling at the date of each contract.'[56] Snowden returned home to Britain to a hero's welcome for standing up to the grasping continentals and demonstrating that they could push Great Britain around no longer.

At a meeting of the German delegation however, Curtius, soon to take Stresemann's place in the German Cabinet, declared that Snowden deserved to be made an honourary member of the Hugenberg committee,[57] for Snowden, so full of moral fervour, had unwittingly given Schacht and the far right the ammunition they needed to discredit the Young Plan.

10.10 The Young Plan Signed

It had been a happy coincidence that while all those large debts were being agreed at the Hague in August there seemed plenty of money in the world's economic system to finance the profits to pay them. True the stock market had taken a dip at the end of May and beginning of June but afterwards it had resumed its path to the stratosphere. Indeed at this

55. Schmidt. *Statist.* p.183. E. Eyck. *The Weimar Republic.* Vol. II. p.207.
56. *Royal Institute of International Affairs Survey.* 1930. p.504–5.
57. E. Eyck. *The Weimar Republic.* Vol. II. p.209.

time the New York Stock Exchange was in a ferment. Paul Warburg had been a lone voice crying out for caution in the Spring, forecasting a period of doom and misery ahead if the present 'unrestrained speculation' was not brought abruptly to a halt.

But how could people believe him when each day brought new paper profits? Indeed 600,000 of the estimated 1,500,000 million American shareowners (out of a population of 120,000,000) were confident enough to deal on margin, whereby they only had to put up a proportion of the capital, so sure were they that the stock market would increase in value the next day.

And it was not only American Nationals who bought. As the Literary Digest declared: 'transoceanic brokerage business has been growing to immense proportions ... But there has been an interlude of uncertainty and inconvenience for speculators crossing the ocean.'[58]

In August 1929 this was eliminated. The Leviathan and the Ile de France became fully equipped for speculation on the stock market even while the boats were tossing about on the high seas.

On 31 August 1929 agreement was finally signed at the Hague. All sides had reason to be happy with the arrangement. France would not now be inundated with reparations under the 'deliveries in kind' formula which had prevented her own industry from maximising its export potential and begun even to hurt the French home market.[59] Britain would not only gain a slight sum more in reparations than originally envisaged in April, but her coal industry, whose export markets had shrunk from Germany's 'deliveries in kind', would also benefit. America felt secure that she had at last commercialised the reparations and secured the payment of the war debts and taken the sting of politics away from them. Germany had in total a smaller sum to pay and all the irksome controls over the German economy removed. Finally, and most gratifying, the Rhineland would be evacuated five years earlier than scheduled under the terms of the Treaty of Versailles. For the British this concession appeared a formality, but for a great many Germans of 'Prussian' outlook, this was the concession most desired from the whole negotiations. Although the German Parliament had yet to ratify the Young Plan, as its negotiators had won acceptance that its implementation should be retrospectively effective from Sunday, 1 September, ratification appeared a formality.

58. Galbraith. *The Great Crash*. p.80. *The Literary Digest*. 31.8.29.
59. *The Economist*. 1929.

10.11   Downturn in American Stock Market

On Thursday 5 September 1929 the New York Times recorded a sudden downturn in the American stock market on 4 September. It declared sardonically:

'Yesterday's general decline was popularly assigned to several different causes, none of which was particularly convincing. The most obvious explanation ... would be that the pace of advancing prices during the past three weeks has been so rapid, and so regardless of the money market position, as to inspire a growing sense of caution even among convinced speculators for the rise.'

The following Monday, under the heading 'Talk of a Future 'Crash' the New York Times produced a serious assessment of the market's reaction. It poured scorn on the idea that the market had reacted to 'one wag' who 'had hit so wide of the mark in the prophecies of a year or two ago' and had now seemed to some to have, single handedly, caused a severe reaction in the market with his prophecies of a crash 'sooner or later.'

The editor of the column then traced previous periods of speculation and collapse on the American stock exchange and he consoled his readers with the differences between then and the present time.

'One is the power and protective resources of the Federal Reserve. They did not avert the prolonged readjustment of 1920 and 1921, but they prevented the disastrous results of overstrained credit which had invariably occurred on previous occasions of the kind. In such older episodes, a highly inflated range of values for commodities ... was always a serious complication' and 'was the most formidable of all aggravating influences in 1920. But with the present methods and circumstances of American industry it is nowadays virtually non-existent. The money market itself is guarded against old-time panics, both by the country's accumulation of gold and by its fund of available foreign credits.'

Although he did regret that 'the spirit of speculative inflation is abroad, in some quarters on a scale beyond the imagination of ten years ago; that a money market, which has this year had to borrow from Europe to meet the home demands, has shown signs of instability; that America, at the climax of a speculative craze, has never failed to overstrain the most seemingly impregnable credit organism' he nevertheless stated:

'There is ... good reason to hope that, if and when the moment for really formidable reaction shall arrive, it will not have the terrors that once attached to it.'

Nevertheless the stock market did continue to fall during the next few weeks. What was more worrying, the funds from abroad which had provided such a comfort and support to the American stock market, began to ebb away.

The Committee to which Curtius had referred when he spoke of Snowden deserving to be 'made an honourary member of Hugenberg's Committee' had been formed in July to fight the Young Plan on the 'moral' grounds that Germany had not started World War I and therefore was not liable to 'reparations.' It was comprised of an odd assortment of individuals and pressure groups to mount such a campaign. It included the head of the Stahlhelm, Seldte, the prominent pan-German, Heinrich Class, and the leader of a minority fascist party, Adolph Hitler.

Hugenberg, himself, was co-founder of the pan-German League and had been in an influential position both before and during the war, being Chairman of the armaments' manufacturers, Krupp, from 1909-19.

Heinrich Class, as leader of the pan-German organization, the Alldeutsche Verband, had been a regular contributor to the far right wing newspaper, *Post*, which had envisaged as the goal of Germany's 'national imperialistic world policy', the 'strengthening of our central European position, the final confrontation with France and Britain; the enlargement of our colonial possessions so as to find new German homes for our surplus population.'[60]

Although he had not set out in detail his list of war aims until a month after World War I had started, Class had discussed with General von Gebsattel what Germany required from the war in July 1914.

General von Gebsattel agreed with him that 'if the coming war (ends) favourably' Germany must acquire 'a strip of land in the east and in the west' to be colonised by German peasants. By this means 'world rule of the Teutons would be established for centuries.'[61]

One month after World War I began, after Germany's initial wartime successes in the West, Class laid down the aims of his executive committee, a high war indemnity from France, Longwy-Brie and the French Channel coast to be detached from France, the ceded area to extend down to the Somme; also the whole line of fortresses from Belfort to Verdun. He also suggested ceding Toulon as a fortified port!

It was astonishing therefore that Class could have the gall to put his name to a document which repudiated all guilt for Germany having started World War I.

It was just as astonishing that the leader of the Stahlhelm, Seldte,

60. *Post*. 25.4.13. Reproduced from *Wars of Illusions*. Fritz Fischer.
61. DZA I, *NL Gebsattel*, No.1. folio 160 ff.; Gebsattel to Class, 23.7.14. Fritz Fischer. *War of Illusions*. p.456.

should have put his name to the document. The Stahlhelm was a paramilitary organisation, many of whose members were former officers in
the Prussian army. They must have known that the military hierarchy
had been preparing for World War I for ages before the murder of the
Archduke. On 15 March 1914 Moltke, Chief of the Prussian General
Staff, had written to the Prussian Ministry of War:

> 'The Reich's economic readiness for war which increasingly preoccupies the
> top level authorities is closely connected with the preparations of the army
> leadership and the direction of the war.' Economic matters to be studied were
> 'the effects of mobilisation on the labour force ... questions arising from the
> disappearance of markets ... transport problems ... (and) marketing prospects
> for commerce if the German ports were blocked.'[62]

At the end of May 1914 Moltke had asked the Foreign Secretary, Jagow,
in the words of Fritz Fischer 'to create the political and diplomatic conditions for a preventative war against Russia and France.'

One could not but have expected the officers connected with the
Prussian General Staff, and the many in the ranks who shared their
views, to have known what was in the minds of their superior officers in
1914. Yet in 1929 the 340,000-strong Stahlhelm gave its support to
Hugenberg's petition against the 'war-guilt' lie. The Stahlhelm's leader,
Seldte, showed his true colours when he joined Hitler's administration
in 1933 as Minister of Labour, and remained with him in that position
till the bitter end of the Third Reich. Hitler rejoiced in the fact that he
had been offered the chance to join this fraternity of bellicose old
Prussians to proclaim to a wider world that Germany was whiter than
white, and had been utterly blameless in causing World War I. The reason for his inclusion appeared to be that Hugenberg had great plans for
Hitler. He would be chosen to lead the popular campaign against the
reparations, once Hugenberg had blazed the propaganda path with the
condemnation of the 'war-guilt' lie in his 550 newspapers.

The tide was running towards socialism in Europe. Germany and
now Britain had majority socialist governments. Hugenberg's party,
the German Nationalists, had lost a third of their voters in 1928 (down
from 6.2 to 4.4 millions) and yet Hugenberg was not happy to let the
socialists try out their principles of running the country, cutting down
the power of the heavy industrial magnates in the process. After the
DNVP was defeated in the national elections in May 1928, it had

---

62. R.A. *Kriegsrüstung und Kriegswirtschaft.* 1st Supp. Vol. pp.287 ff; Moltke to
Delbrück, 14.5.14. See Fritz Fischer. *War of Illusions.* pp.440–1. The Economic
Committee met on 25 and 26 May. The protocol of the session is missing from the docu-
ments. See Cf. Schroeter. *Keig-Staaat-Monopol, 1914–18.* p.51. note 80.

Figure 10.3 Alfred Hugenberg
'Herr Hugenberg offers his follow Nationalists the panacea of dictatorship. He favours monarchism and Hohenzollern legitimism, indeed, but he believes that the restoration of the Imperial throne can only be gained through the preliminary creation of a dictatorial regime akin to Premier Mussolini's in Italy. He is convinced, moreover that this step can be taken legally, or at least without a violent upheaval ... ' New York Times 15th July 1928
© Hulton Deutsch

produced a resolution of its aims, showing its distaste for democracy:

'We hate the present form of the German state with all our hearts because it denies to us the hope of freeing our enslaved Fatherland, of cleansing the people of the war-guilt lie, (and) of gaining necessary living space (lebensraum) in Eastern Europe ... We oppose the political system that regulates the present state, and we oppose those who support this system with all their compromises.'[63]

Herr Hugenberg had been elected by the German Nationalists, the DNVP to get their anti-democratic message across, canvassing external aims to rid themselves of the democratic threat at home.

Formerly the Chairman of Krupps, the armament manufacturers, myopic, bespectacled Herr Hugenberg, was a man of outsized ambitions. He had recently added Ufa (Universal Films) to his media empire so it too could be used to put his propaganda message across:

On the 15 July 1928 the *New York Times* reported:

'Herr Hugenberg offers his fellow Nationalists the panacea of dictatorship. He favours monarchism and Hohenzollern legitimism, indeed, but he believes that the restoration of the Imperial throne can be gained only through the preliminary creation of a dictatorial regime akin to Premier Mussolini's in Italy. In his view, there must first be a German dictator, then a new Kaiser. He is convinced, moreover, that this first step can be taken legally, or at least without a violent upheaval, simply by expanding and strengthening the German President's constitutional right to dissolve Parliament and appoint a dictator if the condition of the country seems to warrant it.'[64]

Hugenberg looked around to find a proletarian, one of the common herd, who the masses could identify with and yet one who could be relied upon to put the boot into the SPD with its democratic principles. Thus he entered into an alliance with the 'hitherto insignificant National Socialists (formerly Volkische) and so entered upon a policy of violence and terrorism.'[65]

10.12 Rise of the National Socialists

The National Socialists had not always been so insignificant. After their

63. Resolution read out at a provincial convention in Furstenwald. Brandenburg. September 1928. E. Eyck. *The Weimar Republic*. Vol. II. p.167–8.
64. *New York Times*. 15.7.28.
65. *Annual Register*. 1929. p.189.

propaganda success in 1923 they had achieved a great success in the polls in the Spring of 1924, attracting 1.9 million votes, but in the 1928 elections their number of votes had slumped to 800,000, leaving the party perilously short of members and money.

'I am not a member of the Reichstag' commented the impecunious anti-Republican Goebbels 'I am a PI and a PRP: a Possessor of Immunity (if he chose to say anything libellous in Parliament) and a Possessor of a Railroad Pass.'[66] (which entitled him to free transport as a member of Parliament.

Goebbels would not have to rely on his free railway pass much longer if he wished to travel. Hitler's party emerged from the Radical fringe of politics into the limelight as Herr Hugenberg's DNVP, the second most powerful political party in the country, elevated it from obscurity with a blast of free publicity. Now the Stahlhelm patriots, that band of aristocratic pro-Monarchists ex-soldiers who counted President Hindenburg among their honourary members, would be encouraged to march side by side with Hitler's brown shirts, for Hugenberg's Committee planned to promote a petition to be called 'The Bill against the Enslavement of the German People' which, if it received enough signatures, had to be submitted by the government to a referendum of the whole nation.

10.13 The Freedom Law

The so-called 'freedom law' contained four paragraphs. The first dealt with the 'war-guilt' lie. It declared that:

> 'the government of Germany should 'notify all foreign powers immediately and formally that the confession of war-guilt forced upon Germany in the Versailles Treaty is contrary to historical truth, rests upon false assumptions, and has no force in international law.'

Germany had not started the First World War. The country was altogether blameless. Indeed Herr Hugenberg's press had decided who the real culprits were. It had been Germany's old economic rivals, the British, who had driven the Germans into the war with their encircling policy in Europe.

In *Der Geist der Englische Politik und das Gespenst der Einkreisung Deutschlands*, reviewed in The Times on 7.1.30 Hermann Kantorowicz tried to dispute the charge made against Britain. He demonstrated through his research that Britain's alleged encircling policy was impos-

66. Bracher, *Auflosung der Weimarer Republik*. p.375.

sible because 'the irrationality of English politics made England inca-
pable of carrying through any far reaching plan, and because the strong
bent of her people towards humanity, objectivity and chivalry would
have prevented it before-hand, had there been any such plans.'[67]

He charged that it was the Germans who had been filled with anti-
British sentiment before the war. He traced this sentiment back to
Bismarck's anti-British 'hertz' (a word for which *The Times* could find
no translation) and he quoted from von Tirpitz's letter of 28 February
1907 in which he said that several decades must pass 'before we are
strong enough to proceed to an invasion of England'[68] to demonstrate
that 'the organised movement against England' developed rather than
diminished after Bismarck's fall. Conversely from the testimony of
German ambassadors and diplomatists he put forward conclusive evidence 'that there was no such movement in England against Germany.'
He stated that in Germany 'it seems ... quite in order that King Edward
(Edward VII) should receive a far reaching plan, which his ministers
and their successors should steadily carry out, to satisfy the envy of
businessmen.'

Hermann Kantorowicz saw a real danger in the 'continuance of the
(Hugenberg) campaign which has for its object the repudiation of all
war-guilt.' So he set his book before his countrymen, bravely, 'without
fear' but also 'without hope.'

Unfortunately he was all too correct. The message of his book was
drowned in a wave of contrary propaganda from Hugenberg's 500 plus
newspaper titles. The German people, who had always been hoodwinked by their leadership anyway, began to think that Germany was
not only, not 'solely' guilty as the Government contended, but was the
victim of gross injustice. After all the British government now had as its
respected Prime Minister, Ramsay Macdonald, whose accusations of
war-mongering against his own establishment in 1914, while little read
at home, had been translated into German and every country Germany
did business with.

The second and third paragraphs of the 'Freedom Law' instructed the
government to make an official protest against the 'war guilt' article,
231 of the Treaty of Versailles, and to reject the Young Plan and the
whole policy of reparation and understanding with Germany's erstwhile
enemies, a policy which had been so successfully built up over the last
few years by Germany's ailing Foreign Minister, Gustav Stresemann.

But the last paragraph of the 'Bill against the Enslavement of the

---

67. *The Times*. 7.1.30. Herman Kantorowicz was Professor of Kiel University.
68. *Riddle of the Sands* by Erskine Childers was published in 1903. It tells of a threatened invasion of England by Germany.

German People' was the most astonishing of all because it proposed that any minister who supported treaties with foreign nations like the Young Plan, and even the Treaty of Versailles, should be tried for treason.[69] All 550 of Herr Hugenberg's newspapers supported his petition. Those who went to his cinemas also received a waft of publicity.

One of Stresemann's last acts at the end of September was to get the executive of his People's Party, the DVP, to pass a clear resolution opposing Hugenberg's 'Bill against the Enslavement of the German People' and so by definition supporting the Republic and its policy of fulfillment of its reparations' obligations.

But Stresemann could do no more. He was a dying man. Antonina Vallentin describes him at Geneva: 'A marked man stood there in the shadow of death. His suit flapped about his shrunken figure ... His breathing came so hard that his sudden coughing often drowned out his words ... One could almost hear the fevered beating of his heart.'[70] A week later he was dead.

Stresemann had been a hawk for most of his life and had shared many of the aspirations of the far right over changing the Versailles boundaries in Eastern Europe, but he had come into contact with enough foreign diplomats to know that 'might is not always right', that friendly persuasion can be more valuable than force, that force indeed can be crude and unproductive. His untimely death at fifty nine was a disaster for the Allies for he was the only man of sufficient stature to be able to stand up to Schacht, Hugenberg and the far right.

10.14   Germany's Role in the New Europe

Under the heading 'Germany's Role in the New Europe', *The Economist* reviewed a book, dedicated to Stresemann's memory by the Democrat former cabinet minister, Dr. Koch-Weser, entitled *Deutschlands Aussenpolitik in der Nachkriegszeit 1919-29*. Dr. Koch-Weser prophesied that Stresemann's style of diplomacy would continue after his death 'because we wish to pursue it' and he gave an outline of the aims Germany would pursue now that the country had gained the right to pay its own bills and run its own affairs in Europe.

The Economist outlined Koch-Weser's new vision of Europe, to Stresemann's memory.

'If war is bad business, it is even more so for Germany than for other coun-

69. For full text, see *Royal Institute of International Affairs Documents*. 1929. p.81.
70. Antonia Vallentin. *Stresemann*. p.278.

tries, and it may be taken as axiomatic that she will pursue a pacifist policy. But pacifism as hitherto preached and practised has been largely a negative creed; Germany proposes to be the protagonist of a more positive pacifism, based on alliances for the active promotion of international cooperation. The question of an Anglo-Saxon alliance to which Germany could be a party is ruled out by the repeated evidence which Great Britain has given of her unwillingness to break with France even when her sense of justice seemed to demand it. Moreover, nothing is more important for Germany than the obliteration of her atavistic feud with France ... '

On the question of the League of Nations Dr. Koch-Weser feared that it might 'degenerate into an instrument for the maintenance of the 'status quo.'

'Dr. Koch-Weser ... visualises the Germany of the future as the champion of oppressed races, and suggests that, in pursuance of this 'role' she should renounce all ambition of ever becoming a colonial power ... he sees a healthier solution in the demolition of economic barriers within Europe, which would open extensive sources of raw material to German industry on the one hand, and would provide markets and an unrestricted field of activity in the enterprise of Germany's abounding and capable population on the other. Bound up to some extent with this is a great eagerness to maintain the German character and culture of those minorities abroad which belong to the German race ... If Dr. Koch-Weser is representative of a substantial section of the German people, it is remarkable evidence of the vitality of the nation that it is prepared ... to rely entirely on its own industry, inventiveness and qualities of leadership to create for it those opportunities which other nations have sought through the means of great overseas possessions. This calls up progressive germanisation of Europe which may seem alarming; but a moment's reflection on the penetration of almost the whole world of recent years, by American methods and influences reveals ... that it is impossible, in modern conditions, to resist the infiltration of economic and cultural influences from any country whose inhabitants have sufficient vitality to originate anything. Germany's influence is bound to grow; growth in the way outlined is likely to be most productive of profit both to Germany and her neighbours. 'The only practicable means of securing this open-door policy is, in Dr. Koch-Weser's view, the formation of a United States of Europe, to be achieved by a gradual series of agreements, and to lead ultimately to much closer economic and political co-operation throughout the world. In this atmosphere of friendship Germany can count on reasonable and fruitful discussion of the four questions whose solution she has most at heart; disarmament, the revision of her Eastern frontier; cultural autonomy for minorities and the 'Anschluss' with Austria.'[71]

Dr. Koch-Weser's vision of the 'Germanisation' of Europe could not be realised unless Germany was immensely strong financially. The British,

71. *The Economist.* 7.12.92.

having given concessions over the Rhineland, must have felt weary at the thought that prominent Germans were already talking of the Allies making new territorial concessions. The revision of Germany's eastern frontier and the 'Anschluss' with Austria seemed particularly hard for Germany to achieve peacefully unless French compliance was ensured by her being reduced to poverty and fearfulness because both had been expressly forbidden by the Treaty of Versailles. Deciding how strong Germany's economy actually was, appeared most difficult to deduce in view of Germany's protestations over the reparations and the large, uncatalogued amount of the nation's money that appeared to be abroad. But *The Economist* had noted how quickly the slide in the German mark had been corrected after Germany had won concessions over the Young Plan.[72] On the economic front, Germany seemed to be moving towards protection, even though Stresemann himself had talked about bringing down trade barriers and the German socialists, currently in Government, had seemed to be in favour of a more open economy.[73]

How far Dr. Koch-Weser's ambitions for Europe reflected those most dear to the late Dr. Stresemann was not disclosed. But Dr. Koch-Weser had promised that Germany would continue Stresemann's pursuit of ambition by peaceful means. Herr Hugenberg, however, with the power of his newspaper empire behind him, was determined to use his power and influence to try and force changes to Germany's advantage, without much regard for the financial stability of the international world.

On 13 October 1929 the German government felt itself sufficiently threatened by Hugenberg's propaganda campaign against the reparations to issue an official proclamation that the petition was a 'monstrous attempt to incite the German people against the government and to annihilate the ten-year good-will policy of the republic with Germany's former enemies.'[74]

On 17 October 1929 counting on the petition to hold a referendum on Herr Hugenberg's so-called 'Freedom Law' began. It was scheduled to take two weeks. In commenting 'that no other post-war political issue has contained an equal amount of mischief in its make-up' the *New York Times* had to concede that the petition would gain the requisite ten per cent of the vote (4 million) because Hugenberg, another of the postwar 'would be Napoleons'[75] could count on Hitler's 800,000 voters and those of other extreme minority right-wing groups if some of his 4.4

72. *The Economist*. 13.7.29.
73. *The Economist*. 7.12.29. From our correspondent. Berlin. December 3. 'The Cabinet is moving towards ever more drastic Protection ... This in view of the Cabinet's semi-Socialistic composition, seems to be an anomaly.'
74. *New York Times*. 13.10.29.
75. *New York Times*. 22.10.29.

million party faithful fell by the wayside.[76] The *New York Times* reported selling on the stock market. There had been a movement to 'force' stocks down. The next day the *New York Times* wrote a leader on Herr Hugenberg's 'Freedom from the Enslavement of the German people' petition. It again stressed its conviction that the petition would succeed and gave its opinion that the reason that Hugenberg had won public sympathy for his petition was because he had opened up the war-guilt issue: 'By coupling rejection of Germany's sole responsibility for the war, they have insured for themselves considerable support among sections of the population otherwise sternly opposed to their mischievous aims.'[77]

10.15 Tight Money Affects America's Stock Market

The American stock market had been ripe for a correction. It had had an unprecedented boom. Not that the economic indicators were forecasting any great tale of gloom in October. John Kenneth Galbraith in his book, *The Great Crash*, asserts that 'until September or October of 1929 the decline in economic activity was very modest.' The Federal Reserve Index of Production was 9 points lower in October than in June, 117 compared to 126. Steel production was also down. So a correction was in order.[78] There had been speculation without much regard for fundamentals for some time. However the stock market collapse was so violent, so deep and it was to last for such a long time that it confounded the experts.

This, however, was only because they looked internally for triggers for the market collapse. They did not realise that with international finance and modern communications, bad political and economic news in one country could not but affect all other countries with whom it did business.

For those Americans with knowledge of Germany, however, Herr Hugenberg's petition could not have spelt anything else but alarm for the American stock market.

Stock markets rely on a ready supply of that precious commodity, cash. Herr Hugenberg was leader of the second largest party in the German Parliament. He was not asking for a lower reparations' bill for Germany. He was stating that no reparations should be paid at all. And America knew that the fate of her citizen's war debts rested with

76. *New York Times*. 17.10.29.
77. *New York Times*. 18.10.29.
78. J. K. Galbraity. *The Great Crash*. p.86.

the reparations. But this was not all. The so called 'Freedom Bill' had stated that any minister who dared 'sign treaties with foreign powers' would be guilty of treason, implying that not only the Young Plan Treaty but all Germany's foreign treaties were under threat. And what faith could one have in Germany honouring her economic obligations if she had so little regard for solemn political treaties? All America's long and short term advances and even her commercial loans could be at risk if other Germans took his attitude. Herr Hugenberg's petition could not have been the only factor triggering the American stock market collapse, but it had to have a major influence.

There were other economic factors affecting the downturn including the increase in European interest rates. The *Deutsche Economist* on 11 October declared that 'the recent fall in Wall Street prices was not due to domestic conditions but to the foreign situation.' 'In particular' according to the *New York Times* 'it ascribes the recent severe reaction on the New York Stock Exchange in the advance in the London bank rate and to selling of American stocks by European holders, who had been frightened by recent scandals in their own markets and by complications coming to light in numerous big European countries.' In England, in the tight money conditions prevailing, the Hatry Group had collapsed while in Austria, which had felt the necessity of raising its interest rates again on 26 September, the Bodencredit-Anstalt Bank had had to be absorbed by the Credit Anstalt Bank, after Bodencredit's customers had started queuing up outside its doors, demanding the return of their deposits.

A European 'strike' against the important American commodity, wheat, was denied as it was asserted that Europe had secured a bumper harvest in 1929. Lack of orders for America's important wheat crop could have affected market sentiment on the American stock exchange, however.

On 2 October 1929 Dr, Hilferding, the German Finance Minister, had promised to enact legislation to counteract the previous high tax on moderate incomes which was 'supposed to check saving' and to encourage 'capital flight to abroad.'

The withdrawal of German funds from the American market since the change in German legislation also had an adverse affect on American market sentiment as it dragged down the value of the dollar. 'Perpendicular' falls were reported on 21 October 1929 after it was reported:

'The outstanding feature of the past week's Berlin money market was the rapid descent of the dollar exchange' in favour of the mark, to 'the lowest of the year to date.'[79]

It could have been other factors which alarmed the Germans however as gold-rich Paris seemed to be attracting money even though its interest rates were only 3½%[80]

As a generality in 1929 America's interest rates had gone up not down. With the exception of France, interest rates had been moving higher practically everywhere. American interest rates had been raised to 6% in August. British interest rates had been raised half a percent higher to 6½% in September. The rate for 'call money' (by which Stock Exchange transactions are financed) in America however had decreased a little from a peak of 9¼% at the beginning of October, and the 90 day rate had been reduced from 9% to 8%.[81] German funds fled the US in search of safer pastures in Europe. The *New York Times* expected that the return of so much cash to Germany would lead to easier money rates. But so far it seemed to have made little difference to Germany's tight money policy as the *New York Times* commented on 21 October:

'Although these withdrawals have increased the supply of money in the Berlin market, money rates have nevertheless remained high.'

German exports were said to be 'very satisfactory.'

But the final straw for the American stock market, however, was not pressure from imports, or Europe's refusal to buy American wheat, or even the removal of the German funds to Europe. It was the raising of a 'political loan.'

10.16 A Political Loan and the Market's Collapse

In early October the Swedish Match King, Kreuger, had reached agreement with Germany by which he lent the German government $125,000,000 to help cover the initial instalment of the new Young Plan

79. *The Economist*. 1929 – gives the following Interest rate figures:
 Berlin raised to 7½% April 1929;
 Vienna raised to 7½% April 1929;
 Warsaw raised to 9% April 1929;
 Brussels raised to 5% July 31 1929;
 Paris remained at 3½%;
 London 5¼% April 1929 raised to 6½% September 26;
 New York Federal Reserve raised to 6% August 8.
80. *New State Economist*. 2.11.29.
81. *The Economist*. 1929. p.737.

reparations' agreement, while receiving, in return, a monopoly of the German match industry. It was said that Kreuger would be able to take care of a large percentage of this loan without resource to the American market.[82] However on the evening of 23 October 1929 'formidable advertisements announced subscription rights in a new offering of certificates in Aktiebolaget Kreuger and Toll.'[83]

This was too much for the American market. Americans had already promised, under the terms of the Young Plan reparations' agreement, to raise one huge loan to help Germany pay her initial Young Plan reparations' instalment. With the prospective success of Hugenberg and Hitler's petition leading to a national referendum, there seemed a doubt as to whether either loan, or indeed any of the money previously lent to help pay the reparations, would ever be repaid. On 24 October 1929 the American stock market collapsed.[84] 19,226,400 shares were sold. The paper loss in October and November, at 26,078,000,000 dollars, was equal to the entire wartime increase in the American national debt.

Not all Germans had removed their funds from abroad in response to higher German interest rates. Much money had been invested by Germans in America over the past year because of lack of faith in the socialist administration in Germany, high taxation at home, and excitement with the booming American stock market. On 31 October 1929 the substantial German bank, the Beamtenbank, crashed, leaving scores of unhappy creditors. The German business world joined the German public in their anger at America. Anti-semitism returned. Because the electrotechnical giant AEG was hit by a cash-flow crisis and was forced to sell part of its business to American concerns, the Siemens finance chief complained bitterly that 'the whole world belongs to the Americans.' 'Denunciations of Yankee penetration of Continental production continued to echo down to the end of 1930.'[85]

On 3 November the results of Hugenberg's petition were revealed. As forecast in the *New York Times*, Hugenberg just managed to scrape together the requisite number of votes to necessitate the Government

---

82. *New York Times.* 3.10.29, 11.10.29. In defence of the monopoly it was said that the Soviet Union was dumping large quantities of matches on the German market 13.10.29. The Bill 'must pass the Reichstag where it will meet heavy opposition, especially from the industrial groups which are exporting goods to Russia.'

83. J. K. Galbraith. *The Great Crash.* p.120. 12.3.32. Kreuger shot himself three months before the final, abortive, Lausanne Conference on the reparations, after heavy selling by Continental interests. J. K. Galbraith. *The Great Crash.* p.152.

84. *Annual Register.* 1929. p.305–6. Followed by a second panic of almost greater dimensions on 19.11.29.

85. Siemens speech 12.12.29 and comment in Stephen A. Schuker. *American 'Reparations' to Germany.* (1988) p.49.

having to hold a debate on the Young Plan in the Reichstag and have a national referendum on the petition.

The Reichstag rejected the bill by an overwhelming majority on 30 November. For under the bill's original wording even President Hindenburg himself could have been sent to prison had he signed the Young Plan. Even the Nationalist Party split over the issue. But still it served its purpose of bringing the war guilt issue back forcibly into the public mind. It had planted a germ. When times grew worse, the German people would blame the reparations for all their misfortunes.

Towards Autocracy

11.1 Introduction

Herr Hugenberg felt he knew what was best for Germany. The American framers of the Young Plan had also had aspirations as to how the German economy should be run. They had promised to make a generous loan available for the first year's Young Plan payment in the hope that the government would use the money to stabilise the budget, fund the reparations, and alievate the deflationary environment.[1]

Dr. Hilferding, Germany's socialist Minister of Finance, was faced with a large deficit because parties such as the German Nationalists had refused sufficient funding for the Spring budget. His subsequent attempt to raise a loan in Germany to cover this deficit was labelled by the DNVP as the 'last, desperate act of a political system which has turned into a runaway pump.' Not unnaturally the loan failed. It was when the regime was considering, in desperation, asking long suffering foreign lenders for yet another loan, that Dr. Schacht suddenly produced his outburst. On the 6 December Dr. Schacht, delivered a bombshell, the details of which he presented to the Press before bothering to disclose them first to the elected Government.[2]

In this address Dr. Schacht declared that after he had signed the Young Plan on Germany's behalf in June, concessions had been made (to the British) at the Hague to Germany's financial disadvantage. He would never have agreed to them. Indeed he made it clear that he had signed the Young Plan in June on the express understanding that the Young Plan document would not be altered and that the German

---

1. *Young Report.* p.22. The new annuities 'start at a level which ... gives immediate and important relief to the German budget ... makes possible an immediate resumption of the tax reduction programme which has been in force since 1924 ... will give a strong stimulus to saving and thereby materially assist in the internal formation of the new capital which Germany still requires' ... and 'provides the greatest possible assurance that the new scheme will function from the beginning without any hitch or disturbance.'
2. E. Eyck. *The Weimar Republic.* Vol. II. p.224.

government would put into effect 'far reaching financial reforms which had not been carried out'.[3]

Britain's *Economist* newspaper spluttered with anger at the iniquity of Dr. Schacht declaring that grave alterations had been made in the final Young Plan agreement to Germany's disadvantage.[4] In Germany, however, with Herr Hugenberg's referendum still to be held, his words could only have an unfortunate effect.

11.2 Concessions to Industry

Dr. Schacht also roundly castigated the elected government for its mismanagement of the economy. He declared that the Reich Exchequer was 1,700,000,000 (£85,000,000) in arrears and yet there was only 1,370,000,000 (£65,000,000) in the coffers. There was a yawning chasm which had been caused by socialist mismanagement. He berated the SPD for their profligacy. Single-handedly he raised the money from German banks to balance the books. The Socialist Finance Minister, Dr. Hilferding, was made to resign.

The budget deficit in fact had been very much of the Right's making. They had refused to vote money to cover the deficit on the arrears of the unemployment insurance they, themselves, had introduced. Some said that the reluctance of Dr. Stresemann's People's Party, the DVP the party of big business, to support legislation raising the unemployment insurance in the Autumn had been instrumental in undermining Stresemann's health. Now with a magic wand Dr. Schacht had coerced all strands of German opinion into following his programme, discrediting the Socialist Party in the process.

Dr. Schacht's proposals were designed to please an America, reeling under the weight of losses on the stock exchange. For under them 450 million marks out of the first year's largesse of 700 million marks would be earmarked to fill a treasure chest to safeguard future payments of the reparations. By 'Schacht's Law' the reparations' reserve fund had to reach the total of 450 million marks by the end of the financial year at the very latest.[5]

3. E. Eyck. *The Weimar Republic*. Vol. II. p.230. Memo by Dr. Schacht.

4. *The Economist*. 14.12.29. 'The "modifications" ... were the renunciation by Germany of the £20,000,000 surplus arising from overlapping of the Dawes and Young Plans; the increase of £2,000,000 of the unconditional part of the Young annuity; the additional cost of the Belgian mark settlement; Great Britain's refusal to refund to the German government the surplus accruing from the liquidation of German property; and the abandonment of Germany's claims in respect to former properties in Poland ...

5. E. Eyck. *The Weimar Republic*. Vol. II. p.232.

Schacht's words stung the government into producing proposals designed to mollify his powerful friends on The Right. Government control over the municipalities would be tightened and unemployment insurance temporarily increased by 1/2%, with a review in March. Company and security taxes would be reduced by 20% and 'the (Aufbringung) levy, a tax imposed on business generally in order to distribute equally the Reparations Bonds burden' under the strictures of the Dawes Plan would be gradually abolished. The industrial debentures which had also helped secure payment of the Dawes Plan demands would be abolished too. Trading and ground taxes were to be reduced, the sugar tax abolished and progressive income tax reductions made during the next five years. These tax reductions were estimated to cost some 800 million marks and exceed in value the benefit which the Allies and America, in their generosity, had given to Germany in substituting the Young Plan for the Dawes Plan. It was to be hoped that the unpopular indirect tax on the poor man's beer and cigarettes would produce enough funds to cover the deficit caused by Dr. Schacht's largesse to industry.

The Economist newspaper declared that Dr. Hilferding 'ought to have resigned in protest, not in humiliation, a year ago when the Reichstag rejected his necessary additional taxation' to fund the unemployment insurance not to suffer humiliation now, from Dr. Schacht 'to whom are attributed, perhaps wrongly, certain political aspirations.'

It refuted any suggestion that Germany was a nation in economic crisis. In July it had quoted from a statement from the Dresdner Bank 'that in spite of the almost complete stoppage of the inflow of foreign capital, German business is able to maintain a level of production and trade which a year or two years ago was only made possible by having recourse on a great scale to the foreign capital market.'[6]

Now it commented: 'The Reichsbank President was, as always, aggressive; (he) was backed, it was proclaimed, by foreign opinion which is naturally inclined to support a Central Bank director against mere politicians; and finally he has the power of the purse. But the fortnight's history casts a new unfavourable light on German political conditions. It is not desirable that a Bank director should be able to dismiss ministers.'[7]

It quoted from the report of one of 'the great Berlin banks, which cannot be named because its communications are confidential' which contained figures showing that 'the year 1929, as compared with the year 1928 ... will show a displacement in a favourable direction in the balance of payments of hardly less than 4 milliards of marks.'

6. *The Economist*. 13.7.29.
7. *The Economist*. 28.12.29.

'The Berlin Bank's report is a mere statement of facts; but there are authoritative opinions, increasing in their number and their emphasis, about the coming favourable development of the balance of foreign payments.

'The editor of the chief banking journal writes that, owing to the rapid accumulation of capital, Germany, 'in a very short time,' will be able 'to meet all the demands of (native) business,' and that 'the time no longer seems far off when German business will be able to do without foreign credit and to begin repaying its foreign debts and buying back the securities and participations now in the hands of foreigners.

'The chief of a Governmental statistical department (in an article mainly devoted to exposing the exaggerated estimates of capital creation) estimates that national savings in the past five years, after the payment of Reparations (and naturally, subtracting the net increase in foreign indebtedness) were £1,000,000,000.'[8]

In the Spring of 1930 *The Economist* would carry a series of articles contrasting German banks with British ones and describing how the German banks had been able to give their industrial customers such excellent service as to enable them to help Germany become a major industrial power again.[9] There had been a number of insolvencies amongst small banking concerns in 1929 but in the words of *The Economist*: 'The productive capacity of industry generally has steadily grown.' Industries such as the steel industry and the cotton industry continued to report an expansion of business and the coal industry reported a record year with coal output up in the Ruhr district by 23% and coke and briquette output up by an astonishing 50%.[10]

It is true that, due to industrial rationalisation, high interest rates, and a cold December, the number of unemployed in Germany had mounted alarmingly. In September Germany had 1,627,439 unemployed[11] (roughly 7.2 of the workforce) but this figure had increased by over a million by the end of December to 2,894,798.[12] In September its unemployment rate had been lower than that of Britain. Now the percentage was higher.[13] The cold weather contributed to the increase in Germany's unemployment, but there was another reason. Industry could see that after the American stock market crash business would contract. With its

8. *The Economist*. 7.12.29.

9. *The Economist*. Jan to June. 1930. p.449, p.572, p.695.

10. *The Economist*. 18.1.30.

11. 1,433,450 covered by unemployment insurance. 194,409 merely covered by sickness insurance.

12. *German Statistical Year Book*. 1930. Arbeitsmarkt. Tables. 1.12.13. (The German figures for those 'in work' would be affected, as the British figures were recorded in 1931 to e, by an allowance for those absent 'from work through sickness and other forms of recorded non-employment other than "recognised" holidays.'

13. Sources. *German Statistical Year Book. The Statesman's Yearbook. The Economist*.

rationalised plants, and less taxes to pay, it would be well equipped to compete in a more difficult market.

The reparations had been paid without pain for the average German taxpayer between 1924 and 1929. Now, however, the burden of paying the reparations was to be switched from German industry to the German salary and wage earner, despite industry's demonstration that it could afford the higher tax burden necessitated by reparations' demands.

Germany's rationalised industry had less need now of willing hands, than it had had in the past, to help it dominate world trade. If the German hierarchy wished to use economic manipulation for political ends, it might feel the urge to demonstrate that the payment of reparations would, in Keynes words, 'degrade the lives of millions of human beings.' In this case the livelihood of the German workforce could be at risk.

On December 22 1929 the Government Referendum on the 'Bill against the Enslavement of the German People' as it was properly entitled, failed. Only 5,825,000 people voted for it, little more than the original petition. The language of the so-called 'Freedom Bill' was too intemperate. Besides, most people held no love for the capitalists of the Far Right. But Herr Hugenberg had planted a germ with his vindictive campaign against the Young Plan. As the financial squeeze began to tighten over the next year, and the burden of paying the reparations shifted from industry to the man in the street, the burden of paying the reparations loomed ever sharper into focus.

11.3 American Deal on Reparations

Parker Gilbert, the reparations' agent, must have been delighted that Dr. Schacht had kept his side of the bargain in forcing those 'profligate' socialists to cut expenditure and balance the budget if America initiated a new deal on the reparations. Schacht's insistence on giving proper priority to the payment of the reparations, by asking the nation to save more to guarantee their payment, (Schacht's Law) was an earnest of his pledge to get the reparations on a happy financial footing if Germany was given a reduction in its payments.

It was this performance of Schacht's in proving that, although he was not a member of Parliament, he could force the elected government to do as he wished in the financial field, which must have prompted the Americans to act with such trusting faith at the final Conference at the Hague.

After Herr Hugenberg's intervention the Allies had become alarmed over the internal situation in Germany and worried whether they had maintained sufficient controls over the German economy. Yet if they wished to strengthen them at this eleventh hour the ground was to be cut from under their feet. For it appeared that America had made a very special private agreement with Germany over her 5% reparations' demands which rendered any united attempt at enforcement impossible. The agreement declared:

> 'The United States accepts the full faith and credit of Germany as the only security for the fulfillment of Germany's reparations.'[14]

Germany's negotiators immediately snapped up the opportunity to broadcast this private arrangement to the world as soon as it had been agreed.

However the 'public', 'private', settlement between Germany and America caused consternation amongst the Allies.

Clearly the 'full faith' of one of Germany's major political parties, the DNVP was lacking so the Allies looked again at some of the economic statistics to see if Germany's 'credit' was reassuring.

The Economist declared: 'It may be rash to conclude that any really considerable part of the 5,000,000,000 marks of long-term and of the 7,000,000,000 marks short-term foreign capital invested in Germany ... has been misapplied.' But it questioned the amount of 'technical' rationalisation of the 'fat' years, 1925–27, (which) led to elaborate programs of plant extension, modernisation of machinery and perfection of processes which involve large capital investments.

This had led to widespread criticism in Germany where it was pointed out that despite productivity increases 'the average share yield of companies (in 1927) was only 4.2%' after allowing about 4.5% for interest on foreign borrowings, and, of course the levy for the payment of the reparations.

It was also pointed out that Germany's wage costs had expanded greatly over five years, the average wage for unskilled labour having risen from an admittedly lowly 44.2 pfennige at the beginning of 1924 to 81.2 at the beginning of 1929, while during the five years the cost of living had risen only from 125.9 to 153.1 per cent of pre-war cost. How much lower Germany's wages for unskilled workers had been in comparison to Britain in 1924 was not disclosed. But the national income per head of population, at $231, was only $13 more than France in 1928 and £204 less than Great Britain[15] so their wages did

14. *New York Times.* 7.1.30.
15. J. W. Angell. *The Recovery of Germany.* (1932) p.320.
$435 in Great Britain;
$231 in Germany;
£218 in France.

not seem unduly uncompetitive. *The Economist* reported that administrative' rationalisation, 'which costs little or nothing and effects immediate economies, is being vigorously continued in Germany.' So industry looked like being able to generate money to repay sums lent to it. But the Allies would have felt safer, in the new, uncertain climate, to have continued with the Dawes controls on the German economy. Clearly the Americans had been acting in good faith over their debt negotiations and Germany's credit looked good. But the fact remained that Germany's agreement with America could not but destroy any Allied attempt to tighten up the small print of the Young Plan document if the 'full faith' lacked. The German Nationalists' machinations to get the entire cabinet tried for treason if they passed the Young Plan Bill had horrified every European. Instead of happy talk at the Hague of nations being able to trust one another to pay their bills without the threat of force, arid harangues ensued as to what economic arrangements should be made should Germany request a moratorium.

Finally, however, the proceedings were agreed at the Hague and the Young Plan was ratified by the German Parliament in March. The exhausted SPD abandoned office.

11.4 German Democracy in the Balance

The SPD appeared to be abandoning office lightly over the flimsy pretext of increasing the unemployment insurance premiums by $1/4$ of 1% to 3%.[16] But there was more to it than this.

President Hindenburg had grown tired of the SPD long before the Young Plan had been agreed. But his soldier's ambition of ridding the Rhineland of the occupationary French troops had overcome all other considerations. He had even offered to fulfil the German Nationalists demands for 'the increase of the power of the President at the expense of the Reichstag'[17] if the Nationalists would agree to take office and ratify the Young Plan but this they refused to do. So Hindenburg was forced to accept the continuance of the SPD cabinet, until the Young Plan was ratified, despite the SPD's unwelcome insistence that his pet project of 300,000,000 marks of aid for agriculture should be financed by taxing incomes of over 8,400 marks.[18] (approximately £420.)

16. E. Eyck. The Weimar Republic. Vol. 2, p.246–7.
17. J. Wheeler-Bennett. *Hindenburg. The Wooden Titan.* p.337.
18. *New York Times.* 2.3.30.

Subsidies for agriculture were a heated issue. Stresemann in 1929 had professed support for a general reduction of tariffs (of all sorts) in Europe in response to Briand of France's talk of a United States of Europe. But the present food minister, Shiele, had declared that Germany 'could not pay her debts, including Reparations, unless she became ultimately more or less independent of foreign foodstuff imports.'

This attitude was a bitter blow to exporting nations like the U.S.A. and Canada. America and Canada were already faced with large stocks of wheat left unsold from the year before. Little did they know that there was a new agricultural supplier whose produce was nearly ready to hit an over-crowded market before the year was over.

Before the war Russia had been a great wheat exporter but between 1917 and 1929 the Soviet Union had exported no wheat and other countries had expanded production to fill the gap. In September 1930 Russian wheat would arrive, in volume, on world markets. For not only was German industry helping with the machinery to create the grain surplus[19] but the firm of Krupp had shown the Soviets how to expand its production.[20]

The Krupp concern had learned its lesson from the early 1920s when Gustav Krupp von Bohlem und Halbach had failed to grasp 'the logic of the inflationary process' or 'position his firm to profit from it.'[21] Now it seemed happy to invest in a country which resorted to the printing press to lower its labour costs. It had renegotiated its agricultural concession in the Upper Caucasus on exceptionally advantageous terms in July 1928, the Soviet government having promised to take over the 'financing as well as the risk of losses.'

It must have distressed Krupp and other concessionaires that Stalin took their success in 1929 in the Northern Caucasus as his model in expanding the role of large collective farms to provide Russia with wheat for export.[22] 'Kulaks' were driven off their land all over Russia and sent to Siberia. Thousands of pacifist Germans who had emigrated to the Russian steppes in previous centuries were faced with a similar fate by Stalin's huge collectivisation program. Their cause was taken up in no uncertain terms by the German Press. Both the SPD who had suffered considerably from Communist agitation in Germany in 1929 and

19. *The Economist*. 25.4.31.

20. *New York Times*. 14.9.28.

21. Stephen A. Schuker. *American 'Reparations' to Germany, 1919–33*. (Princeton 1988) p.21.

22. 'As far back as November the plenary session of the Communist Executive Committee had made a bold stride toward rural socialisation after hearing a report by the representative of the North Caucasus about the growth and success of the communal farms in the region. For the first time it seemed the Kremlin had found the practical means to combat peasant individualism.' *New York Times*. 7.7.29.

the newspapers of the right, joined in their condemnation of Russia.[23]

France was already trying to attract support to stop Russian dumping of other goods. Germany needed to protect its agricultural industry before it was devastated by Russian produce.[24] For, unknown to the wheat exporters of the western world, in the words of *The Economist* of 17 January 1931 'Russia possesses a potential advantage over the United States in having available a larger area of first-grade wheat land' and the German right knew that this land was about to disgorge its wheat onto world markets with devastating results.

Protection for the farming industry was one thing but paying for it by taxing the rich was another. In this matter, Brüning, of the Centre Party, came to the President's rescue. At a dinner party at Willisen's, Meissner, Schleicher, Trevanus, and Groner had all urged Brüning 'to prepare himself to become Chancellor in a few weeks time.' Schleicher even declaring: 'I am afraid I shall have to take office myself' when Brüning remained hesitant.[25]

So Brüning as leader of the Centre Party, refused to support taxation of the rich to pay for the food subsidies and further declared that he would support ratification of the Young Plan only if a comprehensive reform of the economy was carried out. He became the apple of the old President's eye.

'The 'crisis' of March 1930 was provoked by the Reichswehr,' according to A. J. P. Taylor and Brüning was chosen as Chancellor.[26] On 13 March the Young Plan had been finally ratified by the German Parliament. On the 18 March Hindenberg sent the Chancellor, Müller, whose SPD supporters came mostly from urban districts, a peremptory letter which he caused to be published simultaneously in the Press, asking for new aid for 'the agricultural east.'[27] When Müller dragged his feet, Hindenberg lost no time in getting rid of him.

On 30 March, 'at the Chancellor's suggestion, the cabinet voted to resign en bloc without appearing before the Reichstag even one more time.'[28]

Criticism has continued to be heaped upon on the socialists to this day for deserting office on so small an issue as inching unemployment

23. Harvey Leonard Dick. *Weimar Germany and Soviet Russia 1926–1933.* (1966) p.183.

24. 29% of the population worked in agriculture. Jeremy Noakes and Geoffrey Pridham. *Documents on German Nazism. 1919–45.* (1974) p.383.

25. J. Wheeler-Bennett. *Hindenburg. The Wooden Titan.* p.337.

26. A. J. P. Taylor. *The Course of German History.* p.204. (1945 edition). *From Kaiserreich to Third Reich.* F. Fischer (1979) translated 1986) p.92 – on the relationship between the Reichswehr and the State.

27. Dorpalen. *Hindenburg and the Weimar Republic.* (1964) p.175–6.

28. E. Eyck. *The Weimar Republic.* Vol. II. p.248–9.

insurance up by ¹/₄ of 1%. Observers will ponder whether any dramatic gestures by the unloved left could have saved democracy in Germany in March 1930.

11.5 American Stock Market Recovery

After its collapse on 24 October the American stock exchange continued to plummet till the end of the year. But in the first three months of 1930 it staged a good recovery. It reached its peak in the middle of April. Ordinary people in America seemed to have taken little notice of the stock market crash the Autumn before and were still invading the shops creating business. Departmental store sales eased slightly in March, due, it was said to an early Easter but they still showed a healthy 3.7% increase over the average for the frothy stock market period in the first quarter of 1929. Car output was lower than for the same period in 1929 but it was above that for 1927 and 1928. Iron and steel output had also been well maintained. So American buyers returned to the Stock Market. Overseas buyers did too.

On 12 April when the market was at its height the *New York Times* wrote enthusiastically:

'One of the most significant commentaries on the current securities market, contained in market letters sent out yesterday by several brokerage concerns, is that the demand for our securities from foreign sources continues unabated. The magnet of the New York Stock Exchange is attracting investors throughout the world.'[29]

Stock exchange pundits naturally had blamed foreigners for the debacle the year before and were pleased to see that they were bahaving in a different fashion now. *The Economist* had commented on the stock exchange collapse in December: 'It was in the Autumn of 1928 that the flow of foreign short money to Wall Street began, and except for a temporary check in the Spring, when special measures were taken to exclude foreign money, the flow continued until September.' Its disappearance in September had led to a collapse in the market.

Now however foreigners were investing in actual American stocks. Paul Warburg, in January, at the Annual Meeting of the Banking Agency for the Reparations Payments, the International Acceptance Bank, had been unhappy that his predictions of a stock exchange collapse had come true, but he declared:

29. *New York Times*. 12.4.30. p.27.

'Happily now we have turned our backs upon the events of this unfortunate episode. The strength of the Federal Reserve system, and the prompt and courageous action on the part of our leaders, have enabled the country to weather the storm and to devote itself with unimpaired confidence and energy to the task of removing the wreckage and of restarting the wheels of business on their normal course.'[30]

It could be that foreign investors were more fickle than American ones, however. Perhaps they didn't like Republican talk of 'rushing' a new tariff bill through Congress, the highest in American history. The market paused uneasily in mid-April. Then it started to collapse. By Friday 25 April there was general selling. On Monday 28 the *New York Times* pleaded 'Speaking generally, it is possible to say that the country's trade as the end of April approaches makes a better showing than in other recent months.'[31] But on 29 April it had to relate of 'unrelieved selling pressure ... The widest break in the year to date.'[32] The market paused for a while in May but in June, the very month that the Hawley-Smoot tariff bill was being rushed through Congress to protect American industry and ensure for it in the 1930s the protection against dumping that the previous tariff had preserved in the 1920s, the stock market suffered a disastrous collapse.

President Hoover signed the tariff bill on 18 June. On 19 June, the stock market dropped to a new low, below even the level of the previous October and November. Many people held that it was the fall in commodity prices that was responsible for this collapse. The price of cotton fell by 18% between the third week of May and the 17 June. Wheat prices were also at an abysmal level. 'Copper sold lower than at any time since 1902.' Germany had been America's best customer for cotton in 1923. Great Britain had been unable to compete on price and had developed the resources of her Empire in India and Egypt instead. Sales of American cotton to Japan and Germany collapsed in 1930. The other significant drop in American exports to Germany during the year 1929/30 was registered by the car industry. There was another reason given for the drop in the stock market however, European retaliation for America's new tariff law.[33]

30. *New York Times.* 22.1.90.
31. *New York Times.* 28.4.30.
32. *New York Times.* 29.4.30.
33. *Financial Times.* 18.6.30.

11.6 German Dumping Policy

The French, indeed did feel concerned about the higher tariff. The French Minister of Commerce, Pierre Etienne Flandin, had made an impassioned plea to America in January over the proposed inequity of applying an increased tariff to France who had purchased nearly double the amount of goods from America than she exported to her during the first ten months of 1929.[34] There were fears in the US that France might apply a retaliatory tariff to America. However, the *New York Times* commented darkly: 'What Americans fear almost more than the loss of the French market is that the example of France may be followed in other and better European markets.'

Canada had been the US's best export customer world wide in the year 1929/30, followed by Great Britain. Germany remained in third place, despite a 12% drop in exports to that country during the year.

On the import front, America bought most of her goods from Canada, followed by Japan, Great Britain and Germany. Imports from Britain in the year 1929/30 registered a decline. Japan exported much to America while her imports from that country were slight. Germany had also increased her imports to the US by 15% in the year 1929/30 while taking 12% less of American manufactures.

Industrialists had complained of German 'dumping' in America in 1921 before imposing a 'blanket' tariff in 1922. It would have been embarrassing in 1922 to have to explain to American citizens that German industry was threatening American industry so soon after American citizens had gone over to Europe to dictate Europe's peace.

Japan looked the largest threat to American industry in 1930. But there also had been approximately a twenty five percent adverse swing in trade with Germany. It would have been difficult to state publicly, in those days of white supremacy, that Japan was threatening America's industry. It would have been even more difficult to own up to the fact that German industry was threatening America's trade when America had just granted Germany such an advantageous deal over the reparations.

If the Americans hoped that their new tariff against industrial competition would help their own industrial competitiveness with Germany, however, they were destined to be disappointed. Coincidentally, just three days before the new tariff bill was signed by President Hoover, the German iron and steel magnates were allowed to reduce the wages of their 180,000 workers by 7$\frac{1}{2}$% so long as they then reduced their price

34. *New York Times.*

for iron by more than this amount.[35] Talk spread of wage reductions spreading to all other industries.

11.7 Rise in German Unemployment

The Railways Board Commission (set up under the terms of the Dawes Plan and shortly to be disbanded under the terms of the Young Plan) had commented favourably in its final report in January on the state of the German economy and particularly on its export performance in the second half of 1929. But by the Summer of 1930 the Germans felt it necessary to cut domestic costs still further to enable their industry to compete. Responsibility for the lamentable laxity of the domestic economy was naturally given to the SPD who had so lately held power. They had apparently allowed wages to rise by 27% in the last three years besides running the economy in a wanton and feckless manner. Although from the published figures it appeared that there had, in fact, been no yawning chasm in the export/import figures for 1929 when the SPD had shared power – the trade gap stood at 47 million marks in 1929 compared to 1285 million marks when the right-wing DNVP had helped run the country[36] – Dr. Schacht had proved them to be unprincipled as well as incompetent by revealing their plans for the abandonment of socialist principles in the disgraceful pandering to the rich in their budget proposals of December 1929.

After the resignation of the SPD cabinet Heinrich Brüning was made Chancellor of Germany. A former Lieutenant-Commander in the German navy,[37] stiff, upright Brüning had accepted the onerous task of heading his increasingly divided nation with the words 'In the end I could not resist the President's appeal to my soldier's sense of duty.'[38]

Of course, if Brüning was the parliamentary head of the nation, ex-Field Marshall Hindenburg held the supreme authority with awesome powers to override the constitution. *The Times* had commented favourably in the Spring on the responsibility and restraint with which the old gentleman had acted to date. Its rose coloured spectacles were to be shattered as a result of events soon after, however. On the 30 June, the Allied troops were withdrawn from the Rhineland under the terms agreed in the Young Plan. Hindenburg did not use the occasion to make a peaceful gesture of goodwill to the French, however, but celebrated

35. *Financial Times.* 17.6.30.
36. *Royal Institute of International Affairs Survey.* 1930. p.546.
37. J. Wheeler-Bennett. *Hindenburg. The Wooden Titan.* p.303.
38. Beer. *Heinrich Brüning.* p.54. E. Eyck. *The Weimar Republic.* p.254.

the event by forcing the Socialist authorities in Prussia to revoke their ban on the Stahlhelm, Germany's illicit army of ex-soldiers,[39] who then paraded through the Rhineland in an ugly display of force. It was a disgraceful spectacle which brought anger and resentment to the French people.[40] This was ignored by the German Press, however, who merely used the occasion to call for the return of the Saarland.

The new Chancellor, Brüning, had been awarded the iron cross in World War I for bravery but he had a somewhat narrow view of national interests. So, once he had determined what he felt to be right for Germany in the longer term, he was steadfast in his determination to achieve those interests, even if his course was wrong and would cause unendurable hardship to the German people. The Government, he told the assembled Reichstag on 1 April 1930, would 'be identified with no party coalition' ... at the President's explicit request.'

> 'This cabinet has been formed for the purpose of solving as quickly as possible those problems which are generally comprehended to be vital to our nation's existence. This will be the last attempt to arrive at a solution with this Reichstag.'

He was determined to tighten the nation's purse strings. The government had decided that it was more realistic to budget for 2,000,000 unemployed than 1,300,000 as at present. Budgeting for an increased number of unemployed would give a deficit of 750 million marks (38 million pounds approximately). Besides this Brüning wished to cushion the effects of the present and coming drop in world agricultural prices on the farming community. Although many people worked in Germany's vast factories in the Ruhr, many more worked on their own small strip farms, divided into smaller and yet smaller strips through the ages, struggling to make ends meet.

Partially, of course, the long-term drop in world agricultural prices had been aggravated by Germany's own decision to become self-sufficient in agriculture. The German government had increased its tariff on agricultural products in December 1929.[41] Now, Schiele, the agriculture minister, proposed a sliding scale to keep German farmers solvent which would keep the all important rye and wheat prices roughly double the world price. Instead of just increasing taxes on those with incomes of 8,400 marks (£420) to pay for this it was proposed to

39. E. Eyck. *The Weimar Republic*. Vol. II. p.263–4.

40. Foreign Minister, Briand, made a personal protest to the German Ambassador, von Hoesch. *Schulthess' Europatscher Geschichtyskalender*. 1930. p.311. 4.7.30.

41. *Annual Register*. 1929. p.195. 'These include an increase in the duty on agricultural products, in some cases to more than twice the rates in operation before the war.'

increase unemployment insurance and direct and indirect taxes. An additional 5% supplementary tax was to be placed on married men's incomes and 10% on that of unmarried men. A special extra tax of 2% on the salaries of government officials was also said to be necessary. It was to be called 'National Aid.'[42]

Dr. Brüning also wished to seize the opportunity provided by the desire to cut public spending to reform the whole system of local government finance by providing a fixed figure for the Reich, the town councils and the provinces to spend over the next three years. A poll tax would be introduced so that each citizen would feel responsible for the expenditure in his region.

This was a bitter pill for the socialists to swallow. Germany had come a long way as an entity since the four kingdoms, six grand duchies, five duchies, seven principalities and three republics had been welded together by Bismarck into the Prussian Empire.[43] The Reichstag was unhappy about giving the Chancellor a mandate for an unpopular tax like a poll tax. And the National Aid tax they considered deeply unfair.

However, Dr. Brüning, the worthy Lieutenant, considered the measures essential for the future of the country. So he asked his general, President Hindenburg, to invoke the fatal paragraph 48 to save the national economy.

To an outside observer paragraph 48 had not been specifically formulated to deal with such a situation as was now occurring for it appeared to refer to disorder in the country at large rather than disagreement in Parliament. The wording of the paragraph ran as follows:

'In cases where public security and order are seriously disturbed or threatened in the German Reich, the President of the Reich is empowered to take the measures necessary for restoring public security and order ... The President of the Reich must without delay inform the Reichstag of all such measures. On the request of the Reichstag these measures must be withdrawn.'[44]

The SPD, the largest party in the Reichstag, did request that his draconian economic measures be reconsidered They were prepared, unwillingly, to consider some sort of poll tax provided it could be made more equitable, but the tax of 2¹/2% on Government employees, the so-called 'National Aid' enraged them. For so many petty government officials were SPD supporters. They had been reduced to near destitution in 1923

42. E. Eyck. *The Weimar Republic*. Vol. II. Wage reductions over the year averaged 7%, civil servants 6%, Ministers 20%. *Annual Register*. 1930. p.180.
43. Steinberg. *A Short History of Germany*. p.231.
44. *Annual Register*. 1930. p.176.

when both their savings and their income had been reduced to nothing. Since then it had been a long hard struggle to regain solvency. The right wing government dominated by the German DNVP had realised their plight and given them 20% to 25% rises in the Spring of 1927. Yet now, only a little time later, what had been given with one hand was to be taken away again with the other. It would have been better not to have received such large increases in the first place than to have the money taken away, now, when they had just begun to depend on it.

But what particularly incensed the largely urban SPD, was that the money spent on subsidising farming incomes would put up the price of the poor man's loaf of bread while augmenting the incomes of the right-wing Junkers with their great estates who had, according to Poincaré, 'drawn enormous profits from inflation (in 1923) and are the most ardent supporters of Prussian militarism.'

President Hindenburg, however, himself had been given a much-loved great estate over which there had been a tax controversy. He felt he understood the sufferings of those on the land. He therefore issued the financial enactments. He felt secure in his authority in doing this because, although the year before, Bavaria together with other Catholic southern German states had complained vociferously against the 'Berlinization' of Germany,[45] their economies were so dependent on agriculture that they could not afford defiance to central authority. When the SPD called on President Hindenburg to retract the financial enactments, he dissolved Parliament and ordered a general election in two months time.

Alan Bullock in his *Hitler – A Study in Tyranny* found that 'the scale of the depression was not yet evident in the Spring and early Summer of 1930'[46] so it is odd that Brüning's government chose to enact such severe economic measures. *The Economist* had commented in March that, despite emergency action in December, there was still an ongoing debt of some 1,700 million marks but savings of 700 million in reparations would be produced in the year from adopting the Young Plan reparations' deal and if Dr. Schacht's amortization fund of 450 million marks had not had to be reserved, only 550 million, or some £28 million, would have had to be found through taxation or some other means. To take so much money out of people's take-home pay, through pay cuts and extra taxation, would mean an end to all those extra little trips to the shops, upon which so much of the retail trade depended. Only the bare necessities would be bought now.

The Government also chose to force through a 2½% rise in insurance

45. *New York Times*. 25.8.29.
46. Alan Bullock. *Hitler. A Study of Hitler*. p.153.

contributions making it economically irresistible for employers to use new machines rather than old and trusted labour. In September 1929 unemployment had stood at 1,626,488 but as in the year before, in the icy month of January it grew by over a million. A warm Spring must have meant a reduction in the numbers of unemployed yet the government chose this moment to impose a virtual tax on employment. Finally jobs would be slashed by the municipalities if the central power chose to give them strict cash limits. It was not surprising that by September 1930 the number of unemployed had risen to 3 million – and that was before the winter.[47] It was in the this unhappy economic climate that the Parliamentary parties prepared to fight the general election in September.

11.8 Rise of the National Socialists

The splintered moderate parties seemed to have no solutions to offer the voters as the economic storm clouds gathered so it was left to the extremist parties to make all the running. In 1928 Hitler's party had only gained 12 seats in Parliament but he had gained valuable publicity over being identified with the 'Bill against the Enslavement of the German People', the previous Autumn. On 18.8.30. *The New York* Times would express astonishment at the money Hitler found to fight his election campaign:

'He commands by far the best-disciplined campaigning army of any of the big German parties. The one mystery about his organisation is, Who pays its expenses?'[48]

It described how he set about to woo the voters.

'Herr Hitler trims his oratory to the needs of the particular section of the country in which he is speaking. In the lowlands he leads the cause of the downtrodden farmer, while in the urban centers he fiercely rides his familiar hobbies – reparations, anti-semitism and international Jewish capital which he charges is exploiting Germany.'

47. Jochmann. *Brünings Deflationspolitik und der Untergang der Weimarer Republik* in Stegmann *et al. Industrielle Gesellschaft und politisches System.* pp.97–112 – stated that Brüning's policy of slashing wages and prices led to a rapid rise in the unemployed and a contraction of the economy.
48. John A. Leopold in his biography of *Alfred Hugenberg. The Radical Campaign against the Weimar Republic.* (Yale 1977) p.81 – decided that Alfred Hugenberg paid towards the expenses of the rival party's bid for power.

People seemed to associate their increased taxes with the payment of the reparations, which, since industry was no longer carrying the burden, could have been said to have been the case. In a report to his foreign secretary, Arthur Henderson, the British ambassador, Sir Horace Rumbold, observed wryly:

> 'The snowball of 'revision' continues to roll down the electoral slopes, and as it rolls, it is gathering speed and size. It may now indeed be said that the first electoral campaign which has taken place in Germany without the shadow of the Rhineland occupation has brought out into the open, through one party or another, all that Germany hopes for and intends to strive for in the field of external affairs.'[49]

John Wheeler-Bennett, in his book on Hindenburg, says of the importance of the reparations' issue in the September elections:

> 'It was significant that in the General Election which followed ..almost every party went to the polls with 'treaty revision' in its programme; but it was still more significant that the party which made 'treaty revision' the most salient factor of its policy was returned as the second largest in the Reichstag.'[50]

The German Nationalist Party had concentrated on the iniquities of the territorial adjustments of the Treaty of Versailles (particularly the Polish Corridor) in their campaign. The *New York Times* recorded M. Poincaré's views on their campaign: 'revision, however, peaceful be the tone which one affects for that cry, is nothing in reality but a war cry.'[51]

It commented on opinion in France in August:

> 'In some quarters fears are expressed over the possibility of Adolph Hitler and Dr. Alfred Hugenberg combining to form a party of revenge.'

Hitler's National Socialists swept from being a fringe party to the very centre stage of German politics in the elections on 14 September. Hugenberg's DNVP, split in two before the campaign, saw its share of the vote slump. But by October it would not only be Hitler who would be campaigning against paying the reparations.

He had found a vote winner.[52] Other parties hastened to jump on the

---

49. *Documents on British Foreign Policy*. I. p.504.
50. J. Wheeler-Bennett. *Hindenburg. The Wooden Titan*. 1936. p.347.
51. *New York Times*. 18.8.30.
52. See article entitled: 'Reparations issue imperils Brüning.'

band wagon. On 10 October 1929 the *New York Times* declared:

'... the majority of the parties are already pledged to an anti-reparations barrage.'

–12–

The Banking Crisis and an End to Reparations

12.1 American Concern at Hitler's Victory

The news of the victory of Hitler's party, the NSDAP, in the September elections, brought consternation to the American administration. Hitler's vehement condemnation of Germany's external obligations, the Treaty of Versailles, the Treaty of Locarno and the Young Plan Agreement, during the campaign for the so-called 'Bill against the Enslavement of the German People', had been dismissed by the rest of the world as the ravings of the lunatic fringe during the election campaign[1] but now, when he stated, not 'we cannot pay' but 'we will not pay' the reparations, he sent the financial world into a turmoil.[2] For supporting his stance were the third largest party in the Reichstag, the Communists, with 79 seats and the DNVP, who though split, still held 46 seats. The American stock market collapsed, while around 1,000,000,000 marks in funk money poured out of Germany.[3] Only the generous short term funds lent by America managed to stabilise the situation. On 20 October 1930 the Foreign Policy Association of America gave a Dinner Discussion on the 'Young Plan in Relation to World Economy' and invited Dr. Hjalmar Schacht and John Foster Dulles to be the speakers for the evening.[4] Leading Americans wanted to hear the

1. *New York Times.* 21.9.30. 'Here was a clear referendum upon the existing foundations of Europe Peace – the Treaties of St. Germain, Locarno and the Young Plan – and a portion of the German electorate dangerously near to half the voters went on record as strongly in favour of an entirely new deal. Worse than that, these same parties did not conceal their smouldering desire for a 'war of revenge' provided the Allies refused to grant their extravagant demands.'
2. *Annual Register.* 1931. p.183. 'The National Socialists owed a great part of their success to their complete repudiation of all obligation to pay reparations. As the party of national opposition, they won their greatest number of adherents through their campaign against the 'oppression and forcible subjection of Germany.' Not that a large part of the German people were not well aware of the difference between 'Germany cannot pay' and 'Germany will not pay' which was the cry of the National Socialists.'
3. E. Eyck. *The Weimar Republic.* Vol. II. p.284.
4. *Royal Institute of International Affairs Documents.* F/4/1/(193).

man in whom they had placed so much faith, Dr. Schacht, publicly renounce the 'noisy minority which clamours for repudiation of Germany's obligations' (John Foster Dulles). Present were Mr. Sylvester Viereck, Mr. Norton, and many other notables. Paul Warburg, the banker was also there.

The Chairman, James G. McDonald. introduced Mr. Dulles as one who had been against the 'astronomical figures' that the bankers of 1919 had levied in reparations, who were not such 'good economists as those last Fall' who had devised the Young Plan. Mr. Dulles started his address by bemoaning the fact that although the idea behind the Young Plan was to abolish all stigma of the war and even eliminate the word 'reparation' from the reparations' debt, the reverse had happened and the debts' renegotiation had merely rekindled 'the same atmosphere of controversy and the same unpleasant manifestations that have marked this problem during the past decade.'

While he attributed the failure of the Young Plan to achieve its happy purpose of relegating the reparations to the status of an ordinary invoice, partly to the experts inability to find the 'correct formula for Germany's capacity to pay' he did question the goodwill of the German leadership.

He acknowledged that although, under the terms of the Young Plan, Germany was probably being asked to pay no more than the cost of repairing the civilian damage done in wartime in Allied countries, as originally agreed to in the pre-Armistice negotiations, the inclusion of pensions and separations allowances in the original sum had provided fertile ground for German politicians to whip up anti-reparation sentiment.

However in making out his case that Germany could and should pay its reparations he revealed that Germany's exports had overtaken those of Great Britain in 1930 and pointed out that the reparations' charge represented only 'three percent of the national income of Germany.'

He questioned whether Germany was doing its best to manage its economy in order to retain sufficient money to pay its reparations. He alleged that Germany had been paying out lavish social security benefits (in relation to those of America) which had led to 'budgetary deficits' and then had borrowed the money from America to pay the reparations.

Referring to the plebiscite on Herr Hugenberg and Herr Hitler's 'Freedom from the Enslavement of the German People' which Germany's population had repudiated, in December 1929, only nine months earlier, he declared: 'It is inconceivable, that Germany should repudiate, consciously and deliberately, obligations which have been solemnly adopted after a national plebiscite.'

Finally he made the grave charge that some of Germany's leaders had deliberately encouraged an atmosphere of economic depression so as to get rid of the reparations.

'There are leaders in Germany who encourage such an atmosphere – an atmosphere of pessimism ... in which no economic problems can be solved – as a vehicle for ridding Germany of her reparations' obligations. If that policy should succeed ... the leaders would be guilty of a great disservice to the German people. For what is it that keeps Germany great ... It is the self-confidence ... of the German people and the ability to inspire confidence and command credit abroad. That is Germany's greatest asset and if that were traded against a few milliards of marks, Germany would indeed have sold her birthright for a mess of pottage.'

With these ringing words he concluded his speech. All present waited for the man they had pinned so many hopes on, Dr. Schacht, to reassure them that his large and powerful country would remain a responsible member of the international community. However, Dr. Schacht did not give them that reassurance. On the contrary, first of all he promised them another crisis over the reparations, and secondly, he declared that now the Allies had withdrawn their troops from the Rhine there was nothing material they could do about it.

'I think there is no better explanation than to think of what would happen today if because of her bad situation, Germany should be obliged to stop the reparation payments with the French and Belgian troops still standing on the Rhine. I think we would have thrown the whole reparation problem into the old, may I say pre-Ruhr atmosphere. In spite of the faults which were committed at the second Hague Conference, there is one reassuring thing today, that is that if the reparation problem comes up again, as Mr. Dulles has quite rightly said it will, it comes up under more favourable political circumstances than before.'

Dr. Schacht maintained that Germany could not tax the middle classes to provide the reparations due because 'the middle classes have entirely disappeared. They have become extremely poor.' This was no less than the truth since the government had just proposed reducing their salaries and their former savings had been wiped out by the Great Inflation. Of the 80,000 people who Dr. Schacht reckoned were reasonably well off, he predicted that they would 'take some fast train for some foreign country' if they were lumbered with the heavy burden of paying the reparations on their own.

So he declared that America had two choices open to her if she wanted Germany to go on paying reparations to the Allies. Either America could lend Germany the money to pay the Allie reparations or she could let Germany devastate the rest of the world with its exports to generate the surplus to pay the reparations that way. Up to date he declared:

'We have made these payments so far entirely out of borrowings, and it is astonishing to see how the payments for import surplus, the payments on reparation and the payments on interest are exactly equal to what we have borrowed in the meantime.'

Up to the year 1924, it is true, that, by coincidence, the money lost by foreign investors in speculation in the mark had almost exactly equalled the amount that Germany had paid in cash, and kind, in reparations. During the years when the Dawes Plan was in operation, the Allies had extracted the reparations principally through their levies on the German Railways and on exports. If Dr. Schacht seemed to be asserting now that Germany had contrived to borrow from America and the Allies exactly the amount which had been extracted from the country in reparations up till 1930, it posed an awkward question mark over whether some future government, forgetting the scars on the French and Belgian landscape caused by the devastations of the retreating German army, might repudiate even the commercial and sovereign debts as some sort of unjustified reparations' tribute, because in its eyes Germany was guiltless of starting World War I.

. Over the reparations, Dr. Schacht maintained that if the Allies did not lend Germany the money to pay the sums due his country would have to increase 'the present German trade by 50% ... I doubt whether America would like to lose on her foreign trade in order to allow Germany to have a bigger percentage on the world markets.'

He appealed to America for understanding as to why Germany had agree to pay more reparations in August 1929, knowing that she was not going to pay them, merely to get rid of the occupation troops in the Rhineland:

'Can you think of a people which still has some self-respect, standing for having its most important industrial area, one-sixth of its total area – occupied by foreign troops fifteen years after the war?'

He concluded with words which became more and more threatening when German exports conquered the world the following year:

'I must decline to pay the politicians unless they let me earn the money with which to pay them.'

In his address Dr. Schacht had not touched upon the 'war guilt' issue. He had merely emphasised the impossibility of making Germany pay reparations if the country didn't want to. However, in the questions that followed the speeches, Mr. George Sylvester Viereck, who had, in the war, published a newspaper devoted to propagating Germany's cause, went straight to the heart of the matter.

Mr. Viereck asked Dr. Schacht: 'Should Germany pay one per cent of reparation, whether or not she is able to do so, since the obligation to pay reparation is based upon a document that grows from fraud, corruption and trickery?'

Dr. Schacht was more politic in his reply: 'I have abstained from discussing this question outside of my country, and I would always abstain from discussing that question if I am the guest at a party in a foreign country. But if Mr. Viereck will give me the pleasure of coming to see me in Berlin again, I will give him the answer.'

After this the Chairman quickly intervened: 'Well I didn't believe that a dinner meeting could liven up like a Saturday luncheon' and steered the questions on to safer topics before bringing the meeting to a close.

Dr. Schacht had promised to repay 'every cent which has been invested in Germany by a private person, a private bank or private businessman or whoever it may be' but American investors must have been deeply uneasy at his linkage of the reparations with the debt situation, and the preciseness of the sums declared to have been paid by Germany in reparations with those owed in sovereign and commercial loans.

12.2 Buoyant German Economy

One matter was beyond dispute and that was that Germany possessed a powerful economy. Indeed, the economist, Menken, in the *Royal Institute of International Affairs Journal*, estimated that the volume of 'German production in 1929 ... had been 'well above that of 1913' when it still owned the whole of the Silesian coal fields and half of the rich provinces of Alsace and Lorraine. Germany had boasted that before the war its industrial output had been higher than Great Britain's. Now its exports had overtaken Great Britain's. Its chemical industry, he estimated, to be the most powerful in the world.[5]

In May 1930, following his appointment as a member of the Macmillan Committee, Keynes had ranted at the fact that Britain could not compete with Germany at the present wage levels. Money was draining from Britain, attracted by the higher rate of return in investing in German industry.

'Assuming that labour and capital are equally efficient in Germany and England, and in England our wages policy awards three-fifths of the value of the product produced to labour and two fifths to capital, and in Germany it

5. *Royal Institute of International Affairs Survey.* 1930. p.539.

awards three-fifths to capital and two-fifths to labour the rate of profit must be 50 per cent higher in Germany than it is in England and they will be able to offer 7^1/2 per cent when the English borrowers only offer 5 per cent. If that is allowed to go on freely we are bound to get back into the position we are now in, that is to say, either we shall be in a state of chronic disequilibrium ... or we shall have to force down wages in England until capital gets the same proportion of the product as in Germany.'[6]

Statistics bore out his contention that, even with capital securing little return on its investment, British industry was having a hard time competing with Germany. In 1928, while British tariffs operated against German industry, Germany still managed to export more goods to Britain than it imported. In 1930, after the tariffs had been removed, German exports to Britain were nearly double the value of imports. In 1931 German exports to Britain would represent nearly three times the value of imports, although this represented as much the closure of the German market to foreign products as any actual increase in the value of German goods exported to Britain.[7] Germany was operating a siege economy.

In its review of the Leipzig Trade Fair on 4 April 1931 *The Economist* newspaper praised the 'remarkable achievement' of German exports in overtaking those of Great Britain, world wide, in 1931.

'The importance of this great annual Spring Exhibition of German goods is that it reflects at once the determination and adaptability of German industry in its endeavour to capture a growing share of export trade even in conditions of world-wide depression ...

'In pre-war days, when Germany was a lending and investing country, it was estimated that about 10 percent of the total production was exported; and, even then, through the discipline of the cartels, the home market was forced to pay a little more in order that the foreign buyer could be served for substantially less. But, according to recent investigations by the Institute für Konjunkturforschung, the share that export bears to total sales varies as a rule between 20 and 50 per cent ...

'These figures reveal the gradual conquest by German industry of foreign markets.'

6. R. Skidelsky. *John Maynard Keynes.* Vol. II. (1992). p.355. Taken from his collected writings.

7. 1928. German Exports to Britain – 1,180,000,000 million rm.
        Imports   – 893,000,000 million rm.
    1930. German Exports to Britain – 1,219,000,000 million rm.
        Imports   – 630,000,000 million rm.
    1931. German Exports to Britain – 1,134,000,000 million rm.
        Imports   – 435,000,000 million rm.
    Source: *Whitacker's Almanac.*

Although industrial rationalisation in German industry had been continuous since 1924, especially in the huge coal, steel and chemical industries, a sign of Germany's material wealth was evinced by the fact that some three or four more million people were in work in 1929 than before the war, even though the country was smaller than formerly and fewer people were employed in the armed forces. As the great industrial combines had weeded out their excess labour, so the mushrooming building industry, spending about 8.9 milliard marks a year (£450,000,000) welcomed the extra hands to provide homes, shops and factories. All this work stopped, however, after the Summer of 1930. Faced with an ultimatum to accept the draconian economic proposals to which their previous refusal had led to article 48, or be faced with a 'directorate' to run the country, the enfeebled SPD Party humbly accepted even more stringent economic proposals than those agreed in the Summer, including more cuts in the wages of government employees.[8] The wage cuts would cause immense anger and frustration amongst the average German householder who had tried so hard to balance his budget since his savings had been taken from him in the Great Inflation. His success in doing this in the relatively affluent years between stabilisation and the new financial crisis was recorded by an independent witness who wrote to The Economist after visiting Berlin in 1931.

'In general the material, inanimate Berlin is still what it had always been. In the well-to-do quarters the houses still receive that last wash-and-brush-up that are often lacking in the corresponding quarters of London and Paris. And as for the poorer quarters, a Londoner can still walk right through them without realising that he has been exploring 'the slums.' For in Berlin, such slums as disfigure London and New York have always been unknown. A population with less – and today far less – (according to him) purchasing power than the urban proletariat of the English- speaking countries lives in streets where there are no smells, no garbage or waste-paper strewn about and no children whose clothes are not neat and clean.'[9]

Stephen A. Schuker in his *American 'Reparations' to Germany* published by Princeton Studies in International Finance in July 1988 gives his assessment of the strength of the German economy at this time:

'As the Depression deepened, Germany possessed a rationalized industrial plant, a social-welfare system unrivalled anywhere except Great Britain, and

8. *New York Times*. 28.9.30. DICTATORSHIP FOR GERMANY WITH HINDENBURG AT HEAD. BRÜNING'S THREAT TO FOES. Also, *New York Times*. 1.10.30. The new 'spartan' economic proposals included raising the unemployment insurance premium to 6%. Salary cuts for members of Parliament, 6% cuts for civil service employees and 'corresponding cuts for the Reichswehr and State railway employees.'
9. *The Economist*. 20.6.31. (p.1318.)

a conglomeration of municipal amenities that commanded the wonder of the world. The foreigners who had financed much of it held paper claims – just as they had in 1919–23.'

12.3 Rise of Fascism

1931 dawned, a grey dawn. It appeared from the statistics that America was just beginning to claw her way out of the Depression so that she could help other, less fortunate nations.[10] The political situation in Europe, however, was angry and unstable. In Italy the fascist dictator, Mussolini, had given an address on 27 October 1930 obviously aimed at Germany's National Socialists in which he declared that 'Fascism had now become a panacea for Europe.'[11]

Briand felt France threatened and he proposed a federation of European states in March 1931. It was to be hoped that this would defuse Germany's and Italy's selfish ambitions and force the British to become more concerned with Europe. To give material expression to her goodwill the French Parliament voted almost unanimously to join in the credits being raised for Germany by banking groups in the US, Great Britain, Holland, Sweden and Switzerland.[12]

But the plan for a European federation failed. Germany insisted that communist Russia become part of the European federation. Italy wanted Turkey to join. While the British, memories of the 'destitute' Germany of 1923 for ever in their minds, were full of suspicions of the French who had miraculously recovered from their Great Inflation and were now throwing their political and economic weight around. Arnold Toynbee spoke for many when in 1931 he identified with Germany who 'had grasped at world domination in 1914' and 'was now suffering agonies of the 'peine forte and duré' in the iron ring forged round her by France and her post-war Allies.'[13]

Germany's friendship with the Russians, who in Imperial times had been close to France, dated from the war. But it had been reinforced by several post-war treaties. There was the Russian-German trade agreement of 6 May 1921 and the Rapallo Treaty of 1922. The Treaty of Locarno of November 1925 with the West was balanced by the Russo-German Commercial Treaty, signed on 12 October of that year. The entry of Germany into the League of Nations had also been balanced by

10. *Royal Institute of International Affairs.* 1931. p.208.
11. *Royal Institute of International Affairs Survey.* 1930. p.21.
12. *Annual Register.* 1931. p.168.
13. *Royal Institute of International Affairs Survey.* 1931. p.22–3.

the Russo-German Security Pact of 24 April 1926.[14] In commercial affairs the two nations were also close. In the Summer of 1928 the Krupp concern renegotiated its agricultural concession in the Caucasus, the largest concession in that country, on favourable terms.[15] At the 6th World Congress of the comintern in the summer of 1928 the German communists had been forbidden to engage in any 'further collaboration' with German socialists, the enemies of German big business.[16] In international affairs Russia could be relied on to vote with Germany while France's friends were merely the two new underfunded East European states of Poland and Czechoslovakia, sandwiched between two traditionally aggressive Empires.

Briand, however, had another motive when he proposed the concept of a European economic and political federation. He hoped to forestall any attempts at Anschluss – the movement towards a union of Germany and Austria. Briand was acutely aware 'of the unobtrusive but appreciable progress which was being made in the direction of assimilating the administrative and legal machinery of Germany and Austria during the 1920's.'[17] In 1930 an Austrian, Hitler, had come to political prominence in Germany. Frenchmen must have asked themselves whether the promotion given to this Austrian upstart by the German nationalists was not a conspiracy to lure the Austrians into the Prussian lair.

Western opinion was divided over the issue. English Liberals were still guided by the doctrines of ex-President Wilson of America that self-determination and language should be the all important factors governing nationality.[18]

France, however, was pre-occupied with the question of security. If Anschluss was enacted contrary to Article 88 of the Treaty of St. German,[19] Germany and its associates would be in a position almost to completely encircle the erstwhile lesser mortals of Poland and Czechoslovakia. And if Germany engulfed them might not France itself be next?

---

14. *Royal Institute of International Affairs Survey.* 1930. p.126. Under the heading: 'Note on the Rapprochement between Germany, Russian and Italy.

15. *New York Times.* 14.9.28. 'The German firm of Krupp has just concluded a new agreement with the Soviet Government for continuation of the Munich agricultural concession in Northern Caucasus ... Under the original agreement it was found unprofitable ... By the agreement just concluded the Russians will take over the financing end as well as the risk of losses, and the profits will be divided equally ... In case the concession is found unprofitable this (German) invested capital (3,000,000 in buildings and equipment) will be repaid by the Government in gold in 1937.'

16. E. Eyck. *The Weimar Republic.* Vol. II. p.168–9. Alan Bullock etc.

17. *Royal Institute of International Affairs Survey.* 1931. p.298.

18. *Royal Institute of International Affairs Survey.* p.297.

19. E. Eyck. *The Weimar Republic.* Vol. II. p.306.

Map 12.1 'The iron ring forged round her (Germany) by France and her post-war allies' Arnold J. Toynbee.

12.4   Germany and Austria Propose a Customs Union

In the hope of forestalling any decision by the Germans and the Austrians to move towards a closer communion, Briand made the following speech on 3 March 1931:

> 'I used to be told (he said) you are blind. Tomorrow, or the day after tomorrow at latest, the Anschluss will be achieved ... Months and years have passed. Austria has become more solidly conscious of her nationality; she has taken her place more firmly in the circle of the nations; she joins in the discussions on a footing of equality ... The danger which could then be considered a danger of war has gradually diminished. If it has not completely disappeared, it is no longer so acute as it was represented to be two years ago.'[20]

Only two weeks after Briand made his speech the Germans and Austrians announced that they were going to form a customs union. The shocked French nation decided to withhold much needed new short term loans from Austria in an effort to persuade the country to alter its decision.[21]

The American Historian, Gordon A. Craig, in his *Germany 1866–1945* (1978) did not dwell on the international implications of the declaration of the customs union but he wrote of the project censoriously:

> 'It is doubtful whether this project could, even by the most ingenious legal casuistry, have been squared with the provision of the Peace Treaty and the Geneva Protocol of 1922, although it is theoretically possible that the legal obstacles might have been removed by negotiation. But the striking feature of the joint announcement was that it had not been preceded by the kind of diplomatic sounding that Stresemann had always employed, nor had any attempt been made to consult the French or the League of Nations.' He concluded it to be 'a forcing manoeuvre in the Wilhelmine manner' and he maintained that 'its failure was so shattering that it is now virtually impossible to discover who originally inspired it.'

It is true that the idea of the customs union was a failure in that it was eventually abandoned in the Autumn but not before Germany had been granted a moratorium on the payment of its reparations. Dr. Schacht had promised John Foster Dulles 'another crisis' over the reparations just six months before. It had not been long in coming.

20. *Royal Institute of International Affairs Survey.* p.208.

21. E. Eyck. *The Weimar Republic.* Vol. II. Chapter XI. p.308. Curtius. *Sechs Jahre Minister.* p.146. For France's continuing financial pressure see *Royal Institute of International Affairs Survey.* 1931. p.297–323.

12.5 Austrian Banking Crisis

France's decision to withhold short-term loans to Austria helped undermined that nation's shaky financial structure. Its old empire had been torn away and shaped into new, young countries. But the money from America which should have been invested in providing these countries with a healthy, stable future, had gone to Germany instead. Austria's banking system, like her great city Vienna, was top-heavy for its new, small post-war status. It cracked under the strain of providing its ex-colonies help without aid from France. It was in the second week of May that the difficulties of Credit-Anstalt, Austria's largest bank, became known. Depositors queued up for their money. Despite the Austrian Parliament authorising the government to guarantee any credits and advances to the bank, and the promise of a loan from the Bank for International Settlements, the position of the bank was still precarious. The Austrian Chancellor went cap in hand to the French for funds, but as he refused to agree to cancel the proposed customs union with Germany, he came home empty-handed.[22]

For the moment the situation was stabilised by a credit from the Bank for International Settlements but Austria's troubles were not yet over. Yet if her desire for a customs union with her powerful German neighbour had been inspired by the belief that Germany would come to her economic assistance in emergencies she was to be disappointed. Not only did Germany not help Austria out of her economic difficulties but she now declared that she had economic troubles of her own, this despite the fact that the 'pocket battleship' the Deutschland was launched by President Hindenburg with due ceremony at Kiel on the 19 May[23] with plans prepared to produce another one.

It seemed strange that Germany should have been so adversely affected by the demise of the Credit-Anstalt Bank since by far the largest external shareholder in the Credit-Anstalt Bank had been Britain, followed by America. Germany had no more money invested there than Switzerland or Holland.[24] Americans, however, concerned with the security of the loans that they had lent to the Germans, drew too little distinction between one Germanic nation and another and began to call in their loans.

Gold and foreign exchange began to flow unchecked out of the country at an accelerating pace. In the first week of June alone the

22. See *Royal Institute of International Affairs Survey*. Part III. The Project for an Austro-German Customs Union.
23. *Royal Institute of International Affairs Survey*. 1931. p.32.
24. *Royal Institute of International Affairs Survey*. p.211.

Reichsbank lost £9,000,000 in gold and devisen and in the second week £27,000,000.[25] The Government did nothing to check the outflow. However, on the 5 June Hindenburg signed an emergency decree imposing 'drastic' new increases in taxation and cuts in salaries and unemployment benefit. Simultaneously a manifesto was published pointing attention to the heavy demands made of the country under the Young Plan reparations' scheme, when it was already shouldering, so it was contended, more of its fair share of economic distress. The 'psychological effect' produced by the Decree and the Manifesto, according to the Royal Institute observer, was similar to the 'effect produced in his own country, some 17 years before, by the news of the outbreak of war between Great Britain and Germany on the 4 August 1914.'[26]

Chancellor Brüning declared that 'we have reached the limit of the privations we can impose upon our people.' He demanded 'some relief from our intolerable reparation obligations'[27] and on the 6 June he came to England to explain his nation's economic plight.

Since the events of 1923 when the German people's efforts to pay their reparations had been, in British eyes, the cause of reducing the nation to penury and starvation, ordinary men and women in Britain had had great sympathy with their German counterparts. Many of the City of German extraction had fled from bigotry and restriction in Germany in the years before World War I, but their perception of the inefficiencies and failures of their new country had added a rosy glow to their remembrance of the Fatherland. They did not wish to concede, even to themselves, that Germany not doing anything but its very best to fulfil its international commitments. King George gave a warm welcome to the German Chancellor and *The Times* correspondent wrote for the people of Britain as a whole when he described the occasion as 'a happy event which, it is to be hoped, will have contributed as much as the homely week-end at Chequers, to convince the German people that the British Government looks with equal friendliness upon all foreign countries, desiring nothing more ardently than the obliteration of old dividing lines which have separated us.'[28]

During the course of the German discussions at Chequers three cables arrived from Washington perturbed by the Germans' demand for more relief from reparations. However, Sir Montague Norman, governor of the Bank of England, was more sympathetic. He informed the assembled company that he had been telephoned by Britain's Ambassadors in Vienna and Basel who told him that the crisis affecting the Credit-Anstalt

25. *Royal Institute of International Affairs Survey.* p.211–12.
26. *Royal Institute of International Affairs Survey.* 1931. p.69.
27. *The Times.* 10.6.31. E. Eyck. *The Weimar Republic.* Vol. II. p.312.
28. *Documents on British Foreign Policy.* II. 71–7.

Bank was threatening the financial security of the Austrian nation itself. All South East Europe was said to be on the brink of collapse.[29] One week later Britain rescued the Austrian bank. It was a noble gesture, made in the hopes of restoring financial tranquillity to the world but it put Britain's own financial equilibrium in jeopardy.

12.6 Allies Losing Economic and Military Control

On the 19 and 20 June 1931 the Reichsbank lost RM150,000,000 of its gold and foreign exchange reserves and the cover for its note circulation fell to the legal minimum. Panic reigned. It appeared to H.V. Hodson of the Royal Institute of International Affairs that nothing short of a general moratorium on foreign debts coupled with foreign exchange controls could save the German financial system from complete collapse. On 20 June President Hoover offered a one year moratorium on all debts arising from the war. The reason for his action: 'these democratic governments were the base of any hope for a lasting peace in Europe.'[30] Despite the great suffering of the American people it was a principle deserving generosity.

The main beneficiary of the reparations, the allegedly perfidious French, remained cynical. They were aware that 'poor' Germany had felt flush enough to prop up Stalin's regime in Russia with a RM300,000,000 loan in April. Once the reparation payments were halted, they argued, they would never be resumed.[31] Germany would merely use the savings made to finance 'dumping' abroad. They took three weeks to agree to grant Germany a moratorium.

The British public believed the Germans' plea of poverty, but felt it was not in keeping for a supposedly bankrupt nation to be building their second armoured cruiser. It should, at the very least, be postponed, as a gesture of thanks towards the Americans who. though suffering equal deprivation as the Germans, had voluntarily relinquished their hard-earned, much- needed savings. The Germans refused. Such a step they declared might lead to Hindenburg's resignation and the collapse of civilised German life.[32]

The effect of the public proclamation of the Hoover moratorium and

29. *Royal Institute of International Affairs Survey.* 1931. p.212.

30. Herbert Clark Hoover. *The Memoirs of Herbert Hoover.* II. p.65.

31. E. Eyck. *The Weimar Republic.* Vol. II. p.316. 'Later events were to prove this fear completely justified; one can even say that the Germans had hoped the Hoover Moratorium would have precisely this result.' Russian deal reported *The Economist.* 25.4.31.

32. *Royal Institute of International Affairs Survey.* 1931. p.212.

the 100,000,000 short-term dollar credit arranged by the Federal Reserve Bank of New York, the Bank of England, the Banque de France and the Bank for International Settlements,[33] had been to stop speculation but France's delay in accepting the moratorium caused money to start flooding out of Germany again as no foreign exchange controls were imposed.

On the 3 July the Nordwolle, one of Germany's largest textile concerns collapsed in the north of Germany. The Karstadt General Store also found itself in debt to the bank for 75,000,000 marks.

On 7 July a thousand of Germany's larger businesses declared themselves ready to guarantee losses by the Gold Discount Bank up to 500,000,000 Reichsmarks showing that most of Germany's industrialists did not associate themselves with the Government's economic manipulation.[34] Unfortunately, however, the collapse of the Nordwolle concern affected the finances of the Danat Bank (Darmstadter und National Bank).

Before it had been mostly overseas creditors who had withdrawn their funds but now, at last, panic spread to the small German saver. Dr. Luther, the head of the Reichsbank, sped from one foreign capital to another trying to raise yet more money, frightening foreigners and his own countrymen alike. He came home empty-handed.

'It was reported to have been indicated to him in Paris quite unmistakably that, before any financial help would be granted to Germany from the French side, the German government would be required to declare their readiness to make political concessions to France in the two matters of the Austro-Germans customs union plan and the second German ''pocket battleship'', and perhaps also in the matter of ''an Eastern Locarno.'' '

It was unfortunate that the Director of the Danat bank, Dr. Jacob Goldschmidt, was allowed to continue running the bank's finances after its collapse. However much the management valued his integrity and ability, not to make an example of the Jewish Dr. Goldschmidt, and to leave him still seated comfortably at the head of a large banking organisation in which thousands of people had lost their savings, seemed madness.[35] Hitler was preparing for power. By 1934 Jews would fear for their lives. There was a reason for this decision however. There appears to have been an element of collusion between government and banks over the collapse of the Danat Bank. It would not have been fair to ask Dr. Goldschmidt to carry the odium for the failure of his bank if he had

33. *Annual Register*. 1931. p.186.
34. *Annual Register*. 1931. p.186.
35. *Annual Register*. 1931. p.187.

been asked to sacrifice his bank in the hope of saving the rest. According to the *Annual Register*:

> 'The idea was to allow the large bank with least liquid assets to fail, and so isolate the crisis by concentrating it at one point. This step proved to be a serious mistake. The government's declaration that it would assume responsibility for all the debts of the Danat Bank did not avail to maintain confidence. On 13 July there was a run on all banks and savings banks, which were quite unprepared and had for some time been scantily provided by the Reichsbank with means of payment.'[36]

At last, when all the nation's citizens were quiveringly aware of the crisis the government and the Reichsbank acted. Foreign exchange became subject to the control of the Reichsbank. Interest rates were raised. Banks became subject to increasing restrictions. The collapse of confidence had spread to the municipal savings banks, credit co-operative societies etc. The government came to the assistance of these. The *Annual Register* recorded:

> 'This assistance from the Reich entails a considerable reorganisation of the banks and the creation of new machinery of supervision, so that at the end of the year one could almost speak of the nationalisation of German banking.'[37]

The many loans that had officially been repaid by Germany in June and July 1931 had been swelled by the withdrawal of foreign funds during the banking crisis. A conference was therefore called in London on 21 July because of the chasm which was said to have appeared in Germany's finances. Germany's Chancellor, Brüning, first published drastic decrees at home, including 'compelling public authorities, and empowering private employers, to pay no more than a half instalment of wages, salaries which became due on any given date' and 'subjecting tax payers in arrears to a surcharge of 5% a fortnight on their assessments.'[38] Then he went to Paris to ask for a loan. But the French turned down his request.

America's President, Herbert Hoover, had not granted Germany a moratorium on its reparations' payments because of its poverty but because he wished to preserve democracy there.

However, under the influence of his friend, Dr. Schacht, Britain's Governor of the Bank of England, Montagu Norman, had convinced himself that Germany was 'slowly bleeding to death.'[39] Ramsay

36. *Annual Register*. 1931. p.187.
37. *Annual Register*. 1931. p.189.
38. *Royal Institute of International Affairs Survey*. 1931. p.89.
39. J. P. Morgan telegram to Lamont and R. C. Leffingwell. October 13 1932. S. A. Schuker. *American 'Reparations' to Germany*. p.69–70.

Macdonald, Britain's Prime Minister, still sure that France bore the major responsibility for World War I, took a more hostile view of France's refusal to lend Germany money:

> 'Agreement Germany needs help but French never heartily in & Act as freezing mixture. They are solely responsible for the failure of the Hoover Plan & the present position ... Again and again let it be said: France is the enemy; we shall pay with all our honour for that war ...'[40]

Ramsay Macdonald's bitter words must have been influenced by the telegram sent by Hugenberg and Hitler to the Conference, inferring that France had designs on German territory. Outside observers might have been cynical at yet another telegram emanating from Herr Hugenberg at a critical time, especially when he had linked his name with Hitler. Hitler had not yet gained an evil reputation in Britain, however. Montagu Norman, alarmed at the increasing intellectual attraction of Communism in the difficult times prevailing, would look upon Hitler as a friend in the fight against Communism in 1934:

> 'Hitler and Schacht are the bulwarks of civilisation in Germany and the only friends we have ... If they fail, Communism will follow in Germany, and anything may follow in Europe.'[41]

Ramsay Macdonald was wrong to be so prejudiced against France at the Conference, however, because France had not refused Germany a loan. France had merely reiterated its previous precondition that Germany would have to give a formal undertaking not to use Article 19 of the League Covenant as a pretext to alter its Eastern border and claim back the Polish Corridor if it wanted finance.[42] This Germany was not prepared to do.[43]

Although no-one (except France) had the loose change with which to supply Germany with another loan, under the Standstill Agreement negotiated between 21 and 23 July 1931, the Allies and America agreed to refrain from demanding repayment of most of the 'banking credits in Germany expressed in foreign currencies', for a six month

---

40. David Marquand. *Ramsay Macdonald*. (1977) p.608.

41. *Leffingwell Papers*. 4/96. Yale University Library. Quoted in Stephen A. Schuker. *American 'Reparations' to Germany*. p.121.

42. Article 19 stated that 'The Assembly may from time to time advise the reconsideration by Members of the League of Treaties which have become inapplicable and the consideration of international conditions whose continuance might endanger the peace of the world.'

43. *Documents on British Foreign Policy*. II. pp.220–1.

period.[44] After six months had elapsed, however, the Standstill Agreement would be renewed.

Carl Melchior, for whom Keynes had felt such an affinity at the Versailles Conference, expressed disgust at the part he had been called upon to perform, in negotiating a 'Standstill Agreement' on loans which Germany could afford to repay:

> 'What we have just experienced is the destruction of the ground-rules of the capitalistic system. Yet the system depends on the strictest observation of these very rules. This is the first time I have had to refuse to fulfil an obligation to which I had freely committed my name, simply because the state required me to refuse. The capitalistic system in Germany will not survive such a deviation from its rules. For the deviations will constantly increase, and the system will accordingly dissolve.'[45]

There existed a paradoxical situation in Germany at this time with a record number of bankruptcies, increased taxation, wage reductions and iron and steel production 34% lower than the year before. Yet in between the beginning of June to 13 July 1931, before asking for the 'Standstill Agreement', Germany had repaid 3,000,000,000 marks of foreign credits. Between July and December Germany would repay another 1,000,000,000 to 1,500,000,000 of its short term loans, reducing its foreign short-term indebtedness by almost a third.[46] In 1931 Germany was also 'the leading export country.' Its 1931 balance of trade in this year amounted to an astonishing 2,484,000,000 marks. While the quantity of world trade remained stationary Germany's share in it doubled. In August France was forced to fix import quotas to keep out German goods, in September Poland raised her tariffs. Italy, France and Holland followed and finally England imposed emergency duties.[47]

In declaring a moratorium in 1931 Hoover had given Germany a handsome present. Germany therefore should have been able to breathe some life into the internal economy of her country. This did not happen,

---

44. *Royal Institute of International Affairs Survey*. 1931. p.218. The Standstill covered roughly half of Germany's short-term debts. S. A. Schuker. *American 'Reparations' to Germany*. p.65.

Brüning had explained to South German Minister–Presidents on 21 October 1930 that 'he set his sights first on torpedoing the Young Plan in such a way that the short-term lenders would not take fright and that the Bank International Settlement (BIS) would find no handle to impose a financial quid pro quo.' His long-term aims were the 'abolition of the Polish Corridor, some sort of union with Austria, and the extension of German influence in the Danube basin generally.' MA 104218. BHstA. S. A. Schuker. *American 'Reparations' to Germany*. p.54.

45. Carl Melchior to Hans Schäffer, State Secretary to the Minister of Finance. E. Eyck. *The Weimar Republic*. Vol. II. p.323.

46. *Annual Register*. 1931. p.189.

47. *Annual Register*. 1931. p.189.

WORLD TRADE IN 1931.

THE preliminary estimates of the foreign trade of the principal countries during the past year have now been published. The figures show that the economic storm which was raging over the world in 1930 had grown into a devastating hurricane by 1931 :—

VALUATION OF MERCHANDISE TRADE.
(In millions.)

Period.	Net Imports.		Domestic Exports.		Balance.
	Value.	Percentage change on previous Year.	Value.	Percentage change on previous Year.	Export Surplus (+) Import Surplus (−).
			FRANCE.		
	Francs.	%	Francs.	%	Francs.
1929	58,221	...	50,139	...	− 8,082
1930	52,344	− 10·1	42,829	− 14·6	− 9,515
1931	42,199	− 19·4	30,421	− 29·0	− 11,778
			GERMANY.		
	Rm.	%	Rm.	%	Rm.
1929	13,447	...	12,663	...	− 784
1930	10,393	− 22·7	11,328	− 10·5	+ 935
1931	6,721	− 35·3	9,205	− 18·8	+ 2,484
			ITALY.		
	Lire.	%	Lire.	%	Lire.
1929	21,665	...	15,236	...	− 6,429
1930	17,325	− 20·0	12,115	− 20·5	− 5,210
1931	11,620	− 33·0	10,040	− 8·3	− 1,580
			SWITZERLAND.		
	Francs.	%	Francs.	%	Francs.
1929	2,724	...	2,098	...	− 626
1930	2,565	− 5·8	1,763	− 16·0	− 802
1931	2,251	− 12·2	1,349	− 23·5	− 902
			UNITED KINGDOM.		
	£	%	£	%	£
1929	1,111	...	729	...	− 382
1930	957	− 13·9	571	− 21·7	− 386
1931	798	− 16·6	389	− 31·9	− 409
			UNITED STATES.*		
	$	%	$	%	$
1929	4,399	...	5,241	...	+ 842
1930	3,061	− 30·4	3,843	− 26·7	+ 782
1931	2,090	− 31·8	2,424	− 36·9	+ 334
			CANADA.*		
	$	%	$	%	$
1929	1,299	...	1,208	...	− 91
1930	1,008	− 22·4	905	− 25·1	− 103
1931	628	− 37·7	609	− 32·7	− 19

* Includes transit trade.

Figure 12.1 World Trade in 1931

however. The misery for the German population continued. On 1 October the Government decided to reduce the time when they would pay out unemployment benefit from 26 weeks to 20 weeks on assumption that unemployment would top 6,500,000 that Winter. On 7 October the cabinet resigned but Hindenburg asked Brüning to form a new administration. A joint rally of the followers of Hugenberg and Hitler was held at Harzburg attended by the former President of the Reichsbank, Dr. Schacht, amid rumours that President Hindenburg was 'contemplating a National Socialist administration.' However, the aristocratic Field Marshall was not attracted to this 'Bohemian corporal' as he called Hitler after his meeting with him on 10 October. Dr. Brüning announced a new administration on 13 October without SPD involvement. An Advisory Council would be set up to help frame government economic policy in the coming months. A vote of 'no confidence' in the government by the Nationalists, National Socialists and the Communists, 'the National Opposition' failed by 295 votes to 270.[48] The campaign against the Young Plan, however, continued.

Brüning gave what looked like an ultimatum to the American Chamber of Commerce in Berlin on 12 December 1931:

'Either we are allowed to export, in which case we will pay; or we are prevented from exporting, in which case the payment of political debts becomes impossible to us. The time for illusions is past.'[49]

Britain's false illusions as to Germany's weakness and good faith persisted however, fuelled by the memories saddled on them by Keynes, that the British had given Germany a 'dishonourable' peace. But in France there could be no illusion. The Allied troops had been withdrawn from the Rhine, yet Germany's leaders were engaging in a similar struggle as the one the country had engaged in 1923. This time, however, the Allies had no economic controls or military muscle with which to dictate terms.

12.7 Wage Cuts in Germany

On the other side of the Atlantic, influential Senator Borah, who had quoted Keynes in the Senate in 1920, now echoed his sentiments again:

48. *Royal Institute of International Affairs.* 1931. p.189. *Bohemian Corporal.* E. Eyck. *The Weimar Republic.* Vol. II. p.331.
49. *Annual Register.* 1931. p.189.

'I do not believe' he told the French 'that there can be real disarmament in Europe so long as certain conditions arising out of the Versailles Treaty continue ... the Polish Corridor, for instance ... and I would change the situation with regard to Upper Silesia if I could – the plebiscite, in my judgement was all the other way.' As for the reparations he declared that France and Belgium were entitled to damages for actual injury, but that he had never felt that 'indirect damages' had a proper place under reparations.[50]

The British had just experienced a run on their banks, leading to a change of government and a fall from the gold standard. The American economy did not suffer a similar fate. But it was by no means strong. Citizens in downtown America, and all over the agricultural heartland, lost their jobs and looked starvation in the face because there was no comprehensive government unemployment insurance at all.

It has been the banking collapse and the high level of unemployment in the early 1930s which has convinced people that Germany was weak, not strong, before Hitler came to power, although Germany possessed the funds to repurchase around $480 million of dollar and sterling bonds in 1932 at discount prices.[51]

5,059,773 were stated to be unemployed in November 1931. The unemployed included 856,536 workers disallowed for unemployment insurance or even crisis relief.[52] Whereas in September 1929 7.2% of the registered workers available for work had been unemployed, in November 1931 according to the figures in the *Statistische Jahrbuch* 7.8% of the entire population of 64,815,795 was out of work. The Social Democrat vote had remained solid in September 1930. Despite propaganda hardly any of the working class vote had drifted to Hitler. Those in work in Germany still seemed to be earning a good living with the strength that gives to preserve independence of thought.

In December 1931 the International Labour Office published the results of an inquiry into the comparative costs of living in fourteen large towns in Europe and compared them with that of a car worker in Detroit. For Britain they chose Manchester, and for France, Paris. The town with the highest standard of living in Europe and the most expensive prices was Stockholm, followed by Frankfurt-am-Main and Berlin. The standard of living in Cork was surprisingly high. The rest of Europe lagged behind.[53]

50. *Annual Register.* 1931. p.296.
51. Stephen A. Schuker. *American 'Reparations' to Germany.* p.72.
52. *German Statistical Yearbook.* 1932. For 1931 statistics. Arbeitmarkt. Table 8. p.297 and Table 10. p.298. Of these 1,365,535 were covered by insurance, 1,406,453 were covered by crisis relief, 1,565,346 were recognised as being worthy of welfare payments (WE). But 866,536 received no money.
53. *The Ministry of Labour Gazette.* Vol. XL. January–December 1932.

Despite the high cost of living in their country, the German authorities decided, on 8 December 1931, that wages had to be cut. They announced that wages had to be slashed by between 10% and 15%. They argued that the cost of living had already dropped to that prevailing in January 1927 and that Germany had to adopt 'drastic measures for strengthening the competitive position of the country and reducing unemployment.'[54] The 'lives of millions of people' were to be degraded in Germany because of Germany's overseas obligations, even though the whole world seemed to be tariffed, or protected by currency reductions, against the influx of German goods. The German workers now came to believe that their economic misery was due to the burden of paying the reparations. After the 1930 elections international goodwill and democracy no longer seemed so compelling to the skilled artisan in the face of the assault on the living standards of his family.

In his book entitled, *The Weimar Republic*, the German historian, Eberhalb Kolb accused the Brüning government of having 'deliberately aggravated the economic crisis so as to force the solution of the reparations.'

He wrote:

'The view already put forward by W. J. Helbirch (504) that this was Brüning's aim from the beginning of his government is amply confirmed by the latest research from all relevant sources.(497: Glashagen, *Die Reparations politik Heinrich Brünings 1930–1931*).'

Brüning himself confessed his duplicity over the issues of reparations and disarmament in his memoirs:

'to win ... three demands which seemed to contradict each other; elimination of reparations, disarmament of the others, and rearmament for us ... I was now reaching a point where with one false move ... all the French propaganda could revive again ... then the great two-year long approach march, accomplished with endless sacrifice, would have been in vain.'

Brüning's memoirs reveal that he hoped to use his favourable reputation overseas to sell the idea of the desirability of restoring the Monarchy. He urged Hitler, Hugenberg, and the Reichwehr to provide sharp opposition to him, so that he could present the return of the Monarchy as the moderate solution.

The historian Eberhalb Kolb concluded that 'there was a connection between reparations, Brüning's stubborn adherence to policy of deflation, and the objective of a presidential regime.'

54. *The Ministry of Labour Gazette*. Vol. XL. 1932.

It was interesting that, in April 1932, Schacht assured the Reichswehr commanders that, as soon as he had managed to secure the cancellation of the reparations, 'he would devote a share of the resources saved to tripling the secret armaments budget and would authorize an expensive five-year program to create a battle-ready army of a million men.'

The reparations had become subject to a year's moratorium during the banking crash of 1931 but on 20 June 1932 that moratorium would expire. If the German worker seemed to be in even more desperate straights than his counterpart overseas, public opinion in foreign countries would sympathise when the German government declared that reparations could no longer be paid. That his present sufferings could have been imposed, needlessly, by his own government, to persuade foreign opinion to abandon reparations and persuade him to vote for dictatorship, and allow funds for creating a new army,[55] was not something which the skilled artisan imagined in his wildest dreams when he saw his wages slashed in December 1931 and voted for Hitler in 1933.

12.8 The Fight Against Socialism

1932 was a year of extremism in Germany. Brüning was replaced, in May, by von Papen as Chancellor, a former cavalry officer and close friend of President Hindenburg's son Oskar. Von Papen promised no financial respite for the unhappy German people but a fight against Socialism which was given responsibility for the country's unhappy plight.

> 'The German people must be informed of the condition in which the Government finds public affairs. The finances of the Reich, of Prussia, and of most of the other Provinces and of the municipalities are in utter disorder. None of the urgently needed reforms without which there can be no recovery has passed beyond the initial stages. The social insurances are faced with bankruptcy. The continually increasing unemployment is consuming the vitals of the German people. The post-war governments thought that by State Socialism they could relieve both employer and employed of their material anxieties. They have attempted to make the State into a kind of welfare institute ... The disintegrating influence of atheistic-marxist thought has penetrated far too deeply into all cultural spheres of public life.'[56]

Before his departure as Chancellor at the end of May, Brüning had made a speech calling for an annulment of all international debts arising

55. Brüning. Bennett. *German Rearmament and the West, 1932–33.*
56. *Annual Register.* 1932. p.189.

from the war and 'equal' rights for Germany through 'universal' disarmament.[57]

The 'equal rights' part of the disarmament speech alarmed the Allies who had already been approached by Germany to increase her Army by another 100,000 men[58] while on the financial front the Americans declared that Germany had erased her domestic debt and completely modernised her industrial plant. They therefore called for a 'loyal recognition' by Germany of her 'pecuniary obligations.'[59] The Allies decided to have a conference at Lausanne to see if they could sort the matter out.

France had been Britain's ally in the war but since then the countries had reverted to their historical suspicion of each other. Arnold Toynbee had these words to say of the French in 1931:

'She was the dominant military Power in Europe in the air as well as on land; she was executing a naval programme – in submarines, destroyers, and cruisers – which was causing uneasiness to the Admiralty in Whitehall. Above all she had extended her potency into the field of international finance.'[60]

The British Premier, Ramsay Macdonald, must have been aware that though many feared France's capacity as a world power the 'impoverished' Germans had started replacing their ancient battleships with ultra-modern cruisers causing a flurry of activity in French ports.

British socialists, however, in general, felt warmth towards the Germans and suspicion of the French.

Lord Templewood, formerly Sir Samuel Hoare, described the mood of the time in his memoirs.

'We are bad haters. Having been reluctantly drawn into a fight, we wish to forgive our enemies as soon as it is finished, ... The tendency to forgive and forget (between the wars) was further strengthened by the wish to be freed from the financial burden of armaments ... So sure, indeed, were we of the virtues of disarmament that we easily became irritated with other countries, and particularly our former Allies, the French, when they did not agree with us. The anti-French feeling became very strong. Annoyance with our former Allies went very near to becoming affection for our former enemies.'[61]

Before the forthcoming conference with the Germans, however, Ramsay Macdonald had a meeting with the new French Socialist

57. E. Eyck. *The Weimar Republic*. Vol. II. p.348. 'The German government and the German people having been disarmed themselves, now challenge the whole world to join them in disarmament.'
58. E. Eyck. *The Weimar Republic*. Vol. II. p.377, p.458.
59. E. Eyck. *The Weimar Republic*. Vol. II. p.379.
60. *Royal Institute of International Affairs*. 1931. p.22.
61. Viscount Templewood. *Nine troubled years*. p.111f.

Premier, Herriot, to try and find a common approach to the reparations' problem. Ramsay Macdonald proposed offering the Germans the complete abolition of the reparations in return for a 15 year political truce. As a fellow socialist, Herriot could understand the outlook of the former pacifist-minded British Premier. However, he replied that, in the past, Germany had been inclined to treat solemn treaties as scraps of paper.[62] It was better to seek a token of her good faith.

12.9 Lausanne Conference

When the Conference at Lausanne commenced on 16 June 1932 the Allies opened by offering to waive the instalment of reparations due for the coming year. For his part von Papen proposed offering France a bilateral military alliance in return for the abrogation of reparations but his cabinet overruled him.

Beleaguered Herriot, aware that von Papen opposite him carried little real muscle in the Fatherland, whispered to the British delegate, Lord Simon, 'The more I study the face of a German cavalry officer, the more I admire his horse.'[63]

Despite a fellow feeling for the French Socialist, Herriot, Ramsay Macdonald still preserved his views as to the start of World War I. During the disarmament negotiations in 1930 Ramsay Macdonald had been most revealing about his misconceptions:

'I am determined not to drift into the position in which Grey found himself. That gives France a free hand in determining European policy with Great Britain a bound follower. That will mean alliances and war, & I shall prevent it so long as I am in office.'[64]

As Chairman of the Lausanne Conference, therefore, Ramsay Macdonald offered to meet German political objections to Article 231 of the Treaty of Versailles, the 'war-guilt' clause, by implying that if Germany was prepared to agree to pay increased reparations 'the Conference might agree to a political declaration, formally abrogating the hated war-guilt clause of the Peace Treaty.'[65]

When the French nation got wind of the fact that the British and the Germans were trying to drive Herriot into a corner over the 'war-guilt'

62. *Documents on British Foreign Policy.* III. 176.
63. *Documents on British Foreign Policy.* II. 332.
64. Diary. 16.2.30. Reproduced in *Ramsay Macdonald.* David Marquand. p.514–15.
65. David Marquand. *Ramsay Macdonald.* p.722. *Documents of British Foreign Policy. no. 173.*

clause,[66] they were outraged and the matter was dropped.

After lengthy negotiations, however, the Allies agreed to renounce 90% of the original reparations' claims, merely asking for what seemed like a token payment so that Germany could demonstrate her good faith.

Papen, could not turn down this outstandingly generous proposal out of hand without alienating the entire international community. After all, the damage the Germans had inflicted in France while they parleyed with President Wilson on their retreat in 1918 had come to a substantial portion of the Allies original bill, yet here the Allies were, prepared to write off 90% of Allied claims. Other arrangements had been included in the agreement to make sure that Germany's credit remained strong. Germany's delegates signed the document.[67]

It soon became clear, however, that the German Parliament had no intention of ratifying the agreement their representatives had signed. Indeed, after all the propaganda, the German people had decided that they were in no way obliged to pay any of the costs of the wartime destruction that the German armies had inflicted upon the West. The issue merely provided an excuse for Hitler's National Socialists to declare in even more strident form in the violent run up to the Reichstag elections in July: 'We will not pay one more pfennig.' The elections produced a 'total defeat for von Papen's government.' The National Socialists secured 230 seats of the 608 in the Reichstag. There was no more talk of paying reparations.

Under the present order, however, as the world's economy recovered, if Germany wanted to play a responsible part in world affairs, she would have had to start paying reparations again. The reparations had not only been an earnest of Germany's goodwill to atone for her sins, they had also represented an admission that Germans lived in a larger world to which they had responsibilities. The reparations and the imposition of a genuine democracy in Germany – that earnest that each citizen counted in the affairs of the state – were the only relics left of the Treaty of Versailles. It followed, therefore, that almost as soon as the Allies' only hold left over the Germans, the reparations, had evaporated, that democracy should vanish too. After all had not the imposition of a genuine democracy been largely the work of the man who helped the socialists stab the victorious generals in the back in 1918, President Woodrow Wilson of America?

Unfortunately for the French, the Americans did not view events at Lausanne as conclusive proof of Germany's culpability and ill-will. There were reasons for this attitude. America at this time was in a

66. *Documents on British Foreign Policy. 1919–39.* Vol. III. no. 179.
67. E. Eyck. *The Weimar Republic.* Vol. II. p.406–7.

desperate, parlous state. Farmers were over their heads in debt. New York City and Chicago were also said to be on the verge of bankruptcy. One out of seven New Yorkers were being fed by public or private charity. Interested parties had indeed expressed the opinion that a cancellation of the war debts might help their economy. *Annual Register* records the outlook of the cotton trade:

> 'Newspapers began to point out that cotton was the chief export of the United States and that the cancellation of these international debts – which would cost the United States 268,000,000 dollars a year-might prove a small price to pay for the restoration of foreign markets for cotton. Exports of raw cotton had dwindled in 1931-32 to 340,000,000 dollars compared with average yearly exports for the previous five years of 611,000,000 dollars. They said 'forget the debts and restore our foreign markets.'[68]

Initial reports of the Lausanne Conference had been well received in America. If Germany was going to be substantially let off its reparations it would be able to pay a better price for its cotton. But then it became apparent that not only were there going to be difficulties in getting the Germans to ratify the reparations' document but there had also been a proviso agreed before ratification on the part of the seven European Allies. Under what they called a 'gentleman's agreement', arrived at privately among themselves, the Europeans had pledged that they would only sign the Lausanne Agreement if America let them substantially off their war debts.

The Americans reacted angrily to this. The very words 'gentleman's agreement' sent them into a paroxysm of rage. In America such a euphemism was habitually used in low-down deals between businessmen to evade the law. It appeared that, in this case, the low-down Europeans were attempting to avoid their lawful obligations to the American people.[69]

They were especially irate at the French who were refusing to pay their 19,000,000 dollar war debt instalment, when, until gold started to leave the country, France had kept 700,000,000 dollars worth of gold in their vaults. What also bewildered them was the attitude of the previously anti-French British. Despite all the rhetoric emanating from Germany, Ramsay Macdonald had insisted on speaking of 'our German friends' in the same breath as 'our French friends' at the Lausanne Conference. Yet now here were the British and French, apparently

---

68. *Annual Register.* 1932. p.300. After the reparations were abandoned the Germans rewarded cotton-growing Americans, who had put pressure on the Government on their behalf over the reparations, by negotiating to buy American cotton at a premium for discounted German wine and beer. H. James. *The German Slump.* p.411.

69. *Annual Register.* 1932. p.301.

bosom pals, pledging each other to 'complete candour' on all matters 'similar in origins to that now so happily settled at Lausanne.' Americans were sure that the Europeans were out to bamboozle them again as they had been told by Keynes that had happened at Versailles in 1919.

They asserted that the Allies could quite easily pay their war debts if only they would cut down on their military expenditure as they had promised under the terms of the Treaty of Versailles. The Allies, however, weren't prepared to do this. When it was obvious that no more money would be forthcoming from Germany, the Allies, led by France, declared that they would pay no more war debts. Indeed it seems that they had every right to do this because 'on American advice' payments to the USA 'had been based in the Young Plan on German payments to the Allies.'[70]

The American public had not been made aware of this agreement, however. Until now they had supported the French in their just claim for reparations. But the French had been crude and tactless in displaying their monetary wealth to the Americans whose working people were suffering in some cases greater hardship than that endured by the Europeans. Gold had been draining from British and American coffers for a long time. Now the French were accused of creating a 'dollar panic.' Perhaps the French hoped that financial pressure would stiffen American resolve to support France over the reparations. America had sided with the French on the reparations issue until they declined to pay their war debts. But each American citizen, who had mortgaged the future of himself and his family to pay for an Allied victory in 1918, felt cheated when the Allies refused to repay, now when he had such desperate need of the money.

12.10   Food Crisis in America

But it was not only the American middle classes who were suffering from the loss of the income on the loans they had made to help the Allies during the war. The poor were in desperate trouble. So much of the health of the American economy, and so many jobs were still dependent on the health of the farming sector. And now, out of the blue, that had been devastated too.

The Grapes of Wrath by John Steinbeck published in 1939 describes not middle class poverty but a scene of starvation amongst the ordinary

70. G. Borsky. *The Greatest Swindle in the World*. p.60.

people in America in the early 1930s because of the depression in the nation's important farming industry.

> 'The boy was at her side explaining: "I didn't know. He said he et, or he wan't hungry. Las' night I went an'bust a winda an stolded some bread. Made'im chew 'er down. But he puked it all up, an' then he was weaker. Got to have soup or milk. You folks got money to get milk?" '...
> 'For a minute Rose of Sharon sat still in the whispering barn. Then she hoisted her tired body to the corner and stood looking down at the wasted face, into the wide frightened eyes. Then slowly she lay down beside him. He shook his head slowly from side to side. Rose of Sharon loosened one side of the blanket and bared her breast. "You got to." She said. She squirmed closer and pulled his head close. "'There!" she said. "There." '[71]

Out of the blue Stalin's Russia had started dumping wheat on the American market in 1930. The Americans had had no idea that it was going to arrive. Indeed previous to its arrival there had been persistent tales of food shortages and starvation in Russia. Yet Russia was accused of 'dumping' wheat by the Canadians in 1931.[72]

None of the Western Allies would have helped the Soviets modernise their agriculture. But it had been reported that the German Krupp concern had renewed its agricultural concession in the Upper Caucasus, the 'largest agricultural concession in Russia',[73] in 1928 and German machinery imported to help create a modern industrial infrastructure. The success of the farms in the Upper Caucasus was said to have provided the inspiration for Stalin to have adopted a system of 'rural socialisation' in 1929.

Stalin was accused, not merely of trying to obtain foreign currency, but of trying to undermine capitalism itself. The question is whether the German industrialists who were investing in Russia had any influence over Russian governmental policy.

Although the popular Press in Germany was quite unanimous in their condemnation of the Soviet regime in 1929/30, the abject nature of the terms which Stalin negotiated with the Krupp concern, by which Russia would take over 'the financing end as well as the risk of losses' in his project in the Upper Caucasus, and Russia's later acceptance in 1931 that any dispute in connection with purchases of industrial goods from Germany, 'should be settled in German courts', leads one to suspect that they could. After all, Germany had supplied Russia with two years 'clean credit' for £20 million per annum since 1926.[74]

71. John Steinbeck. *The Grapes of Wrath*. p.479–80.
72. *The Times. Royal Institute of International Affairs Survey*. 1931. p.47.
73. *New York Times*. 28.9.29.
74. *The Economist*. 25.4.31. *The Economist*. 7.11.31.

'Collapsed currency' was the one certain way that Russia would make a profit on its operations and pay its German suppliers in the difficult circumstance prevailing. It was also about the only way it could be accomplished without incurring the wrath of public opinion abroad.

Banner headlines in the *New York Times*, such as 'Shortage of food disturbs Moscow' had lulled foreign observers before the Soviet wheat hit world markets. The *New York Times* had relayed Soviet explanations in banner headlines such as: 'Soviet Transportation and Distribution is Blamed as inefficient.'

Popular opinion in Allied countries therefore could not believe that it was the Russian corn that was devastating their farming industry in 1931/32 when they had heard so many tales of Russian food shortages so little time before. Nor did their governments want to elucidate them. For Russia's delegate at the Canada House Conference, Mr. Lubinoff, had laid the reasons for his country's success in exporting wheat exclusively on what was an anathema to Western governments, and an excitement to far left wing elements everywhere, the virtues of the Communist system as opposed to capitalism:

> 'We consider that the present agricultural crisis (in America) is directly due to the contradictions of the capitalist system ...'[75]

12.11 Unpaid German Bills

The Allies and America had tried hard to keep the world a stable place and had spent money for that end. But their aim was difficult to achieve when one of the world's richest countries was not above destabilising it, in order to secure what it considered was its longer term interest. Of Chancellor Brüning's economic policy, the historian Eberhalb had concluded: 'the desperate financial and economic situation in Germany, if not engineered by Brüning, was recognised and used by him as a means of scaling down reparations ...' There had been German engineering, however, both over the aid given to Russia to help it with its wheat exports, and in the structuring of the German economy to protect German farmers from its devastation before they were overwhelmed by the flood. There was little money left in the American financial system, however, to restructure the American farming industry and care for the agricultural population after so many other endeavours by the financial community to keep the world on an even keel. At last, in 1933, the

75. *The Economist*. 30.5.31.

Soviet Union lost interest in purchasing from Germany after it was disclosed at the World Economic Conference that Herr Hugenberg had put forward 'claims for Russian territory.'[76]

During the three years that the Young Plan was in force Germany had paid £140 million in reparations, the £80$^1/_2$ million in cash being £20 million more than the proceeds of the Young Plan loan.

Although £1,038,000,000 had been received by the Allies in total, in reparations, roughly £200 million more than the actual cost of repairing France's devastated provinces, as the Dawes and Young Plans were allowed to lapse in the years before World War II, only £938 million was actually received before another war started.[77] In addition much of the total value of the reparations accredited had been in the value of ceded property and 'deliveries in kind', little in 'actual cash transfers.' 'Cash' transfers have been assessed as amounting to a mere £253 million.[78] Meanwhile, to put the payments in context, Germany's national income in 1929 amounted to 75,900 million gold marks, roughly £3,800,000,000.[79] The country had also received much money from abroad.

The short- and long-term loans and other foreign investments that the country had accumulated were assessed in 1934 to amount to 29,700 million gold marks, £1,985,000,000, more than the sum that the Allies and America had fixed as Germany's total reparations' liability.[80] The economist, Stephen A. Schuker, writing in his study of the period, *American 'Reparations' to Germany* (1986) concluded that Germany received a net inflow of funds 'at no less than 17.75 milliard RM, or 2.1 percent of national income for the whole period 1919–31.'

'... In price adjusted terms' he added, 'this sum approached four times the total assistance that the United States government would provide to West Germany from 1948 to 1952 under the much- heralded Marshall Plan.'

After reneging on the moral debts of war Germany found it easy to jettison its other debts when Hitler came to power. On 9 April 1933 Dr. Schacht declared: 'a complete moratorium seems to be inevitable.' Negotiations dragged on, on the terms for repayment. Investors were offered 40% in cash but the 'Reichsbank reserved the right to withdraw this part of the offer on 30 days notice.' The ensuing collapse in the

76. *Annual Register.* 1933. Section on Russia.
77. G. Borsky. *The Greatest Swindle in the World.* p.61–2.
78. G. Borsky. *The Greatest Swindle in the World.* p.62.
79. *German Statistical Yearbook.* Official rate to the £. – 20.43.
80. *Wirtschaft und Statisk.* 1934. p.134. Creditor countries of German loans. U.S.A. – 55%. Netherlands – 12.3%. G.B. – 11.5%. Sweden – 8.3%. Switzerland – 5.4%. *The Economist.* 23.1.32. Reparations Supplement.

bond price enabled the German government to buy up most of the remainder at a large discount. By 1934, German short-term indebtedness had fallen to less than in 1913.[81]

All America's other loans to Germany suffered a similar fate. We can now understand why Germany had such a spectacular dash to full employment in the thirties, and why other countries, faced with a mass of unpaid bills, had such an arduous task in recovering their prosperity.[82]

Dr. Schacht had an obsession about foreign debt which he felt was akin to some sort of slavery. However, he was aware of the advantages of being a powerful debtor. In 1936 he instituted Germany's 'Drang Nach Sudosten.' In this brilliantly conceived deception, he offered to pay the South-East European countries, Greece, Hungary, Jugoslavia, Rumania and Bulgaria 30% above the world price for their agricultural produce. These countries were naturally delighted at such an opportunity and they offered to underwrite the deal by advancing the money to the producers and wait for Germany to repay them. Dr. Schacht's next move was to sell the commodities which he had thus acquired to Rotterdam or London either at the ruling market price or even below it. His third step was to inform his creditors from South East Europe that he was wholly unable to find the foreign exchange in the amounts required but that he was prepared to pay on his own terms in certain lines of manufactured goods – particularly armaments![83]

Uneasy governments did not like these unpalatable facts to emerge. So the odium for the unpaid German bills in America fell on the 'rich' Allies who had caused the German unemployment, misery and starvation 'leading to the rise of Hitler' by charging those monstrous reparations and refusing to repay their war debts themselves. The famous Johnson Act was passed by Congress forbidding all future credits to the Allies if the war debt payments had not meanwhile been paid. Indeed the bitterness caused by the non-payment of our war debts lasted long afterwards deep into the Second World War. Capital starved America's unemployment soared to 23.6% in 1932 and 24.95% in 1933. In 1937 it was still 19%. Meanwhile, in Germany, Hitler spent a total of 48,911 billion Reichsmarks, on rearming in the seven years before World War II.[84]

---

81. *Royal Institute of International Affairs.* 1934. p.37.

82. *Royal Institute of International Affairs.* 1934. Long-term and Commercial debt. 41.

83. *Royal Institute of International Affairs Survey.* 1936.

84. 'The Schwerin von Krosigk-Overy figures represent a reliable minimum spent on rearmament.' H. James. *The German Slump.* p.383. He gives tables of estimates spent on German rearmament, ranging from that compiled by Dr. Schacht of 34.25 billion RM. to that compiled by the East German, Kuczynski, of 76 billion RM.

In 1919 when President Wilson had campaigned for America's signature on the Treaty of Versailles, he had this to say in Indianapolis:

'If the nations of the world do not maintain their concern to sustain the independence and freedom (of the nations of Eastern Europe) Germany will yet have her way upon them, and we shall witness the very interesting spectacle of having spent million upon millions of American treasure and, what is much more precious, hundreds of thousands of American lives ... to do a thing we will then leave to be undone at the leisure of those who are masters of intrigue, at the leisure of those who are combining wrong influences to overcome right influences, of those who are the masters of the very things we hate and mean always to fight. For my fellow citizens, if Germany should ever attempt that again, whether we are in the League of Nations or not, we will join to prevent it. We do not stand off and see murder done.'ions or not we will join to prevent it. We do not stand off and see murder done.' But by 1939 bitter Americans felt ready to do just that. Their European Allies had let them down.

Conclusions

One must look at events through German eyes. One could say that the reason that Saddam Hussein destroyed 700 oil wells on his retreat from Kuwait in 1991 was because he felt that he should have won the war. If it had not been for the intervention of the United Nations he would have defeated Kuwait.

The destruction of Northern France's mines and industry at the end of World War I is less known than the destruction of Kuwait at the end of the Gulf War, but a similar reason can be given for it. Without the intervention of Britain, America and the rest of the Allies, Germany would certainly have defeated France.

The loss of victory appalled the German hierarchy. At the end of the war Germany still had in excess of 480,000 seasoned troops on the Eastern front, unable to stop the rot in the West. The hierarchy had been so unwilling to contemplate defeat. On 19 September 1918 it had claimed from Russia, the Polish frontier strip on the Werthe-Naras Line, days before its army in the West was forced to sue for peace on terms that envisaged the recreation of Poland as an independent nation state. The country had never fought the war on anything but enemy territory since 1914. It was no wonder that, after the incredible happened, and the army collapsed on the Western front, the leadership ordered the destruction of Northern France and Belgium's mines and industry on its army's retreat. The nation's military dictators put the blame for the country's humiliation on pacifist socialists, and their shop floor friends, who had, in their eyes, been undermining the war effort for years.

Those not in the army could not bring themselves to believe for long that President Woodrow Wilson had rescued the country from defeat. Indeed the army commanders, themselves, soon forgot the crumbling morale on the western front after the fall of Passchaendale in 1918, and convinced themselves that they had made a wrong decision to sue for peace in the first place. Despite the carnage, the home front, from the ordinary man in the street to the Kaiser, had been cocooned from stories of reversals. An innocent bystander reflected popular opinion in

December 1918 when he told an observer from the *New York Times*: 'If the war had gone on we would have won.'

The war had not been won but, in his determination to undermine the Allies too, President Wilson's goal of 'Peace without Victory' gave new hope to Germany. Under the Treaty of Versailles the former Prussian Empire would be cemented into one country, the largest in Europe, a counterweight to the power of the French and British Empires. As Herr Erzberger, the socialist politician soon to be murdered for accepting peace and a policy of fulfilment, stated at the signing of the armistice: 'A nation of 70 million people suffers but does not die.'

The war had cost Germany half what it cost the Allies. It would be in a dominant economic position soon after World War I because the coal-rich country was the O.P.E.C. of continental Europe in the days before the arrival of oil. Victorious France, its mines shattered, would have to come humbly knocking at Germany's door if she wanted supplies of coal. Meanwhile the November 'revolution' was extinguished soon after it had accomplished the abdication of the Kaiser, demanded by President Woodrow Wilson as his price for not commanding 'unconditional surrender.' Cries of 'starvation' secured Germany concessions at the Peace Conference and sympathetic America sighed with relief that its heavy hogs, denied access to Germany via the neutral countries under the stricter controls of 1918, would be profitably exported.

Any losses of German territory, under the terms of the Treaty of Versailles, would have been difficult for The Fatherland to swallow when it had lately been negotiating to accumulate so much more. Deciding to fine the country large sums would be much easier than attempting to extract them from such a strong country.

German citizens had originally been persuaded to change their individual reserves of gold into paper in the confident expectation that the war would be won and the paper would be redeemed with interest as had happened in 1870. It was difficult for them to accept that they could have been foolish in so doing. Civil servants, the judiciary, the rich and the poor, all had faith in the war effort. When the paper reduced in value, the middle classes saw their life savings gradually melt away. Naturally with such an investment in victory, they tended to blame extremist shop floor agitation for their nation's setbacks in the war, and castigated pacifist, intellectual socialism for its naivety in accepting President Woodrow Wilson's woolly promises. Both sections of the populace would come under threat in postwar idealogy. But the country soon united against its external enemy, that American presbyterian President, Woodrow Wilson, who had saved their country from defeat, yet could not deliver them victory, and was now to blame for the loss of their savings, and the rest of the indignities, embodied in the Treaty of Versailles.

Much fuss was made of the £6,600m charged by the Allies in reparation in 1921, after elements in Germany had tried to restore the monarchy the moment America's troops had gone home. Looking more closely at the small print of the agreement, however, one can discern that the true figure asked for, was really £2,500m. The rest was window dressing to allay public alarm. One has to remember moreover that Britain's debts from the war remained at £7,500m, while three quarters of Germany's £7,500m debt had already vanished in currency depreciation.

Paper marks had, in fact, already lost value during the war and it had probably not been originally intended to continue the practice for long afterwards. But as the Allies felt constrained by the strictures of President Wilson's Treaty from seizing the initiative to curb the practice, the Germans felt emboldened to continue it. Gratifyingly, the more the mark toppled, the greater the inroads German exports made into Allied markets. Allied Governments could not explain this embarrassing phenomenon to their electorates. Appeasement seemed a more sensible policy. There must be some sum which Germany would consider 'reasonable' for 'reparation.' So Allied acceptance of German tales of poverty became the norm in the post World War I years when Allied threats proved impotent.

In 1923 France, which had received no 'ready money' at all towards the £830 million repair of its devastated provinces, lost patience and marched into the Ruhr. In the ensuing months the internal value of the mark was reduced to worthlessness. At first German workers in the great coal mines of the Ruhr were paid not to work. But at the end of September the Government agreed to give up 'passive resistance.' However, led by Herr Stinnes, one of the many postwar German 'would be Napoleons' before Hitler came along, the industrialists issued a ten point ultimatum to the Government. They refused to allow their employees back to work until they agreed to their demands for a longer working day, considered vital to compete successfully at a level exchange rate with the Allies. The eight hour day had been the great concession won by labour in the days after World War I ended in November 1918 but, at the end of a cold November in 1923, with no money coming in, and the thin soup from public kitchens inadequate to feed the family, the workers caved in. Germany reverted, in general, to its pre-1918 ten hour day.

Though total reparations' deliveries up to 1924 totalled some £400 million, 'actual cash' deliveries in reparations, as opposed to 'deliveries in kind' amounted to only £80 million, whereas it was disclosed after World War II that Germany had actually netted £400 million from foreigners exchanging their hard currency for German paper marks during the inflationary period. The estimated £500 million which Germany had abroad was ordered to be repatriated.

The British pacifist, Keynes, had predicted that Germany would be reduced to starvation by the rigours of paying the reparations. His astonishing prophecy seemed proved correct in 1923 when heart-rending tales of German food shortages reached Britain. The experts who had originally demanded heavy sums in reparations from Germany were castigated for their inhumanity. Pacifist socialism gained ground in Britain. In contrast to Germany where General Hindenburg was elected head of state by an ecstatic population in 1925, British generals were increasingly pilloried through the gradual perception that Britain had lost much and gained nothing in World War I. Ancient antagonism towards France returned.

Many modern economies seem to indulge in hyper-inflation but stabilisation is less easy. Putting the blame for the individual hardship involved in returning the mark to the 'gold-exchange standard in effect,' on the propaganda issue of the reparations, helped the German government persuade the German people to accept the pain involved. American economic historians such as Stephen A. Schuker are now agreed that Germany gained an advantage from its stabilisation and that in the mid-1920s it was very strong. German high interest rates subjected all European nations within its orbit, including Britain, to deflationary pressures.

It was irksome to much of the German establishment that economic clout was not matched by political muscle. So much needed to be done. Allied soldiers were removed from the Ruhr in 1925 and the Cologne area in 1926 but they still remained in the Rhineland. On 30 October 1930 Dr. Schacht was to make an emotional demand of the Americans, to understand why he had signed the Young Plan reparations' plan in 1929, knowing that the country would almost immediately try to renege on it, merely to get rid of the occupation troops in the Rhineland five years ahead of schedule.

> 'Can you think of a people which still has some self- respect, standing for having its most important industrial area, one-sixth of its total area – occupied by foreign troops fifteen years after the war?'

The Young Plan reparations' agreement had been negotiated with much drama on Dr. Schacht's part in the spring and summer previously. Americans hoped that by transforming the debt into the equivalent of an ordinary loan, the drama of the past war could be forgotten. Germany, now paying less than Great Britain, overall, in debt from the war, would be happy with its reparations, France, which had previously taken the line that it should not be made to repay large sums to America when it had born the brunt of ridding the world of the evils of 'Prussian militarism,' had formally acknowledged its debt. One ugly chapter in the world's history seemed at last to have been laid to rest.

In fact, however, almost as soon as the Young Plan was agreed on 31 August 1929, Alfred Hugenberg, leader of the second largest party in the German Parliament, caused consternation in America by launching a petition for a national referendum to have the whole German cabinet tried for treason for accepting it, on the moral grounds that the imposition of reparations was not valid at all, as Germany was guiltless of starting World War I.

Agreement to the Young Plan by the German Government, up to date, had seemed a formality because the agreement was due to be backdated to start on 1 September 1929, although the German parliament had yet to ratify it. Now the web of payments appeared in jeopardy again and the world's financial stability too. In Britain's democracy the leader of a political party would not have been allowed to own 550 newspapers and a chain of cinemas dedicated to putting out his personal propaganda, especially when he had publicly declared his distaste for democracy.

Indeed, although Herr Hugenberg saved his invective for the Treaty of Versailles, it would not be inappropriate to conclude that his real target was Weimar Democracy itself, ushered in as the price of peace by President Wilson in November 1918, and dedicated to the policy of fulfilment of the terms of the Treaty afterwards.

On 15 July 1928 the *New York Times* had reported Herr Hugenberg's ambitions:

'Herr Hugenberg offers his fellow Nationalists the panacea of dictatorship. He favours monarchism and ... the restoration of the Imperial throne ... but he believes that the restoration of the Imperial throne can be gained only through the preliminary creation of a dictatorial regime akin to Premier Mussolini's in Italy. There must first be a dictator, then a new Kaiser. He is convinced moreover, that this first step can be taken legally, or at least without a violent upheaval ... if the condition of the country seems to warrant it.'

These words by the leader of the second largest party in the Reichstag, had to be a direct threat to the Weimar Republic. And what better way to excite a population which had lost its savings, seemingly in a vain quest to pay reparations, than to stir up the moral issue of the war, when the general public was already in such confusion about how World War I had begun and ended, and were completely unaware of the destruction caused to Northern France and Belgium's mines and industry by the retreating German army?

The question must be asked whether Hugenberg included Hitler on his petition merely to add enough votes to secure a national referendum. Or whether Hugenberg, at this early stage, had envisaged Hitler as the future dictator, akin to Mussolini, which he had outlined in his speech of

1928 to be necessary before 'a new Kaiser' came to the throne. Certainly the free publicity given to Hitler by Hugenberg's five hundred newspapers over the so called 'Bill against the enslavement of the German people' was the shot in the arm which helped to thrust him and his party, suddenly, into the public eye.

The petition, by some of the principle hawks before and during the war, had to have a terrible effect on the American stock market. Not only the American stock market indeed, but to an extent the American economy as a whole, had become reliant on the prosperity of Europe and its repayment of war debts and loans. America needed the reparations to be paid. The sudden dramatic realisation that they might not be, the departure of the German finance which had helped support the stock market, and the request for money for another huge loan to help Germany pay the reparations, when one substantial loan was already scheduled to be raised, all contributed to the sudden dramatic drop in the American stock market in October 1929, despite the nation's healthy balance of trade with other countries.

Hugenberg had declared that 'if the condition seems to warrant it' the country would vote for dictatorship. Hard times had produced a vote for the anti-democratic parties of Hugenberg and Hitler after the inflation of 1923. The question is how far those in authority in Germany augmented the depression in the years after the American stock market crash, using the reparations as a propaganda issue.

John Foster Dulles in 1930 accused the German establishment of aggravating the political misery at home. He asserted: 'There are leaders in Germany who encourage such an atmosphere – an atmosphere of pessimism ... in which no economic problems can be solved – as a vehicle for ridding Germany of her reparations obligations.' And he appealed for Dr. Schacht to help those in Germany who wished the country to behave as a responsible member of the international financial community.

But Dr. Schacht replied by prophesying 'another' German crisis over the reparations 'because of her bad situation' and confidently asserting that it would be bloodless because the Allied troops had been withdrawn from the Rhine. He concluded:

> 'In spite of all the faults which were committed at the second Hague Conference, there is one reassuring thing, today, that is if the reparations problem comes up again, as Mr. Dulles has quite rightly said it will, it comes up under more favourable political circumstances than before.'

Six months later Germany and Austria declared a customs union in direct contravention of the Treaty of Versailles. A horrified France withheld short term finance from Austria. In the ensuing banking crash

Germany was given a moratorium on the payment of its reparations. They were never resumed. In 1932 when America finally agreed to stop demanding reparations, Winston Churchill told the House of Commons,

> 'There has been no Carthaginian Peace. Neither has there been any bleeding of Germany white by the conquerors. The exact opposite has taken place ... It is Germany that has received an infusion of blood from the nations with whom she went to war ... Germany only awaits a trade revival to gain an immense ascendancy throughout the world.'

Eberhalb Kolb, the German historian, writing in 1986, agreed with John Foster Dulles's assertion of October 1930 that Germany was aggravating the economic crisis in order to help rid itself of the reparations. Indeed he went farther and concluded that the reason that the German Chancellor, Brüning, had proceeded with this policy was because he wished to curry favour with Hindenberg and the military establishment, to pave the way for a 'Presidential regime,' using the reparations as a propaganda weapon to justify the temporary individual hardship needed for a popular vote for dictatorship.

Germany's President, Hindenburg, had never concealed his distaste for what he considered to be the partisan nature of democracy. In his acceptance of the Presidency in 1925 he had declared: 'As a soldier I have always had the whole nation before my eyes, and not its parties.'

The German president already had greater powers than an American President. Each time the parties splintered his position grew even stronger. German philosophy had taught that Germans should lead. Many, like him in Germany, looked back to the old days, when under the mantle of the sovereign, the leaders of the country had almost untrammelled ability to do what they considered right for the good of the country without political parties yapping in opposition.

Some elements had tried to restore the monarchy in 1920 as soon as the American troops had gone home. But the war-weary people were not ready for it and the country was still occupied by foreign troops. There had been renewed fears about dictatorship in 1923. Alarm had been raised before Hitler's famous attempted coup in Munich, that the coal magnate, Hugo Stinnes, would not only issue edicts to Parliament, but also grab the reins of government. But Stinnes declared himself uninterested in political power as long as the Government acceded to his demands for industry, and Hitler's coup failed. By the early 1930s however the German hierarchy warmed to the idea of dictatorship again and wished to weaken resistance at home and abroad to the idea.

If Germany was a weak country and wished to create the economic conditions to persuade people to vote for dictatorship it would not have affected the outside world, but if it was a strong one, it could cause repercussions world wide.

Foreign observers have considered Germany to be weak in the late 1920s was because of its apparent need for foreign currency. When the loans from abroad dried up after the American stock market crash, it is asserted, Germany could no longer pay reparations. It is suspicious however that, in the years up to 1924, Germany sucked in capital almost exactly equalling what it paid in total in reparation in ceded buildings, coal, timber and gold, and yet it still defied payment.

After 1924, under the stringent terms of the Dawes Plan, the French ensured that their 'deliveries in kind' would be funded by industrial debentures, a transport tax and a levy on the profitable German railways. The sums raised by these taxes repaid German industry for the goods they delivered free to France in reparation. Britain imposed a tax of 30% on German exports, the proceeds of the tariff being credited against the reparations, but she allowed the Germans to equalise the suffering so that the whole of German industry bore the pain of payment, not just the exporting industries.

Before controls were imposed in 1924 little monetary reparations had been forthcoming. After the controls were removed under the terms of the Young Plan in 1929, attempts at collection soon had to be abandoned.

In October 1930 Dr. Schacht pointed out that Germany 'has regained the entire twelve percent which she had as her share in the trade of the world before the war.' In 1931 Germany was the world's leading exporter. Yet the Allies had no means of insisting on payment if Germany refused to pay.

The dilemma in lending money is that one is always tempted to lend a little bit more, to ensure repayment of the initial sum, if the borrower declares himself to be in temporary financial difficulties. But one cannot go on for ever throwing good money after bad, lest the ungrateful borrower absconds with the cash.

In America Germany had been assessed as having approximately £500 million abroad after its hyper-inflation in 1923 which was ordered to be repatriated.

In 1928 and early 1929 more money left Germany, some to escape high taxes at home and some to be spent allegedly 'in the arbitrage business' over the Young Plan negotiations. The Reich Statistical Office itself estimated the 'capital flight' from Germany between 1927 and 1930 at some £490 million.

Dr. Schacht asserted to his audience in America, in 1930, that cash reparations in the 1920s had been paid 'entirely out of borrowings,' but examination shows that most was paid through the instrument of Allied controls. Much money did flow into Germany, however, during the 1920s. It seemed such a favourable economic area in which to invest. Besides Americans wanted to forgive and forget the war and help Germany build up its tax base so that it could tax its citizens to pay the reparations.

Little did America know that Dr. Stresemann had written in his diary in 1924 that Germany ought to encourage loans from America, not because it needed them, but because 'The granting of a loan would give us an army of 300,000 people in America who would make propaganda for Germany because they were interested in her welfare.'

Germany therefore could be accused of sucking in America's spare change with its high interest rates in the mid-1920s not out of necessity but for political purposes.

Herr Hugenberg had asserted that the Germans could be persuaded to vote for dictatorship but only 'if the conditions warranted it.' The question is how far Germany actually created the conditions in which Germans would vote for dictatorship, and the foreigners would permit it, using the reparations as a propaganda issue.

There are pointers that Allies and American tales of German poverty could have been appeasement in 1931/32. Even before Hitler came to power, the Allies were not only fearful of the cession of their reparations payments but of the fate of all their sovereign and commercial loans. Meanwhile German exports not only devastated foreign competition in industrial goods but Germany also invested in Russia while Russia was pursuing a policy of 'dumping' produce abroad.

In 1928 German industrialists had decided to help the Soviet Union modernise its industrial and agricultural base in return for Stalin persuading the German communists to vote with the German right to undermine Socialism in Germany. By 1930 Stalin's Russia was in a position to export and was prepared to collapse its currency at home to enable it to devastate western markets. France pleaded with Germany to unite with her to try and combat Russian dumping. Germany, after all, had by now declared its abhorrence of inflation and debasement of the currency, and was prepared to go to great lengths to eliminate it at home. However, despite tales of brutality and oppression from Germans driven from their farmsteads in the Soviet Union, and the condemnation of the entire newspaper press of Stalin's regime, Germany refused.

In 1931 Stalin ascribed the devastation of American agriculture by low-priced Russian wheat, to the efficacy of the communist system over capitalism. But in the same year he concluded a new trade agreement with Germany on abject terms. One is inclined to believe that the German negotiators could have influenced how he handled Russia's overseas sales, had they chose, when the country first agreed to help modernise Soviet industry. Even if they failed to foresee events in 1928/29 they could have put pressure on in 1931 when a new contract was signed. It was evident that Stalin was determined to take a short-cut to achieving industrial muscle, whatever the personal consequences for his unfortunate people, and the effect his drastic action would have on the world economy. However some sections of the German far right could have been pleased by the effect of Stalin's policy abroad. The Russian ruin of the American farming economy, not only weakened American fervour to insist on the reparations being paid, but also undermined credence in democracy, in beleaguered economies everywhere.

German citizens had changed their gold marks into paper marks to help fight World War I. These savings had been ruthlessly sacrificed by the German leadership in its bid to eliminate Germany's crushing war time debt and regain Germany's industrial place in the sun. Much of the unemployment that the German people suffered in the early 1930s has been said to have been due to the leadership's belief that hard times would help eliminate the reparations and persuade the electorate to vote for what they euphemistically called a 'Presidential Regime.' Some in Germany are still filled with praise for the early years of Hitler's rule today.

In his speech on 12 November 1988, on the fortieth anniversary of the Kristalnacht pogrom, Herr Jenninger, President of the Bundestag, described Hitler's triumphs in the 1930s.

'The reincorporation of the Saar, the introduction of the general draft, massive rearmament, the conclusion of the German-British fleet accords, the occupation of the Rhineland, the Olympic summer games in Berlin, the annexation of Austria, the Great German Empire, and finally, only a few weeks before the November pogroms, the Munich, agreement, the cutting up of Czechoslovakia – the Versailles Accord was really just a scrap of paper and the German Empire (was) the leading power in the old continent.

'And not only that: Mass unemployment turned into full employment, from mass misery there was something like prosperity for the widest sections (of the population.) Instead of desperation and hopelessness, optimism and self- confidence reigned. Did not Hitler just make reality what was just a promise under Wilhelm II – that is, to bring wonderful times for the Germans? ...

He blamed the Jews and democracy for Germany's economic misery before Hitler came to power.

'And as far as the Jews were concerned: hadn't they in the past measured themselves for roles that did not suit them? Didn't they finally have to accept restrictions? Didn't they perhaps, even deserve to be shown their place? ...

And as for democracy:

'For the Germans who saw the Weimar Republic as a consequence of foreign policy humiliations ... All the astonishing successes of Hitler were – seen as a whole and individually – belated blows to the Weimar System ... '

It must have been infuriating to Americans that the rush to full employment in Germany was helped by reneging on the loans made by American citizens. In America the Allies were blamed for having asked for, in Keynes' words, 'ridiculous and injurious' reparations in the first place, and refusing to repay war debts when those reparations were no longer forthcoming. The City was castigated too for what had essentially been a political decision to try and maintain Germany's international goodwill in the mid 1920s by throwing money at the problem. The Allies and America suffered dreadfully in the 1930s. But Germany suffered most in the longer term. After the initial chimera, the cold hard reality of how they had been duped again, sunk into the consciousness of the German people, as they marched off to war.

After the Gulf War Professor Harold James took a harsher view of the merits of dictatorship in Germany in the 1930s to that espoused by Herr Jenninger in 1988.

> 'The lesson of interwar Germany is that the threat to peace, stability and democracy lies in removing reparations, and not in imposing them. After Lausanne, moderation ceased to be attractive and the stage was set for World War II.'

In the 1930s the American stock market crash and the subsequent European banking crash were ascribed to the failure of capitalism, and they are still ascribed as such in many history books today.

Assuming Germany to be so weak as to be, in Keynes's words, 'reduced to servitude' in 1931 when it was given a moratorium on its reparations' payments, these history books are startled and impressed by Germany's sudden dash to full employment after Hitler came to power, advocating governments at home to take a leaf out of his book and 'prime the pump' to cure unemployment.

Investigation into interwar events however shows that 'priming the pump' is not the simple remedy that Hitler made it appear. This book concludes that Germany had a powerful economy in the early 1930s, mighty enough to fund a dash for growth after Hitler became dictator. It also concludes that, as it was strong in those years before Hitler's ascendancy, its deflationary policy at home, coupled with its assistance for the Soviet Union's undermining of the world's farm economy, were the principle causes of the Great Depression.

However the Allies and America's persistent unwillingness to admit that they had made a mistake in failing to insist on 'unconditional surrender' at the end of World War I, and to take firm steps to control Germany afterwards, must take its share of the blame for encouraging the German hierarchy to play games with the international community in subsequent years, in order to pursue their own nefarious ends.

People such as Alfred Hugenberg knew the power of propaganda and did not hesitate to influence the attitudes of German voters who had no access to documents showing how World War I had begun, how it finished, and whether or not foreigners were trying to 'draw the blood of reparations ... from the veins of the exhausted' German people with extortionate demands. Men like Hugenberg, and even Brüning, felt that the German people had to suffer, and be deceived by their leaders over the reparations, in the greater interest of returning the country to dictatorship.

John Maynard Keynes was also a publicist but of a different sort. He did not deliberately set out to misguide people. But he did put pen to paper without too much regard for his words' effect. Thus 'The Economic Consequences of the Peace' succeeded in alienating Americans towards their former friends in Europe, and encouraging unscrupulous men in Germany to blame the debasement of their currency on the reparations. Then in September 1929, when all the reparations' controls had been removed by the Allies, Keynes made a new pronouncement:

> 'In fact, where a country's difficulties are due to its owing a burdensome sum, readjustment is often brought about by its just not paying it. These are the precedents relevant to the German case ... .When the debt is owed in terms of the home currency, the relief comes by depreciating the currency; when it is owed in a foreign currency, the relief comes by default.'

Keynes should have realised that invitations of this sort, to break solemn agreements in an acceptable fashion, could lead to misery and unemployment in many different countries.

Brief Biographies

Baldwin, Stanley, 1867–1947. Financial Secretary to Treasury 1917. President of Board of Trade 1921–22. Chancellor of Exchequer 1922. Prime Minister 1923, 1924–29, 1935–37. Lord President of Council 1931–35. Lord Privy Seal 1932–34.

Bethmann-Hollweg, Theobald von, 1856–1921. Lord Lieutenant of Brandenburg 1899–1905. Prussian Minister of Interior 1899–1905. Reich Secretary of the Interior 1907. Chancellor 1909–17. Trusted by the left, Bethmann Hollweg managed to convince socialists at home and abroad that Germany was embarked on a war of defence in 1914 by goading Russia into mobilising its army before Germany ordered its own mobilisation. His failure of memory after the war proved crucial in discrediting the Finance Minister, Erzberger, who had expressed himself willing to comply with Allied demands for the trial of wartime leaders and the payment of reparations.

Bonar Law, Andrew, 1858–1923. Arrived in Scotland from Canada at age of 12. Unionist member for Glasgow 1900. Leader of Conservatives 1911. Colonial Secretary in Asquith's Coalition government 1915–16. Chancellor of Exchequer in Lloyd George's Coalition government, December 1916–18. Coalition with Lloyd George's Liberals after war. Lord Privy Seal 1919–21. Retired. Came back into politics to become Conservative Prime Minister 1922–23.

Briand, Aristide, 1862–1932. Very radical when young. Alienated left when Minister of Justice 1907. Premier 1909–10 and 1913. Favoured fighting in Balkans rather than on Western front during World War 1. Premier and Minister for Foreign Affairs 1915–17. Premier 1921–22. Signed Locarno Pact 1925. Shared Nobel Peace Prize with Stresemann 1926. Led ten governments in all and was Foreign Minister for most of the period between 1925–32.

Brockdorff-Rantzau, Count Ulrich von, 1869–1928. Advocated support for Russian Bolsheviks during war believing it to be to Germany's economic advantage. Gained nickname 'Red Count.' Secretary for

Foreign Affairs, December 1918. Foreign Minister, February-June 1919. Sent by Rathenau to Moscow as German Ambassador 1922.

Brüning, Heinrich, 1885–1970. Infantry Officer on Western front 1915–18. Conservative politician in Centre Party, with reputation for financial expertise. Chancellor from 1930–32. Known as 'the hunger Chancellor' because of his savagely deflationary economic policies. Emigrated to USA after Hitler came to power. Taught political science at Harvard 1937–52.

Byng, Julian. Commanded 3rd Cavalry Division 1914–15 – 9th army corps, 17th army corps, Canadian corps 1916, 3rd army 1917–19. Created Baron 1919. 1st Viscount of Vimy 1926.

Chamberlain, Austen, 1863–1937. Member of war cabinet 1918. Chancellor of Exchequer 1919–21. Lord Privy Seal 1921–22. Foreign Secretary 1924–29. 1st Lord of Admiralty 1931. According to Birkenhead: 'Austen always played the game and always lost it.'

Churchill, Winston Spencer, 1874–1965. 1st Lord of Admiralty 1912–15. Chancellor of the Duchy of Lancaster 1915. Commanded a battalion 1915–16. Minister of Munitions 1917–18. Secretary for War 1918–21. Supported Lloyd George on break–up of Coalition and defeated at Dundee. M.P. for Watford 1924–64. Chancellor of Exchequer 1924–29. Understood link between a competitive exchange rate and employment after the inroads made by German competition during the Great Inflation. However, was reluctantly persuaded to return to Gold Standard in 1925 after Germany's stabilisation on a 'gold exchange in effect' and the imposition of a 30% tariff on German goods. In 1932 Churchill would declare that Germany was strong, not weak, despite its unemployment, and 'only waits a trade revival to gain an immense ascendancy throughout the world.'

Clemenceau, Georges, 1841–1929. Elected to National Chamber of Deputies in Radical Party 1876. Minister of Interior 1906. Premier 1906–1909, strengthening ties with Great Britain. After leaving office, although nearly 70, he established newspaper L'Homme Libre, to promote his views on the 'German threat'. Criticised war effort 1914–17. Premier, November 1917–20. Defeated French defeatism in darkest days of war. President of the Paris Peace Conference.

Cunliffe, Walter, 1855–1920. Governor of Bank of England 1913– 18. Member of Reparations Committee 1919.

Cuno, Wilhelm, 1876–1933. Treasury Official before and during war. Director of Hamburg-American shipping line 1918. Represented Germany at Versailles in reparations' negotiations. Reich Chancellor, November 1922 to August 1923.

Curtius, Julius, 1877–1948. Artillery Officer on Western front 1914–18. Welcomed Kapp Putsch. Member of DVP in Reichstag 1919–32. Lawyer for iron producing and industrial combine Gütehoffnungshütte and other industrial clients. Economics Minister 1926–29. Foreign Minister 1929–31. Architect of proposed German-Austrian Customs Union 1931. Failure of the proposal prompted Hindenburg to demand his resignation.

Curzon, George Nathaniel, 1859–1925. Viceroy of India 1898–1905. Earl 1911. Marquis 1921. Lord Privy Seal 1915–16. Lord President of Council and member of war cabinet 1916–18. Foreign Secretary 1919–24. Lord Privy Seal 1924–25.

Dulles, John Foster, 1888–1959. Legal Adviser to US delegation at Versailles 1919. Assisted in preparation of UN Charter 1945. Negotiated peace treaty with Japan 1951. Secretary of State 1953–59.

Ebert, Friedrich, 1871–1925. Former saddler. Became leader of SPD 1912. Backed Peace Resolution 1917. Reluctant head of Berlin armaments strike affecting reputedly over 500,000, January 1918. Accepted help from army to defend Republic from extremism at end of war. President of Republic 1919–25. Personally shattered by court case of December 1924, finding him guilty of high treason for his role in Berlin armament workers' strike in 1918. Died from the aftermath of an appendix operation, February 1925.

Erzberger, Matthias, 1875–1921. Son of tailor. Entered Reichstag as member for Centre Party 1903. Spokesman for heavy industry's annexationist policy in 1914. Supported peace movement 1917. Signed armistice terms 1918. Deputy Chancellor and Finance Minister 1919. Expressed himself willing to comply with Allied demands to try wartime leaders and pay reparations. Accused of personal and professional misconduct 1919–20. Murdered – 26.8.21.

Foch, Ferdinand, 1851–1929. Director at L'Ecole Supériere de la Guerre 1908. Held advance of German army at battle of the Marne – 8.9.14. Relieved of post after setbacks and casualties 1915. Chief of General Staff 1917. Generalissimo of Allied forces. Marshall of French army 1918. President of Allied Military Committee at Versailles 1920.

Gröner, Wilhelm, 1867–1939. Organised war production and labour in collaboration with SPD and unions 1916. Offered to help Ebert defeat perceived threat from Bolshevism, November 1918. Served as Reich Transport Minister 1920–23. Retired. At request from Hindenburg, returned to politics to become Minister of Defence 1928–32. Forced to resign over his prohibition of SA in April 1932.

Haig, Douglas, 1861–1928. Commanded I Army Corps 1914. Commanded First Army 1915. Commander in Chief in France

1915–19 and the Home Forces 1919–21. Created Earl 1919. President of British Legion 1921–28.

Helfferich, Dr. Karl, 1872–1924. Director of Baghdad Railway 1906. Director of Deutsche Bank 1908. Secretary of State 1915–17, preferring to use 'mammoth loans' rather than taxation to pay for war. Minister of Interior and Deputy Chancellor 1916–17. Ambassador to Russia 1918. Unanimous endorsement of Directors of Reichsbank for Presidency after Great Inflation disallowed by President Ebert and Chancellor Stresemann. Died in train accident – 23.4.24.

Henderson, Arthur, 1863–1935. President of Board of Education 1915–16. Member of war cabinet 1916–17. Home Secretary 1924. Foreign Secretary 1929–31. President of World Disarmament Conference 1932–35.

Herriot, Eduoard, born 1872. Minister of Public Works in Briand Cabinet 1916–17. Prime Minister 1924–25. One day Prime Minister 1926. Minister of Public Instruction in Poincaré's Cabinet 1926–28. Prime Minister and Minister of Foreign Affairs, June 1932–December 1932. Minister of State in Doumergue and Flandin Cabinets 1934–36.

Hilferding, Rudolf, 1877–1941. Austrian Jewish extraction. Influenced by Marxist ideas. Published Das Finanzkapital 1910. Protested against SPD approving war credits in 1914. 1916–18, served as military doctor in Austrian army. Became Prussian citizen after war. Member of SPD in Reichstag 1922–33. Helped negotiate Rapallo Treaty with Soviet Union 1922. Reich Minister of Finance, August to October 1923, and June 1928 to December 1929. Compelled to resign. 1933, forced to emigrate to Denmark, Switzerland and finally France. Arrested by Gestapo 1941. Found hanging in cell.

Hindenburg, Paul von, 1847–1934. Chief of Staff of IV Army Corps 1903–11. Retired in 1911. Reactivated, 1914, aged 67. With Ludendorff won the battle of Tannenberg. Promoted Field Marshall Commander in Chief of the Eastern front, November 1914. Chief of General Staff 1916. With Ludendorff 'virtual military dictator' after the fall of Bethmann Hollweg 1917. Helped force abdication of Kaiser, October 1918. Status as national hero consolidated by fallacious 'stab-in-back' legend. President of Weimar Republic – 26.4.25. Despised Republic. Appointed Hitler Chancellor 1933.

Hitler, Adolph, 1889–1945. Co-founded National Socialist Workers' Party 1919. Organiser of unsuccessful putsch 1923. Elected Chancellor 1933. Re-occupied Rhineland 1936. Annexed Austria and Sudetenland 1938, Czechoslovakia, 1939, then Poland, bringing Britain and France into war. Defeated France 1941. Forced to retreat in Russia after Stalingrad 1943. Murdered six million people. Committed suicide 1945.

Hoover, Herbert, 1874–1964. Chairman of Commission for Relief in Belgium 1915–19. Food Administrator for US Member of War Trade Council 1917–19. Secretary of Commerce in US 1921–28. President of US 1929–33. Undertook co-ordination of world food supplies of 38 countries 1946.

Hugenberg, Alfred, 1865–1951. 1890, co-founder of Pan German League. Director of Berg-Metalbank 1907–09. Chairman of Krupp Industrial Empire 1909–19. Became tycoon in his own right early 1920s. Acquired Scherl publishing house and UFA (Universal Film). German Nationalist DNVP. Chairman 1928–33, 'a principal gravedigger of the Weimar Republic.' Received cabinet post in Hitler's government 1933, but was forced out of office later in the year. Survived World War II. Labelled no more than a 'fellow traveller' at de- nazification trials. Died a rich man.

Kahr, Gustav Ritter von, 1862–1934. Right-wing career civil servant. Prime Minister of Bavaria, March 1920–August 1921. September 1923, became General State Commissioner with 'virtually' dictatorial powers. Perceived threat from Hitler's proposed march on Berlin. Prosecution witness at Hitler's trial. Resumed civil service career. Retired in 1930. Arrested during Röhm Putsch. Murdered in Dachau Concentration Camp 1934.

Kapp, Wolfgang, 1858–1922. Founder of Society for Internal Colonisation, particularly in East Prussia. Co-founder (with Admiral von Tirpitz) and Deputy Chairman of the radical right-wing Fatherland Party 1917–19. Joined DNVP after November Revolution. With help of General Walther von Lüttwitz, planned abortive coup 1920.

Keynes, John Maynard, 1883–1946. Became internationally known after his polemic The Economic Consequences of the Peace was used by opponents of President Woodrow Wilson against ratification of the Treaty of Versailles in the run up to the American General elections. Appeared a prophet when outsiders misread Germany's economic strength during and after hyper-inflation of 1923. His opposition to Britain's return to Gold Standard in 1925, after Germany's currency was stabilised on a 'gold-exchange standard in effect', was applauded after Britain was forced to leave Gold Standard 1931. Principal Treasury Adviser 1940–46. Baron Keynes of Tilton 1942.

Lansing, Robert, 1864–1928. Prominent international lawyer. Secretary of State 1915–20. During war, urged policy of friendship towards Britain and peace with Mexico. In 1917 he helped negotiate purchase of Virgin Islands and signed Lansing-Ishiti agreement. Urged non-recognition of Soviet Russia. Differed with President Wilson over aspects of League of Nations. Asked to resign.

Lenin, Vladimir Ilich, 1870–1924. Exiled to Siberia 1897–1900. Subsequently moved to Western Europe. Participated in 1905 revolution in Russia. Settled in Switzerland 1907. 'Sealed train' took him through Germany to power in Russia, March 1917. Concluded peace with Germany 1918. Commanded Bolsheviks in civil war 1918–21. Initiated New Economic Policy 1921. Suffered stroke 1922.

Liebnecht, Karl, 1871–1919. Son of founder of SPD. Imprisoned 1907 for promoting agitation against militarism inside army barracks. SPD Reichstag member 1910–16. 1 January 1916, co-founded Spartacus Group. Sentenced to 4 years' imprisonment for anti-war agitation. Expelled from SPD. Released from prison following amnesty, October 1918. Influenced German Communist Party KPD to attempt to seize power through masses rather than participate in elections. Arrested and murdered by Freikorps soldiers – 15.1.19.

Lloyd George, David, 1870–1945. Liberal M.P. 1890–1945. Chancellor of Exchequer 1908–15. Minister of Munitions 1915–16. Secretary for War 1916. Prime Minister 1916–22. Leader of the Liberal Party 1926–31. Created Earl 1945.

Ludendorff, General Erich, 1865–1937. Quartermaster of Second Army 1914. Chief of Staff under Hindenburg at Tannenberg. Senior Quartermaster General – 28.9.16. With Hindenburg, assumed political powers. Driving force behind Treaty of Brest-Litovsk. Participated in Kapp Putsch. Joined Hitler's abortive coup 1923. Reichstag representative of Hitler's National Socialists 1924–28.

Luther, Hans, 1879–1962. Lord Mayor of Essen 1918–22. Minister of Finance October 1923 till January 1925. Chancellor 1925–26. Forced to resign over flag decree of May 1926 which allowed German missions abroad to use the old Imperial colours. Founded the League for the regeneration of the Reich. President of Reichsbank 1930–33. German Ambassador to Washington 1933–37.

Luxemburg, Rosa, 1879–1962. Jewish revolutionary. Authoress of The Accumulation of Capital and The Tasks of International Social Democracy which was accepted as founding text of Spartacus Group. Imprisoned for most of war for inciting soldiers to disobey orders. Released from prison, November 1918. Murdered in January uprising 1919.

Macdonald, Ramsay, 1866–1937. Leader of Labour Party 1911–14. Had to resign over opposition to war. Leader of Labour Party again 1922–31. Prime Minister and Foreign Secretary of Labour Party 1924. Prime Minister of Labour Party 1929–31, of National Government 1931–35.

Marx, Wilhelm, 1863–1946. Catholic judge. Centre Party Reichstag representative 1910–18 and 1919–32. Chancellor, November 1923–24, assuming emergency powers. Abolished all-lay jury system. Lost Presidential election to Hindenburg by 13.7 million votes to 14.6. Minister of Justice, January-May 1926. Chancellor of 'rightist' administration 1926–28. Introduced unemployment insurance but did not ensure adequate funding.

Melchior, Carl, 1871–1933. Partner of Warburg Bank, Hamburg. In German delegation at Versailles. Alternate for Schacht on Committee of Experts for Young Plan 1929. Part of German delegation at The Hague, August 1929. Unwillingly negotiated 'Standstill Agreement' on short-term loans 1931.

Müller, Hermann, 1876–1931. Editor of socialist newspaper Görlitzer Volkszeitung 1899. Reichstag member of SPD 1916. Chairman of Party 1919–27. Foreign Minister 1919–20. One of two signatories of Treaty of Versailles. Chancellor, March till June 1920. Chancellor, June 1928–March 1930.

Northcliffe, Lord, 1865–1922. Born Alfred Harmsworth. Inspired Daily Mail and made The Times profitable. Created Baron 1905; Viscount 1917. Head of British mission to US 1917. Director of enemy propaganda 1918. Supported charging Germany heavy reparations after World War I – 'If we let her, she will dodge and cheat'.

Noske, Gustave, 1868–1946. Right–wing SPD member. Supported idea of a 'defensive war' in 1907. Negotiated settlement of sailors' revolt 1918. Minister of Defense and Leader of Reichswehr 1919-20. Criticised for using ultra-rightist Freikorps to put down revolts by left-wing radicals. Governor of Hanover 1920–33. Arrested on suspicion of being implicated in July plot against Hitler 1944. Saved by Allies.

Papen, Franz von, 1879–1969. Sent to US as Military Attaché 1913. Ordered home because of involvement in American-Mexican civil war. Chairman of Management Board of Centre Party's newspaper, Germania. Chancellor of Administration, nicknamed 'cabinet of Barons', June till November 1932. Lifted ban on SA and the wearing of uniforms by NSDAP members. Vice-Chancellor, January 1933–34. Escaped murder during Röhm Putsch. Held diplomatic posts in Vienna 1934–39, Ankara 1939–44. Acquitted at Nuremburg Trials 1946. Sentenced to 8 years' hard labour by German denazification court 1947. Released on appeal in 1949.

Pershing, John Joseph, 1860–1948. Served in campaigns against Sioux and Apache Indians and Moro insurgents in Phillipines. Commanded US troops sent to Mexico 1916–17. Commander in Chief of American expeditionary forces in Europe, June 1917–September 1919. Argued for insisting on 'unconditional surrender' in 1918.

Poincaré, Raymond, 1860–1934. Elected to Chamber of Deputies 1887. Minister of Public Instruction 1893. Minister of Finance 1894, 1906. Premier 1912–13. President 1913–18. Premier again 1922–24 during the occupation of the Ruhr. Premier again 1926–29.

Rathenau, Dr. Walter, 1867–1922. Son of Emil Rathenau, founder of A.E.G. Organiser and Director of Division of Military Raw Materials during World War I. Minister of Reconstruction, May–October 1921. Foreign Minister 1922. Murdered – 24.6.22.

Roosevelt, Theodore, 1858–1919. Member of New York Legislature 1882–84. Leader of House 1884. President of New York Police Board 1895–97. Commanded US volunteers in Cuba 1898. Governor of New York State 1898–1900. Vice- President of US 1901. President of US 1901–1908. Progressive Party candidate 1912. Supported Republicans 1916. Expected to be nominated Presidential Candidate of Republican Party for 1920 elections before untimely death.

Schacht, Hjalmar Horace Greeley, 1877–1970. Born in Denmark. Raised in New York. President of the Reichsbank 1923–30, 1933–39. Also Minister of Economy in Hitler's Germany 1934–37. Acquitted at Nuremburg Trials. Founded a bank in Düsseldorf and became financial consultant to developing nations. Wrote autobiography Confessions of the 'Old Wizard'.

Seeckt, Hans von, 1866–1936. Son of General. Married daughter of Jew 1893. Chief of Staff of Turkish army 1918. Member of German delegation at Versailles 1919. Lieutenant-General 1919. Reorganised army into highly professional force, 'a state within a state', but refused to join Kapp Putsch or adventures in 1923. Dismissed in 1926 for giving Crown Prince's son position in army.

Smuts, Jan Christian, 1870–1950. General in Boer War. Minister of Mines, Defence and Interior in new Union of South Africa 1910. Defeated Germans in German South West Africa 1915. Commanded British Army in East Africa 1916. Joined British War Cabinet 1917. Invented 'mandate' system at Versailles. Prime Minister of South Africa 1919–29, 1939–48. Lloyd George refused to propose him Commander in Chief of the American armies in France 1918. However, British made him Field Marshall 1941.

Snowden, Phillip, 1864–1937. Educated elementary school. Prominent member of I.L.P. Chancellor of Exchequer 1924, 1929–31. Lord Privy Seal 1931–32. Created Viscount 1932.

Stalin, Josef, 1879–1953. General Secretary of the Soviet Communist Party 1922–53. Chairman of Politburo 1924. Ousted all rivals by 1927. Initiated first five-year plan for industrialisation and collectivisation of agriculture 1928. Prime Minister 1941–53. Marshall 1943.

Generalissimo 1945. 'Dominant figure' at Tehran 1943, Yalta 1945, Potsdam 1945.

Stinnes, Hugo, 1870–1924. Controlled German-Luxemburg Mining Co. and Rhine Westphalian Electric Co. before 1918. Expansionist during the war, advocating annexing France's northern coast and iron ore deposits. Became richer in Germany's Great Inflation, acquiring Styrian Erzberg, the largest coal-mine in Europe; and having a large share in 69 construction companies, 66 chemical paper and sugar works, 59 mines, 57 bank and insurance companies, 56 iron and steel works, 49 brown coal works, 37 oil fields and petroleum factories, 100 metallurgical factories, 389 commercial and transport enterprises, 83 railway and shipping companies, 150 newspapers and periodicals etc. Defied the Allies over coal deliveries at Spa in June 1920. Used Germany's hyper-inflation to force his workers to accept a return to the ten hour working day in 1923. Died 1924.

Strachey, Lytton, 1880–1932. Author and poet, reviewed books in Spectator 1904–14. Conscientious objector in World War I. Best known for Eminent Victorians 1918, Queen Victoria 1921.

Stresemann, Gustav, 1878–1929. Eighth child of innkeeper. Married daughter of baptised Jewish family. Member of Hansa League 1911–18. Reichstag representative 1907–12, 1914–18, advocating annexations. Helped Ludendorff overthrow Chancellor Bethmann Hollweg 1917. Modified his views 1917–18. Founded DVP after war. Chancellor, 13.8.23 – 23.11.23. Minister of Foreign Affairs 1924–29. Hoped to make changes to Eastern frontier by peaceful persuasion. Awarded Nobel Prize 1926.

Sumner, Viscount, 1859–1934. Born John Andrew Hamilton, impecunious but brilliant. 1st Oxford University. President of Union. Judge 1909. Court of Appeal 1912. Lord of Appeal 1913. Chairman of Committees into matters of national interest 1918, 1921, 1926. Member of British Delegation on Reparations Committee 1919.

Tardieu, André, 1876–1945. Professor of Modern History and Foreign Editor Temps 1902–14. Assistant to Clemenceau at Versailles. Leader of Left Republican Group. Minister for Public Works in Poincaré's Cabinet 1926. Minister of Interior in Poincaré's Cabinet 1929. Premier and Minister of Interior, November 1929. Prime Minister March-December 1930. Minister of Agriculture Laval Cabinet, January 1931–32. Minister for War January–February 1932. Prime Minister and Minister of Foreign Affairs, February till June 1932. Founded Centre Republican Group, May 1932. Promoter of Danube Economic Confederation Plan.

Vögler, Dr. Albert, born 1877. Reichstag representative 1919–24. Chairman of Board of the German and Luxemburg Mining and

Refining Corporation. With Schacht, on Young Plan Committee 1929. Resigned in May in protest against proposals.

Warburg, Paul Moritz, 1868–1932. German-born American banker. In 1902 he emigrated to America and joined Merchant Bank of Kuhn, Loeb and Co. Advocated American banking reforms after panic of 1907. Appointed Member of First Federal Reserve Board 1914–18. Member of Advisory Council 1921–26.

Wilson, (Thomas) Woodrow, 1856–1924. President of Princeton University 1902–10. Governor of New Jersey 1911–12. US President 1912–20. Wish for wartime neutrality changed by German intrigues in Mexico and unrestricted submarine warfare campaign 1917. Offered Germany conditional peace on the basis of the 14 points, provided that the German Kaiser abdicated, October 1918. Lost congressional elections, November 1918 as electorate had wanted 'unconditional surrender'. Would not compromise over wording of League of Nations. His Treaty of Versailles was never ratified and he lost Presidential elections 1920.

Wirth, Dr. Joseph. Chancellor 1921–22. Reich Finance Minister 1920–21. Bitterly critical of Far Right over murder of Rathenau. He was not in sufficient control of the nation's finances to be able to stabilise the currency or to adopt a 'policy of fulfilment' over the reparations.

Bibliography

Official Documents

Great Britain: Foreign Office

Treaty Series, 1930.
>No. 4, 1930. Agreement at the Hague Conference, January 1930. Cmd. 3484, 1931. London: H.M.S.O.
>*Hague Agreements, 1930.* Memorandum on the Receipts of the United Kingdom under the Hague Agreement. Cmd. 3498, 1930. London: H.M.S.O.
>*Treaty Series, 1931.*
>No. 2, 1931. *International Agreements re Financial Obligations* of Germany. Cmd. 3763, 1931. London: H.M.S.O.
>No. 3, 1931. *International Agreement re Financial Obligations of Austria arising out of the Peace Treaties.* Cmd. 3764, 1931. London: H.M.S.O.
>No. 4, 1931. *International Agreement re Financial Obligations of Czechoslovakia.* Cmd. 3765, 1931. London: H.M.S.O.
>No. 5, 1931. *Agreement between United Kingdom, New Zealand, India, and the Austrian Government regarding the Liquidation of Austrian Properties.* Cmd. 3762, 1931. London: H.M.S.O.
>No. 6, 1931. *International Convention to Bank for International Settlements.* Cmd. 3766, 1931. London: H.M.S.O.
>No. 7, 1931. *International Agreement to Geneva 5_ per cent, Loan, 1930.* Cmd. 3761, 1931. London: H.M.S.O.
>No. 12, 1931. *International Agreement re Financial Obligations of Bulgaria under Treaty of Neuilly.* Cmd. 3787, 1931. London: H.M.S.O.
>No. 21, 1931. *Agreement between the United Kingdom, New Zealand, India, and the Hungarian Government regarding the Liquidation of Hungarian Properties.* Cmd. 3845, 1931. London: H.M.S.O.

No. 30, 1931. *Internal Agreement re Financial Obligations of Hungary under Treaty of Trianon.* Cmd. 3910, 1931. London: H.M.S.O.

Miscellaneous, No. 19, 1931.

Report of International Committee of Experts re Suspension of certain Inter-Governmental Debts – due June 30, 1932. Cmd. 3947, 1932. London: H.M.S.O.

Miscellaneous, No. 1, 1932. Bulgaria.

Protocol providing for Suspension of Certain Payments due by Bulgaria. 1932. London: H.M.S.O.

United States: Senate

'Hearings before Committee on Finance, December 16, 1931.' Postponement of Inter-Governmental Debt. 1931. Washington: Government Printing Office.

General Works

Angell, J. W. (1930) The Recovery of Germany. Yale University Press.

Arnot, H. W. (1944) *The Economic Lessons of the Nineteen- Thirties.* University Press.

Bonn, M. J. (1930) *Der Neue Plan.* Munchen: Humblot. viii. 266.

Bowley, A. L. (1931) *Some Economic Consequences of the Great War.* Thornton Butterworth Limited.

Fischer-Williams, Sir J. (1932) 'Legal Footnote to the Story of German Reparations', in *British Year-Book of International Law.* pp. 9–39.

Gribble, F. (1932) *What America Owes Europe.* Hurst & Blackett. xxxiii, 188 pp.

Keynes, J. M. (1925) *The Economic Consequences of Mr Churchill.* As reprinted in 'Keynes: Collected Writings'. Vol. IX. pp. 207–30.

Litter, F. (1930) *Die Verfahransvorschrift für Sachleistungen nach dem Haager Abkommen von 20 January, 1930.* (Kommentar). Berlin: Reichsverbanden der Deutschen Industrie.

Lloyd George, D. (1932) *The Truth about Reparations and War Debts.* London: Heinemann. 150 pp.

McFadyean, Sir A. (1930) *Reparations Reviewed.* London: Benn. 220.

Moulton, H. G. and Pasvolsky, L. (1932) *War Debts and World Prosperity.* (Brookings Institute Publication No. 46). Washington: Brookings Institute. xx. 487 pp.

Mousley, E. (1932) *A British Brief.* Hutchinson. 203 pp.

Myers, D. P. (1930) *The Reparation Settlement*. Boston: World Peace Foundation. 249 pp.

Raab, F. (1930) *Der Neue Plan*. Berlin: Reimar Hobbing. 206 pp.

Raab, F. (1932) *Deutschlands Recht zur Einstellung der Reparationen*. Dresden: Ehlermann. 107 pp. Bwl.

Salter, Sir A. (1932) *Recovery*. London: Bell. xvi, 326 pp.

Schacht, H. (1931) *The End of Reparations*. London: Jonathan Cape. 248 pp.

Stopford, R. J. and Menkin, J. in *Survey of International Affairs*. Oxford University Press:-

1929 (1930. vii, 545 pp.) 'The History of German Reparations from the Dawes Plan to the Young Report', pp. 111–116.

1930 (1931. ix, 605 pp.) 'The History of German Reparations from the Signing of the Young Report to the Coming into Force of the Hague Agree- ments', pp. 499–528.

'The German Economy and Reparations', pp. 528–552.

Wheeler-Bennett, J. W. and Latimer, H. (1930) *The Reparation Settlement*. Allen & Unwin. 253 pp.

Wheeler-Bennett, J. W. (1933) *The Wreck of Reparations*. Allen & Unwin.

Index

Index

Index

Reparations, *see also Reparations* on French occupation of Ruhr, 164, effect of neutrality on German resistance, 168, division of opinion over, 176–7, suspicions over Rhineland occupation, 187, 'die-hard' disquiet over declaration that the Ruhr occupation was illegal, 179–180, British reaction to Smuts's speech, 202, Germany would pay more if 'British Australia' was relinquished, 259

socialists, *see also Labour Party, Macdonald, Snowden, prejudice* admiration for German socialists, 4, against 'unconditional surrender' 25, proposed legislation at Versailles, 69–70, Pressure on Lloyd George at Versailles, 73n, 'die-hards' view of in 1923, 177, anti-French 1929, 272

ships, *see also ships* shortage of, 52, repairers' strike, 53, shipbuilders strike, 80, shipbuilding 210

steel, production 1929, 257, taxes on 272

strikes, 21, 23, 39, 'direct action' 1919, 80, 'direct action' 1918, 82, 'direct action' 103

tariffs, on German goods, credited against the reparations, 1921, 50% 141, 26% 143, 1925, 239–240, amount raised during Dawes Plan, 246, tariff reimposed 1931, 328

taxes, greater total tax burden than Germany 1921, 142, in 1929, 259, burden on industry, 272, 272n

Trade Unions, 6, 10, Conference Jan. 1918, 11, Sep. 1918, 23–24

unemployment, 1920, 137, costs of up to 1923, 178, in 1921 & 1922, 181, 273, unemployed, 294–295

war debts, owed to Britain, figures, 58, 263, France's position, 160, 174, British to America, 58, 127, 263, wealth in 1913, 90

Brockdorf-Rantzau, Count, 56, 70–71, 226

Brüning, 299, 303, tightens the purse strings, 304–305, invokes paragraph 48, 305, publishes drastic decrees, 326, threat of export deluge, 330, territorial aspirations, 328n, Historians over

Brüning's deflationary policy, 307n, 332, 'equal rights' over disarmament, 334

Canada, troops, 52, loyal service of debt, 249n, unsold wheat, 298, America's best trading partner, 302

Cannes, Conference, 145

Central Powers, (Austrian/Hungarian Empire) war costs, 90

Chamberlain Austen, punctilious, 229, 253, on Polish Corridor, 229n

Childers, Erskine, 4

Churchill, 57, 157–8, 240, 246, letter to Lloyd George about German dumping 154–155, a reason for return to Gold Standard, 246, on the German economy in 1932, 351

Class, Justice, 2, 3, aims before and during war, 277

Clemenceau, 27, 38, 39, 51, 67, 119, 125, 230

Coal, 62, American miners strike, 82
    Belgium, 33
    British, 25, 52, 138, miners, 80, shortening working week, 82, anger over British coal exports to France, 114, German competition in 1926, 224, under Young Plan Italy agrees to buy British coal, 274
    French, 31, pumps for flooded mines, 89, Versailles Treaty Memorandum on, 165
    German, 7, 67, 138, 216, 346, production, 63, statistics for women and children in mines, 83, miners' strike 1919, 83, mine pumps, 89, exports, 113, food for miners 135, coal barons in 1923, 169, 1923 domestic coal prices greatly below British, 193, Stinnes demands eight and half hour day underground and ten hours above, 193–194, production in 1929, 294
    Poland, 87

Cohn, Oscar, 128

Communists, *see under country headings* communism, Montague Norman's fears, 327

Coolidge, President, 197, 199, 202, awards Germany Most favoured Nation status 1923, 197

Cotton, *see also individual countries*, America, 1923, Germany best

WITHDRAWN